AN
INDEX MAP
to the following
SIXTEEN SHEETS,
being
A COMPLEAT CHART
of the
WEST INDIES,
WITH
Letters in the Margin, to direct the placing the different Sheets
in their proper Places.

London, Printed for Robt. Sayer, Map & Printseller, N

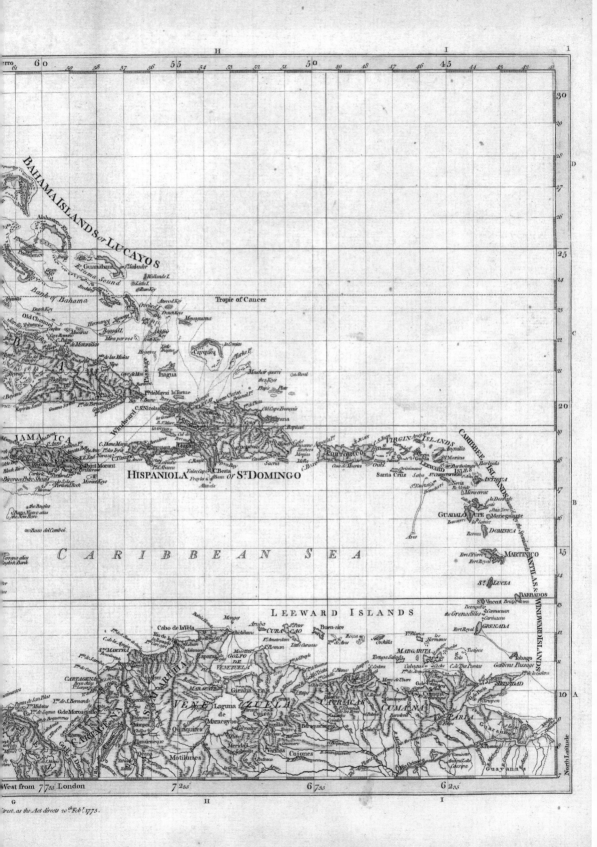

On the Account: Piracy and the Americas, 1766–1835

ON THE ACCOUNT

Piracy and the Americas, 1766–1835

JOSEPH GIBBS

sussex
ACADEMIC
PRESS
Brighton • Portland • Toronto

2 4 6 8 10 9 7 5 3 1

First published 2012 in Great Britain by
SUSSEX ACADEMIC PRESS
PO Box 139
Eastbourne BN24 9BP

and in the United States of America by
SUSSEX ACADEMIC PRESS
920 NE 58th Avenue, Suite 300
Portland, Oregon 97213-3786

and in Canada by
SUSSEX ACADEMIC PRESS (CANADA)
8000 Bathurst Street, Unit 1,
PO Box 30010,
Vaughan, Ontario L4J 0C6

British Library Cataloguing in Publication Data
A CIP catalogue record for this book is available from the British Library.

Library of Congress Cataloging-in-Publication Data
Gibbs, Joseph, 1965–
    On the account : piracy and the Americas, 1766–1835 / Joseph Gibbs.
        p. cm.
    Includes bibliographical references and index.
    ISBN 978-1-84519-476-5 (pbk. : alk. paper)
    1. Pirates—America—History—Sources. 2. Piracy—Atlantic Coast (U.S.)—Sources.
    3. Piracy—Caribbean Area—History—Sources. 4. Pirates—Atlantic Coast (U.S.)—History–Sources.
    5. Pirates—Caribbean Area—History—Sources. 6. Mutiny—United States—History—Sources I. Title.
    E18.75.G53   2012
    364.16′4–dc23   2011040270

MIX
Paper from
responsible sources
FSC
www.fsc.org   FSC® C013056

Typeset and designed by Sussex Academic Press, Brighton & Eastbourne.
Printed by TJ International, Padstow, Cornwall.
This book is printed on acid-free paper.

Table of Contents

List of Illustrations

Cover illustrations: Front – "Burning of the Frigate Philadelphia in the Harbor of Tripoli, February 16, 1804," by Edward Moran. Courtesy of the Naval Historical Foundation KN-10849; back – Map of the harbor of Tripoli. Courtesy of the Naval Historical Foundation, NH 56745.

Endpapers: Map of the West Indies, Printed for Robert Sayer, London, 1775, © Mystic Seaport, G.W. Blunt Library Collection.

Images listed below without acknowledgment are in the public domain; if no artist's name is cited, artist is unknown. In other cases, the author and publisher gratefully acknowledge those named for permission to reproduce copyright material.

The author and publishers apologize for any errors or omissions in the above list and would be grateful to be notified of any corrections that should be incorporated in the next edition or reprint of this book.

Introduction

Alongside a massive technical vocabulary, the Age of Sail spawned a host of euphemisms for the nautical world's darker side. The multi-strand, knotted whip capable of skinning a man alive was called the "cat o' nine tails." Being beaten across a cannon barrel was being made to "kiss the gunner's daughter." To "go on the account" was to turn pirate, making an activity punishable by death sound like a business arrangement.[1]

By the time of the American Revolution, stories of those who had gone "on the account" had long been sensational reading in Europe and its New World holdings. The late 1600s and early 1700s had formed piracy's "Golden Age," so known from not only the material wealth plundered in the New World, but also the lode of characters emerging from the period's chroniclers.[2] Perhaps the most significant of the latter were French writer Alexandre Olivier Exquemelin, who authored 1678's *Americaensche Zee-Rovers*; and the still mysterious Captain Charles Johnson, who produced 1724's *General History of the Robberies and Murders of the Most Notorious Pyrates*. Exquemelin's work was translated from its original Dutch into English by 1684 (as *Bucaniers of America*) and was destined for many reprints. Its reception may have been similar to that given Johnson's work, of which a newspaper commented:

> "I saw a new Book advertised last Week, call'd *The History of the Pyrates*, in the West-Indies, which I had Curiosity enough to peruse; it was not the tenth Part of the Price of a Masquerade, but amus'd me so agreeably, that when I once began I scarce had Power to lay it by, before I had gone thro' it."[3]

Both works are still compelling reading, and remain influential to maritime histories.[4] But just as piracy did not begin with Exquemelin's buccaneers, neither did it end with

---

1   The term or variants of it can be traced back to the 17th century; in 1681, for example, pirate Bartholomew Sharp was reported to "swear on landing in Devon that he would try for another ship to return to America 'upon the same account'" (Williams, *Captains Outrageous*, 57, 129). The term was sometimes rendered as "on the run-away account," as witness John Pigot related it to a Halifax court during an 1809 mutiny-and-piracy trial (*An Interesting Trial of Edward Jordan*, 12).

2   Joel H. Baer (*British Piracy* I:x) noted that the "so-called 'golden age of piracy'" is "sometimes defined narrowly to distinguish the decade 1716–26 when Blackbeard [Edward Teach], [Bartholomew] Roberts and [Edward] Low were in the news." Baer himself addressed materials from 1660–1730 "because, by including Henry Morgan and the buccaneers, it raises important questions about the political construction of piracy as a crime."

3   Untitled article, *The Weekly Journal or Saturday's Post, With Freshest Advices Foreign and Domestick*, 23 May 1724, 1, reproduced in Baer, *British Piracy*, I:359.

4   For examples of historiographical critiques, see Frohock, "Exquemelin's Buccaneers," *passim*; and Turley, *Rum, Sodomy & the Lash*, 3–91.

Johnson's rogues. Almost a century after the *General History*'s first printing, a Baltimore newspaper remarked that there were then so many cases of maritime robbery off the North and Latin American coasts that "The present time seems to be entitled to the appellation of the *age of piracy*."[5] Many chapters were indeed added to the pirate canon during the chaotic years covered in this book, which begin in the period between the Stamp Act and the Boston Massacre, and end at a point where Spain's empire in the Americas had shrunk to just Cuba and Puerto Rico.

Piracy in the Age of Sail continues to fascinate modern audiences. Yet even non-fiction works must be approached with caution, the level of which may depend on the pedigree of the sources employed. Authentic piracy accounts often began with journalists gathering data at dockside. Sometimes they had little more to work with than second-hand reports passed on when vessels "spoke" or met at sea, but luckier writers obtained first-hand interviews with survivors of a pirate encounter. Others got close enough to document trials, preserving or paraphrasing the words of the accused and their accusers, and tracing the proceedings to their final disposition – generally the gallows. Sometimes the victims themselves took up the pen and detailed their own experiences, although they may also have been influenced by their editors' whims or a perception of the public's tastes.

E.H. Carr cautioned that "the facts of history . . . are always refracted through the mind of the recorder."[6] That said, contemporary journalists and other observers were at least on-scene to chronicle their version of events. The problem lies largely with those who came in their wakes and refused to let facts get in the way of a good story. Some not only plagiarized earlier works but "improved" them as well. As a result, pirate chronicles tend to evolve. One cutthroat merges with others; individual acts (some real, some invented) intertwine. Over time dubious or even fictitious figures emerge as archetypes within maritime lore.

Modern historians addressing piracy subjects are gradually setting this aright by emphasizing first-hand accounts and other primary sources. These may be imperfect, but are at least untainted by long periods of embellishment. And by returning to these early texts, different and often complex pictures emerge of seafaring characters and nautical episodes, contradicting the conventions not only of Hollywood but also of mainstream maritime history.

In that same vein, this book aims to present to modern readers original documents concerning piracy in and affecting the Americas in the late 18th and early 19th centuries. It makes no pretense to being a comprehensive omnibus. Rather it presents a sliver of a much larger maritime canon. The texts are rendered with annotations that will hopefully guide general readers through many of the geographical, historical, legal, literary, and nautical references of a past era.

ooooo

5   "Piracy," *Niles' Weekly Register*, 20 October 1821, 118.
6   E.H. Carr, *What Is History?*, 24.

The traditional legal essence of the term *piracy* is that of a felony – at its core, robbery with or without violence – committed on the high seas, i.e. waters outside the jurisdiction of land-based authorities. The texts correspondingly include several accounts of mutiny, an act of piracy as it involved the stealing of a vessel, and sometimes murder as well. Mutinies launched innumerable pirate careers, and those mutineers encountered herein at their trials might have gone on to further maritime crimes had they not been captured. One chapter presents the experiences of American seamen with the Barbary Pirates, the first episodes of cultural clashes that color our own times. Several chapters detail the rise and fall of the Latin American privateers, many of whom functioned simply as pirates. Their contents yield sea fights as vicious as anything in the War of 1812, and glimpses of individuals who may have been as colorful as their "Golden Age" counterparts. Along the way, naval heroes such as Stephen Decatur and Lawrence Kearny emerge, alongside others lesser in rank but not in courage. Also appearing are snippets of life among the crews who went "on the account," generally related by their naval captors, or by victims who survived encounters with them.

The last point introduces a caution: There is little here for those seeking the "romance" of piracy, a *non sequitur*. The remoteness of the crime scene gave incidents of piracy a terrifying edge. At sea in the pre-wireless era potential victims had little hope of assistance (a rare "nick of time" rescue was Kearny's raid, in USS *Enterprise*, at Cape Antonio, Cuba, in 1821, detailed in Chapter 7). Moreover, the perpetrators could, if they chose, let the sea cover up the evidence of their crime. Dead men indeed tell no tales in a courtroom, and by the 1820s many pirates operating in the Gulf of Mexico and Caribbean Sea routinely killed their victims (sometimes after torture) and scuttled otherwise valuable (but incriminating) captured vessels once they had been ransacked. When stopped by pirates in 1829, the officers of one vessel agreed "that in case a massacre was begun, one of them should fire into a barrel of gunpowder in the hold and explode the ship. It was thought to be a better fate to kill all in one general ruin."[7]

ooooo

In editing the *General History* for modern readers, Manuel Schonhorn wrote that his goal was "to present a reliable but also readable text."[8] A similar objective informed the editorial method used to produce the transcriptions in this volume, which was influenced by several works on documentary editing.[9] Generally, the transcriptions are faithful to the originals, with capitalization, including irregularities and variations within an individual text itself, largely reproduced as it first appeared. They are not, however, facsimiles. Bracketed ellipses [...] or editor's notes indicate when material was deleted or

---

7 *Marblehead Messenger*, 21 January 1881, quoted in Bradlee, *Piracy in the West Indies*, 141.
8 Schonhorn, *General History*, xlii.
9 These included Stevens and Burg, *Editing Historical Documents*; and the discussion of methodology in Boyd, ed., *Papers of Thomas Jefferson*, I:xxv–xxxviii.

paraphrased. Paragraph break symbols [¶] appear when sections of text were cut into shorter elements.

In addressing spelling, brackets denote edits made to adjust problematic words; thus *perpretated* becomes the intended "perp[etr]ated," etc. Brackets also show where capitalization was changed, as in instances involving titles placed before names, and where certain acronyms and abbreviations were expanded. Words requiring deletion of surplus characters were corrected using a strikethrough and superscripted brackets, e.g. "marshal[ll]." Some obscure spellings, deemed unlikely to cause confusion, were left, as were certain alternate spellings for place names. The results no doubt reflect imperfect judgment in some cases, but the system adopted does have benefits of consistency of approach. A reader may, for example, find that an edited word such as "g[ao]l" looks unusual, but inserting an obsolete but generally understood spelling for "jail" improved on the original rendering of "goal." At the same time, the legal term "cause," used interchangeably with "case," has been retained.

The original texts occasionally employed erratic, incorrect or (by modern standards) unnecessary punctuation. For clarity and consistency, such problems (though generally not those involving quotation marks and/or hyphens) were silently remedied; run-on and broken ("a gain," "a drift," "to morrow", "a-sleep") words were also silently fixed.[10] Other silent emendations imposed throughout are:

- Replacement of the archaic "long s" (ʃ) with the modern s.
- Replacement of dashes used to end sentences (rather than introduce incidental remarks) with periods; the first word in the following sentence was capitalized if necessary.
- Standardization of multiple short dashes into a single long dash [–].
- Replacement of asterisks used to signify deletions, as in the trial testimony in Chapter 10, with ellipses.
- Elimination of excessive highlighting, such as capitalization and italicization. However, italicization was sometimes added (such as in trial testimony in Chapter 10) for clarity or to keep the formatting style consistent across a chapter. Vessel and periodical names were italicized regardless of how they originally appeared.

To better delineate the editor's modifications to the texts, brackets appearing in the originals were replaced with parentheses. Brackets also indicate short additions to the text when clarification did not require a separate annotation. Besides specific works cited, the annotations made free use of many "common knowledge" sources. These included standard reference works such as Merriam Webster's *Biographical, Collegiate,* and

---

10   However, as noted in a footnote in Chapter 10, quotation marks in a portion of trial testimony were silently eliminated when placed around evident paraphrasing.

Geographical dictionaries; the *Columbia Gazetteer of the World* edited by Saul Cohen; and the Google maps website.

While the annotations attempt to amplify certain obscure points, a conscious effort has been made to let these documents tell as much of their own story as possible. They offer authentic glimpses into their era. Modern readers will hopefully get a sense of what their late 18th and early 19th century counterparts experienced in the densely packed columns of early type, in a time when the sea was a source of adventure, mystery, prosperity – and all too often, terror.

ooooo

A legion of people and institutions deserve my gratitude for their help with this volume, but space limitations allow me to single out only a few. My first such thanks goes to the editors and staff of Sussex Academic Press, who showed confidence in and enthusiasm for this project at every phase. I am especially indebted (again) to maritime historian John Frayler. The staff of the library of the American University of Sharjah, particularly Daphne Flanagan, Alya Kattan and Amar Zahra Ali Shah gave invaluable help over several years. Four other AUS colleagues, Anna Marie Castillo and Drs. Harris Breslow, Rana Raddawi, and Dennis Russell, provided key help at several stages. Finally, my love and thanks to my wife Tanya and sons Michael and Brian for their love and patience.

With those acknowledgements given, please note that any errors herein are the author's responsibility.

1

"Veterans in blood and murder"– The mutiny aboard the *Polly* (1766) and the trial of Joseph Andrews (1769)

Two factors helped close piracy's so-called "Golden Age" circa 1730. One was the period of relative peace between 1720 and 1740, which allowed Europe's naval powers to pit their navies against pirate havens. Another, once the peace ended, was the rise of privateering. This was a form of legalized piracy, in which a government furnished owners of private vessels with either a privateering commission, or a letter of marque and reprisal. The terms were (and are) sometimes used interchangeably, but the former turned a merchant vessel into a warship on the prowl; the latter authorized it to capture enemy-owned craft encountered on its regular route. As much of the 18th century was (in maritime historian Angus Konstam's words) "marked by a near-constant string of wars," the result "was that privateering became extremely lucrative, and by the end of the string of conflicts this form of state-sponsored piracy had become big business."[1] It also kept men who would have otherwise gone "on the account" in the employ of the belligerent states.

The line between privateering and piracy was always blurry, but mutiny was unquestionably an act of piracy before the law. The story of the 1766 mutiny on the sloop *Polly* is a prototype of a tale re-told over following decades, and the account that emerged from Joseph Andrews' later trial contained many elements of classic pirate stories: oaths sworn upon a Bible, hideous forms of execution, and hanging-in-chains. It seems unsurprising that Andrews – who reportedly also gave his name as Anderson – should have tried to kill himself in prison when one considers the fate of his confederate Nicholas Johnson. The latter's grisly execution on St. Eustatius gives some idea of how colonial society on the eve of the American Revolution viewed piracy.

---

1   Konstam, *Piracy*, 272–273. An early study of the legal basis for letters of marque and reprisal is in Alexander Justice's *General Treatise of the Dominion and Laws of the Sea*, first published in 1705. Chapter 11 of its 1710 edition (London: Executors of J. Nicholson, 461–472 – reproduced in Baer's *British Piracy*, III:355–366) includes the text of a letter of marque, with its extensive conditions and restrictions.

ooooo

An Account of the Trial of Joseph Andrews for Piracy and Murder, Together with his Confession to the Gentlemen of the Clergy who visited him during his Confin[e]ment, and to the Keepers of the G[ao]l the Day before his Execution; the Account he gave them of his Parentage and Manner of Life; also his Character and Dying Speech ("Printed for every Purchaser," New York, 1769)

On Wednesday the 17th of May, 1769, by Virtue of a Special Commission from his Majesty, for the Trial of Piracy, &c. at the Hall of the City of New-York, was held a Court of Admiralty, consisting of the following Gentlemen, viz. His Excellency the Governor Sir Henry Moore, President; ten Gentlemen of his Majesty's Council, the Judge of the Admiralty, the Deputy-Secretary, the Receiver General and Collector of the Province, and the Commander of his Majesty's Ship *Deal[e] Castle.*[2]

Joseph Andrews, late of the Sloop[3] *Polly*, Mariner, was brought to the Bar. Richard Nicholls, Esq; Register of the Court of Vice-Admiralty, and John McKisson, Esq; Deputy-Register; and a Notary Public, exh[i]bi[t]ed five several Charges against the Prisoner; fourteen Witnesses were examined on the Part of the Crown, and two on the Part of the Prisoner. It appeared by the Evidence, that in the Month of August 1766, he enter'd himself on board the Sloop *Polly*, Roluss Duryee, Master, bound from New-York to the West-Indies. The other Persons on board were Peter Demilt, jun., Mate; Nicholas Johnson, and William Harris, Mariners, —— Cobbs, a Cabin Boy, Wells Coverley, a young Man; John Van Bunschooten, another young Man, who went for his Health; and an Antigua[4] Captain who had sold his Vessel, and was returning home, Passengers.

Soon after leaving New-York, observing the Captain and Passengers had a good deal of Money, he and Johnson formed the Design of gaining Possession of it by Murdering the People. This Design they concluded to put in Execution as soon as they should make the Land; accordingly about 8 Days after, the Night before they ex-

---

2 The last in a series of four warships to bear the name *Deale Castle*, this one was a 107-foot long, 20-gun 6th rate vessel. Launched in 1756, it foundered in a hurricane off Puerto Rico in 1780 (Colledge and Warlow, *Royal Navy*, 104).

3 Like the twin-masted schooner, the single-masted sloop employed fore-and-aft rigging, with sails hung parallel to the keel. Vessels so-rigged sailed better against the wind than those that were square-rigged, the rigging of which consisted largely of four-cornered sails hung perpendicular to the keel. Also worth noting is that the term *sloop* (like the term *ship*, which in this era was usually applied to square-rigged vessels of at least three masts) was sometimes applied based on factors other than rigging. For example, the Royal Navy used the terms *ship* and *sloop* "depending on the rank of the officer in command. Thus, the donkey frigate *Blossom* was one cruise rated a *ship*, when commanded by a captain – the next, a *sloop*, because only commanded by a commander." A "donkey frigate" was one rated at 28 guns and 600 tons (Smyth, *Lexicon*, 257, 325, 633).

4 According to a 1760 edition of a work by Edmund Burke (*European Settlements*, II:92) Antigua "which we formerly thought useless, has got the start of all the Leeward islands, increasing every day in its produce and inhabitants both freeman and slaves. It has one of the best harbors in the West Indies; on it stands the principal town called St. John's, which is large and wealthy."

Sailors at work on the jib-boom on the end of a bowsprit (or boltsprit), furling and securing a jib (19th century, artist unknown).

pected to get to St. Christopher's,[5] about Midnight, William Harris being at Helm, and the Captain asleep on a Hencoop on Deck, Johnson with one Blow of an Ax killed him, and he expired without a Groan or Struggle. They then in like manner between them Murdered the three Passengers, and Mate with the Ax, and threw the Boy overboard alive. One of them made a Stroke with the Ax at Harris, who ran to the end of the Boltsprit[6] with a Knife, and declared he would Kill the first Man that approached him. They then told him, if he would join them and swear to be secret and faithful, he should be safe, and share the Plunder with them; for Johnson having formerly

5   "The island of St. Christopher's [or St. Kitts] is the chief of those which we possess amongst the Leeward islands. It was first settled by the French and English in the year 1626, but after various fortunes it was entirely ceded to us by the treaty of Utrecht. This island is about seventy-five miles in compass. The circuit of Ant[i]gua is but little inferior. . . . Neither [St. Christopher's] nor any of the Leeward islands yields any commodity of consequence but what is derived from the cane, except Montserrat, which exports some indigo, but of a very inferior kind. It is judged that the island of St. Christopher's contains about seven thousand whites and twenty thousand negroes; that Ant[i]gua has also about seven thousand of the former colour, and thirty thousand blacks; and that Nevis and Montserrat may have each about five thousand Europeans, who are the masters of ten or twelve thousand African slaves. So that the whole of the Leeward islands may be reckoned without exaggeration to maintain about twenty thousand English, of whom every single man gives bread to several in England, which is effected by the labour of near seventy thousand negroes" (Burke, *European Settlements*, II:91–93).

6   A bowsprit or boltsprit consisted of a long spar, or beam, or sprit, extending over the vessel's bow. It provided the foundation for rigging and canvas which helped "in counterbalancing the pressure of the after-sails, thereby tending to force the ship ahead instead of merely turning her round" (Smyth, *Lexicon*, 125).

sail'd with him, pretended to have a Regard for him: But it was previously agreed between Johnson and Andrews, to kill him before they got ashore.¶

Harris them came into the Vessel and assisted in throwing the Bodies overboard; after which they broke open the Captain's and Passengers Chests and Lockers, got a Bottle of Wine, and drank Damnation to themselves and each other if they discovered the Secret. They then got a Bible and made Harris swear upon it that he would not betray them; 3 or 4 Days after this, being in Sight of Land, and several Vessels appearing, they got out the Boat, put into it two Chests, with whatever they thought proper to take, scuttled the Vessel, left her, and sail'd towards the Land, telling Harris to steer clear of the Shore. But he telling them, if they did not get pretty near the Land, the Current would drive them to the Leeward[7] of all the Islands, they left him to steer as he thought best, – but intended to throw him overboard before he got to Land.¶

After some Time, Johnson and Andrews both fell asleep, when Harris, having got near the Shore, stripped himself, took the Opportunity to throw overboard, without Noise, his Clothes, and both the Oars, one of which he had used instead of a Rudder to steer the Boat, he gently let himself down into the Sea and swam on Shore at St. Kitts,[8] where he gave a blind suspicious Account of himself, being afraid to say any Thing that might break his Oath of Secrecy; but at last he applied to a Minister for Advice how a Man ou[g]ht to act in a Case similar to his own. The Minister convinced him that such kind of Oaths were so far from being binding, that it would be highly criminal to keep them. He then went before the Judge Surrogate of the Admiralty and gave his Deposition of all the Circumstances he knew of the bloody Affair. Soon after he quitted the Boat, the irregular tumbling of it waked the two Criminals, who saw their desperate Situation, and were enraged they had not an Opportunity to satiate their Revenge upon Harris. They at first endeavour'd to steer with their Hats, but afterwards did it more effectually with their Sprit,[9] and by that Means got to Eustatia,[10] where they sold the Boat.

Some Days after their Arrival, the St. Christopher's *Gazette* with Harris's Deposition, made its Appearance in Eustatia; Andrews happening to see it, immediately left the Island, in a Vessel bound to Casco-Bay.[11] The Governor of St. Eustatia, on seeing the

---

7   To be "situated, or having a direction, away from the wind, the opposite of windward" (Dear and Kemp, *Companion*, 314).

8   As noted above, an alternative name for St. Christopher's Island.

9   As noted earlier, a sprit was a long spar or beam. A *spritsail* consisted of a sprit "which stretches diagonally across a four-sided fore-and-aft sail … to support the sail's peak" (Dear and Kemp, *Companion*, 551).

10 "Eustatia [St. Eustatius] is but one mountain of about twenty miles in compass; it is amongst the Leeward islands; but though so small and inconveniently laid out by nature, the industry of the Dutch have made it turn out to very good account, and it is fully peopled; the sides of the mountain are divided and laid out in very pretty settlements; and, though they have neither springs nor rivers, they are so careful that they never want proper supplies of water from their ponds and cisterns. They raise here sugar and tobacco; and this island, as well as Curassou [Curaçao], is engaged in the Spanish contraband trade, for which, however, it is not so well situated; and it draws the same advantages from its constant neutrality" (Burke, *European Settlements*, II:54–55).

11 Near Portland, Maine.

Deposition, published by Proclamation an Order for a d[i]ligent Search, and that no Person should carry the Criminals off, under the Penalty of 50,000 Pieces of Eight: [12] He also dispatched a Vessel after Andrews, with a proper Notification of the Charge against him, and Description of his Person. Johnson was soon taken up at Eustatia, confessed the Fact, and was executed on the 15th of November, 1766, by being broke alive on the Rack: He was stretched naked on a Cross, where the Bones of his Arms, Legs and Thighs were broken with an Iron Bar, and he afterwards received up-wards 20 Strokes on his breast, before he expired. Andrews the present Criminal was soon after his Arrival taken up, and imprisoned some Time at Boston, when he at-tempted to cut his own Throat, but was prevented by the Care of his Attendants. From Boston he was sent here, where he arrived the Twenty-sixth Day of May, 1767, and remained a Prisoner till his Execution.

The greatest Part of the clothing found with the Prisoner in his Chest, and by him claimed as his own, in the Presence of the Court, were very fully and circumstantially proved to have belonged to Captain Duryee, and his Mate, or some of the Persons who were Murdered on board the said Sloop; and also many other Things found in the Chest and owned by the Prisoner. Many of the Clothes were marked with the ini-tial Letters of the Names of their former Owners, and many others of them with the plain Marks of those Letters remaining, tho' the Silk of the marking was taken out, and they were marked J.A. the initial Letters of the Name of the Prisoner. [A] Needle work'd Pocket-Book found with, and own'd by the Prisoner, before it was sh[o]wn in Court, was exactly described by the Woman who made it, particularly that a Corner of it was left unfinished for want of Worsted[13] to do it [*]; likewise a Medal of which the Brother of one of the Murder'd Persons, had a Copy. Several things said by the Pris-oner, during the Course of the Trial, and in his Defence, militated much against him. The Trial lasted from Ten o'Clock on Wednesday, until One o'Clock on Thursday Morn-ing, during all which Time his Excellency never left the Bench. The Evidence was full, clear, and particular; the Prisoner was found guilty, and received Sentence of Death.

He was Executed on Tuesday the 23d of May, at the East-Side of Hudson's River, near Domini's Hook,[14] between the ebbing the flowing of the Tide: And his Body was after-

---

12 "The premier coin of the Atlantic world in the seventeenth and eighteenth centuries was the Spanish peso, or piastra – the piece of eight that in the seventeenth century came to be called the dollar and that later became the basic unit of the monetary system of the United States. . . . [I]n the ten years from 1766 to 1776 the Casa de la Moneda in Mexico alone coined 203,000,000 pieces of eight, more than 20,000,000 a year worth £4,567,500 sterling annually. At a guess, perhaps as many as one-half of the coins in use in the colonies were pieces of eight. The intrinsic value of the piece of eight continued almost unaltered for four hundred years." Its approximate value in 1766 was £0.23 (McCusker, *Money and Exchange*, 7, 10).

13 Cloth spun from a type of smooth yarn consisting of long, parallel fibers.

14 Domini's or Dominis Hook is described in a 1775 New York broadside as lying "in the West Ward of this city." The place name seems to have originated under the Dutch (*hoek* means corner or angle in Dutch) as early as 1636. See *To the Public. As the claim of Cornelius C. Bogardus and others to lands at and adjoining to Dominis Hook ...* [New York. 12 June 1775.] Library of Congress Printed Ephemera Collection; Portfolio 108, Folder 29; Digital ID: rbpe 10802900 http://hdl.loc.gov/loc.rbc/rbpe.10802900.

wards hung in Chains, on the most conspicuous Part of the Pest or Bedlow's Island,[15] in New York Bay, as a Spectacle to deter all Persons from the like atrocious Crimes.

The Account he gave of himself was as follows, viz. That he was an Englishman, born at the Town of Swanzey [Swansea], in Wales, of poor but honest Protestant Parents, who brought him up in their own Persuasion, gave him an Education suitable to their Circumstances, and sent him to Sea: That he has led a Seafaring Life ever since, and sailed to many different Parts of the World; that he had some Friends and Connections in Portugal, which led him to frequent and make some stay in that Place, and learn the Language; which gave Rise to the Report, that he was a Portuguese, and a Roman-Catholic, which was not true, as he never professed any other than the Protestant Religion.[16]

For many Years past he has made the City of New-York (where he married and has left a Widow) the place of his Residence, when not at Sea. His Behaviour on Shore was irregular and disorderly.

A Neglect of Religion and all Christian Duties, and a free Indulgence of every vicious Inclination, particularly in keeping bad Company, led him from one degree of Wickedness to another, till his Heart was hardened against Remorse and became capable of harbouring and devising horrid Thoughts and Designs. The restraining Influences of the Divine Spirit, so often slighted and abused, were withdrawn from him, and he was left to be governed by the furious Impulses of his disorderly Passions, and to pursue with Greediness the Desires of his own wicked Heart. The Gratification of these Desires was the Temptation that lead him to covet the Money of the Captain and Passengers, which he hoped would furnish him with the Means; and when that Thought had taken Possession of his Breast he was determined to remove every Obstacle to its Accomplishment, however dreadful the Consequences.

Those Minds must have been most amazingly hardened in Guilt, that could in cool Blood have been so long brooding over such a horrible Purpose, and Persist in it till its final Execution. This caused a Suspicion that Men capable of a Fact like this, must have been Veterans in Blood and Murder, and could not for a first Essay, have been Actors in so dreadful a Scene of Slaughter.

And therefore these Criminals were suspected to be the Authors of several other Murders perp[etr]ated within these few Years, particularly of Anthony De Noyer, Master of

---

15 Bedloe's Island, now Liberty Island, home of the Statue of Liberty. In 1758 New York officials established a "pesthouse" on it to quarantine "people with highly contagious diseases" (Mushabac and Wigan, *New York City*, 26).

16 Such stories appear in a contemporary broadside, *The Last Dying Speech and Confession of Joseph Andrews, who was Executed at New-York, on Tuesday the 23d Day of May, 1769. For Piracy and Murder* (New York: Swiney and Stewart, 1769). Its authors quote Andrews saying that he was 39, that he was born in Spain, and that his father "in his youth had been a Mendicant Fri[a]r, of the order of St. Francis."

a French Schooner, near the Island of St. Domingo,[17] in the year 1765, and of two Men in New Jersey; but they both, till their last Moments, persisted in solemnly denying that they had ever before been concerned in any Murder or other capital Crime.

Joseph Andrews was remarkably ignorant or insensible in Matters of religious or moral Obligation; and though he seem'd heartily to feel the Horror of his Situation; yet all his Distress seem'd to arise from the Dread of personal Punishment – not at all from a proper Sense of his Guilt; and though he confessed the Fact for which he suffered, repeatedly, to both the Ministers, and at the Gallows, ye[t] he always seemed to own it with Reluctance; and to feel something of Resentment against the Witnesses upon whose Evidence he was found guilty, but said he forgave them.

The Excuse he made for throwing the Boy overboard, was, that in the Scuffle he had received a Wound, which he apprehended would have been Mortal, and that therefore it was best to end his Misery at once.

At the Gallows he owned his Crime, desired all People, especially Sailors to take Warning by him, and after repeating the Creed and Lord's Prayer, was executed.

The Night prec[e]ding Andrews's Execution, a Gentleman, whose veracity can be depended upon, went up to the Room wherein he was confined in the New-G[ao]l, and had a very serious conversation with him. And after having joined him in Prayer; he advised him to satisfy the Public, by confessing the Crimes he had been guilty of. Andrews mused for some Time, and then gave the following declaration.¶

["]As a dying Man, I think it is a duty I owe to myself, to say something against the many Crimes laid to my Charge by some Persons, as [a] clamorous and insolent, as they are ignorant and stupid; for if you take the Voice of the People, in general, there never was a Crime committed by mankind but what has been imputed to me. I pray God to forgive them and they have both my Forgiveness and Pity: My name is Joseph Anderson [sic]: I was born in Swanzey in the Southern Part of Wales, near Vaux-Hall, of poor but honest Parents. [I]n my Youth, I came over an Indent[ur]ed Servant to Boston, and served part of an Apprenti[ce]ship to a Capt. of a Vessel; but being very ambitious to be my own Master, I deserted from him when at Lisbon. I always had an insatiable desire for Money, and this unhappy propensity has prompted me to do things, the remembrance of which is now very grievous unto me; but who liveth and sinneth not[?][18] And those who rail most against me, if they will take the trouble of scrutinizing their own Lives, they will find their conduct has not been unexception-

---

17 Hispaniola containing Haiti and the Dominican Republic.
18 An echo of Ecclesiastes VII:20, which appeared in the 1611 King James Version of the *Holy Bible* as "For there is not a iust man vpon earth, that doeth good, and sinneth not." It was often rendered in this period as (to cite one example) "For there is not a just man upon earth that liveth and sinneth not" (Gill, *Sermons and Tracts*, III:184).

able. However they may say of me what they please, as my Time here, in all probability is very short. And after the Execution of my Sentence, when they see my Body Hanging in Chains, they may (as they no doubt will) say ['T]here Hangs the Body of Andrews, the Pirate, who being a Roman Catholic[k], would make no Confession.["] He was then Silent for a short Time, and upon the Gentleman's Asking him whether he was a Roman Catholic or not, he Answered in the Negative. And added that he had lived and should die a Member of the Church of England. He was very desirous to know if his Body real[l]y was to be hung in Chains; if not, he would give a particular account of the Transactions of his Life; but if on the contrary, they persisted in their resolution to Hang him in Chains, the World should have little Satisfaction from him. His Behaviour at the Place of Execution was decent and resigned, he Prayed about fifteen Minutes and then desired the cart to be drove of[f].[19] Upon the whole he seemed to be a daring resolute Fellow.

---

19 Those being hanged were often driven to the gallows in a cart, in which they stood while the noose was placed around their neck. Driving off the cart began the execution process.

2

"All Tory by God!" – Mutiny aboard the *St. Louis* (1778)

From the American colonies' perspective, the Revolutionary War at sea was a continuation of the privateering affairs that had already marked much of the 18th century. Their reliance on privateers also reflected the new United States' lack of a navy; for most of the conflict there were more rebel privateers operating than warships commissioned by the Continental Congress.

Whether their owners were rebel or loyal to King George, merchant captains had more than privateers to worry about, as can be seen by the reward broadside transcribed below, detailing the 1778 mutiny aboard the *St. Louis*. Published in French and English, and released into the chaos of wartime, it originated in Philadelphia, the British occupation of which had ended shortly before the *St. Louis* left Baltimore.

The mutiny occurred just four days out of port, and fortunately for Captain George Ross and the one crewman who remained true to him came off without bloodshed. Mate Francis Rogers, who led the conspiracy, was a mariner with experience aboard an American warship and time served as a British prisoner. The French mutineer's "all Tory" remark to Ross suggests a wry sense of humor, the Tories or Loyalists being those in the colonies who had remained on the monarch's side.

ooooo

FIVE HUNDRED POUNDS REWARD
(BROADSIDE – PHILADELPHIA, JOHN DUNLAP, 1778)

Captured by the crew of the *St. Louis*, a Virginia built pilot boat,[1] burthen[2] about 50 tons,[3] her cargo consisted of thirty eight hogsheads[4] of tobacco whole, and ten

---

1 This term may identify the *St. Louis* as a type of cutter. A "Pilot Cutter" was "a very handy sharp[-]built sea-boat used by pilots." The cutter itself was "a small single-masted, sharp-built broad vessel . . . furnished with a straight running bowsprit, occasionally run in horizontally on the deck; except for which, and the largeness of the sails, they are rigged much like sloops. . . . The name is derived from their fast sailing" (Smyth, *Lexicon*, 229–230, 528.)

2 Or burden. The terms refer to "the quantity of contents or number of tons weight of goods or munitions which a ship will carry, when loaded to a proper sea-trim: and this is ascertained by certain fixed rules of measurement. The precise burden or burthen is about twice the tonnage [see below], but then a vessel would be deemed deeply laden" (Smyth, *Lexicon*, 146)

An armed brig, 1830
(artist unknown).

hogsheads in rolls and bulk, commanded by Capt. George Ross. She sailed from Balti-more the 2d of July instant, and by the 6th left Cape Charles.[5] Being about 25 leagues[6] from the shore, as the Captain was sitting on the quarter-deck, his mate, Francis Rogers, came up to him, seized him by the arms, and desired him to surren-der the vessel, for that he was his prisoner. On which the Captain called to the crew for assistance; but instead of coming to his relief, they all, but one, joined the Mate in accomplishing their wicked design, [and] they tied the Captain by the arms, and threw him and the other young man into the boat, without water or provision.¶

Thus, being left destitute to the seas, he luckily fell in with Captain Hartwell, who re-turned and landed him at New Point Comfort.[7] When he left the vessel, the pirates told him they would go to New-York. Rogers, the Mate, is about five feet five inches high, well set, has black hair, and of a dark complexion, about twenty-nine years of age, speaks English and French very well; he formerly sailed out of Boston in an armed brig,[8] and being taken, was a prisoner at New York for some time, from whence he made his escape.¶

3   In a merchant vessel, tonnage was often calculated by assigning one ton for every 100 cubic feet of cargo. For warships, tonnage figures usually represented water displacement (Dear and Kemp, *Companion*, 587–588).

4   A hogshead was a large barrel usually used to convey a variety of goods, many with unique weight and/or volume standards depending on contents. By 19th century standards, for example, a hogshead of beer contained 54 gal-lons, one of wine 63 gallons (Cousins, "Weights and Measures," 298). Several colonies set forth comprehensive regulations for the construction and size of tobacco hogsheads. The latter seem to have steadily increased in vol-ume until, by 1763, both Virginia and Maryland had established their weight at 1,000 pounds; heavier examples from the period are recorded (Gray, *History of Agriculture*, I:220–2; Kelbaugh, "Tobacco Trade," 16–17). In 1784, a hogshead of tobacco being exported to Britain was worth £5 (Mair, "Virginia Commerce," 88).

5   On the north of the mouth of the Chesapeake Bay; Cape Henry is on the south.

6   Three nautical miles of 6075.6 feet each (Smyth, *Lexicon*, 436, 492).

7   New Point Comfort is on Virginia's Middle Peninsula inside Chesapeake Bay, with the Rappahannock and York rivers to the north and south, respectively.

8   A brig is a two-masted, square-rigged vessel. "The word brig was originally an abbreviation of brigantine before the latter became known as a different type of ship. Brigs were widely used for coastal and short trading voyages and the Scottish clipper brigs were famous for trading to the Baltic" (Dear and Kemp, *Companion*, 67–68).

The rest of the crew, five in number, two of whom are French, both named Andrew, one born in Nant[es], the other in Provence. The other three are supposed to be country born; one of them named [Hozier?], is about five feet three inches high, with curled hair; the other two are tall men, their names forgot.[9]¶

Whosoever will give information, or secure said vessel and cargo so that the owner may have them again, shall be entitled to the above reward; or if any of the accomplices shall make discovery, he shall have One Hundred Pounds reward, on the above condition, and interest made for his free pardon. Or if the vessel and cargo shall be retaken in any foreign port, where our money is not current, I do promise One Hundred Half Johannesses[10] in gold to the person or persons who shall so secure them for me; or ten half Johannesses to any of the crew of said vessel who shall procure a restitution of them. [. . .]

ANTHONY MARMAJOU[11]
Philadelphia, July 16, 1778

N.B. The Names of the Pirates: Francis Rogers, (late Mate) born in Boston; Joshua Berry, an Irishman; Robert Freeman, an Englishman; Andrew Averty, and Andrew Gledermersil, both Frenchmen –– Capt. Ross, while some of these villains were tying his Hands behind him called aloud, "Are ye all against me? – Have I no Friend amongst ye?" To which one of the Frenchmen, with great Vivacity, replied, "No, Monsieur Capitaine, all Tory, all Tory by G-d!"

---

9   However, see the list of "The Names of the Pirates' appended to the handbill.
10   A reference to the gold Portuguese coin known as the *dobra de 4 escudos*, which bore a portrait of Portugal's King John (Johanna) V, and was worth £1.80 in 1766. It was worth half that of the *dobre de 8 escudos*, which also bore King John V's portrait (McCusker, *Money and Exchange*, 6, 12.)
11   Owner of the *St. Louis*, Marmajou was also master and owner of the brig *Little Polly*, and in early 1776 had sought permits from the new American Congress to trade with Martinique, then a source of arms; he later brought in a small amount of military stores. (Augur, *Secret War*, 72, and Horgan, *Forged in War*, 11.)

3

"A heart hard enough to kill a man" – The *Eliza* mutiny and the trial of "three foreigners" (1799–1800)

Philadelphia sea captain William Wheland in 1800 penned a fast-moving, bloody tale based on his experience as the sole living witness to an uprising aboard his schooner *Eliza* the year before. The three sailors who mutinied killed the vessel's mate, another crewmember, and a French passenger; Wheland survived owing to his possession of a pair of pistols. The fact that none of the mutineers could navigate allowed him to bargain with them, he agreeing to sail the vessel in exchange for his life. Wheland ultimately retook the *Eliza* single-handedly, then brought the schooner back to port.

One of the mutineers, Joseph Berrouse (whose name is given as Brous through much of what follows), held a French military commission; his defense was that the mutiny was not an act of piracy but one of war, this being at the time of the Quasi-War at sea between the United States and France. The court rejected this argument, and he joined the other two convicted men on the gallows.

Wheland's story herein is fleshed out by two additional documents, detailing the trio's confessions and executions.

ooooo

A Narrative of the Horrid Murder & Piracy Committed on Board the Schooner[1] *Eliza*, of Philadelphia on the High Seas, by Three Foreigners, Who were tried before the Circuit Court of the United States, on Monday, the 21st April, 1800; Together with an Account of the Surprizing Recapture of the Said Schooner, By Captain [William] Wheland, The only person who escaped from their Barbarity (Philadelphia, Richard Folwell, 1800).

[…]

---

1   The classic schooner is a twin-masted vessel employing fore-and-aft rigging, i.e, with the sails hung parallel to the keel. The term schooner may be derived "from the Scottish verb to 'scon' or 'scoon,' to skip over the water like a flat stone. The name is said to have come from a chance remark 'there she scoons' from a spectator at the launch of the first vessel of the type at Gloucester, Mass., in 1713" (Dear and Kemp, *Companion*, 495).

Schooner *Mohawk* off Sandy Hook Lighthouse, by James E. Buttersworth (n.d.).

On the 27th day of August, 1799, I set sail from the port of Philadelphia, on board the schooner *Eliza*, bound for St. Thomas's[2]: American seamen being at that time very hard to be obtained, I was under the necessity of shipping three foreigners; so that my crew consisted of two Americans, Thomas Croft, (whom I afterwards appointed mate), and Jacob Suster, together with the three foreigners, who entered with me by the names of Joseph Baker, Joseph Brous and Peter Peterson. The name of our supercargo[3] was Charles Rey, a French gentleman, who had long resided in the island of St. Domingo,[4] and had borne the commission of general in the armies of his Catholic majesty, previous to the revolution; but, like many others of his unfortunate countrymen, was under the necessity of seeking an asylum in America, when the Negroes had seized upon the government of that island.[5]

In this country he married an amiable young lady, of Baltimore, of French extraction, with whom he lived in the most perfect state of conjugal felicity, and by whom he had one child. He occasionally resided at Philadelphia and Baltimore; in both of which places, he had endeared himself to a numerous circle of acquaintance, by the cheerfulness of his conversation and the suavity of his manners: his fortunes, however, began to be considerably impaired, by disappointments in his remittances from

2 A Caribbean island, now a part of the US Virgin Islands.
3 "A person charged with the accounts and disposal of the cargo, and all other commercial affairs in the merchant-ship in which he sails" (Smyth, *Lexicon*, 666).
4 Hispaniola.
5 The Haitian Revolution began in 1791.

St. Domingo, and other real losses to a great amount; he resolved, therefore, to go out supercargo, with a view of regaining, if possible, some part of his immense property in the island, and to provide for a beloved wife and [i]ncreasing family.

Neither Mr. Rey nor myself had a good opinion of the three foreigners. They seemed to us to be men of an implacable and revengeful spirit; for, soon after we had sailed, in going down the river, one of them, Peterson, alias Louis Lacroix, having refused to obey the orders of the mate, I struck him; on seeing this, Baker came to his assistance, and Mr. Rey stepped forward to protect me; when I had given Baker a good beating, they both promised to do their duty like good men, if I would forgive them, which I immediately promised to do; after which they behaved themselves for 14 days very well, and there was no more dispute until the 12th of September, being in latitude 28, 30, N[orth] and in longitude 60, 00, W[est]. At about 10 o'clock, p.m. it being the mate's watch on deck, Mr. Rey and myself had gone to sleep in our b[e]rths, one on each side of the cabin. It appears that the three desperadoes, Baker, Brous and Peterson, availed themselves of an opportunity, while the mate was asleep on deck, to give him a blow on the head with an axe; but, as no person was on deck at that time, except the mate and the three ruffians, a circumstantial account of the murder of the mate cannot be obtained. Certain it is, however, that he was murdered and thrown over-board. By their account afterwards to me, Brous is said to have given him the first blow, and Baker, alias Boulanger, the second, which finished his existence; but, by their confession in Philadelphia, before [J]udge [Richard] Peters,[6] it is said, that the mate and Brous, having some quarrel, and Brous declaring himself the master of the vessel, and the mate his prisoner of war, the mate struck him, which caused Brous, alias Berouce, in his own defence, to lift up an axe, and give him a blow on the head: This was a bad plea of self-defence, as the mate was obviously justified in striking a man who acknowledged his intention of turning pirate, and taking the vessel.

As soon as Thomas Croft, the mate, was dispatched, and while he lay lifeless on the deck, they entered the cabin, and, approaching the b[e]rth where I lay asleep, one of them struck me one blow over the head, and another over the arm, with an axe, and immediately I received a stab in the arm with a sword. Upon which, I sprung up, and seized my pistols,[7] which were under my head; at the same time, Charles Rey, awaking from his sleep by the noise which this circumstance occasioned, jumped out of

---

6   Richard Peters (1744–1828) became a federal judge in 1792. In 1807, he published the two-volume *Admiralty Decisions in the United States District Court of Pennsylvania*. For a 20th century study, see Stinson, "Opinions of Richard Peters."

7   Most flintlock pistols of the era were "brass or iron-barreled affairs of about .50 to .60 caliber. At twenty paces a one-ounce pistol ball could spell death as truthfully as any more recently contrived instrument of war. In reality these heavy weapons were as formidable as a shotgun loaded with a single ball, inaccurate over a long range but carrying a killing shock that would knock down an ox" (Woodbury, *Piracy in the West Indies*, 95). Frayler ("Arms Chest," 2) noted that "pistols tended to be heavy and accurate only at very close range, but they did make excellent clubs."

A flintlock pistol (19th century illustration
by George Albert Williams).

his b[e]rth, and cried out in French, ["W]hat is the matter?["] And seeing that I was assailed by the three villains, by the blood on my face and arm, he snatched a pistol
suddenly from my hand, and turning upon them, they retreated from the cabin; but,
in his attempt to follow them, he received a severe blow over the head with the
pump brake,[8] which laid him on the cabin floor; however, he soon revived a little, but,
as it was dark, neither of us durst make a second attempt to go up from the cabin,
thro' fear of meeting with a similar reception. No words can describe the horrors of
my situation for nearly half an hour: my wounds were extremely painful, and I was almost covered with blood, while Mr. Rey seemed a little delirious from the blow he
had received on his head, and I expected every moment to be overpowered by the
ruffians, and finally murdered. We were in this situation, when Mr. Rey, seeing light on
deck, sprung up in a fit of desperation to make a second effort, when he received another mortal blow on the head.

Thinking that my generous friend, Mr. Rey, was murdered, and seeing myself covered
with blood, I wrenched the pistol, with some difficulty, from his dying-grasp, and putting myself in a posture of defence, I begged they would spare my life. Not knowing,
at that moment, that the mate was murdered, I imagined the whole crew had risen
against me, until those murderers informed me, that all, except myself, were killed, –
bidding me come on deck, which I refused, as I was apprehensive that if I did, I
should be immediately murdered. They then ordered me to hand them up liquor,
which I was incapable of doing, on account of the wounds which I had already received; nevertheless, as they saw me armed with pistols, they were afraid of entering
the cabin. A kind of parley then took place betwixt us, in which it was agreed, that I
should navigate the vessel to the Spanish Main,[9] on condition that they would spare
my life. Under an assurance of sparing their lives, they entered the cabin, supplied
themselves with liquor, and removed Mr. Rey upon deck: he was still in life; but it was

8 "The handle or lever of the old and simplest form of pump" (Smyth, *Lexicon*, 548).
9 The term Spanish Main originally "embraced that part of the mainland of the north-east coast of South America
   stretching from the Orinoco to the Isthmus of Panama, and the former Spanish mainland possessions bordering
   the Caribbean Sea and Gulf of Mexico. But by extension, particularly from the sense in which it was used by the
   buccaneers of the late 17th and early 18th centuries, the term came to mean the Caribbean Sea itself. Thus the
   meaning changed completely; where originally it referred to the main land, it later came to mean the main sea"
   (Dear and Kemp, *Companion*, 546).

impossible, even with medical aid, that he could have recovered. He appeared insensible to every thing that was going forward after his last fatal wound. These monsters, eager to finish the diabolical work they had begun, hastened to throw him overboard, although there was evident sign[s] of life. But these wretches were not yet satiated with blood. Jacob Suster, the remaining seaman, who had not joined in the conspiracy, and who had been asleep in the fore-castle[10] during this scene of horror, was now called aft, under a pretence that I wanted him; but, no sooner had he advanced with reach of these wretches, th[e]n he was knocked down with an axe, and immediately thrown into the sea. At that time we had light winds, and the vessel was making very little way, so that I could distinctly hear his groans for at least eight or ten minutes.

Jacob Suster was not known to me previous to his entering on board the schooner; but, from his shipment to the hour of his death, his behaviour was that of a good and faithful seaman. He was born in Germantown, in the state of Pennsylvania, where his parents, I am informed, now reside.

When these villains had finished their work of murder, and conscious of their own incapacity to navigate the vessel, they came into the cabin, and dressed my wounds: they then proceeded to wash off the blood from the floor of the cabin and from the deck, which, when they had finished, they began, as soon as morning appeared, to pillage the property of the deceased.

When day-light appeared, and perceiving that they considered their own safety to depend upon my knowledge of navigation, I began to have some hopes that my life would be spared, and even that the vessel might be regained; but, tho' I found my pistols serviceable to me in keeping them off, I was apprehensive, that, in case of another conflict, they might be used against myself; I, therefore, threw my pistols overboard secretly, – a circumstance which they never found out; for they always understood that I had them in my possession.

In this situation, in mutual fear of each other, we proceeded as they supposed towards the Spanish Main, but in this I deceived them, by telling them that a strong current set in to the westward, and that we must keep a more easterly course, which we did, but without discovering a sail. During this time, though the weather was generally moderate, the sails and rigging not being well trimmed, received considerable damage; for, I was not capable of handling a rope myself, and they were not under my subjection or orders; besides, when my arm, which I had constantly kept in a sling, began to grow better, I endeavoured to conceal it as much as possible from them, thinking that my security consisted, in a great measure, on their ideas of my weak-

---

10   Pronounced "fo'c'sle," on a merchant vessel the term referred to the sailors' living quarters in the forward section, below the deck (Dear and Kemp, Companion, 222; Smyth, Lexicon, 314).

ness. In the mean while, their principal occupation was in rifling the vessel, breaking open packages, in search of any thing valuable, or for barrels of hams or other provisions; whilst I was on the watch or an opportunity to overcome them, and get possession of the vessel.

This opportunity presented on the 21st September, on the ninth day after the murderers had got possession of the vessel. Two of them, Peterson, alias La Croix, and Baker, alias Boulanger, went down the fore-scuttle to bring up some hams, while Brous was stooping down to make a fire in the caboush;[11] I immediately seized a club that lay near me, with my left hand, my right being still in a sling, and gave Brous a severe blow on the back of the head, which laid him flat on the deck; I attempted a second blow, but missed him. Mr. Rey's bull-dog seeing me engaged, flew, barking to my assistance, which so much deterred Brous from turning upon me, that he r[a]n aft, and got up the shrouds;[12] I immediately snatched up an axe, and ran to the fore-scuttle,[13] slipping my arm from the sling, and forgetting my wounds, lifted up the axe, as in act to strike the two that were there, and whose heads were then above the deck, attempting to come out; but the moment they saw the axe over their heads, they sunk down into the hold, and I instantly shut the s[c]uttle over them; and, to make it more secure, I dragged a small anchor from the bow, by means of a rope round the windlass,[14] and laid it over the s[c]uttle.

Having now Peterson and Baker secured, I proceeded to Brous, who was on the shrouds; at first he had no intention of yielding, but cried out to his companions that they might come aft into the cabin, and proceed that way to his assistance, while those below were vociferating loudly to him; but, being in French, I did not perfectly understand.

But, when Brous saw himself entirely at my mercy, he supplicated with great earnestness, that I would spare his life, which I promised to do, on condition that he could come down and submit himself to be confined, and behave in every respect as I direct him. He was some time before he could be persuaded to believe that I would spare him: However, on my further assurances, he was prevailed on to come down; as soon as he was on deck, he fell on his knees, took me by the hand, and kissed it several times, making, at the same time, the most solemn protestations of submission. I then ordered him to put his hands behind him, that I might tie them, which he

---

11   Also Caboose or Camboose. "The cook-room or kitchen of merchantmen on deck; a diminutive substitute for the galley of a man-of-war. It is generally furnished with cast-iron apparatus for cooking" (Smyth, *Lexicon*, 151–152). "It was normally built on deck, and in shape resembled a sentry box. It was originally a wooden box or covering of the galley chimney where it came through the deck, hence probably its association with cooking. The name applied only to smaller merchant ships, all larger ships having space for a galley between decks" (Dear and Kemp, *Companion*, 81–82).
12   See the discussion of *rattling down* in Chapter 5.
13   A scuttle is "a small hole or port cut either in the deck or side of a ship, generally for ventilation. That in the deck is a small hatch-way" (Smyth, *Lexicon*, 599).
14   A piece of equipment, usually located near the front of a vessel, "which serves to ride by, as well as heave in the cable" (Smyth, *Lexicon*, 733).

instantly complied with; I then got a chain, and chained him upon deck to the ring-bolts. Brous being thus secured, I set about taking the necessary precautions for preserving what I had gained; I, therefore, went into the cabin, and brought up biscuit and other provisions, together with my quadrant,[15] books, &c. and secured the cabin, lest they might force a passage that way.

I now saw that I had an arduous task to accomplish, to navigate a schooner alone, and to watch my prisoners; from whom (if they had accomplished their intents) I could expect no mercy; but, when I compared it with what I had already suffered, it appeared a pleasure. The most difficult part I thought was over, and that I had only to suffer some privations, to trust to the protection of the Almighty, and my own vigilance. When I regained possession of the schooner, I found myself in latitude 25 deg[rees] North, and in longitude 60 deg[rees] West. My prisoners below had plenty of provisions; but they were in darkness, and had no water. To prevent them making any attempts regain their liberty, I did not think it proper to drive them to desperation; but to show them that I was willing to let them live, and enjoy as many comforts as was consistent with my own safety: I burnt a hole with a spike in the fore-scuttle, through which I could pour water and other refreshments; so that, after several attempts to break through, and believing that I had killed Brous, and thrown him overboard, they desisted, and seemed to submit to their fate. As for Brous, who was on deck, I suffered him, at meal times, to have the partial use of his limbs, to change his position, &c. but I would by no means suffer him to speak aloud, or be for a moment totally unfettered; for, my greatest fears were from his getting loose, and suddenly surprizing me, while I was in a slumber; for, I never lay down, or had any profound sleep while they were under my charge.

On the 4th of October, being thirteen days after the recapture of the vessel, Providence during all that time having blessed me with favourable weather, except one gale, which lasted twenty-four hours, I discovered the island of St. Bartholomew's,[16] and at 7, p.m. was off the harbour; and, by the assistance of a Swedish schooner, anchored to the leeward of the harbour, and at 10, p.m. John Peterson, Esq., commander of his Swedish majesty's brig *Housare*, sent his barge, with two officers and ten men, to my assistance, in which he was joined by A. Campbell, Esq., commander

---

15 The seaman's quadrant was "the earliest instrument used by navigators for measuring the altitude of a heavenly body. It was in the form of a quarter circle of brass or wood with a plumb line suspended, when the instrument was in use, from the center of the circle of which the quadrant formed part. One radial edge of the instrument was fitted with two pins or sights by means of which a sight of the heavenly body was acquired. This quadrant required two observers, one to bring the observed body into the line of the two pins and the other to note the position where the plumb line crossed the arc of the instrument. ... This simple quadrant could not be used on board ship unless the sea was smooth and the air calm, and even in the most suitable conditions its degree of accuracy was coarse. But it was an instrument which could be easily manufactured by the navigator himself if the need arose and, because the vertical was defined by a plumb line, the quadrant could be used for measuring altitudes when the horizon was obscured by darkness or fog" (Dear and Kemp, *Companion*, 503–4).

16 Saint Barthélemy, an island in the West Indies to the south of Anguilla and north of St. Kitts. At the time of this episode it was a Swedish possession.

of the United States brig *Eagle*,[17] and, on the 5th instant, anchored safe in port; and after being moored, I landed, and entered a protest against the prisoners for murder and piracy, with Job Wall, Esq., consul for the United States of America, who had the murderers put in irons, on board of the aforesaid United states brig *Eagle*, with orders to be delivered up to Thomas Tingey, Esq.,[18] commander of the United States ship *Ganges*,[19] and commodore of the leeward station.

After delivering up my prisoners to [C]aptain Campbell, I was politely treated by the merchants and other inhabitants of the island; but, the government made a claim of salvage, for the assistance the Swedish brig had given me, in bringing the vessel to her anchorage. However, I resisted the claim thus set up, and showed that it was contrary to the treaty with Sweden; but was obliged to pay two hundred dollars to the sailors of the Swedish brig for their assistance. Soon after I sold my cargo, and purchased another of sugars, and having hired fresh hands, I sailed from St. Bartholomew's on the 4th November, and arrived at Gloucester-Point[20] the 25th of the same month.

When the prisoners were brought to Philadelphia, they underwent an examination before [J]udge Peters, in which they confessed the piracy and murder, differing very little in the detail of the circumstances from the foregoing narrative: The plea which they set up in their defence was, that they were French prisoners, and in the service of the French Republic: That one of them, Brous, alias La Roche, bore a commission under that government, and therefore they had a right to make prize of an American vessel, and to kill any person that resisted the attempt. But the judge having considered that they entered voluntarily into the American service, objected to their plea, and ordered them to prison for trial. Peterson, alias La Croix, has not the least appearance of being a Frenchman, though he speaks bad French, having been probably on board a French ship, and it is more likely that he is a Dane or a Swede. As for Boulanger, alias Baker, we have good authority to say, that he is a Canadian, that he was born at Les-trois-riviers,[21] of a creditable family, and was a soldier in a regiment called the Royal Canadians,[22] in the service of his Britannic majesty, from which he deserted in the spring of

---

17 Originally commissioned in the Revenue Cutter Service, the U.S. Navy acquired the 187-ton, 58-foot long *Eagle* in 1798 for service in the Quasi-War. Carrying 14 6-pounder cannon, it was patrolling in the Caribbean at this time, convoying American vessels and hunting French privateers (Mooney, *Fighting Ships*, II:316).
18 London-born Tingey (1750–1829), later a commodore, would have a long tenure heading the Washington Navy Yard (Mooney, *Fighting Ships*, VII:201).
19 The United States Navy in 1798 purchased the *Ganges*, a Philadelphia-built East Indiaman and converted it into a warship. Unofficially listed as carrying 26 guns, mostly long 9-pounders, it served with distinction in the Quasi-War with France (Votaw, "Sloop-of-War *Ganges*," 82–84).
20 Opposite Yorktown, Virginia, on the York River.
21 Trois-Rivières, situated between Montreal and Quebec City.
22 A militia unit of that name was originally raised in 1774. It partook in the defense of Quebec during the Revolutionary War, and by 1777 was one of three regiments on garrison duty there (Untitled article, *Morning Chronicle and London Advertiser*, 11 August 1774 [n.p.]; "Extract of a Letter from Quebec, May 25," *St. James's Chronicle or the British Evening Post*, 22–25 June 1776 [n.p.]; and "Extract of a Letter from Charles-Town, South Carolina, May 14," *Morning Chronicle and London Advertiser*, 2 July 1777 [n.p.]).

1799, and came into New-York state, by the way of Lake Champlain; so that it is not probable that he was ever in the service of France, or at sea before this fatal voyage. And it is highly probable that Brous, alias La Roche, is also a Canadian.

Their trial came on in the circuit court of the United States, before [J]udges [Samuel] Chase[23] and Peters, on Monday, the 21st April; they having for coun[se]l, Messrs. [Alexander James] Dallas, [Jasper Alexander] Moylan and [Peter Stephen] Du[P]onceau;[24] the only evidence against them was myself, and their hardened conduct; and [J]udge Peters, who was called upon to give the substance of their examination before him, previous to their commitment for trial, the jury, after retiring a short time, brought in a verdict of Guilty.

Sentence of Death was passed upon them on Friday, the 25th April, and they are ordered for Execution on the 9th May.

I thought it my duty, not only from repeated solicitations, but that I might be relieved from numerous verbal narrations, to send this to Mr. Folwell's press. I have no emolument in its publication; and so far from setting down "aught in malice," I forgive them, as they are my fellow-creatures; but they must abide by the lenient laws of my country; and hope their God, who is my God, will be merciful.

WILLIAM WHELAND
Philadelphia, April 27, 1800

ooooo

The Confession of Joseph Baker, a Canadian by Birth, who, for Murder & Piracy Committed on the High Seas, on Board the Schooner *Eliza*, Captain Wm. Wheland, in a Voyage from Philadelphia Bound to St. Thomas, was Tried on the 25th of April, 1800, Before the Hon. Samuel Chase and Richard Peters, Judges of the District Court of the United States, for the District of Pennsylvania, and now [is] under sentence of Death, in the solitary cells of the Penitentiary House of the City and County of Philadelphia[25] (Philadelphia: Richard Folwell, 1800).

---

23   Born in 1741, Samuel Chase was an associate justice of the U.S. Supreme Court from 1796 until his death in 1811. The U.S. House of Representatives impeached him in 1804–05, but the Senate acquitted him (See Knudson, "Jeffersonian Assault").

24   All three attorneys were Philadelphia residents who had been admitted to the bar of the Supreme Court of the United States in 1791. Dallas (1759–1817), began practicing law in Jamaica in 1780 and joined the bar of the Supreme Court of Pennsylvania in 1785; he later became secretary of the U.S. Treasury. Moylan (ca. 1759–1812) joined the bar of Philadelphia in 1782 and that of the Supreme Court of Pennsylvania two years later. Du Ponceau (1760–1844), who had a background as an interpreter, joined the Philadelphia bar in 1785 and a year later was admitted to the bar of the Supreme Court of Pennsylvania (Marcus and Perry, *Documentary History of the Supreme Court*, Vol. I, part 1:189n79, n80, and n82).

25   Built in 1790, the Walnut Street Jail's "penitentiary-house . . . was built of brick, three stories high, raised on arches. It contained sixteen solitary cells, each six by eight by nine feet high. They were quite dark as the only light admitted came from above through a peculiar, narrow form of blind. Below this block as well as under the two wings were dungeons. In 1797 several brick buildings were erected in the jail yard to serve as workshops.

Considering the awfulness of my situation, the dreadful tribunal before which I must appear, there to give an account of a jealous and much-offended (but just and merciful God) of all my vile and wicked crimes, committed at this early time of life I deem it a duty I owe to [C]aptain Wheland, and to the community in general, to give a clear and circumstantial account of the horrid act, and of all the circumstances leading thereto, so that such of my fellow-men as follow the seas, might take warning at my fate, and learn to fear God; to shun such wicked practices, and thereby avoid those disagreeable feelings which I have and am now suffering, and the ignominious and untimely end to which I must shortly be brought.

I was born in the year 1779, at Les-trois-riviers, in Canada, in a street called Forge-street. I was eighteen years old when I left my father, and went to Lake Champlain, from there I went to Virginia, on Lake Champlain, being sixty miles from the line of Canada: In June, 1799, I worked my passage in a boat from thence to Albany and New-York, where I went to work in company with another Canadian, at making staves, and continued in that employment 8 days, at two dollars per day; to the other man, with whom I worked, I lent money to pay for his lodging, and gave the remainder of my money and clothes in his charge, with all which he run off: I then went in the country to one [C]olonel Robins, twenty-one miles from New-York, and got from him a recommendation to obtain work at the ship-carpenter's business.¶

On my return to New-York, there I became acquainted with one Pierre Lewis Lacroix, (who is now under the unhappy sentence with myself, for the same crime.) One evening I went to a tavern in company with Lacroi[x]; and in conversation, he asked me where I lodged. I told him where my lodgings were, and the next day he (in company with Brous, now under the same sentence also) called upon me: they told me I was a fool to stay in such a country as this was, when, if I would go [to] the West-Indies and work at my trade, I could get five dollars per day. They told me of an English vessel at New-York, mounting eighteen guns, which was bound to Jamaica,[26] with a cargo of flour and lumber. I went and entered on board of this vessel as ship-carpen-

---

A wall, some twenty feet high, surrounded the entire prison, save for the facade. The wall was topped with a sort of fragile wooden shed, extending a few feet into the interior yard for the purpose of preventing escape by throwing ropes over with hooks attached. The two-storied central building was crowned with a pediment in which was a semi-circular arched fan window. A one-story cupola rose above the entire structure on which was placed a copper weather vane in the shape of a key which was gilded" (*Teeters, Cradle of the Penitentiary*, 19).

26 "Jamaica . . . is in length, from east to west, a hundred and forty English miles; in breadth about sixty; and of an oval form. This country is in a manner intersected with a ridge of lofty mountains, rugged and rocky, that are called the blue mountains. On each side of the blue mountains are chains of lesser mountains gradually lower. ... [O]n one hand the mountains are very steep; so the plains between them are perfectly smooth and level. In these plains the soil, augmented by the wash of the mountains for so many ages, is prodigiously fertile. None of our islands produce so fine sugars. They formerly had here cacao in great perfection, which delights in a rich ground. Their pastures after the rains are of a most beautiful verdure and extraordinary fatness. They are called savannas. On the whole, if this island were not troubled with great thunders and lightnings, hurricanes, and earthquakes; and, if the air was not at once violently hot, damp, and extremely unwholesome in most parts, the fertility and beauty of this country would make it as desirable a situation for pleasure, as it is for the profits, which, in spite of these disadvantages, draw hither such a number of people" (Burke, *European Settlements*, II:61–63).

ter. There were seven Italians and Frenchmen on board this vessel, who proposed to me to enter into a secret conspiracy for surprizing the captain and crew on her voyage to the West-Indies, and make ourselves masters of the ship and cargo: But I would not agree to their proposal, and, therefore, quitted the ship; in consequence of which, Pierre Lewis Lacroix and Joseph Brous, quitted her also.¶

I came to Philadelphia on the twentieth of August, 1799, and took up lodgings at a boarding house in Water-street, in company with Pierre Lewis Lacroix: The before-mentioned Brous, having found out where we lodged, came and took lodgings in the same house. As I did not like the company of Brous, I told Pierre Lewis Lacroix, to let us go, and look out for a vessel that was going to the West-Indies, and quit Brous. We found one [C]aptain Wheland who was bound to St. Thomas. I enquired of him if he wanted any hands: he told me he wanted two, and shipped Lacroix and myself at twenty-five dollars per month, [and] Lacroix and myself then went to another part of the city to lodge, till the vessel should be ready to sail; but, unfortunately, we me[e]t with Brous in the street, and he asked me to lend him three dollars, for the purpose of paying his board. I accordingly lent it to him, and told him I never wanted to see him any more.¶

The next Monday morning Lacroix and myself went on board the vessel to stay; and, to our great surprize, we saw Brous on board at work. I then asked him if he was shipped with the vessel [and] he told me he was to work his passage. We told him that this was not the way to go to the Havannah,[27] as he said he meant to do. He told he would find some vessel at St. Kitts that would be going to the Havannah. After which, the captain took him to the merchant to sign articles to work his passage. The merchant asked him what countryman he was; he told him he was an Italian. The merchant told him it was not true, for he was a Frenchman, and he had no passage for him. Afterwards the captain told him to go on board to work, and he would pay him for what he did: the captain that afternoon told him he would give him his passage, although the merchant had refused it. He accordingly went on board the vessel, and we sailed from Philadelphia, bound to St. Thomas, on the 27th of August, 1799.¶

The 4th September following, being at sea, Brous asked me if I would assist him in taking the vessel. I told him I would not. After which, he put the same question to Lacroix. He also told him he would have nothing to do with it; but he continually har[r]assed us for three days to consent to his wicked proposal: Lacro[ix] then told

---

27 An administrative center in Spain's Latin American colonies, by the turn of the 19th century Havana was becoming one of the continent's busiest ports. Within a few years, it would rival Charleston for activity, and by 1816 it would handle "more commercial maritime traffic than Boston, Baltimore, New Orleans, Philadelphia, or Savannah. Havana's principal exports in this era were sugar, coffee, molasses, and wax." It was also a waystation for the import of slaves, an estimated 15,000 arriving in 1817 (Gibbs, *Dead Men*, 52–53). Cuba itself had been a haven for pirates for more than a century, a Dutch chronicler in the late 1600s noting that "Cuba is surrounded by innumerable small islands, known as Cays, frequently used by the buccaneers as bases from which to harry the Spaniards" (Exquemelin, *Buccaneers*, 127).

him, that if he would take the vessel, he (Lacroix) would take her into port. He then asked me to take some poison out of the medicine-chest, and put some in the soup, for the purpose of destroying the captain, and the three other men. I told him that I had not so hard a[n] heart as to kill any man. I then asked him if he had a heart hard enough to kill a man. ["Y]es,["] says he, ["]and if I had fifty of them tied hand and foot, I could kill them all, and my father at the head of them too.["] I told him that my heart was not so hard as all that come [to?]¶

Brous then told me that he was an officer in the service of the French Republic; and said, that if I did not consent to assist in taking the vessel, that the first French cruiser they came up with, he would report me thereto, and have me shot. I told him I was not a Frenchman, but was a Canadian. He told me that he would report me to be a French-man, and not a Canadian, and that [G]eneral de[s] Fo[u]rneaux[28] would take his word before he would mine. I told him that I would see that, and he said it was very well.¶

I was in hopes every day that some American or English vessel would come in sight, as I intended to have reported to [C]aptain Wheland what Brous had said; but unfor-tunately for us, we met with none.¶

About two days after Brous and I had had the foregoing conversation, Brous again asked me (at about 10 o'clock at night) if I was ready to help him to take the vessel. I told him I would have nothing to do with it. He then replied, "I will begin, and you must take care of yourself," and called me a coward. Next night, about ten o'clock, he called me to light a candle. I, accordingly, was about doing so, when the mate asked me where I was going: I told him I was about lighting a candle for the binnacle,[29] and when I brought up the candle, I found the mate lying dead on the companion.[30] Brous had an axe in his hand, and Lacroix had a handspike[31] in his, standing side by side. They told me to go down and take the captain's sword, and if he was a-sleep, to

---

28   General Desfourneaux commanded a French division on Haiti (Rainsford, *Hayti, passim*).
29   A binnacle is "a wooden case or box, which contains the compass, and a light to illuminate the compass at night. . ." (Smyth, *Lexicon*, 102). Various navigational instruments, including charts, "were also properly stowed in the binnacle" (Dear and Kemp, *Companion*, 46). This compass, divided into 32 points of direction, would have been a "dry card" one; according to one maritime expert the "wet" or "spirit compass," in which the magnetized needle floated in a mixture containing alcohol – intended to dampen sudden sharp movement – did not come into use until about 1830 (correspondence with Norman Bliss, 30 December 2010).
30   "COMPANION. The framing and sash-lights upon the quarter-deck or round-house, through which light passes to the cabins and decks below; and a sort of wooden hood placed over the entrance or staircase of the master's cabin in small ships . . . COMPANION LADDER. Denotes the ladder by which the officers ascend to, and de-scend from, the quarter-deck. COMPANION-WAY. The staircase, porch, or berthing of the ladder-way to the cabin" (Smyth, *Lexicon*, 204–205).
31   "A lever made of tough ash, and used to heave round the windlass in order to draw up the anchor from the bot-tom, or move any heavy articles, particularly in merchant ships. The handle is round, but the other end is square, conforming to the shape of the holes in the windlass" (Smyth, Lexicon, 365). It differs from a marlinspike, which Smyth noted (470) is "an iron pin tapering to a point, and principally used to separate the strands of a rope, in order to introduce the ends of some other through the intervals in the act of knotting or splicing . . ."

run it through his body, and if I did not do it, they would kill me: I went down, but I could not find it in my heart to kill the captain, but struck him on the hand with a hatchet: he then jumped up, and made a catch at me, and I then struck him on the head. Immediately I ran up on deck: Brous then attempted to kill me, because I had not killed the captain: I told him I had not the heart to kill him

Lacroix stood on the companion, with a handspike in his hand, to kill the first man that came up. The supercargo came up, with a pistol in each hand, and Lacroix knocked him down with the handspike: Lacroix then told me to lower the peak of the [m]ain-sail; but, just as I was going to do it, I observed the supercargo coming after me, with a pistol in each hand, to kill me. I then looked behind me, and saw a stick, which I picked up and struck him with, and knocked him down.¶

All this time the captain was below, and called out to Lacroix. I asked what he wanted; he told me to save his life. Brous told the captain to come up; the captain said, "[Y]ou will kill me if I do." I told him to stay down, and surrender himself a prisoner of war. The captain then said he would. Lacroix then went down to bring up some liquor and called me down to help to bring up the supercargo on deck. Brous and myself went down and brought him up. We then laid him down till Lacroix brought some liquor to wash his wounds, but Brous said he would give him liquor enough; and immediately threw him overboard, though he was yet living. Brous told us to come along with him and kill the sailor in the for[e]castle: I told him I would not. Brous bid me go down to the sailor. I accordingly did so; the sailor asked me if I wanted to kill him? I told him, that I did not, but that Brous did. He asked me where Brous was: I told him he was on deck, laying in wait to kill him: he then jumped on deck to catch Brous, but, before he could get to him, Brous struck him with a handspike, and killed him. He then threw him overboard. We had now killed all but the captain, who considered himself as a prisoner of war.¶

About four days after, Lacroix found a bottle of opium[32] in the medicine-chest; he told me to take care of it. I took it, and hid it. Brous came to me afterwards, and asked me where the bottle was; he said he wanted to give some to the captain to drink, so as it might kill him. I told him I had lost it; but, a little time after, he found another bottle of the same kind, which he said he would keep himself, and give it to the captain to drink, as soon as we saw a vessel heave in sight; so that he might say that all hands had died on board, except us three. I told the captain of his danger, that Brous was determined to kill him the very first vessel we saw. The captain said he would not help it; but he would do the best he could to save himself.

The next day the captain told me he was sick, and desired me to go and get some ham for him: Lacroix and myself went down to get some for him, and when we went

---

32   A standard element in most vessels' medicine stores, opium was "commonly included in pain medicines such as Laudanum, and as addictive then as it is now" (Frayler, *Medicine Chest*, 9).

down, the captain took the axe and knocked Brous down. He then immediately locked down the forecastle, so that we could not get up. Lacroix told me to assist him below, in cutting the mast down, so that it might fall, and tear up the deck, that we might get out: I told him that I did not want to do so, and, in consequence of my refusal, he abused me very much, and said I was a coward.¶

We were fourteen days in the hold before we got to St. Bartholomew's, and, during that time, we lived upon flour and water, and some liquor. After we arrived at St. Bartholomew's, the captain put us on board an American armed vessel, the lieutenant of which abused us in a violent manner, and put ropes round our necks: [W]e remained in this situation three days, and then we were taken to St. Kitts, where we were put in prison and kept in irons, on five ounces of bread and water per day for nineteen days. We were then put on board the United States sloop of war[33] *Ganges*, and were in irons eighteen days, sleeping on deck all the while. Brous and Lacroix told me to declare myself a Frenchman, at the peril of my life. They also told me, if I would consent to this declaration, each of them would give me 700 dollars; to which I consented.¶

We arrived at Philadelphia on the 12th of November, 1799, and were landed from on board the *Ganges*, conducted to prison under guard, and immediately lodged in the cells. 'Tis but justice I owe to the inspectors, and to every keeper about the prison, to say, that we have always been treated with every degree of humanity, and, in every respect, as well as the nature of our situations could admit of, received full allowance, nor were we ever put in irons until after we received the fatal (tho' just) condemnation of death, (and that by order of the court.)

And now, having finished my narration, and the time approaching fast when I must suffer the just reward due to the horrid crime in which I have been too great a participator, there remains nothing more for me to add, but to declare that I die in the full belief of the Roman Catholic religion [and?] that I have truly and sincerely repented of my manifold sins and transgressions, and, as I place a firm reliance on the mercies of Almighty God, I humbly beseech him to manifest his blessed declaration upon me, and be to me "The Lord, the Lord God, merciful and gracious, delaying indignation, and abundant in goodness and truth, keeping mercy for thousands, forgiving iniquity, transgression and sin; that it may please him to number me amongst those thousands for whom he has declared he will keep mercy; and that, through the blood and merits of my blessed redeemer, my sins may be purged away, and my soul admitted into the mansions of eternal bliss. Amen.["]

Joseph Baker.

Solitary cells of the Prison of the City and County of Philadelphia, May 5th, 1800.

---

33   A term used to refer to any warship smaller than a frigate, the latter generally being a three-masted, square-rigged warship.

ooooo

Execution of La Croix, Berrouse, & Baker, for Piracy. The Last Words and Dying Confession of the Three Pirates Who Were Executed This Day, (May 9th, 1800.) (Philadelphia: Richard Folwell, 1800).
[. . .]

Joseph Baker, alias Boulanger, on the day before his exit, dictated to a French gentleman, of this city, a letter to his Brother, with injunctions to send it forward immediately after his execution; which we have faithfully translated from the original.

Copy.

Philadelphia, May 8th, 1800.

Dear Brother,

I hasten to make known to you my situation, for the last time, and about eighteen hours before my death.

Having committed an action against the commandments of God, and the laws of civil society, I send you this, in order to keep you at a distance from the like misfortune, and that you should acquaint my father, brothers and sisters of my death, without telling them the cause of it: I trust that they will pray for me on earth, as I hope to pray for them in heaven. I have complied, in every thing, with the rules of our religion, and bid you a last adieu, – hoping that my poor family, and all my friends, may enjoy eternal life: so no more from your unfortunate brother, who is only thinking on God.

Joseph Boulanger.

To Mons. Pierre Boulanger, in Captain Destmonville's Company of Volunteers, Canada

The same day, Joseph Berrouse dictated the following letter to his Uncle, in Paris:

Copy.

Philadelphia, 8th May, 1800.

My Dear Uncle,

I write you these lines, at this time, which is likely (by an accident which has befallen me) to be the last day of my life.

Wishing to support that unfortunate Republic, and seeking to return to my own country, I was induced to commit an action, contrary to the laws of God, and of civilized nations – which hath shortened my days.

I pray you, my dear uncle, not to forget to make known my unfortunate lot, to my relations and guardians, that they may take possession of my property. I hope they will not forget me in their prayers – that they will cause mass to be said, and give something to the poor, for me. – Make my respects to all my dear relations, and salute my dear cousins, for me. I am sorry that I have made no will, but hope that you will agree together.

I am your unfortunate
And dear Nephew,

Joseph Berrouse, Cadet.

To Mons. Depuis le Jeune, Saddler
And Coach-maker, Fauxbour, St. Germain, Paris.

These three unfortunate young men were attended, from the time they received their sentence, to the day of their execution, by clergymen of different persuasions, and they employed themselves almost unremittedly in acts of devotion; and appeared truly penitent, and anxious to obtain favour from an offended God, through the merits of Jesus Christ.

Peter La Croix, shortly before his execution, gave the following account of his life.

"I was born in Flanders; my parents gave me a good education; and my mother, particularly, never failed to give the best admonitions; but, unfortunately, I did not comply with them; on the contrary, I followed my own wicked inclinations. I was only a boy when I went to sea, and I engaged at last in the Low-Dutch, or Holland service; but, not liking this, I went over to England. I soon returned from thence to Holland; and, in order not to be brought to punishment as a deserter, I changed my name, and called myself Peter Peterson. My restless spirit soon drove me away from Holland again; and I wandered from one place to another.

"During the whole time, after I had left my parents, I led a very ungodly life. I had not, nor did I care for, any good book; and, particularly, I never read in that book, which is now my only consolation, – the Bible.

"God and Eternity were only my sport. I was a true blasphemer; and I now recollect, with horror, that I actually lifted up my fist against the Almighty; and, in the tumult of my passion, challenged his vengeance.

"I could say a great deal about the dreadful murder on board of the *Eliza*, but I think it unnecessary: This one circumstance I cannot, however, conceal, that I never actually killed one, myself, of those who were murdered: But this does not excuse me, because I could have saved their lives: Yet, though it was in my power, as I did not prevent the murder, but, on the contrary, sided with those who perpetrated it, I have certainly deserved death, and shortly shall justly suffer what my actions merit."

To the above, we have to add, that the name of La Croix was no more his real name that that of Peterson; and he certainly had his reasons why he changed his name the second time – reasons which were obviously not founded on his good behaviour. He disclosed his real name to one of the ministers, who visited him; but begged that it might be kept a secret, as he did not wish to expose his relations to that disgrace which the publicity of his unhappy end undoubtedly would.[34]

According to his account, he is of a respectable family; and his mother, brethren, and sisters were yet alive, as far as he knew.

The author of this short account did not see the prisoner until sentence had been passed on him; and, therefore, can only relate what situation he found him in, during that short space of time.

The unhappy man was, in those days, as much as appeared, quiet, and perfectly re-signed. His chief occupation was the study of the Scriptures; and, in these, the Old Testament as well as the New, he was surprisingly versed. He made many sensible and striking remarks upon some texts, which might otherwise be accounted difficult; and it appeared, plainly, that he understood what he read. It was a great advantage to him, that, in his early days, he had been well acquainted with the Bible; for, although he afterwards reviled the same, and even scoffed at it, yet, at the hour of death, it was his only refuge; and this, without a doubt, because the blessed recollection of what it had been to him in his youth, encouraged him thereto. He confessed that he never had cared for the Scriptures since his infancy, until he was confined in the cell of the Philadelphia Prison. In this distress, he knew of no other remedy to allay his apprehensions. He read, and the more he read, the more he wished to read; and he must really have been very industrious, in this his employment, or else it would have been impossible, that, in so short a time, he should have become so well acquainted with this book, as he really was.

When visited, he complained of nothing more than of the hardness of his heart. This he looked upon as the severest judgment of God, which the Lord had inflicted upon him for his enormous iniquities. He acknowledged how great the difference was be-tween faith of the head and of the heart: He complained that the latter remained so strange to him. He prayed frequently; yet, according to his own declaration, altho' the words proceeded from his mouth, his heart and sentiments had no share therein. He believed in Jesus as his Saviour; but this belief made no impression upon his heart. He sh[o]wed great concern, lest the Lord should reject him, and that he would hardly accept of a sinner like him. His approaching end, did not, according to his acknowl-edgment, occasion in him any fear. He confessed that he had perfectly deserved this

---

34 In 1831, condemned pirate and mutineer James Jeffers would maintain a similar alias (Charles Gibbs) until his execution, citing the same reason. See chapter 9.

punishment; but, that the judgment[s] of God, and of eternity, were dreadful to him: That the recollection of his sins, and the damnation which he had deserved, were the gnawing worm of his heart.

In this sorry and dreadful situation of mind, he was found constantly, until about three days before his execution; when beamed a small glimpse of grace upon his darkened soul. A very applicable German Hymn was read to him, which drew the first tears from his eyes, and his heart was considerably rel[ie]ved by it. From that moment, he began to be more easy. He now perused the Scriptures with more sensation: Reading Luke 11, I, 12,[35] he exclaimed: "Now this must be true, what Jesus has said, for he never spoke an untruth; and so the Almighty God will, for all, hear my prayers." And here his eyes were bathed in tears.

The above-mentioned Hymn gave great consolation to him; he read it himself, and he caused it to be read to him repeatedly.

On the [last?] morning of his life, when he was visited, and asked how it was now with him, his answer was, "Oh, it is better, – much better with me. I had a very good night; I have prayed the whole night. The Lord Jesus ordered me to watch and pray! No sleep came into my Eyes, and I feel now much easier."

Particularly important it was to him, that which he had read that morning in H[e]rvey's *Meditations on the Night*,[36] where he introduces a Latin Motto on a Sun-dial. The translation of which is, "On this moment depends an eternity." ["]Each moment,["] said he, ["]is now, for certain, to me, an eternity; and, for that reason, I like to do nothing better than praying.["]

During this conversation, a woman came in, who said that she was his mother. He looked at her without the least emotion; and only said, "[N]o, – no, – that is not my mother. I know that my mother could not be in Philadelphia." It is said that the woman, herself, afterwards, acknowledged her error.

As one of those, who visited him took his leave, (bursting into tears) he said, "Ah! I hope and I believe we shall see one another again in bliss with the Lord. Farewell – farewell and thanks for your kindness."

---

35 Luke 11:1–12 includes the Lord's Prayer and Jesus' assertion that God is generous to those seeking aid.

36 English Methodist James Hervey's work *Meditations and Contemplations* was originally published in two volumes in 1746–47. In a footnote in the section "Contemplations on the Night," Hervey wrote (198): "I remember to have seen upon a sun-dial in a physician's garden at Northampton, the following inscription; which, I think, is the most proper motto for the instrument that measures our time; and the most striking admonition that can possibly be represented to every eye: *Ab hoc momento pendet Eternitas*. The weighty sense of which, I know not how to express in English, more happily than in those words of Dr. Watts: Good God! on what a slender thread (Or, on what a moment of time) Hang everlasting things!"

He had given to the same person, the evening before, a Letter, with a request to forward the same to his brother, and to desire him to inform his mother of his fate; at least, of his death. Here follows the translation of the letter, which was written in the Low-Dutch language.

Philadelphia, 28th Germinal [18 April],[37] 8th year of the French Republic.

Dear Brother,

This is the last letter which you will receive from me; and I hope that the great and Almighty God, will let you come to a better end that that which I am come to: Because I forsook the Almighty God, my latter end is truly unfortunate. I hope you will take this to heart, and, with your whole soul, cleave to God, who can deliver us from evil. Dear brother, I write this in chains and fetters, about twenty hours before my death, in hopes that you will take the same to heart, and trust in him, whom I had forsaken, – but on whom I now place my only hopes, and confide in his unmerited mercy. I hope that you will remember me with brotherly love. I herewith conclude, recommending you, as likewise my poor soul, into the hands of the God of my fathers, and wish you an eternal good night. And, as I hope to obtain the grace of God, I recommend you into the hands of my Saviour, Jesus Christ; and I now go to eternal rest – Amen. – Greet all friends and acquaintances in the name of the Lord my God, and your God – Amen.

Your servant and brother,

To eternity,

Peter La Croix.

Reader! The crimes of these young men were the greatest that can be committed in civil society – and highly aggravated by many atrocious circumstances. Although they have not furnished the world with a particular account of their past lives, it is almost certain, that, though young men, they had pursued a dissolute and abandoned course, – regardless of God, before whom they are now to be judged – and who, in his all-wise Providence, stopped them in their vicious career.

---

37   *Germinal* (from the French word for germination), representing late March to late April on the traditional or Gregorian calendar, was the seventh month of the year by the Revolutionary Calendar of the French Republic, in use from 1793 to 1805. "The old years and months were to be abolished by decree, replaced by a system of twelve equal thirty-day months, while the extra five or six days at the end of the year, running up to the autumnal equinox (when, fortuitously, the Republic had been created) would be given over the national festivities. The week was to be replaced with a ten-day period (the *décade*, with just one day of rest – storing up trouble for the future popularity of the measure), and, within each day, the twenty-four hours would be replaced by ten segments, each themselves divided into ten smaller periods (of just under fifteen 'old' minutes), and then further subdivided as necessary *ad infinitum* 'down to the smallest measurable units of duration'" (Andress, *The Terror*, 219–221).

Murder is a crime of so deep a dye, that it seldom or never escapes a temporal punishment; – though God, in his infinite mercy, may grant repentance, and, thereby, the unhappy perpetrator may not be finally shut out from eternal happiness.

How much reason had these persons to rejoice, that they were brought to a city, where the consolation[s] of the gospel were held out to them, by pious divines; – that they were not snatched into eternity, from their wicked courses, in a moment, without time or opportunity to reflect on, and repent, of their misspent life, and the disregard they had paid to the commandments of God, or the laws of man.

It is sincerely hoped, that their untimely fate may be a warning to all young men, to forsake the paths of vice, and to remember their Creator in the days of their youth – to gain a living by honest industry, rather than by violence upon the persons or property of others in whatever stations they are allotted to, – whether by Land or Sea.

They were taken from the cells about 11 o'clock, dressed, in white, in one cart, accompanied by two clergymen, to Market-street wharf, where they were put on board a boat, and conveyed to the place of execution, on the Island, opposite Dock-street, and guarded by the marshal[*], sheriff and other peace-officers. They continued in prayer until near twelve o'clock; when the executioner performed his last office to them, and they were launched into eternity, in the view of an immense concourse of spectators, who cro[w]ded the wharfs and the shipping. They made no other speech, than begging the world to forgive them, as they forgave every person in it.

Captain Wheland was present, with whom they shook hands, as they did with each other, previous to the last moments of their existence.

4

"The most abject slavery . . . " – The United States and the Barbary Pirates (1793–1804)

The North African states acquired the name "Barbary" after the Berbers, a designation loosely applied to a range of different nationalities driven out of the Iberian Peninsula late in the 15th century. While their expulsion helped expand Mediterranean piracy, by then it had already long been a practice in North Africa.[1] By the early 1600s, the Barbary pirates' ranks began to swell with Europeans, who at one time actually constituted a majority within their crews. "Worse yet," maritime historian Joel H. Baer observed, "they taught their hosts to sail European tall ships, which displaced their traditional galleys and greatly extended their range." The result was that by the middle of the 17th century, "Barbary pirates had seized European merchantmen as far north as Iceland and as far west as Newfoundland." Alongside robbery at sea, the Barbary pirates specialized in ransoming Christian prisoners and slave-trading, "a trifecta of enterprises that heightened the terror and loathing they inspired in Europe."[2]

Barbary pirates had long seen non-Muslim captives as chattel, to be made to work in shipyards or man galley oars, or simply sell for a profit.[3] In 1698, almost a century before the first of the documents presented in this chapter, Cotton Mather published a pastoral letter to "English Captives in Africa," expressing sympathy but emphasizing that under no circumstances should they convert to Islam to secure their freedom. "We had rather a Turk or a Moor should continually Trample on you," he observed at one point, "than that the Devil should make a prey of you."[4]

Distracted with wars among themselves, Europeans generally responded to the Barbary pirates with appeasement via tribute. The American colonies enjoyed paid-for protection under the British umbrella, but when they broke with the mother country their vessels became targets. In March, 1783, Algerine corsairs chased two American

---

1 Chidsey, *Wars in Barbary*, 6–9, 10–12.
2 Baer, *British Piracy*, I:xxvi.
3 "Islamic law . . . forbade the enslavement of free members of Islamic society, including *dhimm* s (non-Muslims) residing in the abode of Islam. The *sharī'ah* (divine law) regarded as legal slaves only those non-Muslims who were imprisoned or bought beyond the borders of Islamic rule, or the sons and daughters of slaves already in captivity." The Ottoman Empire would not outlaw slavery until 1887 ("Slavery," *Oxford Encyclopedia of the Modern Islamic World*, IV:79–81). For more on the use of slaves by both Christian and Muslim navies in the Mediterranean, see Muscat and Cuschieri, *Knights of St. John*, *passim*.
4 Mather, *Pastoral Letter*, 4.

An English ship in action with Barbary Pirates, by Willem van de Velde the Younger, 1680.

ships on their way out of Marseille. In October 1784 Moroccan corsairs captured a Philadelphia-based brig off Cadiz. With Spanish diplomatic help, the situation was eventually resolved with the release of the imprisoned crew and restitution for the impounded cargo. However, not long after, Algerine pirates took a pair of American ships and sent their crews into slavery. Encouraged by this first success, the ruler of Algiers, Dey Muhammad Pasha, declared war on the United States. A US envoy sent to negotiate a peace was allowed to come ashore in Algiers only to redeem American slaves.[5]

It was the start of a long contest. More than 600 Americans were captured and enslaved in 1785–1815, the author Richard Zacks likening the situation to "a near-constant hostage crisis."[6] While there were sporadic treaties and truces, the larger Barbary menace to international shipping would end only with the French invasion and occupation of Algiers in 1830.

The United States' wars with the Barbary Pirates, the subject of several fine books, extend beyond the time frame addressed here, which covers only a narrow but intense segment of the conflict. The earliest elements in this chapter, from the 1790s, offer accounts by some of the American seamen who fell into the Barbary Pirates' hands, along

---

5 London, *Victory in Tripoli*, 27–30.
6 Zacks, *Pirate Coast*, 12.

An American warship engaging a Barbary Pirate vessel (19th century, artist unknown).

Cutlasses are prominently displayed in this illustration by N.C. Wyeth for Robert Louis Stevenson's *Kidnapped*. Historian John Frayler notes that these examples are based on the US model 1860 navy cutlass, itself based on an 1833 French model, which had a similar iron cup handguard painted with black lacquer.

with some editorial discussion of the situation. Note author Matthew Carey's condemnation of the American practice of slavery, amid his discussion of that in the Barbary states.

The contents then shift to two episodes involving William Bainbridge: the first, his forced cruise in the USS George Washington under orders of the Dey of Algiers, flying an Algerine flag, to deliver presents and slaves to Constantinople; the second, his loss of the USS Philadelphia in Tripoli harbor.

The chapter closes with a report detailing Stephen Decatur's daring, and successful, mission to burn the Philadelphia. Decatur would return to North Africa in 1815, heading a squadron which would defeat the Barbary fleet and – literally at gunpoint – secure a lasting American treaty with Algiers.[7]

ooooo

[From Carey, *A Short Account of Algiers* . . . , 37–38]

Letter from William Penrose, captain of the ship President, *to his owners, dated Algiers, November 4, 1793.*

On the 23d October, at nine o'clock a.m. a sail to windward bore down upon us, which we thought was a Spanish privateer; when he came nigh,[8] hoisted Spanish colours, fired a gun to leeward, and brought us to. As soon as he saw the American colours hoisted, he hoisted out his launch immediately. It being then nearly calm, as it had been for eight days before; in an instant there was nearly 30 armed men on board, the first saluted me with a dreadful stroke with his cutlash,[9] made me jump over the rail into the boat and all hands after me, without ever suffering any one to go below, and carried us on board the cruizer, where they stripped us to the skin, and gave us a few old rags, that would scarcely cover our nakedness, let alone keep us from the cold. In this situation, we were obliged to lay on deck; the people they let go below, and Mr. Barry by some means or other, got below for two nights – I was forced to lay on the pump, and the wind being at E[ast] N[orth] E[ast] it almost per-

---

7   See Leiner, *Barbary Terror*, for a recent study of the 1815 campaign against North African piracy.
8   Synonymous with near and close. Partridge, *American Slang*, 792.
9   The cutlass or cutlash was the standard edged weapon at sea in this era. It had a relatively short blade, making it suited to fighting below decks. On the cutlass "a rounded brass guard like that of a Scottish claymore protected the hand and wrist. It was a lethal weapon, for the swordplay it afforded was both cut and thrust, brute strength as well as skill" (Woodbury, *Great Days of Piracy*, 95). Frayler ("The Arms Chest," 2) describes the cutlass as "a short, handy chopping sword." The Royal Navy, after a pirate attack on the tender to *HMS Tyne* in September 1822 (see chapter 8) copied their enemy's habit of fighting with a cutlass in one hand and a long knife in the other. A British captain remembered in his 1849 memoirs that "The crews of the vessels employed in the West Indies for the suppression of piracy, from 1822 to 1825, had a bayonet and scabbard always attached to the cutlass belt. The bayonet had a becket worked to it, like the cutlass sufficiently large to go firmly on the wrist. The men were taught to use the bayonet in the left hand, while attacking or repelling the enemy with the cutlass: and in this way the bayonet was always in its proper place, if required to be used with the musket" (Francis Liardet, *Personal Recollections on Seamanship, Discipline, etc.*, quoted in Lubbock, *Cruisers, Corsairs and Slavers*, 76).

ished me; but at length an old man, more humane than the rest, lent me a blanket, which they had taken out of the ship. The provisions they gave us was black bread and water, sometimes a few rotten olives, and that we thought was a treat. In this situation we continued eight days.

On the 31st we arrived at Algiers: we thought ourselves hardly treated on board the cruizer, but alas, our sorrows were but coming on; for we were not on shore scarcely, when they [almost?] loaded us with irons, and the second day made us go to work like criminals, and murderers: we are in the most abject slavery ever people were, in the world. The same day arrived two frigates[10] and a brig, who had taken nine more American vessels; so that our number now is above one hundred, and are expecting more daily. They have several cruizers out now, and there are several in the harbour equipping with the utmost speed. [. . .]

There is part of two ships' companies here, that was taken eight years ago, but the plague and hard usage hath carried them all off but ten. The small pittance they had from the United States, has been taken off nigh three months, so that we have nothing to subsist on, but a little black bread and water, and sometimes nothing; for it is against their religion to give Christians any flesh meat; and if you will be so kind as to supply me with a few dollars for the present, I shall take it as the greatest favour any person every conferred on me, for it is impossible to subsist long in this miserable situation.

Spanish xebec (18th century, artist unknown).

ooooo

[From Carey, *A Short Account of Algiers* . . . , 39–40]

Extract of a letter from John McShane, captain of the Minerva, *to William Bell,*[11] *dated Algiers, November 13, 1793.*

---

10   A frigate was a three-masted, square-rigged warship, "normally armed with from 24 to 44 guns carried on a single gun-deck. In navies where ships had a rate according to the number of guns they carried, they were fifth- or sixth-rate ships, and thus not expected to lie in the line of battle" (Dear and Kemp, *Companion*, 227)

11   The *Minerva's* owner (Carey, *Short Account of Algiers*, 44).

On the 18th October, about five leagues from Gibraltar,[12] we were boarded by a ze-becque[13] of 20 guns, belonging to this place, who after coming within musket-shot,[14] kept up a constant firing with small arms, until they manned our yards from theirs, then the firing ceased, and they came down sword in hand, spared our lives, but nothing else, having stripped us of the clothes we had on, and put us on board the zebecque, which brought us to this place on the 30th ult.[15] when we were taken be-fore the dey,[16] from thence to the banyon,[17] where the slaves are kept locked up at night: next day we were all sent to the marine, and kept at hard labor from day light till dark, with an iron chain which reaches from our legs to our hips; about 50 lb. weight, and treated with great severity by our masters, who allow us nothing but bread and water for our subsistence. The wheel-barrow men in your city lived a gen-teel life to what we do.

Our situation is truly shocking – and how long we can exist, God only knows. The car-penter, John McFarlane, a Scotchman, was taken out of the marine, by the British consul[18] – the sail-maker, John Fogereaux, and two Spaniards, G. Romeo and B. Gazona, were sold at public auction. On the evening of the same day, I arrived here,

---

12 Located at the entrance to the Mediterranean, Gibraltar has been a British possession on the Spanish mainland since 1713.

13 According to Peter Kemp (*History of Ships*, 112–113) the "true xebec was a development of the pirate's brigan-tine, with a pronounced overhanging bow and stern, somewhat like a galley. They were built with a narrow floor to give them extra speed through the water, but with a considerable beam in order to provide a base for the ex-tensive sail plan which they carried. They were also built with turtle decks to make water shipped on deck while sailing run down into the scuppers, and above these decks gratings were rigged to allow the crew to work dry-shod." A xebec had a complicated "variable rig which it set according to the weather and point of sailing." An Algerian captain told William Falconer, who compiled one of the first maritime dictionaries, that "the crew of every Xebec has at least the labour of three square-rigged ships, wherein the standing sails are calculated to an-swer every situation of the wind." Kemp concluded that "Nevertheless, there was no other ship of the times to touch them for speed."

14 The individual smoothbore musket's effective range in this era was about 100 yards (Hess, *Rifle Musket*, 16).

15 An abbreviation for *ultimo mense*, Latin for "last month."

16 Turkish for "maternal uncle" (*Oxford English Dictionary*, IV:588), *Dey* was the title given to rulers of Algiers from the late 17th century until the French conquest of 1830. A 1971 book summarized the political nomenclature sit-uation like this: "Morocco was governed by a sheriff [sharif] or emperor; Algiers by a dey; Tunis by a bey; Tripoli by a pasha, sometimes, since there was no *p* sound in Turkish, called a 'basha' or 'bashaw.' These men were to all intents and purpose independent princes, though they had no blood claims to their thrones and were only mili-tary adventurers or, at best, the sons or grandsons of such. They were all under the nominal suzerainty of the Grand Turk, or Padishah, or Sultan, seated at Constantinople, who also governed Egypt; but in fact the Barbary potentates – though they sometimes flew the Padishah's flag and always paid him an annual tribute in cash and expensive presents, such as slaves – did pretty much as they pleased. They were absolute monarchs, answerable to nobody, who possessed, and often used, the power of life and death" (Chidsey, *Wars in Barbary*, 2).

17 The word *bagnio* (sometimes spelled banio) was intended; the *Oxford English Dictionary* (I: 884) defines it as "An oriental prison, a place of detention for slaves, a penal establishment."

18 "There were large numbers of foreign nationals, including British subjects, working as seamen on American ves-sels, even including ships of war, in this era. Captain William Bainbridge of the ill-fated *Philadelphia* [see below], for instance, estimated in 1804 that three-fourths of the crew being held prisoner in Tripoli were British and wondered whether it might be 'policy' to ask [British] Admiral [Horatio] Nelson to seek their release. Similarly, Captain Edward Preble of the *Constitution*, when in the process of recruiting her crew, remarked in July 1803 that of the 165 men he had on board, he did not believe he had more than twenty native-born Americans" (Parker, *Uncle Sam in Barbary*, 62).

the following masters with their crews were brought in – Captains Wallace, Virginia; Newman, Boston; Taylor, Rhode-Island; Furnace, New-Hampshire; Calder, Gloucester; Burnham, New-York; Bailey, Newbury; Moss, ditto; Penrose, Philadelphia.

The whole number of Americans is between 120 and 130. They treat the Dutch in the same manner they do us. – Captain[s] O'Bri[e]n and Stephens,[19] with their crews are here, ten of them are living, the rest dead. – If their small number could not be redeemed, we have no hopes of relief; therefore endeavour to make ourselves as happy as possible: they ask for my ransom 4000 dollars, first and second mate, 3000 dollars each, and for each man, 1500 dollars. If a peace is not made, or our ships protected, we may expect to [i]ncrease daily, as we are all employed in the marine department, fitting out cruizers. I have not yet learned their force; but as there is no check on them, no American vessel will be able to go to Europe in safety. A courier is arrived from Alicant[e],[20] informing the dey that [C]olonel [David] Humphreys[21] is there with full power from Congress, to make a peace, and waits his permission to come; but the dey, I am informed, had refused him.

I remain
Your humble servant, [. . .]

John McShane, master [. . .]

[**Editor's note:** As captain of the Philadelphia-registered ship *Dauphin* (or *Dolphin*) Richard O'Brien spent 1785–95 as the captive of Algerine pirates; he was allowed considerable liberty and his letters – such as the one reproduced here – were a conduit of information to American officials. He eventually functioned "as an ad hoc U.S. agent in the matter of obtaining funds in Europe to conclude the peace in Algiers, and then as a peace negotiator with Tunis and Tripioli."[22] He would formally become U.S. consul general in Algiers in January, 1798, and the consulates at Tunis and Tripoli reported to him.[23]]

ooooo

---

19 Isaac Stephens had been captured in 1785 (Carey, *Short Account of Algiers*, 42).
20 Mediterranean port in south-eastern Spain, "the principal port of embarkation for Algiers." (Parker, *Uncle Sam in Barbary*, 80.)
21 A Revolutionary War aide to George Washington, David Humphreys had been minister to Portugal in 1793 when President Thomas Jefferson sent him to Algiers as a negotiator to arrange a treaty and secure the release of enslaved Americans. He was, in fact, Jefferson's third choice, the others dying before they could undertake the task (Allison, *Crescent Obscured*, 18–19).
22 London, *Victory in Tripoli*, 54.
23 Parker, *Uncle Sam in Barbary*, xxiv; Lambert, *Barbary Wars*, 94.

[From Carey, *A Short Account of Algiers*..., 40–41]

Copy of a letter from [C]aptain O'Brien, to James Simpson,[24] Esq. At Gibraltar, dated Algiers, the 28th November, 1793.

Your letter of the 12th inst.[25] I received the 25th. It is a long period since I heard from you; but I hope you will be this way shortly from Toulon.

The Algerines, in their October expedition, captured ten sail of American vessels; nine of them have safely arrived. The crews of these ten vessels, amounting to 102, are at present in Algiers, experiencing what we have suffered for upwards of eight years. – I have repeatedly, for these five years past, forewarned the United States of the impending danger; for the Portuguese have been trying a long time to effect a peace with Algiers;[26] but the Americans in general would put but little confidence in the assertions of a poor victim captive; but they now find that they contained the truth.

On the 11th instant, Mr. Humphreys, the Ambassador for Algiers, sent hither a courier to obtain the dey's permission to come hither in order to make peace. The dey answered, that he would not receive him, either to make peace or redeem the American slaves – that he had been soliciting the Americans to come and make a peace with this regency for three years past, and they had treated his propositions with neglect and indifference; and that since he had made a truce with the Dutch and Portuguese, and captured ten sail of Americans, and likely to take many more, he could not and would not make peace with them: that he made the truce with Portugal for the purpose of capturing American vessels,[27] and could not therefore be at peace with all nations. The courier returned to Mr. Humphreys at Alicant[e] with the dey's reply – but we have heard nothing more since.

---

24 Then American consul at Gibraltar, Scottish-born James Simpson would be later appointed U.S. consul to Tangier. "Early in 1793 . . . at the request of Col. David Humphreys, he had taken over supervision of affairs in both Morocco and Algeria" (Hall, *United States and Morocco*, 97).

25 An abbreviation for *instante mense*, Latin for "this month."

26 The danger of a Portuguese peace with Algiers was the removal of the Portuguese-enforced blockade of the Straits of Gibraltar against Algerine cruisers. "Following the Spanish-Algerine truce and the eruption of the Algerine corsairs into the Atlantic in 1785, the Portuguese, to protect their ships coming from Brazil, began to assume responsibility for guarding the Strait of Gibraltar in 1786 and had kept the Algerines bottled up in the Mediterranean. Their commitment to do so was formalized in a letter of August 2, 1787, from Queen Maria I to Congress. For this reason, and perhaps others, there had been no American ships captured since 1785, and many of them were frequenting Atlantic ports in 1793. In the absence of a peace treaty between the United States and Algiers, a truce under which the Portuguese allowed the Algerines out into the Atlantic would again expose American shipping to capture" (Parker, *Uncle Sam in Barbary*, 74–75).

27 Hasan Pasha, who was Dey of Algiers from 1791–97, indeed wrote to Britain's King George III on 27 March, 1794 that the objective of peace with Portugal (which the British helped negotiate) "was to Revenge ourselves on Yours and our Enemies the Americans in the open seas by harassing and destroying them in such a manner so as to reduce them to the necessity of submitting to be your subjects again" (Parker, *Uncle Sam in Barbary*, 231).

The terms prescribed by the dey for the relief of the Portuguese, is as follows: 1,200,000 Mexican dollars[28] for the treasury; 600,000 dollars for the dey's voice and the great officers, of the regency, ambassadorial and consular presents – equal to what Spain gave; and the redemption of 75 Portuguese captains, at 2000 dollars each. On the 7th inst. the Portuguese frigate sailed from Algiers for Lisbon, with the dey's propositions.

The day following the dey called [C]aptain Logie,[29] and desired he would immediately write to Portugal, [and] that he demand for his family and friends 600,000 dollars in addition to the terms above expressed.

The Algerine politicians are of [the] opinion that Portugal will not agree to the dey's demands; but, sir, I think they will, as they wish to extend their commerce, and well know the difficulty of blocking up the Str[ai]ts, and the vast sums they expend in keeping up the fleets against the Barbary States.

The Dutch truce will expire in twelve days from this date;[30] and if Van Trump[31] is not here in the limited time, away go the rovers in quest of Dutchmen.

The Danes, in my opinion, are on the verge of losing their peace with Algiers. Should these three nations be baffled, relative to Algerine affairs, then the United States might probably have an opportunity of establishing a peace; but never on so favourable terms as they might have had three years past; which neglect will cost them four millions, together with loss of trade, insurance, armaments, and peace re-demptions. At all events, the United States have no alternative but to fit out twelve of the best sailing vessels that can possibly be built; these cruizers to be properly ap-pointed and completely manned, for all depends on this measure. At the same time the door for obtaining a peace should be kept open, and care taken that the United States do not become the dupe and buffoon of all Europe.

---

28 See the note on Pieces of Eight in Chapter One.

29 Charles Logie, British consul at Algiers, who helped negotiate the Portuguese truce. American officials alleged that Logie had "told the dey that with independence the Americans no longer enjoyed British protection and were fair game," but Parker (*Uncle Sam in Barbary*, 43) held that such a charge cannot be substantiated from the British records.

30 The Dutch had negotiated a six-month truce with the Dey of Algiers on 11 Sept., 1793; assuming it became ac-tive about that date, it should have been valid until March (Parker, *Uncle Sam in Barbary*, 229).

31 Possibly a cryptic reference to Dutch naval power. The Dutch navy at this time had a 54-gun warship called *Tromp*, named for 17th century Dutch Admiral Maarten Harpertszoon Tromp, who was "accounted the greatest seaman of the age" (Hainsworth and Churches, *Anglo Dutch Naval Wars*, 4). Some 18th century English sources called Maarten Tromp "Van Trump," and used the same appellation for the warship named for him. For example, the 30 July, 1781 *Courant and Westminster Chronicle* contains an extract (3) from a letter by Capt. Thomas Hall, commander of the 22-gun privateer *Tygress*, to the vessel's owners, relating an encounter with "a frigate of 50 guns, calld the *Van Trump*. She cha[s]ed us almost out of sight of the two ships, and sh[o]wed English colours, when we brought to, taking her to be an English frigate; but soon found our mistake, by their summons to strike our colors; . . . " The British would capture *Tromp* at the Battle of Saldanha Bay in 1796 (Winfield, *British War-ships*, 114).

ooooo

[From Carey, *A Short Account of Algiers* . . . , 41–42]

Letter from sundry captive American captains, to [C]olonel David Humphreys, dated Algiers, December 29th, 1793.

We the subscribers, in behalf of ourselves, and brother-sufferers, at present captives in this city of human misery, return you our sincere thanks, for your communications of the 29th ult. And for the provision you have been pleased to allow us, in order to alleviate somewhat our sufferings in our present situation.

We have drawn up and signed two petitions, one to the Senate, the other to the House of Representatives, and we shall esteem it, among the many favors you have rendered us, that you will please to forward these petitions to their respective address, so that no time may be lost, but that they be laid before the Representatives of our country, hoping that the United States, will fully provide funds for extricating [us] from captivity, and restore us to our country, families, friends and connections.

We have perused with sentiments of satisfaction and approbation, your memorial to the regency of Algiers, and have to observe, that its contents fully coincide with our sentiments on this business, which we trust, in the Almighty, will terminate to the honour and interest of our common country, notwithstanding the insinuations (of others in this quarters) to the prejudice of the United States.

We trust, and hope, that the United States will adopt such effectual plans, in order to prevent any more of our brethren, sharing our unhappy fate, which unavoidably will happen, if some speedy and decisive means is not immediately put in execution, as we understand the Portuguese truce, with this regency, was agreed on for one year. What damp[en]s our spirits in some degree, is, that we are informed, that the plague, that fatal and tremendous disorder, has given its awful alarm in the country adjacent. And as your unfortunate countrymen are confined during the night time, in the slave-prisons, with six hundred captives of other nations, from our crowded situation, we must be exposed to this contagious disorder; which necessitates the subscribers, to [e]ntreat you, sir, that in this case, those our friends, and of influence in this regency, will be authorised by you, and our honoured countrymen, Mr. C[h]armichael,[32] and Mr. Short,[33] to have a house taken for the residence of the American masters and mates,

32   William Carmichael was U.S. *chargé d'affaires* in Madrid from 1783–1794. In 1785, when O'Brien and Stephens and their crews first became prisoners of the Algerine corsairs, on Carmichael's request the Spanish representative in Algiers arranged separate quarters for the captains and the mates, although the captured sailors were not provided for (Parker, *Uncle Sam in Barbary*, 46, 68).

33   William Short was U.S. *chargé d'affaires* in Paris in 1790–92; he became minister resident in Madrid in late 1794 (Parker, *Uncle Sam in Barbary*, 68).

and, if possible, the mariners, to shield them from the threatening storm of mortality and danger.

We make no doubt, but in case of the Almighty's wrath, visiting this city of iniquity, but the dey and regency would acquiesce to the proposed plan of humanity, which would be establishing an example for the general welfare of mankind – and would to posterity be recorded to the immortal honor of the United States.

[At t]he same time, honoured sir, and friend, be you assured, for your consolation, that we the American captives, in this city of bondage, will bear our sufferings with fortitude and resignation, as becoming a race of men endowed with superior souls in adversity.

We are much indebted to Mons. Skjoldebrand,[34] and brother, his Swedish majesty's agents, in this city, for their humanity, and attention to the American captives; and feel ourselves particularly obliged to you for recommending us to the good offices of consuls Skjoldebrand, and Mr. Mace,[35] whom you mention to us as friends.
With sentiments of gratitude and the most profound respect, we remain,

Honoured sir,
Your most obedient
Most humble servants,
The subscribers in behalf of ourselves, and brother-sufferers.

Richard O'Brien,	1785[36]	Moses Morse,	1793
Isaac Stephens,	do.	Joseph Ingraham,	do.
James Taylor,	1793	Michael Smith,	do.
William Wallace,	do.	William Furnass,	do.
Samuel Calder,	do.	John Burnham,	do.
William Penrose,	do.	John McShane,	do.

To DAVID HUMPHREYS, Esq., &c.

ooooo

AGREEABLE INTELLIGENCE (Broadside – New Bedford: "Printing Office" of the *Medley* newspaper, Tuesday, 31 December, 1793)

Last evening the Sloop Hazard, *George Folger, jun. Master, arrived from New York. – He has favored us with a Paper printed there, of the 21st inst. which contains the*

34 Mattias Skjöldebrand was Swedish consul general in Algiers who intervened on behalf of the American captives; he gave several key tasks to his brother, Per Erik Skjöldebrand, who "was not there in any official capacity but was very familiar with political affairs and channels of negotiation" (Parker, *Uncle Sam in Barbary*, 80–81).
35 British diplomat Charles Mace had been designated to succeed Charles Logie as British consul in Algiers but would not arrive until early 1794 (Parker, *Uncle Sam in Barbary*, 78, 227).
36 The numbers refer to the year in which the signer was taken captive.

following interesting particulars. – Convinced an early knowledge of any circum-
stances relating to the Algerines, would be gladly received by the promoters of the
Medley, the Editor presents it [to] them in this manner.

NEW YORK, Dec. 21
Mr. Phillips arrived here yesterday in the Danish ship *Stadt Altona*, 56 days from Lis-
bon, charged with dispatches to the Government of the United States, from Mr.
Church, our Consul at Lisbon.

(The following Letter from our Consul at Lisbon, appears to have been received by
the above vessel – directed to Peter S. Livingston, Esquire, New[Y]ork:)–

Lisbon, 22d Oct. 1793.

"Dear Sir,
"I have the pleasure to inform you, that I have this day obtained a promise from
the court of a convoy for our ships, about 16 in number, to be provided as soon
as they shall be ready to sail. My letter, and the very polite and friendly answer
from the Portuguese Minister,[37] go by this conveyance to the Secretary of State;
the vessel sails tomorrow. I pray you to communicate this pleasing & very important intelligence to all the merchants, &c in your city. I am, Dear Sir, most sincerely
yours,

"EDWARD CHURCH.["][38]

We learn from Mr. Phillips, that the Peace made between the Regency of Algiers and
the Queen of Portugal,[39] was wholly effected without her knowledge or consent, by
the agents of the British and Spanish courts. That the captain of the Portuguese
frigate who had bro[ugh]t the news of the peace into Lisbon, first obtained it from an
Algerine cruizer he fell in with, and who produced him his authority for the peace,
being papers signed by the British and Spanish agents; upon this the frigate quit her
station and went into port, where the captain was immediately imprisoned for having
done so.

Mr. Phillips further adds, that it was currently reported, and generally believed in Lisbon, that her Majesty of Portugal, would immediately order a 60[-]gun ship and a

37 Luis Pinto de Sousa Coutinho had been Portugal's foreign minister since 1788 (Maxwell, *Naked Tropics*, 130–131).
38 The following is inserted as a footnote in this broadside's original text: "N.B. The two following vessels arrived here the 20th inst. without seeing the enemy: viz. the schooner *Elsey*, Capt. Wells, of Boston, but last from North [C]arolina, 7 weeks passage; and the brig *Betsey*, Capt. Bunhury, of Portsmouth, last from Virginia; same passage spoke Capt. Aikins, bound from hence to Boston, 40 leagues N.W. from the Rock of Lisbon."
39 Maria I, who reigned from 1777–1816. "Owing to her insanity, however, Maria I ceased to govern in 1792 and her son, the prince of Brazil, ruled in her name, assuming the title of Prince Regent in 1799" (Goodwin, *New Cambridge Modern History*, 378).

frigate to cruize off the Str[ai]ts' mouth, to protect the vessels of the United States, bound to and from her ports.

We are sorry to add to the foregoing, that nine American vessels have been seen in the Mediterranean with Algerines on board, who were taking them into their ports. One of these unfortunate vessels is said to be the brig *Nancy* of Philadelphia.

ooooo

[From Carey, *A Short Account of Algiers* . . . , 15–16]

When an Algerine pirate takes a prize, he examines into the quality and circumstances of the prisoners. If he disbelieves the account that they give of themselves, they are bastinadoed,[40] till he has met with an agreeable answer. Having obtained what information he is able, he brings them on shore, after having stripped them almost naked. He carries them directly to the palace of the dey, where the European consuls assemble, to see if any of the prisoners belong to their respective nations, who are at peace with Algiers. In that case, they reclaim them, provided that they were only passengers; but if they have served on board of the ships of any people at war with "the mighty and invincible militia," they cannot be discharged without payment of the full ransom.

Matters are thus settled between the dey and the consuls, what part of the prisoners are to be set at liberty, and what part are to be considered as slaves. The dey has next his choice of every eighth slave. He generally ch[oo]ses the masters, surgeons, carpenters, and most useful hands belonging to the several prizes. Besides his eighth, he lays claim to all prisoners of quality, for whom a superior ransom is to be expected. The rest are left to the corsair and his owners. They are carried to the slave market; the crier proclaims their rank, profession, and circumstances, and the price set upon each of them. They are then led to the court before the palace of the dey, and there sold to the best bidder. If any sum is offered beyond the price first set upon them, it belongs to the government. The captors and owners have only that which was originally set upon the slaves. For this practice of buying and selling slaves, we are not entitled to charge the Algerines with any exclusive degree of barbarity. The Christians of Europe and America carry on this commerce an hundred times more extensively than the Algerines. It has received a recent sanction from the immaculate Divan[41] of Britain. Nobody seems even to be surprised by a diabolic kind of advertisements, which, for

---

40 "The manner of inflicting this punishment is as follows: The person is laid upon his face, with his hands in irons behind him, and his legs lashed together with a rope. – One task-masker holds down his head and another his legs, while two others inflict the punishment upon his breech, with sticks some what larger than an ox-goad. After he has received one half his punishment in this manner, they lash his an[k]les to a pole, and two Turks lift the pole up, and hold it in such a manner, as brings the soles of his feet upward, and the remainder of his punishment, he receives upon the soles of his feet. Then he is released from his bands, and obliged to go directly to work among the rest of his fellow-slaves" (Foss, *Journal*, 24–25).

41 The term *dīwān* (*Oxford Encyclopedia of the Islamic World*, I:381–2) has commonly been used "with respect to certain offices that administered important governmental functions." Its use here may be an ironic comment on

some months past, have frequently adorned the newspapers of Philadelphia. The French fugitives from the West-Indies have brought with them a cro[w]d of slaves. These most injured people sometimes run off, and their master advertises a reward for apprehending them. At the same time, we are commonly informed, that his sacred name is marked in capitals, on their breasts; or in plainer terms, it is stamped on that part of the body with a red hot iron. Before therefore we reprobate the ferocity of the Algerines, we should enquire whether it is not possible to find, in some other regions of the globe, a systematic brutality still more disgraceful?

[Editor's note: In this article, onetime Algerian prisoner Richard O'Brien, discussed earlier, functions as a diplomat. The episode gives some idea of the difficulty and complexities of arranging peace with the North African states, not to mention in conveying tribute.]

ooooo

[Hartford, Connecticut *American Mercury*, 8 May 1797, 2.]

BOSTON, April 29
History of the ALGERINE BUSINESS

An obliging correspondent has favoured us with the following communication from Capt. O'Brien, so well known for his sufferings in Algiers, and so justly celebrated for his exertions to support, the honor and advance the interests of the United States. It is dated at Philadelphia the 15th instant, and says, "I left this city in June last – arrived in Lisbon, and took on board 220,000 dollars, besides presents, destined for Algiers, but was captured on the 18th of August, adjacent to Algiers, by a corsair of Tripoli – and I, brig, money and crew carried to Tripoli, and, with the crew of the ship *Betsey*, of Boston, made slaves of. But, sh[o]wing the Dey of Algiers' passport, and making appear I was still the slave of the Dey of Algiers; that the money being delivered to me by the United States, was the same as if delivered to the Dey, and it becoming under the Dey's guarantee, and not for the ransom of the captives, I was after two days examination, liberated, and arrived in Algiers the 1st of October – delivered the money, and by the well-timed and well[-]adapted plans of Mr. Barlow,[42] I sailed the 10th of October, commissioned on the business of the peace of the United States, with the regencies of Tunis and Tripoli. I arrived at Tunis the 16th of Oct. The Dey of Algiers wrote to the Bey of Tunis to make the peace on the terms prescribed by the

failed efforts in Britain in 1791–1794 to abolish the slave trade. See Michael J. Turner, "The Limits of Abolition: Government, Saints and the 'African Question'," c. 1780–1820, *English Historical Review* 112:446 (April, 1997).

42   Then American consul in Algiers (to be replaced by O'Brien in January, 1798), Joel Barlow was born in Connecticut in 1754 and was a member of Yale's Class of 1778. He had "a remarkably varied career as a military chaplain, poet, publisher, lawyer, politician, businessman, and diplomat." He died late in 1812 while minister to France, succumbing to pneumonia while en route to Napoleon's winter headquarters at Vilna (Parker, *Uncle Sam in Barbary*, 181, 252 n10).

Dey. Tunis would not, but demanded equal to three times the sum. After many audiences and conferences to have the government of Tunis' demand for the peace lowered, I found that the terms, so tendered, were the voluntary terms on which Tunis would make a peace with the United States, and that Tunis would not make a peace on the terms which the Dey of Algiers prescribed. I forwarded to Mr. Barlow in Algiers, who communicated the Tunisian demand to the Dey, who would not admit Mr. Barlow to acquiesce. Leaving the Tunis business in this situation, I proceeded to Tripoli, and with much difficulty made the peace there the 4th November. Left in Tripoli, Capt. Joseph Ingraham as American charge des affairs,[43] and sail from Tripoli the 27th November; brought away the remaining part of the crew of the ship *Betsey*.

"Arrived at Tunis the 7th of Dec. [T]here I received Mr. Barlow's and the Dey's orders, to demand a definitive answer from the Bey[44] of Tunis, if he would make the peace with the United States, on the terms prescribed by the Dey of Algiers – The Bey of Tunis would not. Having discretionary powers, I tried what could be done; but the Bey of Tunis's demands were not within my limits. I sailed from Tunis and arrived in Algiers 3d January, and explained all requisite affairs to the Potent Dey, and to Mr. Barlow. The Dey was much enraged at this non-compliance of the Bey of Tunis; and on account of some old grudges, and his rejecting the Dey's intercession in our affairs, the Dey ordered his Eastern camp of sixty thousand men to enter the Tunisian territory. His troop[s] plundered, cut of[f] many heads and ears, and returned to the Algerine territory. This was to feel the political pulse of the government of Tunis; to know if it would still continue to be biased, or dependent on the Dey of Algiers. The Dey declared, that the business of Tunis relative to its making peace with the United States, was under his guarantee, and in consequence gave me orders to proceed for the western world. I left Algiers the 18th January – arrived, performed quarantine at Lisbon, and sailed from thence the 18th February – arrived here the 1st of April. The brig and O'Brien is under repair.

"I now tell you candidly that no American vessel should enter the Mediterranean, until our peace with all the Barbary States is fully established, and published by the authority of the United States."

[**Editor's note:** American naval officer William Bainbridge's luck and judgment failed him on at least two occasions in his dealings with the Barbary states. The first time came in 1800 when, in command of the 24-gun light frigate *George Washington*, he dropped anchor in Algiers too close to the port's cannon-studded fortifications, thus allowing

---

43 On the scale of diplomatic ranks, a *chargé d'affaires* is below ambassador and minister, but might conduct high-level diplomatic business in the absence of a higher-ranking official (*Oxford English Dictionary*, III:39). During the first U.S. presidency, "Washington and his cabinet had decided that the United States should maintain its diplomatic representation at the lowest possible level, appointing chargés d'affaires rather than ministers or ambassadors wherever possible" (Parker, *Uncle Sam in Barbary*, 73–74).

44 "A Turkish governor of a province or district: also a title of rank" (*Oxford English Dictionary*, II:161). As noted above, it was the term used for the ruler of Tunis.

the Dey to force him to essentially commandeer his and his ship's services in bringing tribute to Constantinople, simultaneously requiring Bainbridge to fly the Algerine flag from his masthead. "Bainbridge carried out the onerous task with considerable credit to himself," one author has noted, "but it was, nonetheless, an unmitigated affront to American sovereignty and could not be ignored."[45] Later documents in this section show how his bad luck reared itself again on Halloween, 1803, when he ran the frigate *Philadel-phia* aground on a reef in Tripoli harbor, and surrendered it to the corsairs. The incident led to Lt. Stephen Decatur's successful effort, using a captured ketch to infiltrate the harbor, to set the *Philadelphia* alight.]

ooooo

[New London CT *Bee*, 17 December 1800, 2]

SKETCH OF ALGERINE SPOLIATIONS FOR THE LAST TWO YEARS.

27 sail of Neapolitans, Sicilians and Maltese, having British passports from [L]ord Keith;[46] vessels and cargoes condemned; crews, 215 condemned to slavery, claimed by the English, and not given up.

17 sail of Greeks; vessels, cargoes and crews condemned; the Greeks employed as slaves, and after a service of 15 months given up to the grand seignior. [47]

13 sail of imperialists,[48] valued at one million of dollars; vessels and cargoes condemned; crews given up to the grand seignior.

At Tunis, they have taken 11 Danish vessels valued at six hundred thousand dollars. At Tripol[i], they have captured 24 sail of Swedes.

A Danish frigate by mistake chased an Algerine corsair ashore near Tunis; for which the Danish government will have to pay to the Dey *eighty thousand*, and to his ministers *twenty thousand* dollars!

Three hundred and sixty-eight Frenchmen were made slaves in July last at Algiers, but were released at the conclusion of the peace with France.

---

45 Martin, *Most Fortunate Ship*, 83.

46 Admiral George Keith Elphinstone, 1st Viscount Keith. For a recent study of his performance in the Egyptian campaign, see Piers Mackesy, *British Victory in Egypt, 1801: The End of Napoleon's Conquest* (London: Routledge, 1995).

47 *Seigneur* was originally a French term for a "feudal lord; a noble taking his designation from the name of his estate" (*Oxford English Dictionary*, XIV:891). It was commonly used to refer to the head of the Ottoman Empire – e.g. "the Grand Signor of the Turks," as it appeared in "The Turkish Fast," in the *Monthly Mercury*, Dec. 1697, as reproduced in Brooks, *Barbarian Cruelty*, 90.

48 The word *imperialist* at this time generally referred to the Germans and the German Emperor, at that time Francis II, the last Holy Roman Emperor (*Oxford English Dictionary*, VII:712).

The Spanish consul was [55?] days in chains on account of the French taking the brig *Bashaw*. Spain returned the brig and crew to Algiers, accompanied with presents to [to] the amount of 60,000 dollars, which released the poor consul.

Look out! United States of America! or you will share the fate of the Swedes at Tripoli; the Danes at Tunis, and of many other nations at Algiers! *"Millions for defence, but not a cent for tribute!"*[49]

The United States should immediately have six stout frigates in the Mediterranean, to keep the rogues in awe. Should any accident happen to the *George Washington*[50] in her passage to or from Constantinople, the government of the United States will be obliged to reimburse the Dey all damages he may sustain thereby, or his most potent majesty will order his corsairs to capture American vessels.

Among the presents sent to the grand seignior were *one hundred* black slaves, 50 of them females; lions, tygers, leopards, ostriches, &c, &c, valued at several millions of dollars. *Precious cargo for an American government ship!*. Captain Bainbridge[51] was obliged to hoist the *standard of Algiers* at his maintop gallant mast head,[52] instead of the *American pendant!*[53]

The *George Washington* sailed on the 19th of October, upon her new voyage, and may return to this country possibly in July next. She had carried out to the Algerine government large supplies of stores, which were received on account of the annual stipulated payments from the United States. The English had offered a frigate for this purpose, but the Dey did not like to trust them, for fear they would secure the treasure to themselves, as there had been a serious misunderstanding with them. Several

---

49 This is a rendering of a slogan which originated in Charles C. Pinckney's "No! No! Not a sixpence!" response to French demands at the time of the XYZ (or WXYZ) Affair that preceded the Quasi-War of 1798–1800. The "Millions for defense . . . " line came in the form of an 18 June, 1798 toast to honor John Marshall, who had accompanied Pinckney and Elbridge Gerry on the mission to France. The true authorship of the quote is unknown (Beveridge, *John Marshall*, II:348–9).

50 A converted merchant vessel, the USS *George Washington* was a 624-ton, 108-foot long 32-gun warship. It would be sold in Philadelphia in 1802 (Mooney, *Fighting Ships*, III:80–81).

51 Bainbridge (1774–1833) "joined the Navy in 1798 and was subsequently given command of the *Retaliation*, *Norfolk*, and *George Washington*." Following the loss of the *Philadelphia*, "he remained a prisoner until June 1805. After a stint as commander of the Charleston Navy Yard, he commanded the frigate USS *Constitution* and defeated HMS *Java* off the coast of Brazil on November 29, 1812. He later commanded ship-of-the-line USS *Independence*, held a number of shore posts, and established a school for naval officers in 1817. He served as president of the Board of Navy Commissioners from 1832 until his death the following year" (Morris and Kearns, *Historical Dictionary*, 19).

52 The topgallant-mast was the "third mast above the deck; the uppermost before the days of royals and flying kites." Correspondingly, topgallant-sails were the "third sails above the decks; they are set above the topsail-yards, in the same manner as the topsails above the lower yards" (Smyth, *Lexicon*, 687).

53 An alternate spelling for pennant. Commodores – the senior officer commanding a squadron – had distinctive pennants to signify their presence. Similar designs caused confusion during the Tripolitan War when American fleets met. This caused Commodore John Rodgers to suggest successfully that the navy adopt three distinctly different types and assign them depending on seniority (Paullin, *Commodore John Rodgers*, 245).

Danish vessels were forcibly taken into their possession and ordered for the Isle of Rhodes[54] upon similar business with the *Washington*.

The English consul was at first refused a reception at Algiers, but was finally permitted to remain there.

Notwithstanding the treatment [C]aptain Bainbridge received from the Dey, the American consul, and flag is more respected there than any of the European nations. The Algerines observed to [C]aptain Bainbridge that he ought to consider it a great mark of the Dey's favor, to go upon his majesty's special business to the grand seignior; adding, that it was an honor he would confer on very few others. There are about 2300 European slaves in Algiers; some of them from the first families in Europe. The place appears very strong, but 6 or 8 seventy-fours[55] could batter it to pieces. The policy of the English government is against a measure so important to the commercial world. A petty despot of a piratical state, with a small marine force, commands homage and respect from all the [C]hristian world. *Oh tempora! Oh mores!*[56]

Mr. O'Brien had written home to the American government, requesting that another consul might be sent out to supercede him.

ooooo

[Washington D.C. *National Intelligencer and Washington Advertiser*, 24 December 1800, 3]

Salem, December 11
Late from Algiers and Gibraltar

On Tuesday arrived at this port, the ship *Brutus*, William Brown, commander, in 32 days from Gibraltar, and 40 from Algiers. Captain Brown informs, that the United States frigate *George Washington*, [C]aptain Bainbridge, sailed for Constantinople on the 19th of October; having on board the Algerine General of Marine and suite, with presents, &c. for the Grand Seignior. The Dey of Algeirs, by force, compelled [C]aptain Bainbridge to perform this service, and threatened in case of refusal, War to the United States, and slavery to the Officers and Crew of the *George Washington*. The Dey also insisted, that the ship *Brutus*, [C]aptain Brown, should unlade, and go to the Isle of Rhodes, for a cargo of Turks – no pay or freight to be allowed – but the voyage

---

54 A Greek island near the Turkish coast, Rhodes was part of the Byzantine Empire in 1308 when the Knights of St John turned it into a base. Rhodes fell to the Barbary corsair Hizir "Barbarossa" Rais in 1523. It was an Ottoman possession until near that Empire's end (Konstam, *Piracy*, 74, 83–84; and Muscat and Cuschieri, *Naval Activities of the Knights of St. John*, *passim*).
55 i.e., 74-gun warships, "ships of the line."
56 Generally rendered as *O tempora o mores* [Oh the times, oh the morals], from Marcus Tullius Cicero, *Oratio in L. Catilinam Prima, Habita in Senatu* (Cicero, *Orationes Selectae*, 1).

to be considered as a favour granted by the United States. Through the influence of the American Consul, Mr. O'Brien, and the ship's being private property, and having a perishable cargo on board, she was excused from this service. Captain Brown embraced this favourable moment, fearing a further requisition and quitted Algiers, on the 25th of October. Captain Brown brought dispatches to the secretary of state containing the particulars of this extraordinary affair. – Mr. O'Brien, the Consul, and Captain Bainbridge, had remonstrated, but were obliged to comply, to prevent a more serious difficulty. Two days out from Algiers, Captain Brown was brought to[57] by the British brig *Carmelia;*[58] the lieutenant of which informed – that he was bound for Egypt, with dispatches from Lord Keith; and that his Lordship, with the fleet and transports under the command, was destined for Egypt. On arriving at Gibraltar, no one was permitted to land from the *Brutus*, because she was from the Barbary coast... .
[...]

ooooo

[New York *Mercantile Advertiser*, 28 April 1801, 2]

[...]
"Algiers, 10th Oct. 1800.

"Sir,

"I wrote you on the 25th ult. informing that the arbitrary Dey of Algiers had made a demand, that the United States ship *George Washington* under my command, should carry his presents to the Grand Signior at Constantinople.

"By my letter of the 25th you will see the responsibility this Regency considers the United States at on this embassy, although forced into it by the power of the Regency. Every effort that it was possible to suggest, has been attempted by Consul O'Brien and myself, to obviate my going.

"An English ship of war arrived here and offered to carry the embassy; but her they would not accept, supposing they would be under some obligations to the British. "The light that this Regency looks on the United States is exactly this; you pay me tribute, by that you become my slaves, and then I have a right to order as I please. Did the United States know the easy access of this barbarous coast called Barbary, the weakness of their garrisons, and the effeminacy of their people, I am sure they would not be long tributary to so pitiful a race of infidels.

"[E]nclosed you have the letter of Richard O'Brien, Esq., Consul-General, of the 9th

---

57   To bring to is "To make a Ship stationary, stopping her way by bracing some of the Sails a-back, and keeping others full, so that they counterpoise each other" (Lever, *Young Sea Officer's Sheet Anchor*, 119).
58   No Royal Navy vessel appears to have had this exact title. A candidate for the vessel referred to is the 16-gun "brig-sloop" HMS *Cameleon*, which took part in Egyptian operations in 1801 (Winfield, *British Warships*, 282; Colledge and Warlow, *Royal Navy*, 74).

Oct. to me on the business of this embassy; my answer and his reply, by which you will see that I have no choice in acting, but I am governed by the tyrants here.

"Consul O'Brien and myself had a very warm dispute with the Dey and Minister of Marine, (which was very near causing a declaration of war) respecting hoisting the mission flag; the consul and myself insisted that if the Dey forced us to go, to wear our own flags, or if it was meant as a compliment to the minister of marine to hoist it at the fore-top-mast head; but no arguments could avail; their despotic will must be complied with; the Minister of Marine came on board with his admiral and several Algerine captains, who went into the main-top, and hauled down the American pendant, and hoisted the Algerine mission flag.

"Had we 10 or 12 frigates and sloops in those seas, I am well convinced in my own mind that we should not experience those mortifying degradations that must be cutting to every American who possesses an independent spirit.

"This forced cruise compelled by the Dey, will cost 14 or 16 thousand dollars in expenses for pay and provisions, and after effected, will have no tendency to promote the interest of the United States with this Regency; it is not in the nature of those people to regard any favors done to them by a [C]hristian nation.

"I hope, Sir, you will consider the very unpleasant situation that I was fixed in, having no alternative but compliance or war – the fear of slavery for myself and 131 under my command, was the least alarming to me; but a valuable commerce in those seas that would fall a sacrifice to the pirates of this port on account of our not having cruisers adjacent to protect it.

"I sincerely hope on my return from the Levant, that I shall see some of our frigates off Algiers; it is my candid opinion that in no part of the world there is more need to sh[o]w them than in the Mediterranean sea.

"It is the opinion of Consul O'Brien, should any accident happen to the *Washington* against the interest of Algiers, by whatever cause it may be, the Algerine cruisers will immediately capture our vessels, unless they are prevented by our cruisers being in these seas. I candidly believe, on the safety of the embassy in the ship under my command, hangs the preservation of our peace with Barbary. I have the honor to be, with great respect, your most ob't servant.

Wm. BAINBRIDGE
Hon. Benjamin Stodd[e]rt,[59] Secretary of the Navy.["]

---

59   Cavalryman-turned-merchant Stoddert (1751–1813) was the first Secretary of the Navy, being appointed by President John Adams in May, 1798. He obtained "Congressional authorization for a new Navy of 13 frigates and 12 74-gun warships." He also "acquired property for the development of navy yards in Portsmouth [New Hampshire] and Kittery, Maine; Washington, Boston, Gosport, Va., New York, and Philadelphia. He also drafted the important bill for the government of the United States Marine Corps and commenced the construction of the United States Navy Hospital at Newport, R.I." He stepped down as Secretary of the Navy in April 1801 when he "resumed his commercial activities" (Mooney, *Fighting Ships*, VI:642).

A Barbary Pirate (artist unknown).

Commodore John Rodgers (Courtesy of Louisa Alger Watrous).

ooooo

[Randolph, VT *Weekly Wanderer*, 7 May 1804, 2]

Domestic Intelligence.
CHARLESTON, (*S. Carolina*) March 24.

A LETTER was yesterday received from Mr. Saunders Osborne, of this city, who was a midshipman on board the frigate *Philadelphia*,[60] and is now a captive in Tripoli. He writes that Capt. Bainbridge [on 31 October 1803] defended his ship for five hours, with the greatest gallantry, after she had struck on a sunken rock, which was unnoticed in the charts, but at length was obliged to yield to the superior force.[61] That their situation at the time he wrote was not so distressing as their fears led them to believe it would be; that the reason it was so, was owing entirely to the unremitted exertions & friendship of the Consul of the Danish Majesty, who had left nothing in his power undone to serve them.

---

60   As launched in 1799, USS *Philadelphia* was a 1,240-ton, 130-foot long, 28-gun frigate. Commanded by Stephen Decatur, Sr. (father of the man who eventually led the successful effort to destroy it), it captured five French warships and recaptured six prizes to them during a cruise on the Guadaloupe Station during the Quasi-War. Prior to running aground in Tripoli Harbor on 31 October 1803, *Philadelphia* had taken a 24-gun Moroccan warship, *Mirboka*, and recaptured an American brig *Mirboka* had taken as a prize (Mooney, *Fighting Ships*, V:282).
61   Zacks (*Pirate Coast*, 18, 20–23, 25–27, 45–48) cites contemporary sources questioning Bainbridge's handling of the *Philadelphia*'s grounding in Tripoli harbor; the frigate floated free within hours of its surrender.

ooooo

[Albany (NY) *Centinel*, 22 May 1804, 3]

Extract of a letter from one of the officers of the Philadelphia *frigate to his friend in*
Philadelphia.
TRIPOLI, Nov. 24, 1803.

I mentioned in my last, under date of the 15th that, in consequence of orders from
the Bashaw, communicated to us on the evening of the 13th we were on the following morning conducted to the castle. The object of this removal was to punish us, by
way of retaliation, for ill treatment which they say the Tripolitan officers, taken in the
ship captured by the *John Adams,*[62] received from Capt. [John] Ro[d]gers.[63] The
prime minister, a few days previous, had written to Captain Bainbridge informing him
that a letter had been received from the Tripolitan Captain at Gibraltar, in which he
complained of being ill treated by Captain Ro[d]gers; and in consequence of this, by
way of satisfaction, the prime minister requested Capt. B[ainbridge] to write and order
Commodore Preble[64] to deliver up all the prisoners taken in that ship; in which case
we should continue to be treated as heretofore; but should Capt. B[ainbridge] not
comply he would be compelled to exercise retaliation upon us. – No exchange was
proposed; but we were to deliver up seventy-eight prisoners to insure our not being
ill treated. Capt. Bainbridge declined compliance, and we were conducted to the castle. The change was indeed an unpleasant one, from a large commodious house to
what they call a castle, which in fact is nothing less than a loathsome prison. We were
placed in the same place with the ship's company. How well calculated the room was
to contain such a number you may judge, when I tell you that it was about 30 by 25
feet; how comfortable, when the only place to admit the air was at two holes in the
ceiling, grated over. However, it was not intended that we should remain there any
time, and was only done under the idea that we were to be frightened into a compliance with the prime minister's demand.

---

62 Launched in 1799, USS *John Adams* was a 544-ton, 139-foot long frigate, originally armed with 24 12-pounder
    and six 24-pounder cannon. It served with distinction in the Quasi-War, and at the start of 1803 joined a
    squadron operating against Tripoli, in which it saw extensive action over the next two years. The Tripolitanian
    capture referred to here may have been the *Meshouda*, a 20-gun warship USS *John Adams* captured in May 1803,
    or a 22-gun warship it took in June in partnership with USS *Enterprise*. After the War of 1812, it returned to the
    North African theatre in the second Barbary War, then shifted to anti-piracy activities in the Caribbean and
    Gulf of Mexico. In 1817, it expelled privateers from Amelia Island off the Florida coast; it later served as David
    Porter's flagship in the "Mosquito Fleet." After serving in a variety of capacities, it was sold in 1867 (Mooney,
    Fighting Ships, III:521–523).
63 Then commander of the USS *John Adams*. In early 1803 Rodgers, in company with Commodore Richard Morris
    and Consul General-designate James Cathcart, spent several days under house arrest in the Tunisian bey's palace
    during an awkward phase in negotiations. In 1805 he would command the American Mediterranean squadron
    (London, *Victory in Tripoli*, 117, 119, 216).
64 Edward Preble (1761–1807), who commanded the American Mediterranean squadron.

"While we were there, Lisle,[65] the Tripolitan admiral, *accidentally* passed that way, and was very much *surprised* to see us there. He came up to inquire the reason of our removal, and said that he understood a letter had been received mentioning that the Tripolitan prisoners had been ill treated. Capt. Bainbridge told him that it was an infamous falsehood; that the laws of the U[nited] States absolutely forbid any prisoner being treated ill, and that he knew Capt. Ro[d]gers had given no just cause of complaint; that if such a letter had been written, it was without foundation, and the writer had affected a most malicious falsehood: That even supposing they had been treated ill, that could not justify their retaliating upon us; that it would not tend to produce a reconciliation; but would have a quite contrary effect; that we were within their power, and they might sacrifice the whole of us, but the United States had officers and men enough to find out. He said that the Bashaw was out of town, and would not return till evening, when he would see what could be done.

"In the evening we were re[-]conducted to our lodging. Shortly after Capt. Bainbridge received a note from the prime minister, in which he affected to be entirely ignorant of our removal until after it had taken place. He expressed his *grand* surprise at hearing it; and to use his own phrase, [']could not have felt more hurt if one of his own limbs had been taken off, or if one of his own family had been taken away;['] and concluded with assuring us, we might rely upon our not being disturbed in that manner again. The Danish consul, in company with the French consul, waited upon the prime minister the day we went to the castle, and assured us we need be under no apprehension of a second removal. – We feel ourselves perfectly secure. I cannot say which was greatest, our contempt for a character so replete with duplicity, or our indignation at the prime minister, for supposing us so weak and credulous as to believe him unacquainted with our removal, until after we had gone. He and the admiral are both renegadoes;[66] the former a Prussian, the latter a Scotchman.

ooooo

---

65   Then 42, Scottish-born Peter Lisle (or Lyle) served Tripoli under his conversion name of Murad Rais; he appeared before the prisoners with a full beard, wearing a turban and "billowy pants" and carrying a curved dagger. "He had a decade earlier been chief mate of an English ship, *Hampden*, but after being twice accused of embezzling, he had jumped ship in Tripoli harbor. To gain the protection of the Bashaw, he had converted to Islam the same day and had been immediately circumcised in a rushed ceremony and clothed in Barbary finery. He had taken the Moslem name of a great sixteenth-century corsair, one who had hounded the Popes' own flagship and terrorized even the Atlantic. Murad . . . eventually became admiral of Tripoli and married the Bashaw's daughter. (British records indicate that Lyle had apparently left behind a Christian wife and five children in Wapping Old Stairs in London.) He was described as a 'slight' man, of 'indifferent morals,' with a blondish beard, a foul temper, and an above-average thirst for hard liquor. Reports of his drunken, violent behavior – such as beating servants or cursing strangers – often bobbed up in consular reports" (Zacks, *Pirate Coast*, 46).

66   Or *rinigado* – renegade – in what Zacks (*Pirate Coast*, 1) called "the Lingua Franca slang of the Mediterranean." Cotton Mather in 1698 referred to "Those Wretched Renegado's, who have abandoned the Christian Religion, Expecting thereby to mend their Condition in the world…" (*Pastoral Letter*, 3–4).

An example of a ketch (19th century, artist unknown).

[*Philadelphia Evening Post*, 24 May 1804, 2]

Copy of a letter from [L]ieutenant [Stephen] Decatur[67] to [C]ommodore Preble, containing an official account of the destruction of the frigate *Philadelphia*, dated

On board the Ketch[68] *Intrepid,*[69]
At sea, Feb. 17th, 1804.

Sir,

I have the honour to inform you that in pursuance of your orders of the 1st inst. to proceed with this ketch off the harbour off Tripoli there to endeavour to effect the de-

---

67 Stephen Decatur Jr. (1779–1820) "began his naval career as a midshipman in 1798 on Captain John Barry's 44-gun frigate *United States*. By 1804 he had gained command of the *Enterprise*. . . . During the War of 1812, Decatur, now a captain, commanded the *United States* in its famous battle with the British frigate *Macedonian*, forcing the enemy vessel to surrender. Thereafter he and his crew transferred to the best frigate available, the 44-gun *President*, but were forced to surrender to the British after a chase. When the war ended, Decatur headed a squadron on his flagship, the new 74-gun *Washington*, as the Americans returned to the Mediterranean to end their conflicts with the Barbary pirates once and for all. He achieved this by peace treaties with Algiers, Tunis, and Tripoli. Thereafter assigned to the three-man Board of Navy Commissioners, Decatur later died in a duel with James Barron, court-martialed ten years earlier, on March 22, 1820." The duel had stemmed from Decatur's presence on the earlier court-martial "that found Barron guilty in the *Chesapeake-Leopard* Affair and Decatur blaming Barron's absence during the War of 1812 to cowardice. Barron was wounded in the encounter but recovered and became a senior officer in the Navy" (Morris and Kearns, *Historical Dictionary*, 72–73).

68 A two-masted vessel often used for coastal trade; later a favorite type of yacht. There was also a "bomb ketch" type of warship, mounting a mortar in the "large open space forward of the mainmast" (Dear and Kemp, *Companion*, 302).

69 The *Intrepid* was a French-built 60-foot long, 64-ton ketch. Named *Mastico* while in Tripolitanian service, the U.S. Navy captured it in December, 1803, and after quarantine and condemnation as a lawful prize, Commodore Edward Preble renamed it and fitted it out for the mission inside Tripoli harbor. Its career ended in the same place, in September 1804, when it blew up prematurely while on a mission to explode in the middle of a pirate flotilla (London, *Victory in Tripoli*, 159; Martin, *Most Fortunate Ship*, 97–98; Mooney, *Fighting Ships*, III:445; and Morris and Kearns, *Historical Dictionary*, 136).

struction of the United States late frigate *Philadelphia*. I arrived there in company with the United States brig *Syren*,[70] [L]ieutenant-[C]ommandant [Charles] Stewart, on the 7th, but owing to the badness of the weather, was unable to effect any thing, until last evening when we had a light breeze from N[orth] E[ast]. At 7 o'clock I entered the harbour with the *Intrepid* (the *Syren* having gained her station without the harbour, in a situation to support us in our retreat) at half past nine laid her alongside the *Philadelphia*, boarded, and after a short contest carried her. I immediately fired her in the store-rooms, gun-rooms, cock-pit,[71] and b[e]rth-deck,[72] and remained on board until the flames had issued from the spar-deck,[73] hatchways and ports, and before I got from along side, the fire had communicated to the rigging and tops; previous to our boarding, they had got their tomp[io]ns[74] out and hailed several times, but not a gun was fired. The noise occasioned by boarding and contending for possession (although no fire arms were used) gave a general alarm on shore and on board their cruizers, which lay about a cable and a half[75] length from us, and many large boats filled with men lay round, but from whom we received no annoyance. They commenced a fire on us from all their batteries on shore, but with no other effect than one shot passing through our top gallant sail. The frigate was moored within half a gun shot[76] of the bashaw's castle and their principal battery, their two cruizers lay within two cables length on the starboard quarter, and their gun boats within half a gun shot on the starboard bow; she had all her guns mounted and loaded, which, as they became hot, went off, and as she lay with her broadside to the town, I have no doubt but some damage has been done by them.

---

70 Launched on 6 August, 1803, the 240-ton brig USS *Syren* left Philadelphia on 27 August for Gibraltar, which it reached on 1 October. Two weeks later, *Syren* "sailed via Livorno to Algiers carrying presents and money to the Dey of Algiers. She then sailed to Syracuse, Sicily, where she arrived early in January 1804. . . . *Syren* and ketch *Intrepid* got underway from Syracuse on 3 February 1804 and proceeded to Tripoli which they reached on the 7th. However, before the American ships could launch their attack, they were driven off by a violent gale and did not get back off Tripoli until the 16th" (Mooney, *Fighting Ships*, VI:709).
71 "The place where the wounded men are attended to, situated near the after hatch-way, and under the lower gun-deck" (Smyth, *Lexicon*, 198).
72 The berth-deck was the "'tween decks" location "under the gun deck, where sailors usually mess" (Smyth, *Lexicon*, 97, 703).
73 "In the US Navy the term applied to the weather deck of its frigates, where the flimsy gangways formerly used to connect the forecastle and quarterdeck had been so expanded and strengthened as to create a continuous deck capable of supporting guns. The ships themselves were sometimes referred to as 'spar deck frigates'" (Dear and Kemp, *Companion*, 547).
74 Tompions were round wooden plugs used to seal cannon muzzles to keep water out (Smyth, *Lexicon*, 685–686).
75 In estimating distances between ships, a cable was approximately 100 fathoms, the latter being a nautical term for six feet; however, on charts "a cable is deemed 607.56 feet, or one-tenth of a sea mile" (Smyth, *Lexicon*, 151, 290).
76 Smyth, who had served in the Napoleonic Wars era, wrote in his *Lexicon* (358) that as a term of measurement *gun-shot* "formerly [meant] the distance up to which a gun would throw a shot direct to its mark, without added elevation . . . " He added that "this range was about 800 yards." However, the point-blank range of cannon depended on factors such as shot weight and powder charge. Frayler ("Armed to the Teeth," 2) noted that a cannonball from a small four-pounder "when fired almost level with the ground (or water) would land about 500 yards distant." Another source held that the point-blank range of a 32-pounder of 1805 "was 350 yards, the distance at which decisive sea engagements then were fought" (Grahame, "Evolution of Naval Guns and Armor," 52).

"Burning of the Frigate Philadelphia in the Harbor of Tripoli, February 16, 1804," by Edward Moran (Naval Historical Foundation KN-10849).

Before I got out of the harbour, her cables burnt off, and she drifted in under the castle where she was consumed. I can form no judg[e]ment as to the number of men that were on board of her. There were about twenty killed; a large boat full got off; and many leapt into the sea. We have made one prisoner, who I fear, from the number of bad wounds he has received, will not recover, although every assistance and comfort has been given him. I boarded with 60 men and officers leaving a guard on board the ketch for her defence, and it is with the greatest pleasure I inform you, I had not a man killed in this affair, and but one slightly wounded. Every support that could be given, I received from my officers, and as each of their conduct was highly meritorious, I beg leave to enclose you a list of their names. Permit me also, sir, to speak of the brave fellows I have the honor to command, whose coolness and intrepidity was such as I trust will ever characterize the American tars.[77] It would be injus-

---

77 A "tar" was slang for a seaman, a term that originated among the British (e.g., Jack Tar) but is here applied to the Americans. "Tar is the shortened form of tarpaulin, the tarred canvas which seamen, and especially topmen, used to wear as protection against the weather during the days of sail. Also, when pigtails were the fashionable hairstyle afloat, seamen always dressed theirs with tar" (Dear and Kemp, *Companion*, 287).

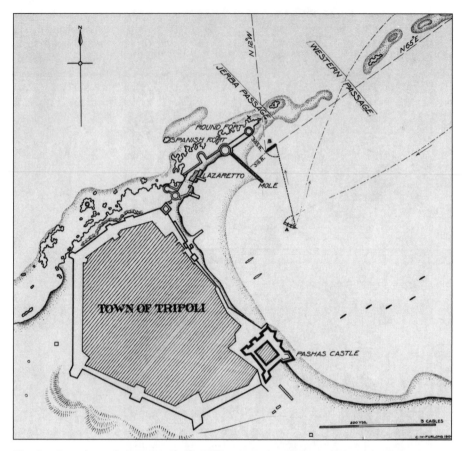

This chart by explorer-scholar-writer Charles Wellington Furlong shows the harbor of Tripoli, with Intrepid's path given in dots and dashes (– · – · –). The Philadelphia was set afire at point A; the heavy dotted line (······) shows how far it drifted to point B, where Furlong found its wreck a century later (Naval Historical Foundation, NH 56745).

tice in me, were I to pass over the important services rendered by Mr. Salvadore, the pilot[78] on whose good conduct the success of the enterprize in the greatest degree depended. He gave me entire satisfaction.

I have the honor to be, sir,
With great respect,
Your most obed't humble serv't.

STEPHEN DECATUR, Jun.

---

78 Sometimes treated as synonymous with navigator, a pilot is "an experienced person charged with the ship's course near the coasts, into roads, rivers, &c., and through all intricate channels, in his own particular district"(Smyth, Lexicon, 528).

5

"A horrible crime to think upon" – The mutiny on the George Washington (1812)

Born circa 1770, Philadelphia mariner Samuel Tulley was serving as mate of the Delaware-registered schooner *George Washington* in early January 1812 when it anchored at the "isle of May" – Maio, one of the Cape Verde islands off Africa's west coast – with a cargo aboard of Tenerife wine and Spanish money. Tulley had clashed with captain Uriah Phillips Levy at some point during the voyage, so when Levy visited another American vessel at anchor after dark one night, Tulley seized his chance. He caused both the *George Washington*'s anchor cables to be cut, then headed the schooner to sea, allowing two unwilling crewmen to take a boat ashore.

Now heading west, the *George Washington*'s crew at this point consisted of Tulley, cook John Owen, and two remaining sailors: George Cummings, described in court testimony as a "foreigner," and Englishman Jack Heathcoat, who later used the name John Dalton. Owen, who became a witness for the prosecution, later testified that Cummings became depressed and began acting erratically: he "used to go two or three times a day and kiss the Mate's hands or feet and those of Jack." Shortly before reaching the West Indian island of St. Lucia, Cummings intimated that he would commit suicide. But Cummings (who gave Owen his earrings and a breastpin as a parting gift) turned his violence not against himself, but against the former mate. Wielding a knife and hammer, he wounded Tulley in the head and hand before Tulley and Heathcoat-Dalton overpowered him and threw him overboard.

On St. Lucia, the remaining mutineers concocted a story of being shipwrecked. Owen, however, became uneasy enough to tell the whole story to an American ship captain. The result was that he and the other two were arrested and sent to Boston for a trial which ended in Tulley's and Heathcoat-Dalton's convictions; both were sentenced to hang at South Boston. Shortly after Tulley was executed, his body still suspended in mid-air, the marshal read out a presidential reprieve for Dalton, who had the gallows rope around his neck. He later received a full pardon.

ooooo

The Trial of Samuel Tulley & John Dalton on an indictment for Piracy and Murder; Committed January 21st, 1812. Before the Circuit Court of the United States, at Boston, 28th October, 1812: Containing the Evidence at large, a Sketch of the

Arguments of Counsel, and the Charge of the Hon. Judge Story, on pronouncing sentence of DEATH. ("Printed for the Publisher": Boston [?], 1814)

At the Circuit Court of the United States, for the first circuit, holden at Boston within and for the district of Massachusetts, on the fifteenth day of October A.D. 1812, before
   Hon. Joseph Story,[1] Presiding Judge,
   Hon. John Davis,[2] District Judge,
the grand jurors returned three bills of indictment against Samuel Tulley and John Dalton, of Philadelphia, in the State of Pennsylvania, mariners. One for Piracy, on the statute of the United States passed 30th April, 1790 – for piratically and feloniously running away with the schooner *George Washington*, from the care, custody and possession of Uriah Phillips Levy, her master.[3] Another for the murder of George Cummings, on the high seas, on the 20th day of January last. Another for feloniously scuttling and casting away said vessel on the high seas, on the 21th day of January last, against the provisions of a law of Congress in such case made and provided. Copies of these several indictments and a list of thirty six jurors to be called at the trial were given to the prisoners, and in pursuance of a statute provision for the assignment of causes, James T. Austin,[4] and Peter O. Thacher,[5] Esquires, were assigned them by the court to assist them in their defence. On Tuesday, 28th October, the prisoners were brought into court and arraigned on the first indictment. [. . .]

[Editor's Note: The first indictment – the only one on which the prisoners would be tried – was signed by grand jury foreman Humphrey Devereux and US Attorney George Blake. It set forth the charges that on the previous 10 January, Tulley and Dalton took the schooner *George Washington* "with force and arms upon the high seas, near a place called the Isle of May, one of the Cape Verd[e] Islands, and out of the jurisdiction of any particular State . . . ." Besides the schooner itself, the two men were also charged with the theft of its cargo, which included "fourteen quarter casks of Teneriffe wine" valued at $1,000 – along with "two thousand Spanish milled dollars."]

1   Joseph Story (1779–1845) had been appointed in November 1811 an associate justice of the United States Supreme Court. When that court was not in session, he presided over the First Circuit Court – which covered Maine, New Hampshire, Massachusetts and Rhode Island; it generally met for two terms each year (Story, *Joseph Story*, I:221–222). Later a professor of law at Harvard University, he delivered the Supreme Court's decision on the *Amistad* case.
2   John Davis (1761–1847), a member of the Massachusetts convention that adopted the United States Constitution, represented Plymouth in the state legislature, and became Comptroller of the U.S. Treasury in 1795. President Washington appointed him the state's district attorney, and from 1800–1841 he served as a federal judge. Fellow circuit court judge Joseph Story dedicated his 1839 *Commentaries on the Law of Agencies* to Davis (Gannett, *Good Old Age*, 27–30).
3   A navy veteran of the Barbary Wars, Levy (1792–1862) would re-enter the service during the War of 1812 and rise to become the first Jewish commodore in the United States Navy. He was also a noted philanthropist. See Ira Dye, *Uriah Levy: Reformer of the Antebellum Navy* (Gainesville: University Press of Florida, 2006).
4   A lawyer since graduating from Harvard in 1802, Austin (1784–1870) later served as Massachusetts' attorney general from 1832–1843 (Duyckinck and Duyckinck, *Cyclopedia*, II:61).
5   In addition to his work as an attorney, by 1814 Thacher was a trustee of the Boston Athenaeum and sat on the Boston School Committee; by 1834 he would be a municipal court judge in Boston (Burdick, *Massachusetts Manual*, I:110, 161; and "Judge Thacher's Charge," *Niles' Weekly Register*, 27 December 1834, 281).

Whereupon the Clerk of the Court asked them if they were guilty or not guilty? to which they severally answered, not guilty; and it was then demanded of them, how they would be tried? to which they said, by God and their country; and the clerk rejoined, God send you a good deliverance. The prisoners being ready for trial a Jury was empanelled ... after several challenges by the prisoners. ...

The case was then opened by George Blake, Esq.[6] Attorney for the United States. He said it was his painful but necessary duty, to lay before the Court and Jury, the Law on which the Indictment was founded, and the evidence which would support the charge against the prisoners at the bar, and in order to enable them more fully to understand the story which the witnesses would substantiate, he should present them with a general outline of what he expected the government would be able to offer in evidence. The Attorney then read the Law as follows.

"If any person or persons shall commit upon the high seas or in any river, haven, bas[i]n or bay out of the jurisdiction of any particular state, murder or robbery or any other offence, which, if committed within the body of a county, would be punishable with death; or if any Captain or mariner of any ship or other vessel shall piratically and feloniously run away with such ship or vessel, or any goods or merchandise to the value of fifty dollars, or yield up such ship or vessel voluntarily to any pirate, or if any seaman shall lay violent hands upon his commander, thereby to hinder and prevent his fighting in defence of his ship or goods committed to is trust, or shall make a revolt in the ship, every such offender shall be deemed, taken, and adjudged to be a pirate and felon, and being thereof convicted, shall suffer death. And the trial of crimes committed on the high seas, or in any place out of the jurisdiction of any particular State, shall be in the district where the offender is apprehended, or where he may first be brought."

The Attorney then gave a summary and candid statement of the expected evidence, and proceeded to call the witnesses.

JAMES HOLMES, CALLED AND SWORN

He said he brought the prisoners at the bar, together with John Owen, a black man, from the Island of St. Lucie[7] to the United States; that they were delivered to him as prisoners, by the authority of the Island, to be brought to the United States; that the first port he made was Martha's Vineyard;[8] that the three men were delivered to the civil authority, and committed to prison in New Bedford,[9] and afterwards brought to Boston.

---

6   Blake (1769–1841) was a 1789 Harvard graduate who joined the bar in 1792; he became a U.S. attorney in 1801 (Kerber, *Toward an Intellectual History of Women*, 280).

7   Saint Lucia, in the Windward Islands.

8   A large island off the south coast of Cape Cod, Massachusetts.

9   Major port in southern Massachusetts, best known for its whaling industry; Herman Melville's novel *Moby Dick* opens in New Bedford.

URIAH PHILLIPS LEVY, CALLED AND SWORN

He said he was the master of the schooner *George Washington*, and a part owner jointly with two other American citizens; that she was a new vessel, American registered [and] was built in the State of Delaware, and had not been to sea till the voyage in question. On the 17th October, 1811, he sailed from the Delaware on a voyage to Teneriffe[10] and elsewhere. His crew consisted of Samuel Tulley his mate, John Dalton a foremast hand – the prisoners; a sailor called [Joseph] Neal, Daniel Hopkins, George Cummings, and John Owen, cook. On the 13th December the schooner arrived at Teneriffe, landed the cargo, and took on board fourteen quarter casks of wine and $2500 in specie. On 23d December sailed from Teneriffe to the Isle of May,[11] one of the Cape de Verd[e] Islands, where they arrived on the 4th of January. That a proper and convenient place for anchorage was pointed out to him by an American captain who lay there, and the schooner was moored in about ten fathoms[12] of water, by two cables, one 9½ the other 8½ inch, 75 and 60 fathoms [respectively]. On the 9th January,[13] at 3 o'clock, p.m. went on shore and left all hands on board directing the Mate to send the boat on board the brig *Lambert*, Captain Levi Joy, then laying there, at sundown. Joseph Neal and Daniel Hopkins came with the boat at that time, and he ordered them to return and come again for him in an hour or two. At eight o'clock, Joseph and Daniel came again; they stated to him a conversation between themselves and the Mate on board the schooner, which the witness was not permitted to repeat. That he immediately looked out for his vessel, but saw she had gone from the place she was moored in, and he never has seen her from that time to the present. That the next day he caused the search to be made for the anchors, which he found and weighed. The cables were fastened to them, but both cables had been cut with some sharp instrument, and from the examination of the length, he had not the least doubt they had been cut at the windlass.

On cross-examination he said the anchorage in the Isle of May was in an open road;[14] that there is a strong current which is felt immediately on leaving the bay; that the

---

10 Tenerife is the largest of the Canary Islands, off the north-west coast of Africa.

11 Maio, or Mayo "is raised considerably above the sea, but a great part is level, excepting three inland mountains, of considerable height. On the S[outh] W[est] side is a sandy bay, called English Road, within which is the town and extensive salt-pans. The soil of this isle is generally dry and unproductive, and there is but one spring of water in the island. The coast is, however, plentifully stocked with fish, which supply, with a few vegetable productions, subsistence to the poor inhabitants. . . . Mayo is about 4 leagues in length from N[orth] to S[outh], rising most towards the middle. On approaching the island from the S[outh] E[ast] the appearance is very different; you may descry, in the north part, two hummocks, which appear like two islands; but, when nearer, the land is perceived, by which they are connected. Southward of these, is a mountain, (Monte Mayo,) with very low ground to the south, over which two hillocks are seen" (Purdy, *Memoir, Descriptive and Explanatory*, 228).

12 Sixty feet of water, a fathom being the nautical equivalent of six feet.

13 The indictment dated the episode to January 10.

14 A road, or roadstead, was an off-shore anchorage "where ships may await orders . . . [or] where a well-found vessel may ride out a gale." However, an "open roadstead" was one that "afforded no protection either from sea or wind" (Smyth, *Lexicon*, 507, 576).

Shrouds and ratlines, and the dead-
eyes and lanyards fastened to the hull
by which they were adjusted (19th
century, artist unknown).

schooner was a good sailer, required some pumping, and on her outward passage
with a cargo of corn, they used to pump every half hour; that the last time he saw the
vessel, they had been swaying up[15] the foresail;[16] the topsail[17] was in the cabin; the
foreyards,[18] [j]ib-boom[19] and foresail were on deck; the fore-rigging had been set up
and rattled down;[20] that the vessel might have been got ready for sea in five minutes;
that at the time there was only a moderate breeze, and all sail could have been set;
that when he first knew the schooner had gone, it was rather dark, yet light enough to
have discovered her if she had been in the bay; that no vessel was there capable of
pursuing with any hope of overtaking her; that there was generally a heavy sea and

---

15   To sway up a sail was "to apply a strain on a mast-rope in order to lift the spar upwards, so that the fid [itself a
      wood or iron bar supporting the topmast's weight] may be taken out, previous to lowering the mast" (Smyth, Lexi-
      con, 293, 668).
16   The foresail was the main sail on the schooner's foremost mast (Smyth, Lexicon, 316).
17   On a fore-and-aft rigged schooner a topsail was any one set above the main sails. A "topsail-schooner" had a
      square sail at the top of its foremast, and a "two-topsail schooner" carried an additional square sail on top of its
      main mast (Dear and Kemp, Companion, 589; and Smyth, Lexicon, 688).
18   The term may refer to assorted rigging from the bow-end of the schooner, including the foremast's foresail and
      the canvas that would normally have been hung from the jib-boom (see below).
19   The jib-boom "runs out through the Cap of the Bowsprit . . . ; it is generally rounded all the way" (Lever, Young
      Sea Officer's Sheet Anchor, 31). See illustration in Chapter One.
20   Rattling down referred to preparing a vessel for travel by securing the ratlines – the rope ladders that allowed
      sailors to access the masts and yards – to the thicker rope shrouds that comprised "the standing rigging of a sailing
      vessel which gives a mast its lateral support in the same way as stays give it fore-and-aft support" (Dear and
      Kemp, Companion, 459, 531–532).

swell running into the bay, and that the windlass had been whelped[21] with four pieces of board over each end. He often left the schooner in the care of the mate before this time. Dalton complained of being sick on the voyage, but always did his duty. Joseph and Daniel left the Isle of May with his consent, in a vessel bound to the United States; he has made very careful inquiry for them, but has not been able to gain any intelligence of them, nor can he say where they are. He sent circular letters respecting his loss into every part of the United States and the West Indies,[22] but has never obtained any information respecting his schooner. The American consul gave such intelligence respecting men detained at St Lucie[23] as induced him to go there, where he received from the commanding officer 1350 dollars and his clothes, the balance being detained for expenses. The prisoners had left the Island before his arrival.

JOHN OWEN, CALLED AND SWORN

He said that he lately belonged to the American schooner *George Washington*, commanded by [C]aptain Levy, and a few months since sailed from Philadelphia in the said vessel to the island of Teneriffe, and from thence to the Isle of May. Whilst lying at the Isle of May, one day after dinner, the Captain went aboard an American vessel likewise lying there, and desired the mate to send the boat for him at sunset, which was done accordingly; but the captain did not return, and desired the boat again to be sent for him, at eight o'clock. The witness, being cook of the vessel, prepared supper at about eight o'clock in the evening, of which the mate, Samuel Tulley, partook; but the captain not being arrived, the provisions were left waiting for him on the table, and this witness went to sleep; sometime afterwards, when it was dark, he was called upon by Samuel Tulley, to hold a lantern to the pigeon hole,[24] through the cabin, on deck, in order for him to see by the compass how the vessel was lying, it being then still at anchor; some considerable time afterwards he was called up again by the mate, as were all hands, and ordered to make sail on the vessel, the mate declaring that she was drifted.¶

Sail was accordingly made, until one of the sailors, named Neal, being forward in the vessel, exclaimed that he would not hoist the sail, for that both the cables were cut. The mate then insisted upon their continuing to hoist the sail, which Neal and a man named Dan refused, unless he would give them some satisfaction as to what he was going to do with the vessel, which the mate refused, saying it did not signify, and still

---

21 In this case, whelping refers to the practice of bolting pieces of wood (whelps) onto "the main-piece of a windlass, or on a winch, for firm holding, and to prevent chafing. . . . " (Smyth, *Lexicon*, 729).

22 The West Indies refers to groups of islands – Cuba is the largest – that mark the north and east boundaries of the Caribbean Sea (the western and southern limits of which are the coasts of Central and South America). *West Indies* and *Caribbean* were often used interchangeably to designate the same region.

23 St. Lucia changed hands several times between France and Britain but by this time had been occupied by the British since 1803.

24 One source (Bradford, *Mariner's Dictionary*, 194) gives two meanings for this term, but neither directly applies on this occasion. In this context, the "pigeon hole" may have been a slot allowing someone belowdecks to see the compass in the binnacle, situated near the helm.

insisting on the sails being hoisted; adding, ["A]fter the sails are up I will give you the boat.["] The sails were accordingly hoisted by all hands, after which the mate gave the two men, (Neal and Dan) the boat, in which, having put their clothes, these two men departed. Owen declared that he also requested permission to go in the boat, which the mate positively refused and declared that no other person should quit the vessel. After this, the Mate himself continued at the helm the greatest part of the night. The men remaining on board the vessel were the Mate, Samuel Tulley; Jack, who is now here and calls himself John Dalton; George, and this deponent.

About two weeks were spent at sea, during the last part of which time he observed that George became uneasy in his mind and fell from his appetite, and used to go two or three times a day and kiss the Mate's hands or feet and those of Jack.

One evening when it was expected aboard the vessel soon to see land, George went to Jack and asked him when the land would be seen. Jack replied ["T]omorrow["]; whereupon George replied ["G]ood bye, you will not see me any more.["] Jack, who was steering, treated what George said lightly, asked him what was the matter, and said he was foo[l]ish; but George persisted in saying the same things. The witness then went own below to sleep, leaving George sitting on one side of the deck and the Mate sitting opposite to him on the other side, on the hen coops. During the night, he thinks about eleven or twelve o'clock, he heard a noise upon the deck and himself called for; he came upon deck, when Jack said to him, that George was killing the Mate, and the Mate and Jack together had George upon the gunwale[25] of the vessel, throwing him overboard. This witness was much confused, and did not know what to do; he replied to what was said to him by Jack, that it could be no such thing, ran to the helm which had been abandoned, then in his confusion, left it again. In the mean time the Mate and Jack continued throwing George overboard; the Mate saying "overboard he shall go at the ris[k] of my life;" and George was, in this manner, by them thrown overboard and left in the sea.

The next day after George had been thus thrown overboard, land was seen from the vessel; it was time of evening, and the Mate made the vessel lie to[e][26] till morning. The Mate then caused the long boat[27] to be hoisted out, put into it the Captain's large chest and several other things according to his wish, together with the trunks of Jack and this witness. Then made this witness get into the boat, fastened it to a line, and let the line run out (he, Owen, remaining in the boat) to a great length; then, the

---

25 Pronounced and sometimes spelled *gunnel*, this is the upper edge of the vessel's side (Dear and Kemp, *Companion*, 253).

26 To "lie to" is synonymous with to "bring to": to keep the vessel stationary (Lever, *Young Sea Officer's Sheet Anchor*, 119, 122).

27 A merchant vessel's long boat was "carvel-built, full, flat, and high, and is usually the largest boat belonging to a ship, furnished with spars and sails, and may be armed and equipped for cruizing short distances; her principal employ, however, is to bring heavy stores on board, and also to go up small rivers to fetch water, wood, &c. At sea it is stowed between the fore and main masts" (Smyth, *Lexicon*, 454).

line being made fast, the boat was towed by the vessel; afterwards the boat was hauled up along side the vessel, and the Mate and Jack came into it; and he knows, by what was said by the Mate and Jack afterwards, whilst in the boat, that during the time he was towed in the boat, those two men bored holes in the bottom of the vessel, in order to occasion her to sink; but so long as she remained in sight from the boat the vessel did not sink.

When the boat had thus quitted the vessel, the Mate distributed, to Jack and this witness, money, consisting of dollars, which he knew to have belonged to the Captain; the Mate saying they must all keep secret every thing that had happened, and keep the money for themselves. The same evening the boat came near to land, but being afraid of the reefs, it was made to stand out to sea again; and the next day again approached, and coming ashore, they found the land which he did not know before, to be the Island of St. Lucie in the West Indies. After they got on shore, they went to the first house on the Island, which was inhabited by persons who spoke only French, and they could not make themselves understood. The Mate and Dalton repeatedly enjoined upon the witness not to tell what had happened, but to keep it secret and say they had run foul of a wreck and were cast away, and that the Captain had taken one boat and they another. The Mate went to town. Witness and Dalton sta[ye]d till he returned, which he did after a short time, in company with the harbour master, who took them all in a boat and towed them round to the town. Dalton then went to one place to live, and the witness and the Mate lived together at another. He continued to repeat the story in which he had been instructed. He however grew uneasy in mind at being obliged to tell a lie to every body who questioned him, and resolved to disclose the whole affair; for which purpose he went one evening to [C]aptain Taylor's, an American captain, and told the truth as he has now related it. Thereupon they were all arrested, and after sometime being confined were brought here as prisoners.

On his cross-examination he said that when the vessel was said to be adrift, it was candle light, but that he could see the land from the deck. That Dalton assisted in lowering down the boat, but cannot say whether he asked for leave to go ashore or not. The night was dark, cannot tell what course they steered; they set the mainsail, foresail and [j]ib. During most of the night the Mate kept the helm; when he left it, Dalton stood at helm. He does not know if any attempts were made to put back, but the next morning there was no land in sight. From the remains of the cables, he knows both must have been cut with an axe or knife. George, the deceased, was a foreigner; the morning before he died, he gave the witness his earrings and breastpin and said he should not live to see land. When the witness came upon deck, and saw George struggling, he had in one hand a knife and in the other a hammer; the Mate was wounded badly in the cheek and back of his ear with the knife, and on the back of his head with the hammer; he also received a wound across his hand, which has left a scar. To a question of one of the Jurors, witness said he never heard either the Mate or Dalton express any regret for the loss of the man, or seem to lay it to heart.

The money which he received of the Mate, the witness said he never expended, nor did he go into any company or place of amusement in St. Lucie; and when he was arrested there, the money was taken by the officers of government.

The Attorney for the United States rested the case on this testimony.

The counsel for the prisoners then called [C]aptain Benjamin Harris, who was accordingly sworn. He stated that he was an experienced seaman, having been for many years conversant with the sea; that he had been at the Isle of May and the other Cape de Verd[e] Islands. That there is a pretty regular trade wind prevailing there, which blows off the coast; that there are what is called heavy rol[l]ers, which he explained, by saying they were great billows or waves, driven by the force of the winds or other causes, and that these were frequent in the hurricane months, but not usual in the month of January. That the anchorage in the Isle of May is very bad, by means of many anchors being lost there, which are apt to cut off the cables of vessels riding there. Vessels are apt to part their cables and drift out. His own vessel was driven out in that manner at Bona Vesta.[28] That when a vessel was found to be adrift, an experienced seaman would in the first place make sail and endeavor to beat to windward. That in moderate weather, although there is a strong current off the Isle of May, he should not think it difficult to get back or to make the Isle of Jago,[29] where vessels usually touch.

CAPT. MICHAEL HOPKINS, CALLED AND SWORN
He corroborated the testimony of captain Harris. He said that the anchorage ground was bad, that there were many foul anchors in the bay, vessels frequently part their cables and drift out; that in the month of August, September, and November it is very rough, with heavy swells and rol[l]ers; and that it is not incredible that a vessel, situated as the George Washington was, and short manned, might be driven off and find it difficult to return; though he should think there would be no great difficulty, in moderate weather, in returning. That when the vessel was found to have parted her cables, it was judicious and seamanlike to make sail.

At this stage of the cause, the court adjourned for one hour. The Jury were directed to continue together and not to converse on the case before them, but to keep their minds perfectly unbias[s]ed until the whole cause was finished, and with the consent of the prisoners they were permitted to take moderate refreshment.

AFTERNOON
COURT OPENED. – PRESENT AS BEFORE.
James T. Austin, and Peter O. Thacher, Esquires, severally addressed the Jury at great length, on behalf of the prisoners; and the Reporter regrets, that he has not been per-

---

28 Bonovista, one of the Cape Verde islands.
29 St. Jago, the former name for Santiago, the largest of the Cape Verde islands.

mitted to make an extract from their briefs. Three points, however, were relied upon in their defence.

1st, That the whole evidence, if the witnesses for the government were credited, was not inconsistent with the accidental departure of the Schooner, or at least without any criminal agency on the part of the mate or Dalton; and that whatever events might have occurred at sea, rendering a concealment necessary when they arrived at St. Lucie, that the fact of feloniously and piratically running away was not made out in evidence.

2dly, That the principal witness from whom alone the facts came, by which the defendants could be charged, was John Owen, the cook, who was a single witness, suspicious in his character, and from his own testimony, although he does not confess himself guilty, must be deemed to be an accomplice in whatever crimes were committed. The Jury, therefore, were not only warranted in laying his evidence out of the case, but it would be their duty so to do. That to convict one man of a capital offence, on the credibility of a single witness, even of honest character, was risking too much, and incurring a greater responsibility and hazard than a Jury were warranted in assuming; but to condemn two men on the testimony of a single witness of very suspicious character, a perfect stranger, of a class of society not usually well instructed in moral principles and the obligation of an oath, swearing for his own liberty and deeply interested in the event of the prosecution was an event which no Jury would venture to produce; and that although it might be possibly [be] true, that this dark[-]coloured accomplice had told a correct story, yet that on evidence so suspicious and so liable to mistake, it was the safest and most rational judgment to pronounce, not indeed that the defendants were innocent men, but that they were not provided by satisfactory and unimpeachable evidence to be guilty.

3dly, That the facts in credited, do not amount to the crime of Piracy. The defendants, it was said, were indicted on the statute piratically, as well as feloniously, running away with the schooner *George Washington*, from the care, custody, and possession of Uriah Phillips Levy, the master. The word feloniously referred to the disposition and temper of mind, what in law is called *animus furandi*;[30] and the word piratically, to the manner in which this disposition was exercised; and that nothing could amount to the c[r]ime of piratically running away with the vessel, but a larceny of the property, together with such personal violence or putting in fear, as would change the crime of larceny into the more aggravated crime of robbery, if it had been committed on shore. The distinction was illustrated by the following case. If a gentleman left his horse in the care of his servant while he alighted, and the servant went off with the horse and sold him, or converted him to his own use in any other way, it would be larceny in the servant, but not robbery; but if the servant or any other person, while the master was

30 Intent to steal.

riding his horse, had with force and violence, or by threats, compelled the master to dismount, and the servant had then rode off with the horse, this would be robbery. The addition of force changes the nature of the crime and increases the punishment – and by the laws of the United States the robber is punished with death, while the thief is subjected to a limited imprisonment. The Counsel contended that the same distinction existed between the crimes of larceny and piracy; and they quoted from a variety of law writers and from analogous reasoning to prove their position, and finally said, that if the Mate or seamen who were the servants of [C]aptain Levy, had exercised any personal violence upon him and threatened him, and then run away with the schooner, it would be piratical; but if they had watched [for] an opportunity in the absence of the captain, when they could get possession without such fo[r]ce or threats and had run away with her, it was not piracy, but larceny; and the prisoners, although amenable to justice on another Indictment, for an offence less heinous and not capital, could not be found guilty of the crime charged upon them in this indictment.

A distinction was also attempted to be made in the operation of the evidence on the defendants separately, with a view to sh[o]w that in whatever light the conduct of Tulley might be viewed, Dalton was not a principal, but only accessory.

In concluding his remarks, Mr. Austin, of counsel for the prisoners, addressed the Jury in words of the following import, as nearly as we can repeat them from our minutes.

["]The defendants, gentlemen, are in your hands. If there exists a reasonable doubt as to the law or the evidence, that doubt will save them. Fortunately for our country, a scene like the present rarely presents itself in our Courts of Justice. I persuade myself, the times in which we live have not destroyed the sensibility which such a scene should excite. We hear, indeed, almost on every gale, the dreadful deeds of war and battle, and grow more and more familiar with death. Among the many who are falling around us, two lives like those of the unhappy men at the bar, may not be thought much addition to the melancholy catalogue. Yet, gentlemen, when the law, which is made for the protection of human life, deems it necessary, to put that life in jeopardy, not for any injury to the lives of other members of the community, but for a mere injury to personal property; there is much, very much for a Jury to consider. If by your verdict, the defendants should be called to pass through the dark valley of the shadow of death, they will at least have the consolation of knowing, that their fate has been sealed by an impartial and honourable Jury. But if the reverse of this should be the case; if your verdict opens their prison doors, and restores to them a new existence, chastened by the dangers they have incurred, and bound to honesty by the perils they have passed, the reflection of having returned to them their lives, which the law this day puts into your hands, will be to you a source of the sweetest consolation, at that awful hour when your lives shall be required by the great Judge of nature. Gentlemen, the defendants are in your power: I can only repeat for them the humane wish of the law – 'God send them a good deliverance.'["]

After the defence had been concluded by the counsel for the prisoners, George Blake, Esq., addressed the Jury on the part of the prosecution, and applied the evidence to the several points on which it was necessary for the Jury to be satisfied. He contended that it was utterly impossible, under the circumstances which had been stated, that the schooner could have drifted by accident from her moorings, and equally so, that any other persons than the prisoners could have been instrumental in the perpetration of the crime. He enforced to the Jury the strong and violent presumptions of guilt which the testimony of Captain Levy alone furnished against the prisoners. From his testimony it was beyond contradiction, that the vessel had been at the Isle of May, and that suddenly she departed, and had never since been heard of; that the Mate and Dalton were on board, and the Mate having her in charge. That the Captain's chest of clothes, and some of his money had been carried by the prisoners to St. Lucie, where they were found by Captain Levy, who received them from the hands of the legal authority. That the vessel was feloniously taken, is also apparent from his testimony, because the fact to which he swears positively, that on examination the cables were found to have been cut, is irreconcilable with any other supposition. The testimony of Owen, the cook, is therefore not necessary, although in a case of this kind it is satisfactory to obtain all the information which the nature of the case admits. His statement is in affirmance of Captain Levy's, and is corroborated by it so far as both witnesses were capable of knowing the same facts. It is only an enlarged and more circumstantial story to which he testifies. The Captain had given the outlines of the horrible picture, Owen had filled up the dark particulars of the scene. In law, even an accomplice was admissible as a witness, and by every principle of common sense, his evidence would be credited if it was probable, consistent, and corroborated by facts independent of it, and known to exist. His statement of the departure from the Isle of May and arrival at St. Lucie are not only probably, but certainly true; his story is consistent, clear, and uncontradicted in any of its parts; after an able and most ingenious cross-examination, nothing appears to make his statement in the least degree ambiguous or uncertain. He tells a plain, unvarnished tale of his whole course of life. The great advantage of a trial by Jury is, that Jurors have an opportunity of seeing the witnesses, and judging of the credit due them by the manner in which they testify. In this instance he left it to the Jury to determine whether they ever saw a more unembarrassed, and intelligent, and cautious witness; and whether he was an accomplice or not, it was impossible to resist the force of his testimony. But was he an accomplice? His own statement, and the circumstances he has related, sh[o]w that he was not. He had, probably, no will of his own. In the most menial capacity, a mere drudge, necessary to the new masters of the vessel, but too insignificant to be for a moment consulted, he had no choice but to obey their commands. He was a man more sinned against, than sinning; and as soon as he had an opportunity, evinced his regard for the laws of God and man, which he had seen so flagrantly violated, by voluntarily giving evidence to the first American Captain whom he was able to meet, by means of which, the defendants were arrested and brought to the bar of their country.

The Attorney considered at large, and replied to the various arguments which had been urged by the Counsel for the prisoners, and contended that every felonious running away with a vessel on the high seas, was a piratical act within the Statute; and if the Jury believed the testimony which had been adduced, the crime contemplated by Law and charged in the indictment had been perpetrated, and the Jury would not hesitate in a verdict of Guilty.

After the arguments had closed, the learned judges several[l]y addressed the Jury. Each of them recapitulated the testimony, and stated in a very fair, perspicuous, and impartial manner, the operation and effect of it, as well in favour as against the prisoners at the bar. On the question of law, which they said had been very properly raised by the Counsel for the defendants, they had bestowed as much attention as was possible during the course of the trial; and both their Honours stated explicitly their opinion, that a felonious running away with the vessel, was a piratical act within the meaning of the act of Congress, and subjected the perpetrators to capital punishment.[31] The prisoners had had a fair and patient hearing; the Jury had paid close attention to the evidence, and the arguments which had been addressed to them. It was a question of evidence, and they were the sole and exclusive arbitrators. It was also a question to be settled by the judgment, and not by the feelings. The powerful appeal, that had been made to their sensibility, might cause them to regret the obligations imposed upon them; but as Jurors, the oath of God was upon them. They had a duty to do, which it would be criminal in them to omit. They were bound as well by their allegiance to their country, as by their tenderness for the prisoners. This duty might be painful, but it was, nevertheless, imperious. If in their consciences they believed the defendants were guilty, they were bound to say so, and leave the consequences to Providence. Theirs was a duty prescribed by justice; the more delightful attribute of mercy was, by the law, placed in other hands; in hands which never failed to exercise it, where the circumstances of the case warranted the interposition of executive favour. A reasonable doubt would operate in favour of life – but the doubt must be reasonable; not the mere suggestions of fancy, and the air creations of mere possibility, but a reasonable and conscientious doubt. To such, a Juror was bound to listen; with such a doubt, he never ought to condemn. If such a doubt remained, the prisoners were entitled to an acquittal.

The trial commenced at ten o'clock in the morning, and it was eleven at night when the case was given in charge to the Jury. Officers were sworn to keep them in some

---

31 "Many nations used the death penalty in various incarnations to deter seamen from piracy. Decapitation and hanging were common punishments, sometimes accompanied by other horrors. Brigands captured by the Danish in one medieval antipiracy campaign were forced inside herring barrels, which were nailed shut and sent by ship to the gallows. The English routinely left executed pirates hanging by the shore as a warning, sometimes encased in chains that kept the corpses intact as they rotted"(Gibbs, *Dead Men*, 56). As seen in an earlier chapter, in 1766 the authorities on St. Eustatius killed convicted pirate Nicholas Johnson by strapping him to a cross and breaking his bones, then beating him until he died.

convenient place until they had agreed upon a verdict, and not to suffer any person to speak to them unless by order of Court, and the Court adjourned until the next day (Wednesday), at nine o'clock, a.m.

Wednesday. The Court opened. Present Judges Story and Davis. The prisoners were brought into Court and [the] Jury came in; being called, they severally answered to their names. It was then asked of them whether they had agreed on a verdict, to which the foreman answered they had not. The Court thereupon inquired if any further explanation of the law was necessary, to which the foreman replied that the Jury could not agree, that the facts in the case amounted to Piracy. The Court then repeated the substance of their former charge on this point, and ordered the Jury to withdraw for further consideration. The Jury accordingly retired. In about three hours they came again into Court. The prisoners were also brought in, and answered to their names.

Clerk:	Gentlemen of the Jury, have you agreed upon a verdict?
Jury:	Yes.
Clerk:	Who shall speak for you?
Jury:	The Foreman.
Clerk:	Mr. Foreman, rise and look upon the prisoners. Prisoners, look upon the Foreman. Mr. Foreman, what say you? Is Samuel Tulley, one of the prisoners at the Bar, Guilty or not Guilty?
Foreman:	Guilty!
Clerk:	Mr. Foreman, what say you? Is John Dalton, one of the prisoners at the Bar, Guilty or not Guilty?
Foreman:	Guilty!

The next day the following motion was filed by the Prisoner's counsel.

United State of America
District of Massachusetts.

Circuit Court of U.S. October Term, 1812.

The United States By Indictment, vs.
SAMUEL TULLEY AND JOHN DALTON.

And now, after verdict and before judgment, the said Samuel and John, by their counsel assigned them by the court, now move the court here for a new trial of the issue joined on the said indictment, for the following causes, viz.

Because the honorable Court, in committing the cause to the Jury who tried the same, misdirected them in a material point of law; in this, that they directed the Jury if they believed, from the evidence in the case, that the defendants feloniously r[a]n away with the vessel and merchandize mentioned in the Indictment, it constituted the crime of piracy, within the meaning of the Statute on which the Indictment is founded.

Because the verdict of the Jury was rendered against the weight of evidence, they having found the defendants guilty of piratically and feloniously running away with the vessel and the merchandize mentioned in the indictment, from the care, custody and possession of Uriah Phillips Levy, the master thereof, although no evidence was offered them to show that any force or violence was exercised on the said Levy, or that he or any other person was thereby put in fear, but the evidence on the part of the government provide the contrary.

PETER O. THACHER,
JAMES T. AUSTIN.

J.T. Austin addressed the Court. He said that having had a very fair and full opportunity of addressing the Court, through the Jury, at the trial, on the subject matter of the present motion, the Counsel for the prisoners did not propose to occupy the further time of their Honors, with the recapitulation of former arguments. In justice, however, to the defence which the Court had entrusted to their care, they deemed it proper to present these objections in the present shape, that they might command the deliberate reflection and judgment, which their immense importance to the prisoners entitled them to receive. They were the only planks in the shipwreck of their hopes, on which they had any prospect of floating to a shore of safety. It would be for their Honors to decide, whether this too should fail them.

On the subject of a new trial, he would merely remark, that although in capital cases it had not been very usual, yet the case of the United States vs. Fries,[32] in the Circuit Court of the United States, for the District of Pennsylvania, and the case of Commonwealth vs. Hardy,[33] in the Supreme Judicial Court of this State, in both of which cases, after verdict of Guilty, new trials had been awarded, were in point to sh[o]w the power and practice of the Court, where circumstances authorized the interference of their discretion.

The motion was received by the Court and held under consideration until Monday, 9th November. The prisoners were then again brought into the Court, and the opinions of their Honors were severally delivered.

---

32   A former Continental Army officer, John Fries was tried for treason in 1799 in Philadelphia in connection with an insurrection in Bucks County; convicted, he won a new trial, which took place in 1800, but was again found guilty. Sentenced to hang, President John Adams pardoned him. See Jane Shaffer Elsmere, "The Trials of John Fries," *Pennsylvania Magazine of History and Biography* 103:4 (October, 1979), 432–445.

33   An 1807 case which resulted in a mistrial (Gulliver, *Supplement*, 22).

His Honor Judge Davis.[: "]A pirate is one, says Hawkins,[34] who, to enrich himself, either by surprise or force, sets upon merchants or other traders, by sea, to spoil them of their goods; this description, as is observed by a respectable writer of our own country, is applicable merely to piracy by the law of nations. Piracy, by the common law, consists in committing those acts of robbery and depredation upon the high seas, which, if committed on shore, would amount to felony there.

["]The description of the offence, in the first part of the 8th Section of our Statute,[35] is analogous to the common law description; but the Statute proceeds, in correspondence with the Statute of 11 and 12 of William 3,[36] to make certain other acts piracy, which would not be so at common law, and among the rest, an atrocious breach of trust by any Captain or mariner of any ship or vessel, in running away with such ship or vessel, or any goods or merchandize to the value of fifty dollars. To constitute this offence, the act must be done, as the Statute expresses it, piratically and feloniously. Unlawful depredation, says a respectable writer of the civil law, is of the essence of piracy; and this I apprehend is true, relative to piracy thus created by Statute, as to piracies by common law. The *anim[o]us depredandi*,[37] as it is expressed by Molloy,[38] is to be determined by the Jury, from facts and circumstances given in evidence, and is comprehended in the term feloniously, which refers to the mind, will or intention. If the Jury find the act of running away with the ship or vessel and goods to be done feloniously, they find it to be done without any justification or excuse; they find it to be done willfully and fraudulently, *animo furandi, lucri causa*;[39] and having been committed with the other qualities and incidents mentioned in the Statute, i.e. at sea, by persons bearing the relation to the ship, Captain or mariners, and the property plundered, amounting to fifty dollars – such felonious act is, in contemplation of the Statute, piratical.

["]Thus the Jury were instructed, and after the serious deliberation which the nature and magnitude of the case necessarily impose, I do not think the direction erroneous.

["]In regard to the second objection, if force were necessary to be proved in order to constitute piracy, there was sufficient evidence in the case of a forcible taking of the

---

34   William Hawkins, A *Treatise of the Pleas of the Crown*, first published in 1716.
35   This refers to the 30 April, 1790 U.S. law, created by an Act of Congress, which established the legal basis for trying and punishing cases of piracy.
36   The act 11–12 Will. III, c.7 of 1700 was known as "An Act for the More Effectual Suppression of Piracy," and replaced legislation dating from Henry VIII's time. It "allowed prosecution in all of England's colonies, trading posts and ships at sea," and established comprehensive new rules for piracy tribunals, or commissions. The act would "put into place a system that controlled British piracy prosecutions for the next 170 years" (Baer, *British Piracy*, II:ix–xi).
37   *Animus depredandi*: Intent to commit depredation
38   Charles Molloy, *De Jure Maritimo et Navali, or A Treatise of Affairs Maritime and of Commerce*, first published in 1676.
39   With intent to steal, for the sake of gain.

property in question; nor can it be contended, I think, from the evidence, that no person was put in fear. But it is said that no evidence was offered, to sh[o]w that any force or violence were exercised on Levy, the master, in whose care, custody and possession the vessel and goods were alle[d]ged to be, or that he was put in fear. This objection is grounded on an analogy to robbery on land; an analogy too strictly pursued in the argument on this head. Even at common law, piracy might be committed without the characteristic[k]s which this objection considers as [e]ssential. If a ship shall ride at anchor, says Molloy, and the mariners shall be part in the ship's boat and the rest on shore, and none shall be in the ship; yet if a pirate shall attack and rob her, the same is piracy. And on this Statute there can be no question; as appears to me, that actual force on the master, or other person in possession, is not necessary to constitute the offence. The Statute had in view the prevention of atrocious violation of trust, by persons standing in particular relations to the ship. Officers and mariners may combine feloniously to run away with the ship and cargo without any person being put in fear, in the sense considered in the objection, and yet it would be clearly a piratical act, within the true intent and meaning of the Statute.

["]It is not necessary now to consider whether a new trial could properly be directed by the Court, if the objections, or either of them, were well founded. Being persuaded that the Jury were not misdirected in matter of law, and that the Indictment is legally maintainable without proof of actual force or violence on the master or others, or that they were put in fear, I am of [the] opinion that the motion be overruled.["]

The honorable Judge Story stated at full length his reasons on this point, which, concurring with those of Hon. Judge Davis, it is not necessary to recapitulate. The motion was accordingly overruled.

George Blake, Esq. then rose and addressed the Court in a solemn and impressive speech, in which he recapitulated the proceedings on the Indictment, the verdict of the Jury, and the law which [pro]nounced capital punishment on such conviction; and concluded, by stating it to be his duty to move, and he accordingly did now move the Court to proceed to pronounce the sentence of the law.

His Honor Judge Story then addressed the prisoners as follows:

["]Samuel Tulley – John Dalton,

["]You have been charged by the Grand Inquest of the United States, for the District of Massachusetts, with the crime of piratically and feloniously running away with the schooner *George Washington*, commanded by Uriah Phillips Levy, against the Statute of the United States in such cases made and provided. You have been duly furnished with copies of the Indictment, and also with lists of the Jury, who, upon your trial, were to pass between you and the United States. You have had Counsel assigned you by the Court, according to the benign provision of the law in capital cases. You have been arraigned on the Indictment, and have severally pleaded not guilty. You have been tried by an impartial Jury of your country, and at the trial had assistance and arguments of able, and learned, and eloquent Counsel in your defence. You have been severally found guilty of the verdict of your peers. You have excepted to the opinions of the Court in matters of law at your trial. These exceptions have been fully considered by the Court, and upon mature deliberation have been over-ruled. You have now been brought into Court to receive the judgment of the law, and the District Attorney has now, in your presence, moved the Court to proceed to judgment.

["]What reasons have you now to sh[o]w to the Court, why they should not pronounce sentence against you?["]

No reason being shown, the learned Judge proceeded as follows:

["]Before I proceed to the painful duty imposed upon me by the law, a cup of bitterness which I would most willingly put aside, I shall make a few remarks, which I hope will impress your minds with the most solemn conviction of the turpitude of your offence, and with the mercy of God, incline your hearts to contrition and repentance.

["]The crime of which you have been convicted is of a most odious nature; it is willful, malicious, deliberate piracy. Among all civilized nations, it is esteemed as an offence which places you in enmity with the whole world, which banishes you from the hospitality and the protection of society, and consigns you to an ignominious death. In the present case, it has been attended with still more aggravated circumstances than usually attend the depredations of unauthorized plunderers of the property of their fellow men. You were part of a crew of a vessel navigated under the flag of the United States, entrusted by the owners with their confidence and property, and urged, by every honorable motive, to an honest discharge of your respective duties.

["]The security of the commerce of the country, the maintenance of the good order of society, and the lives of thousands of your fellow citizens are intimately connected with the good faith and honesty of seamen. How have you repaid the confidence reposed in you by the esteem of your commander? You have been treacherous and deceitful. You have had no adequate temptations, and no apology for your deliberate violations of the law.

["]You sought the darkness of night to cover deeds which would not bear the light. You had time to consider and reflect. The midnight stars shone with disastrous light on your wickedness; the deep silence of the hour, when nature pauses as upon the brink of dissolution, gravely warned you of your fate. The morning rose in its splendour to call you back to repentance; yet you returned not; yet you sought not the forgiveness of the world, by returning to the bosom of society, and repenting of your sin. Shall I stop or shall I proceed? One crime leads on the way to another, and every step in guilt is but a new incitement to urge another. One of your companions bowed down in spirit, overwhelmed with self humiliation, approached you in the ful[l]ness of his sorrow, and repented and implored your mercy. Did your bowels yearn with mercy towards him? Did you endeavor to soften his woe or seek with him the path of future peace, by a return to virtue? I dread even to remember the hateful tale! His tears and entreaties were of no effect.

["]I would not willingly accuse, much less would I unheard condemn you. The hour of his fate drew nigh; in the deep gloom of the night, there was a most foul and unnatural murder.[40] You heard his dying groans; you saw his last struggle; you took his lifeless corpse and plunged it amid the sullen waves. The ocean received him to its bosom, and returned back its short but awful murmurs. Were you guilty of this atrocious crime? I will not say; let your own hearts and consciences declare.[41] The morrow saw no tears and no contrition. The deeds of night were but the precursors of a new destruction. The vessel was herself the next object of ruin; and she was wantonly scuttled and left to sink to the bottom of the sea. Foul and deliberate falsehoods closed the horrible history of your crime.

["]Yet though these transactions were veiled from human eyes, think not they escaped the all seeing eyes of that Being who createth and governeth the universe.[42] At the solemn hour when deep sleep falls upon the sons of men, his ever watchful mind is awake. When darkness surrounds the plunder of the public pirate, he is ever present and marks the wanderings of wickedness. When murder riots in supposed security, he hears the voice of dying innocence, and His own right arm shall avenge the deep damnation of the dead.

---

40 An invocation of William Shakespeare's *Hamlet*, Act I, Scene 5:
   GHOST: . . . If thou didst ever thy dear father love—
   HAMLET: O God!
   GHOST: Revenge his foul and most unnatural murder.
   HAMLET: Murder!
   GHOST: Murder most foul, as in the best it is;
     But this most foul, strange and unnatural.
41 This statement, and the question that preceded it, is a reminder that the prisoners were tried and convicted only on the first of three grand jury indictments – in this case, for piracy.
42 Phrases similar to "createth and governeth" turn up in several period religious tracts; the phrase itself appears in Scottish theologian Samuel Rutherford's *A Free Disputation Against Pretended Liberty of Conscience*, first published in 1649. In it, Rutherford observed (7) that the conscience naturally recognizes "that there is a God, that he createth and governeth all things, that there is but one God, infinitely good, more just rewarding the Evil and the good."

["]I would not willingly afflict you in your fallen condition, but I must awake your consciences to an awful sense of your impending fate. You are now soon to be cut off from life; and these cheering beams which now surround you, will soon be shut from your sight. The grave will become your cold and solitary residence, and the places that now know you shall know you no more. You are in the bloom and vigour of your days, yet society has found it necessary to arrest them, and to send you, with all your imperfections on your heads, to another world. Think, oh think, after what has happened, how can you appear before that dread tribunal, and that Omnipotent Judge who searcheth the hearts, and trieth the reins of all men[?][43] From his sentence there is no appeal, and before him you must soon appear to render an account of all the deeds done in the body. There can be no concealment or shelter there; the accusing spirit of conscience will rise in judgment against you, and the voice of your poor unfortunate brother will be heard from the very depths of the ocean.

["]Let me entreat you, tenderly and earnestly entreat you, as dying sinners, to turn from your wicked thoughts; to ponder on the errors of your ways, and with penitence and humiliation to seek the altars of our holy religion. Let me entreat you to pray for mercy and forgiveness from that righteous God, whom you have so justly offended. The time, perhaps, may not be too late. The glory of Christianity may yet brighten your declining days, and the spirit of reigning grace may drop a tear on your sins and blot them out forever.

["]I now proceed to pronounce the awful sentence of the law upon your crime:["}

SENTENCE

["]Whereupon all and singular the pr[e]mises being seen, and by the said Judges of the said Court here fully understood – it is considered by the Court here, that the said Samuel Tulley, and John Dalton be, and they hereby are severally deemed, taken, and adjudged to be pirates and felons; – and that they, the said Samuel Tulley and John Dalton, and each of them, be hanged by the neck until they, and each of them, be dead. And it is further ordered and considered by the Court here, that the Marshal of this District do, on peril of what may fall thereon, cause execution to be done in the pr[e]mises aforesaid upon them, the said Samuel Tulley and John Dalton, on the tenth day of December next ensuing, between the hours of ten o'clock in the forenoon, and three in the afternoon of the same day; and that they, the said Samuel Tulley and John Dalton, be now taken from hence to the g[ao]l in Boston, in the District of Massachusetts, from whence they came, there, or in some other safe and convenient prison within the District aforesaid, to be closely kept until the day of

---

43 A possible rhetorical nod to Revelation 2:23 in the King James Version of the *Holy Bible*, in which Jesus addresses the church in Thyatira, and says of Jezebel: "And I will kill her children with death, and all the Churches shall know that I am hee which searcheth the reines and hearts: and I will give unto every one of you according to your workes."

execution, and from thence, on the day appointed for execution as aforesaid, to be taken to the place of execution in Boston aforesaid, there to be hanged as aforesaid.

["]I recommend you to the mercy of Almighty God, before whom we shall all one day appear; and I pray that he may succour and support you in the hour of trial, and I now bid you an eternal farewell.["]

APPENDIX
Some account of the conduct and conversations of the Convicts especially since their conviction, having been deemed interesting, the following particulars have been obtained from an authentic source.

Tulley, the mate, is an American by birth, of respectable but poor parents, in the State of Pennsylvania, and is forty-two years of age. Dalton, or rather Heathcoat, which is his true name, is an Englishman, and was twenty-four years old. The mate had received a tolerably good education, was a capable seaman, having most of his life followed the sea. – Dalton was very ignorant.

Immediately on their conviction they were removed by the consent of his Excellency the Governor and the Directors of the State Prison, to that place, for safe keeping, and were confined there till they were taken out for execution. Every accommodation and comfort which their situation would permit has been afforded them. They were fed from the officers' table, and the indulgence and humanity of the Marshal of the District, the Warden, and the Officers of the prison according to them every reasonable gratification.

To secure to these unhappy convicts the advantages which the interval between their sentence and its execution offered for their spiritual and eternal good, has been the earnest desire of the government of the prison, and in this they were indefatigably and most humanely assisted by Clergymen of various sects in and about the metropolis. [. . .] The conduct of the prisoners has been uniform, patient, and resigned. They have acknowledged their faith in the Divine Redeemer, and that the first awakening of their minds to the great duties that should prepare them for eternity, was excited by their awful situation, and the monitions of their disinterested and unexpected friends.

They acknowledged with gratitude, the fairness and impartiality of their trial, the free will labours of their Counsel, and the justice of the law; and though they persisted to the last moment in denying the truth of some parts of the testimony at their trial, they acknowledged the propriety of their condemnation.

Tulley, who has expiated his offence with his life, confessed that he cut the cables and ran away with the vessel, but that the treatment he received from Captain Levy, and his repeated refusals to discharge him instigated him to that act.

As to any concern in the murder of George Cummings, he absolutely refused to confess himself guilty. But on the contrary, protested that Cummings had free access to the wine, got intoxicated, made the first assault, and wounded and bruised Tulley to the great danger of his life; and, that without any participation further, than his not opposing it, Dalton and the Cook threw him overboard. The scuttling of the schooner, or any attempts to do it he absolutely denied, and persisted in declaring that the testimony of Owen in this respect was totally false. He said further, that his original intention was to have brought the vessel to the United States, but that being short handed, the Cook no sailor, and Dalton being sick, he was not able to do it. The crime, however, for which he was condemned he acknowledged, and acquiesced in his sentence.

On Thursday morning at 11 o'clock, prayers were offered in the State Prison, and the convicts taken under care of the Marshal and his officers, accompanied by the Sheriff of Suffolk [County] and his Deputies, and conducted to the place of execution, at South Boston. – The Rev. Mr. Collier, with his wonted kindness and humanity, rode with them in the coach. When the Prisoners had ascended the scaffold, the Marshal read the Death Warrant. Tulley then wished to read a paper which he had prepared but his strength failing him, he desired one of the Deputy Marshals to read it for him, (as his dying words) as follows:

"As a man and criminal now going out of this world, I do think it my duty to acknowledge that I have been guilty of taking, and assisting to take, the property which is mentioned in the first Indictment, but the murder, which was charged in the second Indictment, I do not see that I am any ways guilty of, although it was plead so hard against me, and I have reason to believe was the means of my being condemned; but if not, I acknowledge the justness of my sentence; but if other ways, I pray that the Almighty God will forgive those who have done me this wrong, and I freely forgive them from the bottom of my heart, as I hope the Almighty God will forgive me, not only this, but all the sins and wickedness that I have done in the world. This crime, for which I now suffer, is a horrible crime to think upon, and I beg that it may be a warning to every one that may hear of it, or witness my sad fate – And I do think that it is my duty to express, with gratitude, my sincere thanks to the Marshals, and to other gentlemen, in whose hands and charge I have been since I first came to Boston, and particularly to the Wardens and Keepers of the State Prison in Charlestown, and Col. Gardner in particular, for his kindnesses shown to me. I give my sincere and hearty thanks to all the Ministers, and other pious people of different denominations, who have assisted me with their repeated visits, and their good advice, their prayers, their sermons, and their pious and godly books, to bring me to a due sense of myself, and to open my blind and wicked heart, and to soothe my sorrows, to bring me to true repentance for all my sins and wickedness, and to prepare me to meet my awful sentence and death, and to meet the Almighty God who gave me my existence, and has been my whole support through this veil of life. – And undoubtedly it has been his good will and pleasure that I should suffer [on] this side [of] the grave, to expiate for the sins and wickedness which I have willfully committed against so good and merciful a Creator; and to bring me to his only Son, Jesus Christ, the Redeemer and Saviour of the world, in whom I put my whole trust, hope and confidence, well knowing there is no other name under Heaven whereby I can be saved. Therefore I resign myself to his gracious disposal, with my body to the earth from whence it came, and my spirit to the Lord who gave it; and may the Lord Jesus Christ have mercy on my poor soul. – Amen.

SAMUEL TULLEY."

The Throne of Grace was then addressed by the Rev. Mr. Collier. The rope was first placed round the neck of Tulley, who ascended the platform and continued fervent in prayer, and in the presence of an immense concourse of spectators, he was launched into the eternal world.

Dalton, who was not desirous of saying any thing at the place of execution, was then taken and his neckcloth removed, the rope fixed, his arms pinioned, the cap drawn over his eyes – an awful moment of anxiety was felt by the assembled crowd; one instant more, and he would have followed his companion to the world of spirits; when the Marshal stepped forward, and thus addressed the spectators.

"Friends and Fellow Citizens.

"The good people of the United States, when they formed their National compact, wisely ordained among the duties assigned the President, that he should execute the laws with judgment and with mercy; while therefore has he left that man (pointing to Tulley), who is now suspended between heaven and earth, a spectacle for men and angels, to suffer the pains adjudged him by the law; he has been disposed in mercy to respite the sentence of this man (pointing to Dalton) for a few days, that he may gain that information which may perhaps incline him to extend further favours."

The Marshal then read a reprieve, by order of the President of the United States, till the 10th day of January, 1813.

Within the time limited, Dalton received his full pardon, signed by the President, and issued under the great seal of the United States.

A public execution is a very rare occurrence in the town of Boston; it on Thursday spread a gloom throughout the capital of this State! The sight was affecting, even to a degree of awfulness! To see a fellow creature pinioned that he should not destroy himself, or in the bitterness of his soul, madly to destroy another; his halter about his neck; his coffin by his side, and going to be hung, is one of the most shocking sights that can meet the weeping eye in civilized society! The bell to be tolling for the death and funeral of men still living and passing the streets, had an effect that few could support without tears! It is, at all times, a dreadful thing to die! Death, said an ancient philosopher, is like the sun – it cannot be looked at steadily![44] The strong fibred, philosophical [Samuel] Johnson always thought so. He said, they who appear un-moved at the idea of death, do not show so much a strength of mind, as a want of thought.[45]

---

44 *Le soleil ni la mort ne se peuvent regarder fixement* is Maxim 26 in François de La Rochefoucauld's *Réflexions ou Sentences et Maximes Morales* (10–11), first published in 1665.

45 The writer may be citing the following exchange:
   BOSWELL: Then, Sir, we must be contented to acknowledge that death is a terrible thing.
   JOHNSON: Yes, Sir. I have made no approaches to a state which can look on it as not Terrible.
   MRS. KNOWLES: (seeming to enjoy a pleasing serenity in the persuasion of benignant divine light:)
       Does not St. Paul say, "I have fought the good fight of faith, I have finished my course; henceforth is laid
       up for me a crown of life?"
   JOHNSON: Yes, Madam; but here was a man inspired, a man who had been converted by supernatural
       interposition.
   BOSWELL: In prospect death is dreadful; but in fact we find that people die easy.
   JOHNSON: Why, Sir, most people have not *thought* much of the matter, so cannot *say* much, and it is
       supposed they die easy. Few believe it certain they are then to die; and those who do, set themselves to
       behave with resolution, as a man does who is going to be hanged: – he is not the less unwilling to be
       hanged (Boswell, *Life of Johnson*, III:321–322).

6

"The greatest villains that ever blackened the human character" – The privateers of the Gulf and Caribbean (1814–1821)

At the same time the War of 1812 raged, Central and South America had for several years already seen a series of revolts against Spanish colonial power. As was the case with the American colonies in 1775, the new states that emerged lacked navies and the funds required to establish them. As a result, they offered privateering documents to ship owners willing to capture Spanish vessels in return for a percentage of their value after being condemned by a prize court. Such forms were especially easy to get from such former Spanish colonies as Cartagena in New Granada (modern Colombia), and Buenos Aires, capitol of modern Argentina.

Like their North American and European counterparts, the Latin American privateers were subject to restrictions and regulation, including the posting of bonds. But these received little enforcement as the region slipped into chaos. Privateer craft, failing to find Spanish prey, and with crew members clamoring for prize money, often slipped across the line into piracy and attacked whatever vessels hove into view. Many ostensible privateering cruises originated in U.S. ports, with American investors backing them.

Louisiana especially became a host for smugglers and pirates, the colorful but deadly Laffite brothers, Pierre and Jean, among them, operating first with French and later with Carthaginian documents. Prior to the War of 1812, the Laffites moved operations from New Orleans to Grand Terre Island, renaming it Barataria (or Barrataria) for its location in the *Grand Lac de Barataria*, or Barataria Bay.[1] Fearing the Laffites would accept an offer from the British, a United States squadron in mid-September 1814 scattered the Laffites' settlement; the brothers, who often played one side against the other, would still opt to assist the United States against the British as the campaign for New Orleans unfolded.

The treaty that ended that war also unemployed a horde of American and European sailors, many of whom found new posts on Latin American "patriot" privateers.

---

1 Barataria Bay "was linked to the Mississippi River by a network of small rivers and bayous, and [Laffite] and his colleagues used these waterways to transport goods between the Gulf of Mexico and the city [of New Orleans], and stood ready to use them as a means of escape if the authorities came looking for them" (Konstam, *Piracy*, 276).

Map of the Grand Lac de Barataria, showing Grand Terre Island (The Historic New Orleans Collection, accession no. 1993.2.28, DETAIL).

For a while the privateers found acceptance, even praise, from American editors, but soon proved a greater threat to American shipping than their North African counterparts had ever been. They also earned a reputation for brutality and sadism.

What follows begins with reports of the U.S Navy's September, 1814 assault on Barataria island. Subsequent accounts detail the rise of the Latin American privateers, and their piratical excesses. The shift of editorial opinion about their nature, from praise to condemnation, is also visible. The documents continue to a point in late 1821 when the American response to their threat was about to come ashore on Cuba itself.

ooooo

[Hallowell, Maine *American Advocate*, 3 December 1814, 4.]

Copy of a letter from Cdm. Patterson to the Secretary of the Navy, dated New Orleans,[2] Sept. 10, 1814

SIR – I have the honor to inform you that I departed from this city on the 11th ult. accompanied by Col. [George T.] Ross[3] with a detachment of seventy of the 44th regt.

---

2 At the time of the Louisiana Purchase, New Orleans, at the Mississippi river's mouth, was "itself made up several dozen square blocks of creole and colonial houses on the northwest side of a crescent bend in the Mississippi River, all still encased in the remnants of an earthen rampart remaining from its earlier defenses. The Place d'Arms sat just back from the river, an open square on which stood the Cathedral Church of St. Louis, with the territorial prison and guardhouse to one side and an ecclesiastical charity house on the other. Street names redolent of French and Spanish history . . . paralleled the levee road at the river's edge. Intersecting them were others of equal association . . . " (Davis, *Pirates Laffite*, 8–9).

3 Ross was "colonel of the United States Forty-fourth Infantry Regiment and the senior regular army officer in Louisiana. A native of Pennsylvania, following service with the First Artificers & Engineers (1796–1801) and Second Infantry (1802–1804), Ross had migrated to Louisiana, where he was appointed colonel of the newly formed Forty-fourth Infantry on August 1, 1813" (Vogel, "Raid on Barataria," 158).

of infantry – on the 12th reached the sch[oone]r *Caroline*[4] at Plaquemine [Louisiana], and formed a junction with the gun vessels at the Balize[5] on the 13th – sailed from the south west pass on the evening of the 15th, at half past 8 a.m. on the 15th, made the Island of Grand Terre (Barrataria) and discovered a number of vessels in the harbor, some of which sh[o]wed Carthag[i]nian colors[6] – and at 9, perceived the pirates forming their vessels, ten in number, including prizes, into a line of battle near the entrance of the harbor, and making every preparation to offer me battle – at 10, wind light and variable, formed the order of battle with the 6[-]gun vessels, viz. *No. 5, 23, 156, 162, 163*[7] and [85?], the *Sea Horse* tender,[8] mounting one 6[-]pounder[9] and 15 men, and a launch mounting one 12[-]pound carronade; the schooner *Caroline* drawing too much water to cross the bar – at half past 10 perceived several smokes along the coast as signals, and at the same time a white flag hoisted on board a schooner at the fore, an American flag at the main mast head, and a Carthag[i]nian flag (under which the pirates cruise) at her topping lift;[10] replied with a white flag at my main; at 11, discovered that the pirates had fired two of their best schooners; hauled down my white flag and made the signal for battle – hoisting with it a large white flag bearing these words, "Pardon to deserters," having heard there were a number from the army and navy there, who wished to return if assured of pardon, and which the President's proclamation offered till the 17th. ¶

---

4   Officially the USS *Carolina*, commanded at this time by John Dandridge Henley. USS *Carolina* was an 89-foot long, 230-ton schooner which the US Navy bought, as yet unfinished, in 1812 at Charleston. On its cruise to New Orleans it captured the British schooner *Shark*. Following the raid on Barataria, it played a major role in the subsequent defense of New Orleans. British artillery fire destroyed it in late December, 1814 (Mooney, *Fighting Ships*, II:38).

5   "The Balize refers to the entry point where ships entering [the Mississippi River] from the Gulf of Mexico stopped for inspection before proceeding to the port of New Orleans. Over time this simple checkpoint developed into a settlement, known during the nineteenth century as Pilottown, Louisiana" (Buman, *To Kill Whites*, 62n155).

6   The Cartagenian flag at this time "contained a white eight-pointed star on a green rectangle surrounded by yellow and red borders. This flag is sometimes mistakenly identified as the Venezuelan flag" (Spain, "Flags").

7   The flotilla consisted of "Gunboat *No. 5*, 5 guns, Sailing Master J. D. Ferris; Gunboat *No.* [23], 5 guns, Acting Lieut. Isaac McKeever; Gunboat *No. 156*, 5 guns, Lieut. Thomas ap [Catesby] Jones; Gunboat *No. 162*, 5 guns, Acting Lieut. Robert Spedden; Gunboat *No. 163*, 3 guns, Sailing Master Ulrick. . . . The gunboats were shallow-draught 'Jeffs' [i.e. part of the Jefferson Administration's attempt to build a coastal force of small vessels] mounting three to five guns and carrying crews of between thirty and forty men. Individual gunboat service records have not been published; all five veterans of the Barataria Bay action were captured by the British in the Battle of Lake Borgne on December 14, 1814" (Vogel, "Raid on Barataria," 164–5, 165n25, citing Wilbur S. Brown, *The Amphibious Campaign for West Florida and Louisiana, 1814–1815* [Tuscaloosa: University of Alabama, 1969]), 77–81).

8   The Navy bought the schooner *Sea Horse* in 1812; it was employed during the defense of New Orleans until mid-December 1814, when "after repelling two attacks by armed British launches, she was beached by her commanding officer... and burned to prevent capture" (Mooney, *Fighting Ships*, VI:403).

9   Cannon "were usually designated by the weight of their solid shot rather than the diameter of their bore. Thus an 18-pounder gun fired a ball weighing 18 lbs. The heavier the gun the more powder it could take and hence the longer the range and greater the velocity of its shot. Thus guns of the same size bore usually appeared in a variety of different classes" (Tucker, *Handbook*, 6).

10 Lifts are "ropes which reach from each mast-head to their respective yard-arms to steady and suspend the ends. Their use is to keep the yard in equilibrium, or to raise one of its extremities higher than the other if necessary, but particularly to support the weight when a number of men are employed on it, furling or reefing the sail." Topping-lifts are "lifts which support a spar, davit, etc." (Smyth, *Lexicon*, 443–444, 687).

At a quarter past 11, gun vessels *No. 23* and *156* (the latter bearing my pendant) grounded, and were passed agreeably to my previous order, by the other four, which entered the harbor; manned my barge and the boats belonging to the grounded vessels, and proceeded in, when to my great disappointment, I perceived that the pirates had abandoned their vessels and were flying in small boats in all directions. I immediately sent the launch and two gun barges with small boats in pursuit of them – at meridian took possession of all their vessels in harbor, consisting of six schooners and one felucca,[11] cruizers and prizes of the pirates, one brig, a prize, and two armed schooners under the Carthag[i]nian flag, both in the line of battle with the armed schooners of the pirates, and apparently with an intention to aid them in any resistance they might make against me, as their crews were at quarters,[12] tompions out of their guns, and matches[13] lighted. Col. Ross at the same time landed, and with his command took possession of their establishment on shore, consisting of about forty houses of different sizes, badly constructed, and thatched with Palmet[t]o leaves.

When I perceived the enemy forming their vessels into a line of battle, I felt confident, from their number and very advantageous position, and their number of men, that they would have fought me; their not doing so I regret; for had they, I should have been enabled more effectually to destroy or make prisoners of them and their leaders; but it is an object of great satisfaction to me, to have effected the object of my enterprize, viz. capturing all their vessels in port, and dispersing the band, without having one of my brave fellows hurt.

The enemy had mounted on their vessels 20 pieces of cannon of different calibres; and as I have since learnt, from 800 to 1000 men of all nations and colors.

Early in the morning of the 20th, the *Caroline*, at anchor about five miles distant, made the signal of a "strange sail in sight to the eastward;" immediately after, she weighed anchor and gave chase, the strange sail standing for Grand Terre, with all sail; at half past 8 the chase hauling her wind off shore to escape; sent acting [L]ieut. Robert Spedden with four boats manned and armed to prevent her passing the harbor; at 9 a.m. the chase fired upon the *Caroline*, which was returned; each vessel continued firing during the chase, when their long guns could reach – at 10 the chase grounded outside the bar, at which time the *Caroline* was, from the shoalness of the water, obliged to haul her wind off shore, and give up the chase – opened a fire upon the chase

---

11 A felucca is "a small sailing or rowing vessel of the Mediterranean, used for coastal transport or trading." Large feluccas might have carried multiple masts; smaller ones "were propelled with six or eight oars, though some of the smaller sailing feluccas used oars and sail simultaneously." The felucca is "still in use on many eastern Mediterranean rivers, particularly the Nile" (Dear and Kemp, *Companion*, 203).

12 At battle stations; sailors were usually summoned by use of a "short, quick, and determined roll" on a drum, hence the term *beat to quarters* (Miller, *Broadsides*, 53).

13 A match used to fire cannons consisted of "a twisted cotton wick soaked in lye that rested on the edge of the water tub [kept between the guns] until needed. . . . Beginning in 1780, the British replaced matches with the more efficient flintlock, which was triggered by jerking a lanyard" (Miller, *Broadsides*, 54).

across the Island from the gun vessels – at half past 10 she hauled down her colors, and was taken possession of by [L]ieut. Spedden – she proved to be the armed schooner called the *Gen. Bolivar*,[14] under the Carthag[i]nian flag – by grounding she broke off both her rudder pintles,[15] and made water – hove her off in the course of the day, and at day light on the 21st, sent out a small prize schooner to lighten her – took from her her armament, consisting of one long brass 18[-]pounder, one long brass 6[-]pounder, two 12[-]pound carronades, small arms, &c. and twenty one packages of dry goods, and brought her into port; and as I could not wait for the repairs necessary for her rudder, ordered her to this port for adjudication. I am well convinced that she is one of the vessels belonging to, or connected with the pirates, as signals of recognition for her were found on board one of the pirates' cruizers; and at the time she was discovered, she was standing directly for Grand Terre, which she still endeavored to gain, after being chased by the *Caroline*, not knowing of our being in possession of it; she fired several shots at the *Caroline*, after the latter had sh[o]wn her colors.

On the afternoon of the 23rd got under way with the whole squadron, in all seventeen vessels – (but during the night one schooner under Carthag[i]nian colors escaped) – on the morning of the 24th entered the south west pass of this river, and on the 1st inst. arrived opposite this city with all my squadron.

The amount of the prize goods will probably be considerable; but at present cannot be ascertained.

Three of the schooners are admirably adapted for the public service on this station, being uncommonly fleet sailers and light draught of water, and would be of infinite public utility.

I cannot speak in too high terms of commendation of the good conduct of the officers, seamen and marines whom I have the honor to command; nothing could exceed the zeal shown by all on this occasion.

Great credit is due to [L]ieut. Louis Alexis, and Mr. Thomas Shields, purser,[16] for gallantly leading in, in the face of the enemy, the former in the *Sea Horse* tender, and the latter in the launch, when they had every reason to believe the enemy would open their whole battery upon them, supported by gun vessel *No. 5*, astern of them, commanded by Mr. J.D. Ferris; Mr. Shields very handsomely volunteered his services

---

14 Venezuelan revolutionary Simón Bolívar (1783–1830), central to the Latin American wars of liberation. For a biography, see John Lynch, *Simon Bolivar: A Life* (London: Yale University, 2006).

15 "The rudder is hung on to a ship by pintles and braces. The braces are secured firmly to the stern-post by jaws, which spread and are bolted on each side. The pintles are hooks which enter the braces, and the rudder is then wood-locked; a dumb pintle on the heel finally takes the strain off the hinging portions" (Smyth, *Lexicon*, 529).

16 "The old name by which the paymaster, and officer responsible for provisions and clothing, was known in both the British and US navies during the days of sail" (Dear and Kemp, *Companion*, 448).

on this expedition, and has from his being a seaman, rendered me great assistance in taking charge of and bringing one of the prizes to this city.

Lieut. Thomas A.C. Jones[17] particularly distinguished himself by boarding one of the schooners, which had been fired, and extinguished the fire after it had made great progress; a quantity of powder being left in her cabin, evidently designed to blow her up; he is also with Lieut. Norris, and acting Lieut. Thomas S. Cunningham, entitled to my thanks for the severe duty performed by them in open boats for several days and nights.[...]

I have the honor to be, with great consideration and respect, your obedient servant,

DANIEL T. PATTERSON.[18]

The Hon. Wm. Jones,[19]

Secretary of the Navy, Washington

BARRATARIA

In a late paper we gave an account of the breaking up, and capture of the band of pirates at this place. For the information of such of our readers as are unacquainted with the history and nature of the establishment, we copy the following interesting narrative from the *National Intelligencer*.

Barrataria is a bayou, or a narrow arm of the Gul[f] of Mexico. It runs through a rich but very flat country, until it reaches within a mile or two of the Mississippi river, fifteen miles below the city of New Orleans. This bayou has branches almost innumerable, in which persons can be concealed from the severest scrutiny. It communicates with three lakes which lie on the southwest side, and these with the lake of the same name, and which lies contiguous to the sea, where is an island formed by the two

17 Thomas ap Catesby Jones (1790–1858) had "one of the more famous and colorful careers in the nineteenth-century navy," becoming a midshipman at 15 in 1805. His "entire 1808–15 career was spent in gunboats and small craft on the New Orleans station." The latter part of that period was spent weathering misconduct charges brought initially in late 1813 by one Philip Philibert, "a troublesome acting midshipman against whom Lieutenant Thomas ap Catesby Jones had recently taken disciplinary action . . . " Philibert spent much of 1814–15 under arrest – reinstated to duty for the New Orleans campaign, he (like Jones) would distinguish himself in battle. Philibert ultimately in 1815 "produced sworn depositions by four enlisted men . . . recounting in specific and realistic detail homosexual encounters between themselves and Lieutenant Jones." Ultimately, Secretary of the Navy Benjamin Crowinshield ruled the evidence was "malicious and vindictive and destitute of any proof upon which a court martial or any other tribunal could condemn the said Lieutenant Jones . . . " (McKee, *A Gentlemanly and Honorable Profession*, 82, 157, 438–439). See also Gene A. Smith, *Thomas ap Catesby Jones, Commodore of Manifest Destiny* (Annapolis, MD: Naval Institute Press, 2000).

18 Patterson (1786–1839) joined the Navy as a midshipman in 1799, and was among those taken prisoner on the *Philadelphia* in Tripoli Harbor. Released in 1805, he "spent much of his following years on station at New Orleans. . . . " Promoted to captain in 1815, Patterson "remained on the southern stations until 1824 when he became fleet captain and commander of flagship *Constitution* in Commodore John Rodgers' Mediterranean Squadron." He was in command of the Washington Navy Yard at the time of his death (Mooney, *Fighting Ships*, V:229).

19 Secretary of the Navy from 1813 to 1814.

arms of this lake and the sea. The east and west points of this island were fortified in the year 1811, by a band of pirates, under the command of Monsieur La F[fit]e. A large majority of those out-laws are of that class of the population of the state of Louisiana, who fled from the Island of St. Domingo during the troubles there, and took refuge in the Island of Cuba. And when the last war between France and Spain commenced they were compelled to leave that island with the short notice of a few days. Without ceremony they entered the United States, the most of them the state of Louisiana, with all the negroes they had possessed in Cuba. They were notified by the Governor of that state, of the clause of the constitution, which forbade the importation of slaves; but at the same time, received the assurance of the Governor, that he would obtain, if possible, the approbation of the general government for their retaining this property. The conduct of this part of the favored emigrants, and the refusal of those who could not from local causes, join in the illicit confederation to obey the draft in that state, which was required by the general government, and ordered by the state herself, prove the fidelity of the allegiance which was promised by these fugitives to the United States. The island of Barrataria is situated about lat[itude] 29 deg. 15 min. lon[gitude] 93, [30?], and is remarkable for its health, as for the superior scale and shell fish with which its waters abound. The chief of this horde, like Charles De Moor,[20] had mixed with his many vices, some transcendent virtues.

In the year 1813, this party had from its turpitude and boldness claimed the attention of the Governor of Louisiana [William C. Claiborne];[21] and to break up the establishment, he thought proper to strike at the head. He therefore offered a reward of 500 dollars for the head of Monsieur La F[fit]e, who was well known to the inhabitants of the city of New Orleans, from his immediate connection, and his once having been a fencing master in that city, of great reputation, which art he learnt in Bonaparte's army, where he was a captain.[22] The reward, which was offered by the Governor for the head of La F[fit]e, was answered by the offer of a reward from the latter of 5000 dollars for the head of the Governor. The Governor ordered out a company to march from the city to La F[fit]e's Island, and to burn and destroy all the property and to bring to the city of New Orleans all his banditti. This company, under the command of a man who had been the intimate associate of this bold captain, approached very near to the fortified island before he saw a man, or heard a sound, until he heard a

---

20   Karl von Moor/Charles de Moor was a character in German playwright Friedrich Schiller's 1781 melodrama *Die Räuber* (The Robbers). "Gifted with every noble quality of manhood in overflowing abundance, Moor's first expectations of life, and of the part he was to play in it, had been glorious as a poet's dream. But the minor dexterities of management were not among his endowments; in his eagerness to reach the goal, he had forgotten that the course is a labyrinthic maze, beset with difficulties, of which some may be surmounted, some can only be evaded, many can be neither. Hurried on by the headlong impetuosity of his temper, he entangles himself in these perplexities; and thinks to penetrate them, not by skill and patience, but by open force" (Carlyle, *Life of Friedrich Schiller*, 17–18).

21   Governor of Louisiana from 1812–16.

22   Laffite's life and career is shrouded in myth, and there were colorful tales of his existence after his presumed death. For a modern biography, including an analysis of Laffite legends, see Davis, *Pirates Laffite, passim.*

whistle, not unlike a boatswain's call.[23] Then it was he found himself surrounded by armed men who had emerged from the secret avenues which led into this bayou. Here it was that this modern Charles De Moor developed his few noble traits; for this man, who had come to destroy his life, and all that was dear to him, he not only spared his life, but offered him that which would have made the honest soldier easy for the remainder of his days, which was indignantly refused. He then, with the approbation of his captor, returned to the city. This circumstance, and some concomitant events, proved that this band of pirates were not to be taken by land. Our naval force having always been small in that quarter, exertions for the destruction of this illicit establishment could not be expected from them until augmented; for an officer of the navy, with most of the gun-boats on that station had to retreat from an overwhelming force of La F[fit]e's. So soon as the augmentation of the navy authorised an attack, one was made; the overthrow of this banditti has been the result; and now [that] this almost invulnerable point and key to New Orleans is clear of an enemy, it is to be hoped the government will hold it by a strong military force.

ooooo

[Essex (Mass.) Register, 22 October 1814, 3]

Copy of a letter from John K. Smith,[24] Esq., to the Secretary of the Navy, dated New Orleans, Sept. 23d. 1814

> SIR – Captain Patterson left this place on the 11th inst. with three barges, and was joined at the Balize by six gun boats and the sch[oone]r *Carolina*, from whence he proceeded against Barrataria. He has been completely successful in breaking up the nest of pirates at that place, and has taken nine vessels, some specie, and a quantity of dry goods. The principal (Laf[fit]e) escaped; but the second in command, Dominique,[25] is taken. – The number of prisoners taken is not known, nor are any of the particulars. A letter from that place states that Capt. Patterson would leave them on the 20th. He will therefore, no doubt, have the honor of giving you the result by the next mail.
>
> The breaking up of this piratical establishment is of great importance to this country. It is ascertained that vessels clearing out from this port with passengers have been captured and every soul on board murdered;[26] they took indiscriminately vessels of every nation, and the fact was perfectly known at Pensacola. The com-

---

23 The boatswain (pronounced "bo'sun") was "the officer who superintends the boat-sails, ship's-sails, rigging, canvas, colours, anchors, cables and cordage, committed to his charge. . . . He pipes the hands to their several duties, seeing that they attend his call, and ought to be in every way a thorough seaman. (Smyth, *Lexicon*, 113).

24 Navy agent at New Orleans since 1809 (Madison, *Calendar*, 346; Allston, *Ready for Sea*, 39).

25 Privateer captain Dominique or Frederick Youx, active in the West Indies since at least 1805; he was not, as some legends would have it, Pierre Laffite or a third Laffite brother (Davis, *Pirates Laffite*, 30, 199, 493).

26 Patterson repeated this allegation in an 1815 letter to Secretary of the Navy Benjamin W. Crowninshield, quoted in Allen, *Our Navy*, 9–10. Faye ("Privateersmen of the Gulf," 1034, 1043) contests this charge.

manding British officers at that place recently made a communication in writing to Laf[fit]e, requesting his aid in an attack upon N[ew] Orleans, which was refused.[27] That correspondence, which is in the hands of Governor Claiborne, no doubt has been communicated to the government.[. . .]

I have the honor to be, sir, your obedient servant;

J.K. SMITH

Hon. Wm. Jones, Secretary of the Navy.

ooooo

[Boston *Daily Advertiser*, 19 September 1816, 1]

NOTICE. – The Spanish brig *Infatigable*, Capt. Don Matias De La Torre Y Rio, bound on a voyage from Havana to New-York, was captured soon after sailing, about the 16th June last, by an armed schooner called the *Bellona*, Capt. Luis Aury,[28] and the crew and passengers landed at Campeachy.[29] The *Infatigable* not arriving there, it was supposed that the prize crew might have brought her into some port in the United States, a circumstance which it is very desirable to ascertain. The *Infatigable* was formerly the American brig *Elizabeth*, of Baltimore, a full[-]built[30] vessel, of about 270 tons burthen, and her cargo at the time of her capture consisted of the following articles, which are here enumerated as a means of identifying the vessel: –

461 hhds.[31] Molasses and 35 bbls.[32] [Molasses]} Part without marks – part with the marks DS.T.M.
14 bbls. Honey, part of the mark T.
7 tierces[33] Jalap,[34] of the mark T.

---

27 The British, then occupying Pensacola, delivered an offer to Laffite prior to Patterson's raid, prompting Laffite to open correspondence with Claiborne (Sugden, "Jean Lafitte and the British Offer of 1814," *passim*; and Vogel, "Raid on Barataria," 162–163).

28 Born in 1788 in Paris, French navy veteran Luis-Michel Aury operated a number of privateer schooners based at Galveston, which sailed initially under Venezuelan commissions and later under ostensible Mexican ones (Faye, "Privateersmen of the Gulf," 1033, 1044–1045; Rodriguez, "Louis Aury"; and Konstam, *Piracy*, 275–276).

29 Campeche: a city (and a corresponding state in modern Mexico) on the Gulf of Mexico.

30 In vessel design, the term "full" was synonymous with rounded, e.g. "a full bow is a round bow as opposed to a fine or sharp bow" (Lenfesty and Lenfesty, *Nautical Terms*, 183).

31 As noted earlier (see note in Chapter 2), hogsheads had different weight and volume standards depending on contents. In 1772, a hogshead of molasses from the sloop *Catherine* contained 107 gallons; a court appraised it at £8.0.6 (Reese, "Court of Vice-Admiralty," 310).

32 Like the hogshead, the barrel was an often imprecise unit of measurement. Late in the 19th century, an observer noted that "a 'barrel' of beef is 200 pounds; butter, 224 pounds; flour, 196 pounds; gunpowder, 100 pounds; soft soap, 256 pounds; beer, 36 gallons; tar, 26¼ gallons; whilst a barrel of herrings is 500 herrings" (Cousins, "Weights and Measures," 298).

33 A 42-gallon cask (Flett, "Arithmetic Exercise Book," 5).

34 From an 1805 book: "Jalap is the root of the convolvulus jalappa. It derives its name from Xalapa, a town of Mexico, in the environs of which is grows plentifully. [. . .] [The roots] are cut into slices in order to dry them. They

70 boxes Sugar, of the mark NP.

84 bags Coffee, of the mark A.O.

8 [bags] [Coffee], of the mark P.T.

300 quintals[35] Logwood [. . .]

ooooo

[*Niles' Weekly Register*, 28 December 1816, 289–290]

Case of the *Romp*.

From the *Richmond Enquirer*.

United States vs. Wm. Hutchings.[36]} An indictment for piracy.

This case was brought on before the circuit court for the United States for this district, on Thursday, the 12th December inst. As it had excited a considerable sensation in this part of the country, a brief account of it may be acceptable to your readers. It may also be of service to a portion of our countrymen, who have been concerned in this species of adventure, to know in what light it is viewed by the courts of the United States.

The prosecution was conducted by William Wirt,[37] esq., district attorney. The counsel for the prisoner, were Messrs. [Abel Parker] Upsh[u]r,[38] of Richmond, and Murdaugh,[39] of Williamsburg.[40]

The leading facts proved on the part of the prosecution, were the following: –

The schooner *Romp* armed with six eighteen[-]pound carronades[41] sailed from Baltimore early in April last ostensibly, on a commercial voyage for Buenos Ayres. She

---

then acquire a brown colour and a resinous appearance. Their taste is rather acrid and excites a nausea. [. . .] Jalap is an active and violent purgative, and is given only in small doses. There are seven thousand five hundred quintals [see below] of Jalap consumed annually in Europe, which cost £45,000 sterling" (Kauffman, *Dictionary of Merchandise*, 185.)

35 A quintal was the equivalent of a "long" or "imperial" hundredweight of 112 lbs (Nicholson, *Men and Measures*, 105–108).

36 The prosecution of Hutchings and Mitchell described in this article was part of a United States legal response to Spanish protests about American-based privateers operating against Spanish shipping. Two other former crewmen of the *Romp* also faced trial, but when juries acquitted the first two the district attorney "refused to prosecute the others" (Henderson, *Congress, Courts and Criminals*, 125–127).

37 In 1817, Wirt (1772–1834) would become attorney general of the United States.

38 Abel Parker Upshur, after being expelled from Princeton in 1807, "studied law in Richmond and was admitted to the bar. In addition to his legal practice, Upshur held several political offices including commonwealth attorney for Richmond, member of the Richmond city council, and member of the Virginia state legislature. In 1826 he was elected a judge of the General Court of Virginia. . . . " He later served as U.S. secretary of the navy and secretary of state (Leeman, *Long Road*, 149–150).

39 Possibly James W. Murdaugh, a Williamsburg attorney referenced in Robert Saunders to Henry Clay, 23 February 1822, Hopkins, *Papers of Henry Clay*, III:172–174.

40 As a federal circuit judge, Supreme Court Chief Justice John Marshall sat on the case (Rubin, *Ethics and Authority*, 95; Wheeler, *Reports*, II:543).

41 A carronade was "a short-barreled, long-bore, muzzle-loaded gun manufactured by the Carron Iron Founding and Shipping Company and introduced into the Royal Navy in 1779. These were mounted on slide, instead of

took with her an American register, and was in all respects documented as an American vessel. About 12 days after leaving the capes of Virginia, her crew were mustered, when they were informed of the destination of the vessel against the commerce of Spain. A salute was fired, the colors of Buenos Ayres[42] hoisted, the name of the vessel changed from the *Romp*, to the *Santafecino*,[43] and articles under the government of Buenos Ayres signed by the crew.

There was some disagreement between the witnesses as to the manner in which the crew received the intelligence of this change in the national character of the vessel, some affirming that the colors of Buenos Ayres were saluted with cheers, and others affirming they were saluted with murmurs. The *Santafecino* however proceeded on her cruise, and in the course of it, captured five Spanish vessels, out of which they took every thing valuable, sent two of them to Buenos Ayres for condemnation,[44] and gave up the rest to the prisoners. Near an hundred vessels, American, Portuguese, Dutch, English, and others, which were neutral between Buenos Ayres and Spain, were spoke during the cruise; all of which were treated politely. The general conduct of the *Santafecino*, appeared to be that of a regularly commissioned vessel, her prisoners being treated humanely, and their private property restored to them, and perfect respect always paid to the vessels of neutral nations. Some of the witnesses who were of the crew of the *Santafecino*, farther proved that the crew were dissatisfied with the colors under which they sailed, and that the revolt among them was in consequence of this dissatisfaction.

---

41   wheeled, carriages. Their large, low-velocity ball produced greater destruction of wooden hulls at short range than previous high-velocity guns that made a cleaner hole" (Lenfestey and Lenfestey, *Nautical Terms*, 80). Another source (Tucker, *Handbook*, 8) noted that "The lightness of the carronade enabled it to be employed where a heavier gun could not be supported, as on the poop or forecastle. Savings in weight made it especially popular for smaller vessels, and in fact the carronade became the principal armament of brigs. Generally speaking it replaced the small 4- to 12-pounder long guns on board naval vessels. . . . All carronades were short, only about seven calibres (one calibre being the diameter of the bore) in length. Royal Navy carronades weighed about 50–60 lbs of metal for every pound of shot. US Navy carronades were closely patterned after those of the Royal Navy but were heavier, 60–70 lbs of metal for every pound of shot. This is in contrast to as much as 150–200 lbs of metal for every pound of shot in long guns."

42   The flag of Buenos Aires from 1812 consisted of a set of blue-white-blue horizontal stripes; in 1818 a sunburst was added in the center. "That symbol recalled the brilliant 'Sun of May' that had shone through clouds in 1810, when the Spanish governor ceded control to the Patriots. Argentina has used the flag ever since" (Smith, *Flag Lore*, 11).

43   *Santafecino* (or *Santafesino*) means "one from Santa Fe." The vessel's title likely refers to Santa Fé de Bogotá, (now simply Bogotá, the capital of Colombia), which Simón Bolívar, late in 1814, established as the capital of New Granada, modern Colombia (Harvey, *Liberators*, 132). "The *Romp/Santafecino*'s actual owner appears to have been Bermuda-born Thomas Taylor, a former British seaman whose 'Buenos Ayres squadron' spent part of 1817 blockading the south Cuban coast. Taylor frequently stopped American craft but conducted himself well, paid for appropriated supplies, and was said to have disciplined one of his captains for an unspecified transgression. Prodded by Spanish officials, American authorities eventually arrested Taylor in New York and charged him with piracy. The episode the prosecutors used involved the *Fourth of July*, a brig 'built, armed, equipped and owned in Baltimore by sundry merchants of that place and com[modore] Taylor.' Taylor enlisted a crew in Baltimore and Norfolk in December 1816 and set sail for the Caribbean, where he ran up the Buenos Aires flag and changed the *Fourth of July*'s name to *Patriota* before embarking on a cruise against Spanish shipping. The jury acquitted Taylor after finding his Buenos Aires commission valid" (Gibbs, *Dead Men*, 43–44).

44   Condemnation refers to an admiralty (naval) court's declaration that a captured ship was taken legally, as in a time of war, and was therefore a "lawful prize" (Smyth, *Lexicon*, 207).

The only evidence offered on the part of the prisoner, was a paper, purporting to be a commission to the *Santafecino*, and a commission to the prisoner, as sailing master on board of her, from the government of Buenos Ayres. – The district attorney objected to their going to the jury, because

1st. There was no evidence of their being genuine papers, as there was no proof that Buenos Ayres was an independent government, nor that the seals attached to these commissions, was the seal of Buenos Ayres.

2nd. If the commissions were genuine papers, they obviously did not belong to this vessel, for they bore date in November 1815, and the name of the *Santafecino*, was not borne by this vessel, till the April following.

These points Mr. Wirt pressed with his usual eloquence and vigor.

Mr. Upshur for the prisoner, contended that the papers ought to go to the jury as evidence to be allowed whatever weight they should be found entitled to. He contended, that the question whether Buenos Ayres was independent or not, was for the executive to decide, and not the judiciary. That a late correspondence between Don [Luis de] Onis, the Spanish minister, and the American secretary of state [James Monroe], proved that the people of Buenos Ayres were in a state of revolution, exerting themselves to throw off the yoke of Spain. That there was an exact and perfect analogy between that contest, and the revolutionary contest of our country. That by the treaty of 1783, by numerous decisions of our courts, recognizing the validity of laws passed during the revolution and by express decisions on the point, the principle was settled that our existence as an independent nation commenced with our declaration of independence in 1776, and not with the definitive treaty of peace in 1783. That by parity of reasoning, the independence of Buenos Ayres commenced with their declaration of independence, and as that declaration was [a] matter of notoriety throughout the world, and was more particularly proved by the correspondence between Don Onis and Mr. Monroe, we were bound to consider them an independent people. That the seal of an independent people proved itself, and was not the subject of proof by any other sort of evidence. That it was in its nature the highest species of evidence, because no nation could delegate to subordinate agents a greater power or authority than it possessed itself. That this principle was fully recognized in the supreme court, and it was indeed an offspring of the comity of nations, which all civilized nations acknowledged. – That of course the seal attached to the commissions in the present instance proved itself – proved the genuineness and object of the commissions, and that it was incompetent to the prosecution to call for any other evidence as to these points. This argument, Mr. Upshur considered, applied to both points made by the district attorney, but even if it did not, that there was nothing in the second point, because these commissions were executed and dated in Buenos Ayres, in blank, and were left to be filled up by the agent of that government in this country. That this was a satisfactory mode of accounting for the difference of time between the date of the commissions and the adoption of the name of the *Santafecino*, and that there could be no reason to believe that the commissions had ever been used on board of any other vessel.

The court decided that the commissions should go to the jury, merely as papers found on board the vessel. But on the main question; the court was of opinion, that a nation became independent from its declaration of independence, only as respects its own government, and the various departments thereof. That before it could be considered independent by the judiciary of foreign nations, it was necessary that its independence should be recognized by the executive authority of those nations. That as our executive had never recognised the independence of Buenos Ayres, it was not competent to the court to pronounce its independence. That, therefore, the court could not acknowledge the right of that country to have a national seal, and of course that the seals attached to the commissions in question, proved nothing.

Upon this state of the testimony, the case was argued before the jury. The cause occupied the whole of Thursday and Friday. In the course of the argument, Mr. Upshur made the point, whether by the act of congress, under which the prisoner was indicted, a robbery on the high seas amounted to piracy in any case. The words of the act are, that "if any person shall upon the high seas, or in any haven, bay, or river, out of the jurisdiction of any particular state, commit murder, robbery, or any *other* crime or misdemeanor, which, if committed in the body of a country, would by the laws of the United States by punished with death, it shall amount to piracy.["] The argument of Mr. Upshur was, that it was necessary that robbery should first be made punishable with death by the laws of the United States, when committed on land, before it could amount to piracy, when committed on the sea, which was not now the case. That [J]udge [William] Johnson had so decided it in South-Carolina, although a contrary decision had been subsequently pronounced by [J]udge [Bushrod] Washington.[45] – That

---

45   This refers to two 1813 trials, both involving officers of the privateer *Revenge*. In April, the vessel's first lieutenant, John Jones, went on trial in the Philadelphia Circuit Court for piracy involving the robbing of a Portuguese brig. The second trial, which took place in June in the South Carolina Circuit Court, was of William Butler, the *Revenge*'s captain, indicted for piracy in robbing a Spanish ship. According to a modern legal text: "Although the Constitution and the Judiciary Act of 1789 gave admiralty jurisdiction to the federal courts neither spelled out what substantive maritime law these courts were to apply. . . . Both prosecutions were founded on section 8 of the Penal Act of 1790 which provided the death penalty for robbery on the high seas. In each the chief question made was whether the act of Congress reached these cases. And if not, was there no means of punishment for a crime which from time immemorial had been regarded as piracy? In Jones's trial before Justice Bushrod Washington and District Judge Peters, Jared Ingersoll, counsel for the defense, argued that robbery was not piracy by the laws of the United States since the offense of piratical robbery was not defined by statute. . . . [H]e emphasized that the criminal common law of England was not the law of the United States and therefore no resort could be had to that code for the punishment of such an offense. Absent Congressional definition of this crime, the indictment could not be supported within the language of the Act of 1790. His associate William Rawle added: 'There is no other source of authority, no other code of law, from which what is deficient or doubtful in the act of Congress can be supplied.' Alexander Dallas, the prosecuting attorney, had no difficulty with the matter. The act of Congress, he asserted, specified the offenses to which federal criminal jurisdiction reached; the language employed by Congress to define a crime must be explained in doubtful cases by the source from which

the conflict between these two learned judges, proved that the law was at least doubtful; that the jury in a capital case, were judges, as well of the law as the fact, and were bound to acquit, where either was doubtful.

The court being appealed to for the interpretation of the law, decided that it was not necessary that robbery should be punishable by death when committed on land, in order to amount to piracy if committed on the ocean – but as two judges, (for both of whom the court entertained the highest respect,) had pronounced opposite decisions upon it, the court could not undertake to say that it was not at least doubtful. Mr. Murdaugh contended that the acceptance of these commissions amounted to an act of expatriation.[46] Mr. Wirt, on the other hand, insisted, that it was not competent to any one to change his national character by his own act alone without the concurrent act of the government he adopted.– The court indicated an opinion against Mr. Murdaugh, founded ch[ie]fly upon the opinion already pronounced that the government of Buenos Ayres could not be recognized by the court as existing at all. The facts w[h]ere commented on by all the counsel at considerable length.

The jury retired at candle light on Friday evening and in about ten minutes returned a verdict of NOT GUILTY – which was received with applause by the surrounding crowd. The next day, John J. Mitchell was put on his trial, for the same offence, and was defended by the same counsel. He also was acquitted. But from the whole course of the trials, the court obviously thought that the conduct of the accused had been highly illegal, though no piratical design seemed to be attributed to them. – Before the discharge of Mitchell the court gave him an impressive admonition, which it is to be regretted, was not heard by those of our countrymen, who seem to have considered themselves perfect at liberty to endanger the peace of the country by these imprudent enterprizes.[47]

---

the language was derived. To fix the legal import of the word 'robbery' therefore, it was necessary and appropriate to resort to the common law. Justice Washington, charging the jury, made short shrift of the contention of defense counsel. It is true, he said, that unless the offense charged in the indictment be made punishable by some law of the United States, the prisoner must be acquitted. 'But nothing can be more clear than that robbing on the high seas, is declared to be felony and piracy by the 8th section of the act. . . . ' Doubtless mindful of the punishment and very likely because of conflicting testimony of witnesses regarding the identity of the accused, the jury acquitted Lieutenant Jones. . . . [I]n June, 1813, the second *Revenge* case came on for trial in Charleston before Justice William Johnson. Here, Captain Butler, the prisoner, went free when Johnson ordered the indictment against him dismissed. Johnson deliberately used the case to counter Washington's views in *Jones* and to impress on Congress the necessity of passing amendatory criminal legislation. More importantly, he seized the opportunity not only to affirm elaborately his denial in [a previous case] of a federal common law power over crimes but to extend that doctrine considerably into a new area, the criminal admiralty law" (Preyer, "Jurisdiction to Punish," 249–251).

46 I.e., losing one's citizenship by having joined a foreign military service.

47 Marshall "chided the men saying that they owed their clemency to the juries and not to the law 'for that the act which had been proven upon them was, unquestionably, piracy'" (Henderson, *Congress, Courts and Criminals*, 127).

Action at sea (as depicted by illustrator George Varian).

ooooo

[*Lloyd's List*, 16 May 1817, 1]

Insurgent Cruizers.

The English Brig *Jane*, Johns, arrived at Havannah from London on the 19th March, after being attacked by a Carthag[i]nian Privateer (Alme[i]da,[48] Commander) which made the Master pay 200 dollars for the shots fired at his Vessel. The Mate and one Seaman on board the Brig were severely wounded.

The *Catharine*, Eldred, arrived at Charleston 30th March, from [Le] Havre, was boarded 20th February in lat[itude] 36. 2. long[itude] 17. 10. by the *Patriota* Mexican Privateer, of 18 guns. She had made one Prize.

The English Ship *Cyrus*, M'Laren, from Jamaica, arrived at Charleston 4th ulto. The day after she sailed she was boarded from a Schooner by 18 armed men, who took pos-

---

48 Joseph Almeida was one of several Latin American privateer commanders who "attained a kind of celebrity in American newspapers. . . . [He] apparently served under commissions from both Cartagena and Buenos Aires at various times. On one occasion in 1818, when his well-armed vessel *Louisa*, its decks crammed with about one hundred men ready to make mischief on Spanish shipping, spoke with another ship at sea, Almeida dryly asked to be reported as 'bound round Cape Horn, on a sealing voyage.'" Almeida had bought the *Louisa* (itself captured by a Buenos Airean privateer), armed and equipped it at Ensenada, near Buenos Aires, and refitted it in Baltimore. Almeida later lost the *Louisa* to mutineers (Gibbs, *Dead Men*, 37, 162n7). Almeida was a Baltimore resident (*Brig Wilson v. United States*, in Marshall, *Papers*, IX:31).

session of the Ship, and compelled the crew to assist them in taking from her 2 6-pounders, the Privateer having thrown her own guns overboard whilst chased by a British man of war. She was a Baltimore-built schooner, commanded by a Frenchman, her crew 95 men, principally blacks. [. . .]

ooooo

[Niles' *Weekly Register*, 26 July 1817, 346–347]

"SPANISH" AMERICA [. . .]

A brig belonging to the royal fleet at Havana, formerly the *Chasseur* of Baltimore, returned into port on the 5th inst. in a very crippled state, and with the loss of 60 men in killed and wounded in an engagement with a Carthag[i]nian privateer. This vessel was probably the *Hotspur*,[49] [C]apt. Rapp, since spoken, which had 24 men killed and wounded.

A vessel has arrived at New-York that was boarded by the Carthag[i]nian privateer, commanded by Almeida, who put on board of her two Spanish state prisoners taken out of a vessel bound for Cadiz, which he had captured.

The schooner *Hannah*, of Baltimore bound to La Guayra [Venezuela], with her cargo, was captured within a day's sail of her port by a Spanish privateer, carried to Puerto Cabello [Venezuela], and condemned as [a] good prize. Mr. Wilson, the consignee at the former, proceeded to the latter place, and made an investigation into the matter, and unfolded a scene of great villainy on the part of the captors to make a robbery complete – for this he was deprived of his papers, and thrown into prison by "the worse than savages" where he nearly died of disease – but was recovering, and had strong hopes of bringing "these wretches to condign punishment." [. . .]

FLORIDA

The capture of Amelia Island,[50] by [G]en. M'Gregor,[51] is certain. He landed his men on the 30th of June, in the rear of Fernandina, marched them through the marsh, breast-

---

49 "Hotspur" was the nickname of medieval English warrior Henry Percy, the antagonist of William Shakespeare's *Henry IV, Part I*. Faye ("Privateersmen of the Gulf," 1071–1072) identified the *Hotspur* as a fore-topsail schooner that carried a long brass 18-pounder and three long 9-pounder cannon. It was commanded by Henry B. Rapp, a former U.S. Navy lieutenant who resigned his commission in late 1816 at New Orleans; Rapp may have sailed with Mexican papers from Aury, then based on Galveston Island.
50 Then a Spanish-held island on Florida's Atlantic coast, near the Georgia border.
51 The eccentric "Sir" Gregor MacGregor, "a Scottish adventurer replete with kilt and bagpipes" served under Simón Bolívar and married the latter's niece. A modern historian describes him as "an extraordinary man, only half-sane; besides making a sizeable profit, like the other recruiters, by selling commission in what was at that stage a phantom army, he also arranged a series of expeditions to America on his own account . . . in the course of which he would dump his recruits and sail away with any available booty. Of the 2,200 in total who went with him, including a hundred women and forty children, only two ever returned – apart from MacGregor himself" (Harvey, *Liberators*, 142–3, 153–4).

deep, and entered the town by capitulation, without firing a gun. There were only about 70 Spanish soldiers on Amelia. He was rapidly recruiting his little army, and intended immediately to march for St. Augustine, a strong place, and said to be defended by 500 men, where he will probably have warm work. He has with him a ship of 22 guns, and some smaller vessels. [. . .]

Two schooners were captured at Amelia by McGregor, who has already established a court of admiralty there, with a post office, &c. John D. Heath, formerly a member of the bar, at Charleston, is the judge.[52] A newspaper, in the English language, is intended to be printed. One privateer had received a commission at Amelia and sailed on a cruise.

Forty African slaves taken at Amelia, were condemned as prize and sold at auction. Later accounts say that every thing was tranquil at Amelia. Gen. McGregor was sending off troops to St. John's[53] for St. Augustine,[54] which was closely blockaded by a patriot frigate and a sloop of war – they were thought a match for any naval force that Spain has in the western hemisphere.[55]

ᴏᴏᴏᴏᴏ

[*Niles' Weekly Register*, 1 August 1818, 392]

SOUTH AMERICA

[Venezuelan Admiral Louis] Brion[56] has notified the governor of St. Thomas' that Cumana, Laguira [La Guayra], and all the other ports of the Main, in possession of the royalists, are in a state of blockade.

---

52 "This court ... became significant to MacGregor's operation because it provided a means of raising money. With Heath as admiralty judge, the court charged a fee, 16.5 percent against the gross value of the prizes, as a source of revenue to operate the government of Amelia Island. The judiciary also levied regular court costs." Heath later "resigned in a dispute over a French vessel, supposedly carrying Spanish cargo" (Owsley and Smith, *Filibusters*, 128, 131).

53 "About 1590 the Spanish mission San Juan del Puerto, 'St. John of the harbor,' was established and ultimately gave its name, in shortened form, to the river. For a time in the mid-1700s, both San Mateo and San Juan were shown on some Florida maps as two names for the one river. It was during the 20-year period of British ownership of Florida, 1763 to 1783, that San Juan finally became St. John's and since has remained save for the dropping of the apostrophe" (Morris, *Florida Place Names*, 212).

54 "St. Augustine . . . is situated on the eastern coast of Florida. The town is built on a small peninsula between the St. Sebastian river and the harbor. . . . England obtained the province of Florida by treaty in 1763, and when the red-coats came to St. Augustine, the Spanish inhabitants nearly all left. Many of them or their descendants, however, returned when the English had decided to get rid of the troublesome colony, and recession to Spain occurred in 1783, in exchange for the Bahama islands" (King, *Great South*, 390–392).

55 Amelia Island subsequently became a base for privateers under Aury's command. It remained so until December 1817, when the USS *John Adams* "appeared off Amelia Island and demanded its surrender. It was evacuated without resistance, but under protest by Commodore Aury." The latter subsequently "established himself at Old Providence, a small island in the Caribbean Sea" (Allen, *Our Navy*, 14, 15).

56 Brion was a Curaçao merchant who joined Simon Bolívar's cause late in 1815, offering him "a number of ships at his disposal, including a 24-gun corvette and a small frigate." Brion reportedly ordered his officers to execute prisoners, a reflection of Bolívar's "War to the Death" policy (announced in 1813) against Spaniards who fought against the Latin American revolutionaries (Harvey, *Liberators*, 141, 155).

A Spanish brig, the *Manuel*, of 12 guns and 35 men, with a valuable cargo, lately blew up in a battle she had with a patriot privateer, near Puerto Cabell[o] – eight of her crew were saved.

A small vessel, under very suspicious circumstances, was lately scuttled and sunk, in Jekyl Sound,[57] with a probable view of raising her hereafter. It seems that she was a privateer, or rather a pirate, under commission from McGregor, which had robbed a Spanish ship from Spain for Cuba, with 200 passengers on board, of every thing valuable, even stripping the women and children. – After this she was met by the Buenos Ayrean brig *San Martin*, [C]apt. Stafford, who seized upon and treated her as a pirate, putting a prize crew on board, &c. But the pirates left on board rose upon the prize crew, secured them and bore away for the United States – arrived off Jekyl, landed and concealed what property remained, scuttled the vessel, and having armed themselves, left her. – Our naval officers on the southern coast are attending to the affair in searching for the villains, and intend to raise the vessel.

We regret to observe, because it injures the patriot cause, that the West India seas appear to be filled with pirates under the independent flag, who rob ships of all nations.

ooooo

[*Niles' Weekly Register*, 29 August 1818, 9]

Savannah, Aug. 17

"Last evening our city was all in arms. The Patriot privateer *Gen. St. Martin*, came up to town yesterday, her crew having mutinied in the West Indies, had put her commander, Captain Stafford, and most of his officers, ashore at Port-au-Prince [Haiti], threatening at the same time to murder the rest of the petty officers. When she came within the Bar, it appears that the crew deputed five of their number to come up to a mercantile house in this city, who had claims upon the brig, and threaten unless they received $30,000, to scuttle her below; they however compromised for $18,000, for which they took a note, to be discounted on Tuesday, the first discount day. This satisfied them, and induced them to bring the privateer up opposite the town, but being a turbulent set, they would not permit the civil authority to board them, and appeared determined to resist. This induced the Mayor, ([James Moore] Wayne)[58] to call upon the volunteer companies; two pieces of artillery were brought to bear upon the brig, and were all ready for a fight, when they thought proper to submit. They were brought on shore and confined in the guard-house, and now all is quiet."

---

57 Jekyll Island, off the Georgia coast.
58 James Moore Wayne (1790–1867) began his legal career in 1810 and served in the War of 1812; he was Savannah's mayor from 1817–1819. He held a variety of legislative and judicial positions during his lifetime, and in 1835 became an associate justice of the Supreme Court. For a biography, see Alexander Lawrence, *James Moore Wayne, Southern Unionist* (Chapel Hill: University of North Carolina, 1943).

ooooo

[*Newport Mercury*, 26 September 1818, 3]

Ship News.

[...] Arrived at Bristol [Rhode Island] on Monday last. Schooner *Columbia*, Gilbert, 31 days from Trinidad, (Cuba) – Capt. G[ilbert] informs, that on his passage he was robbed by a piratical sch[oone]r called the *Pelican*, mounting 5 guns, with 45 men, mostly negroes. – They took from the schooner what cargo there was on board, besides 1700 dollars, and also robbed Mr. Williams, a passenger, of 700 dollars. – The sch[oone]r *Alonzo*, Capt. Smith, of New-York, was also robbed by the same privateer, and Capt. Smith was very illy treated. – The crew of the privateer informed Capt. G[ilbert] that they had killed their former captain 20 days previous. [...]

ooooo

[*Niles' Weekly Register*, 31 October, 1818, 156]

SOUTH AMERICA.

[...] A paper, printed at Easton, in the state of Maryland, (on what authority we know not) gives the names of eleven vessels, carrying 153 guns, and 1535 men, which, it says, were fitted out and owned by certain citizens of Baltimore, to cruise against the Spaniards, under the patriot flag. Several of the vessels named, and perhaps nearly the whole of them, have been at Buenos Ayres, and there received regular commissions.[...]

A vessel, called the *Columbia*, with five guns mounted and fourteen in her hold, and sixteen men, has been taken possession of by the revenue cutter *Monroe*,[59] and sent into Norfolk,[60] for want of papers. It appears that she was one of Brion's squadron, but abandoned him, as it stated by her commander, because the officers and crew could not get any pay.

ooooo

[*Niles' Weekly Register*, 21 August 1819, 430]

WEST INDIES

[...] Several pirates are reported to be captured by the British and Dutch and a French squadron is looking out for them. Some of them have been executed at Nassau. At which place M[a]cGregor has been indicted as one.

---

59 The *Monroe* was built in Norfolk in 1816, and cruised regularly in the Chesapeake Bay with the revenue cutters *Active* and *Vigilant* (King, *Coast Guard*, 76).

60 Port at Hampton Roads near the Chesapeake Bay, home to what was then the Gosport (later Norfolk Naval) Shipyard.

A certain person called John Louis Dupuis was recently executed at Jamaica, for piracy and murder on the high seas. He was an officer on board a vessel called a patriot privateer, and in his cruise boarded an English vessel, in which a man and his wife were passengers. The woman was violated by the savages in the presence of her husband, after which both of them were taken on board the privateer. The man was then beaten and abused in a dreadful manner – but finally the rascals becoming *merciful* shot him and threw him overboard. After which, Dupuis seized upon the woman as his property, and had compulsory intercourse with her!

In the confession of Dupuis we see a specimen of the manner in which the war in Venezuela is carried on. He was with the patriots when they captured La Guiria – and stated that "every woman was violated, every house plundered, and nearly every human being murdered."

The "patriot flag" is now so much abused by the greatest villains that ever blackened the human character, that it is time for decent men sailing under it to come to a pause, and resolve to abandon it – unless means are taken to prevent a recurrence of such terrible outrages.

ooooo

[*Niles' Weekly Register*, 11 September 1819, 31]

New Orleans, Aug. 4. Extract of a letter – We have received a report in the city, from Barrataria, that the renegado Mitchell[61] has collected together upwards of 150 desperadoes, and has fortified himself an island with several pieces of cannon, and that he has declared they will all perish within their [e]ntrenchments, before they will surrender to any force. There are now about 100 men out in search of the late pirates, four of whom have been taken and are now in custody – *but it will require good friends to get hung.* A few days ago, one of them, with a pistol in each hand, marched boldly through the city guard of eight men, with fixed bayonets, and they boldly stood still and let him go off clear – all true disciples of Hudibras.[62] It is thought here, that it will require five hundred men to destroy this nest of pirates. [. . .]

Balt[imore]. Pat[riot].

ooooo

---

61 William Mitchell was another questionable captain who operated under Cartagenian privateering commissions. "Early in 1816 the English-born Mitchell successfully attacked the Spanish island of San Andrés, executing its governor and garrison of six soldiers. Like many of his profession, he dabbled in running slaves, fourteen being aboard Mitchell's schooner, *Cometa*, when the USS *Boxer* captured it in 1816. But a New Orleans court acquitted Mitchell that June, and he made trouble near New Orleans and British Honduras for the next few years, at one time operating a fleet of open boats" (Gibbs, *Dead Men*, 44). According to Davis (*Pirates Laffite*, 451), Mitchell "supposedly died May 1, 1821, on Great Corn Island, off Nicaragua."

62 *Hudibras* was a satirical epic poem by Samuel Butler, published between 1663–78; the title character was a knight errant whose deeds are described in exaggerated (and mocking) terms.

[Springfield Massachusetts *Hampden Patriot*, 21 October 1819, 2]

A Pirate Taken

A New Orleans paper of the 15th ult. furnishes the following information:–
"The U[nited] States Revenue Cutter *Louisiana*, Captain J. Loomis, and the *Alabama*,
also a Revenue Cutter,[63] arrived at the Bay of St. John[64] yesterday having in company
the Spanish sch[oone]r *Philomela*, which they re-captured from a pirate on the 29th
ult. off the Dry Tortugas.[65] The pirate is also brought in. On that day they fell in with
an American sch[oone]r bound from this port, on board of which the pirate had
placed a number of Spanish gentlemen and ladies, who had been passengers in the
Philomela. From their information Capt. Loomis supposed that the pirate could not be
very distant, and determined to look out for her. Eight hours afterwards, accordingly,
he espied two sail, one of which stood for him, and on being required by the
capt[ain] of the *Alabama* to send her boat on board, fired a volley of small arms; she
was soon silenced, however and taken possession of. – She proved to be a
sch[oone]r called the *Brave*, fitted out at New-Orleans, carrying two guns and twenty-
four men, and commanded by a man who calls himself Le Fage.[66] The prize, the
Philomela, was about a mile astern during the action, but was soon overhauled and
re-captured. In the slight contest, which prece[e]ded the capture of the *Brave*, the *Alabama* had four men wounded, two of them including the first lieutenant dangerously;
the pirate lost six men killed. The remainder of her crew, to the number of eighteen,
were safely lodged in prison last evening. – *The Brave* had on board a number of
Spanish prisoners, who are thus happily relieved from a captivity, which most probably would have terminated, if they had not fallen in with the revenue cutter, by their
being compelled to walk the plank.[67] The pirate had a printed commission, the date
of which was blank, signed Humbert,[68] *governor of Texas!*"

---

63 "Built in New York for $4,500 each in 1819, they [*Louisiana* and *Alabama*] were an extreme type of Baltimore
    clipper. . . . The *Louisiana* and the *Alabama* were 51-tonners, measuring 56.8' on deck, with a 17'4" beam and 6'
    depth of hold. Rigged as fore-topsail schooners, they had fine lines, square sterns, raking [slanted] masts, and light
    rails in place of heavy bulwarks. . . . [They] were armed with 12- or 18-pound carronades or with long nines,
    twelves, or eighteens. They were designed to carry a pivot gun amidships, which was supposed to have been the
    heaviest gun carried, but the *Louisiana* did not have a pivot gun when she first went to sea, a shortcoming that
    caused her captain, Harris Loomis, a great deal of anxiety" (King, *Coast Guard*, 66–67). A pivot gun was a can-
    non "[m]ounted on a frame carriage which can be turned radially, so as to point the piece in any direction"
    (Smyth, *Lexicon*, 531).
64 Bayou St. John, in the city of New Orleans.
65 "Discovered by Ponce de León in 1513 and named for the many turtles found there, the Dry Tortugas are located
    seventy miles west of Key West in the Gulf of Mexico. The low-lying islands, devoid of any source of fresh water,
    lie in the midst of a large area of shoals and treacherous coral reefs" (Viele, *Florida Keys*, 33).
66 *Le Brave*, owned by Jean Laffite and captained by Jean Desfarges (Davis, *Pirates Laffite*, 398, 404–7).
67 Walking the plank seems to have been a rare practice. A 1788 reference to it places it in the context of mutiny:
    "WALKING THE PLANK. A mode of destroying devoted persons or officers in a mutiny on ship-board, by
    blindfolding them, and obliging them to walk on a plank laid over the ship's side; by this means, as the mutineers
    suppose, avoiding the penalty of murder" (Grose, *Vulgar Tongue*, n.p.) An 1822 episode is detailed in a later chap-
    ter in this book. Cordingly (*Under the Black Flag*, 130–131) describes an 1829 incident involving a Dutch brig
    taken off Cuba.
68 French expatriate Jean Amable Humbert, a confederate of the Laffites who had served at the Battle of New

A passenger in the *Emma*, arrived at New-York from New-Orleans, who conversed with Capt. Loomis, states, that at the time the above pirate was captured, she had not been in possession of her Spanish prize long enough to commit the outrages upon the passengers which were threatened, but had stripped them of nearly all their clothes. The pirate approached with sweeps[69] within pistol shot of the cutter before she fired – Only three men in the cutter were wounded, one of them, it was feared dangerously. The pirates were all lodged in prison at New-Orleans. The vessel had been regularly cleared out at New-Orleans, for Pensacola.

N.Y. pa[pers . . .]

ooooo

[*Niles' Weekly Register*, 23 October 1819, 128]

SOUTH AMERICA

[. . .] There was a report at Havana that the Spanish government brig *Fernando* had captured an "insurgent" vessel called the *"Pagaro,"* after a combat of 4 hours – and that all the prisoners were *put to the knife!* The victor had 25 killed and 50 wounded. About 450 prisoners captured in "insurgent" vessels, are said to be at Porto Rico.[70]

CHRONICLE

[. . .] *The pirates*, noticed in our last as having been brought to New Orleans by the U.S. revenue cutter *Alabama*, [C]apt. Loomis, were committed to prison. A stir was made to liberate them, as *patriots*, by writ of *habeus corpus*,[71] but it does not appear that they were enlarged at our latest dates.[72] Their vessel, it seems, belonged to John Laf[fit]e, and was commissioned at Galvezton;[73] and [G]en. Long,[74] commander of the adventurers in Texas, is said to have approved of her equipment. They deny the enormities imputed to them, and say that they did not fire upon the cutter defensively, and that none of their crew were killed – but this differs from the account on which we rely; and if what is said of them is true, we hope that none of them will escape.

---

68 Orleans, commissioned privateers under Mexican colors (Allen, *Our Navy*, 14; Vogel, "Jean Laffite, the Baratarians, and the Battle of New Orleans," 267, 269, 270; and Davis, *Pirates Laffite, passim*).
69 Oars.
70 The Caribbean island of Puerto Rico was then a Spanish possession.
71 "From [the Latin for] *you have the body*, the *writ of habeas corpus* or *habeas corpus* is a writ to bring a person being confined before the court for an inquiry into the legality of the person's confinement and the extraordinary writ that can be used to determine the legality of any confinement, custody, or detention, civil or criminal" (Nolfi, *Legal Terminology Explained*, 349–350).
72 "latest dates" – i.e., the most recent newspapers received.
73 Laffite had moved his operations to Galveston Island, on Texas' coast with the Gulf of Mexico, after the U.S. Navy's 1814 raid on Barataria.
74 Dr. James Long, a Natchez, Mississippi businessman who led filibustering expeditions into Texas from New Orleans in 1819 and 1820. Spanish troops captured him late in 1821; he died in captivity, shot by a guard, the following year (Chipman and Joseph, *Spanish Texas*, 254; and Davis, *Pirates Laffite, passim*).

ooooo

[*Niles' Weekly Register*, 8 January 1820, 308–309]

Barataria. We learn that Laf[fit]e has lately received a commission from [G]en. Long[75] – that he (Laf[fit]e) has four or five small vessels, generally cruizing, and about 2 or 300 men. Two open boats, bearing commissions of [G]en. Humbert from Galvezton, having robbed a planter on the Marmento river,[76] of negroes, money, &c. were captured in the Sabine[77] by the boats of the U.S. schooner *Lynx*[78] – 6 of the men are now in custody awaiting their trial – one was hung by Laf[fit]e.[79] The *Lynx* also captured a small Galvezton privateer and her prize, that had been for a length of time smuggling in the Marmento.

ooooo

[*Niles' Weekly Register*, 5 February 1820, 400]

Sixteen pirates condemned. – A letter from New Orleans, dated 1st Jan. states that on the 30th of December, [J]udge [Dominick A.] Hall,[80] of the U.S. district court, pronounced sentence of death on the 16 pirates taken at Barrataria[81] some time since by [C]aptain Loomis. To prevent any attempt to rescue them from the hands of justice, the military turned out to guard them. They are to be hanged on the 2[4]th of next May, unless pardoned by the president. After the judge had finished pronouncing sentence upon the hardened wretches, several of them cried out, in open court, "murder, by G-d;" and in no respect did they appear to be in the least affected. The letter adds, there is a patrol[e] kept up by the citizens every night to prevent any conspiracy, which it is feared, may be formed, to effect their escape.

---

75 Late in 1819 Long named Jean Laffite governor of Galveston, and authorized him to grant letters of marque against Spain; the Laffites were in fact planning to betray Long to the Spanish (Davis, *Pirates Laffite*, 399–401, 420).

76 The Mermentau River, in Louisiana.

77 The Sabine River flows along the Texas-Louisiana border and into east Texas.

78 USS *Lynx* was a 150-ton, 80-foot long "6-gun Baltmore Clipper rigged schooner," launched in 1814, but which did not see service before the War of 1812 ended. Dispatched to deal with the Barbary Pirates, that conflict was also resolved by the time it arrived. It performed survey duty in 1817, then operated against Gulf and West Indian pirates. It disappeared without trace after leaving St. Mary's, Georgia, in January 1820 bound for Jamaica (Mooney, *Fighting Ships*, IV:172–173).

79 Following an improvised trial, on 6 Nov., 1819, Laffite hanged one George Brown for a robbery in New Orleans which he feared would be used as a pretext for a U.S. Navy strike at his Galveston base (Davis, *Pirates Laffite*, 413–415).

80 In 1814, Hall had helped arrange an amnesty for Baratarians willing to assist Maj. Gen. Andrew Jackson in defense of New Orleans. But in early 1815, Jackson himself had Hall arrested and jailed for six days for ordering the release of a Louisiana legislator Jackson had imprisoned (Vogel, "Jean Laffite, the Baratarians, and the Battle of New Orleans," 264; and Deutsch, "U.S. vs. Andrew Jackson," 967–968).

81 The original news stories refer to the pirates being captured off Dry Tortugas rather than at Barataria.

ooooo

[*Niles' Weekly Register*, 27 May 1820, 240]

Pirates. Three persons are condemned to be executed at Boston on the 15th of June, as pirates and felons. Four were hung for similar offences at Charleston, on the 12th instant, and the additional crime of murder. Six persons have been executed at Malta,[82] for piracies in the Mediterranean. Eighteen were to be hung at New-Orleans on the 2[4]th instant, unless reprieved. Other executions may be looked for at other places. One of those hung at Charleston, in his address to the people, denied that he ever had been guilty of the crime of murder; but admitted that he had, with others, been deluded into a service which eventuated in piracy, for which he was about to pay the forfeit of his life; *while thousands who projected the scheme, were now walking at large in the country with impunity.*

ooooo

[*Niles' Weekly Register*, 5 June 1820, 256]

New-Orleans. General [Daniel] Bissel[83] has ordered detachments of the regular army from St. John's[84] and Baton Rouge[85] to New-Orleans to resist an attempt that has been threatened to rescue the pirates now confined there under sentence of death.

ooooo

[*Niles' Weekly Register*, 17 June 1820, 288]

New-Orleans. We have accounts from this city to the 24th ult.[86] Numerous attempts to fire the town had been detected. The public mind was exceedingly agitated, on ac-

---

82 Malta (consisting of the Mediterranean island of that name, coupled with the smaller adjacent island Goza) was then a British possession.

83 Daniel Bissell (1768?–1833) served in the American Revolution as courier and fifer. He rose through the ranks and by the War of 1812 had received a brigadier general's commission. After the war he served at Baton Rouge and New Orleans (Christensen, *Missouri Biography*, 76).

84 St. John the Baptist parish ("parish" being an administrative term in Louisiana, akin to counties in the rest of the United States) is on the Mississippi River about 30 miles from New Orleans; it was the scene of a major slave insurrection in 1811. See Lubin F. Laurent, "History of St. John the Baptist Parish." *Louisiana Historical Quarterly* 7 (1924), 316–331.

85 Baton Rouge was "some seventy-five miles upriver from New Orleans . . ." (Davis, *Pirates Laffite*, 13).

86 That was the date set for the execution for piracy of Jean Desfarges and Robert Johnson, respectively captain and lieutenant of *The Brave*. According to a modern account, "at noon the marshal brought the two condemned to the riverfront. A rumor held that a family had been adducted out in the bayous to be ransomed for the lives of the condemned, but the ceremony went ahead. The doomed men stepped aboard a navy barge, and a substantial crowd, including the biggest military assembly since the war and perhaps Pierre Laffite, looked on as a distraught Desfarges first asked a marshal for a pistol to shoot himself. Then, though bound, he jumped overboard, perhaps hoping to drown rather than hang. Sailors fished him out of the water and he and Johnson met their ends without further incident. In time most of the others would be hanged as well" (Davis, *Pirates Laffite*, 434).

count of the threats made to release the pirates, at every hazard. There had been one alarming fire near the jail, and another at the arsenal, both of which did much damage. The latter endangered a great part of the city and shipping. One hundred barrels of powder were in the magazine, which was fire-proof; but six hundred muskets in the arsenal, strangely left loaded with ball cartridges, were destroyed. Happily they were stacked, so that they were discharged in the air. Twenty buildings were consumed on this occasion.

∞∞∞

[*Boston Columbian Centinel*, 17 June 1820, 2]

Execution. On Thursday last, sentence of death was executed in this town, on William Holmes, Edward Rosewaine, and Thomas Warrington, alias Thomas Warren Fawcett, for the crimes of piracy and murder committed on board a prize schooner under one of the South American flags, some time since.

The criminals left the jail about 10 o'clock in an open wagon, accompanied by the Rev. Mr. Lahasey. They were preceded by a Deputy-Marshal, and two Deputy-Sheriffs, on horseback, Marshal Prince, in a carriage, accompanied by Sheriff Austin, of Middlesex [County], and a carriage with Surgeon Austin, of the U.S. Navy; and followed by a car[t] in which were their coffins; and the procession was closed by a Deputy-Marshal, on horseback. The prisoners were clad in new sailors' dress, and appeared very suitably impressed with their situation. They were all young men, one born in the U.S., one in England, and the other in Scotland. On arriving at the place of execution, the Marshal read their Death Warrant, and then addressed the spectators in his usual impressive and compassionate manner, and the execution took place about twenty minutes before twelve. Ho[l]mes and Rosewaine appeared to die easy; but Warrington, who was an extremely stout and robust man, struggled some time, and had a hard death.

The spectators were extremely numerous, and orderly. As the procession was passing our streets, the bell of the Old South [Church] tolled a solemn knell. The bodies have been delivered to the surgeons for dissection, agreeably to the sentence.[87]

∞∞∞

[*Niles' Weekly Register*, 24 June 1820, 298–299]

Piracies. Three persons have just suffered death at Boston for piracy and murder, committed in consequence of their having joined the "patriot" service, and several

---

87 In America murderers had been dissected as early as 1733, though the dissections were not part of the sentence, but a post-execution arrangement. Massachusetts in 1784 passed the first law allowing judges to specify dissection as part of a sentence (Banner, *Death Penalty*, 77–78; and Sappol, *Traffic of Dead Bodies*, 100–101).

others are just taken up at Norfolk, Georgetown, Charleston, &c. – in all twenty or thirty men, charged with similar offences from similar causes! The case appears to be as follows:

The officers of the brig *General Rondeau*,[88] under the flag of Buenos Ayres, were lat[el]y risen upon by the crew, who murdered some of them and sent the rest afloat in a boat, about twelve miles distant from the island of Grenada. New officers were then appointed, who shaped the brig's course to the United States. They arrived off the coast of North Carolina – when, having plundered the brig, they scuttled her and made their way to different parts of the neighboring country, laden with their ill-gotten wealth. Various suspicious circumstances caused their arrest, to end their lives on the gallows. It appears that not many of the crew of the *Gen. Rondeau* were Americans – most were British subjects. When is this miserable business – this wretched privateering-piracy, which so much corrupts the morals of sea-faring men and leads them into every excess, terminating so often in murder and punishment by the executioner – to end? The "patriot" service, as of late fitted for in some ports of the United States, is a disgrace to the country, but unhappily it has been so managed in general as to elude our laws intended for its suppression. The *Gen. Rondeau*, however, it should be observed, was last fitted at Buenos Ayres.

Since writing the preceding, we have the following in a Norfolk paper of the 19th inst. "The Buenos Ayrean armed brig *Wilson*, [C]apt. Wilson, cleared at Norfolk on Saturday last for Margaretta [Margarita].[89] On Wednesday night last, while she was lying at anchor in the bite[90] of Craney Island,[91] 27 of her men got ashore by some means or other, and made their escape; the remainder, consisting of about a half dozen, together with the landlord who shipped them, were on Friday last arrested by the marshal of the U.S. for this district, under a warrant from Judge [St. George] Tucker,[92] and are now confined here in prison.["]

ooooo

---

88 Named for Argentine soldier-statesman José Casimiro Rondeau Pereyra (1773–1844), this was a 202-ton Spanish *bergantin* (Carranza, *Campañas navales*, II:199).

89 Margarita: a mountainous island off Venezuela's north coast. "By 1816 . . . it was in chaos, and was a way station for anyone considering a career in Caribbean privateering and its close cousin, piracy" (Gibbs, *Dead Men*, 40). A contemporary work described it as "about 30 leagues in circumference. . . . The possession of Margarita was an object of great consequence to Spain, as it is separated from the continent by a strait only 8 leagues wide, and to windward of all the best ports of Caracas, and forms the channel through which all vessels coming from Europe or windward, to Cumana, Barcelona, and La Guayra, must pass, though it is not navigable in its whole breadth . . . " Bell, *A System of Geography*, 322.

90 Bight; a curve in the shoreline.

91 Island in Hampton Roads, Virginia, near the mouth of the Elizabeth River.

92 Bermuda-born Tucker (1752–1827) began to practice law in Williamsburg, Virginia, in 1775. In 1790, he became a professor of law at the College of William and Mary, which he had attended. He is best remembered for a 1796 proposal for the abolition of slavery, and for producing in 1803 an annotated edition of Sir William Blackstone's *Commentaries on the Laws of England, 1723–1780* for an American audience (Bauer, *Commentaries on the Constitution*, 170–182).

[*Newport Mercury*, 1 July 1820, 3]

The Privateer Gen. Rondeau.

We have collected the following particulars of this so much talked[-]of vessel, from the accounts related by the seamen who have arrived in the United States from her. These accounts say, that the *General Rondeau* was originally a prize brig, and mounted 18 guns; that having arrived at Buenos Ayres she was commissioned under that government; that her commander was Captain David M. Miles, of Baltimore; her Lieutenants Mallard, an American; Sweeney, an Irishman, and Latterman, an American; that persons bearing the names of Smith, Riley, Davis and Wright, held subordinate situations on board; and that her crew consisted of 160 men, white, black and yellow; of which about 30 were Americans, and the others of all nations and tongues. That after leaving Buenos Ayres, (in Dec. 1819) they cruized in the Atlantic and the Mediterranean seas, and made many captures, from which they took about $10,000 in cash, and put the prisoners on board a vessel bound to Teneriffe; – That on their passage from the Mediterranean to Margaretta [Margarita], after having landed, and had a row at Grenada,[93] the crew mutinied, (complaining that Miles had ill[-]used them, and had left George Perkins, one of their messmates, ashore drunk,) killed Lt. Sweeney, and threw him overboard; then put the Captain, the officers, and some of the marines (11 persons in all) into a boat, and ordered them to make for the land (Grenada) then about twenty miles off; – That the crew then gave the command of the brig to Robinson, the gunner; but who appeared to have shared his authority[94] with Tom Brush, David Leyall, and Charles Nelson; – That they divided the Spanish dollars &c among themselves (refusing to give the marines any) and then directed their course to the U.S. to have an opportunity to spend it. That this money amounted to 214 dollars, a share; which the sharers generally quilted into belts, which they wore under their jackets: – That when they approached the American coast, they put part of their crew on board a English vessel – part on board a New-York vessel, sixteen on board Capt. Gibb's schooner: the rest then landed in parties, in Virginia and the Carolinas, until the crew was reduced to 14, when those scuttled the brig and went ashore in the boat with nothing but their clothes; the able-bodied of the crew, having, as they say, previously robbed them of their share of the money: – That soon after they had landed, most of the crew had been apprehended, and now stood committed for trial, as mutineers and murderers.

Boston Centinel.

---

93   Grenada is a Caribbean island off Venezuela's northeast coast; it had been a British possession since 1763.

94   Shared authority was historically common among Caribbean pirates. Captains generally earned a slightly larger share of loot, and some emerged as larger-than-life figures with their era's chroniclers, but the title itself conveyed few privileges. The original Caribbean *boucaniers* allowed the captain "no better fare than the meanest on board," according to Exquemelin (*Buccaneers*, 70–71). "If they notice he has better food, the men bring the dish from their own mess and exchange it for the captain's." Johnson, in the *General History* (Schonhorn, ed., 138–39, 194–95, 213–14), discussed how pirate crews elected a man captain solely to command them in battle, when he would be strictly obeyed. At other times, the quartermaster regulated all non-combat activities.

A pirate destroying a merchant ship (19th century, artist unknown).

ooooo

[*Niles' Weekly Register*, 20 October 1821, 118–119]

PIRACY. The present time seems to be entitled to the appellation of the *age of piracy* – caused chiefly by the spewings out of the late wars, and especially so of the contests between Spain and her late "American colonies." The coasting trade of the United States is almost daily insulted – the voyage to and from New Orleans cannot be made in safety: and indeed, we are deficient in present means to protect it and bring the marauders to justice; for we have few vessels fitted for the purpose, notwithstanding the weight of our naval establishment. We want more strong, but "flying" schooners, to scour the coasts, and cause the property and persons of our citizens to be respected. The instances that reach us are of the most provoking description, and we can hardly open a newspaper without seeing "piracy" or "more piracy" staring us in the face. In the south seas,[95] too, it appears by a circular of [C]ap-

---

95   The South Pacific Ocean.

tain [Charles G.] Ridgely, of the *Constellation*[96] frigate, dated at Valparaiso [Chile], 20th of April last, that the "island of St. Mary's and the shores of Arauco[97]" are "infested with people who have committed the grossest outrages on neutral flags and rights – several American and British vessels have been plundered by them. We cannot fully reach those persons, but such as depredate on our coasting trade should be brought to judgment.

To recapitulate all the cases of piracy that have occurred in our neighborhood, and give a list of all the vessels plundered within the last two months, would, perhaps, fill a whole page! They are well known at "head quarters." We may notice, however, the two following:

The ship *Orleans* of Philadelphia from New Orleans, was robbed off [C]ape Antoni[o],[98] by a piratical corvette[99] of 14 guns, of goods to the value of $40,000. The marauders appeared to be Spaniards. After robbing the ship, the chief of the pirates penciled in the French language and delivered or sent to a United States' officer, a passenger on board the *Orleans*, the following note, which is correctly translated into English:

> *"At sea, and in good luck.*
> SIR – Between buccaneers, no ceremony; I take your dry goods, and, in return, I send you pimento; therefore we are now even: I entertain no resentment.
>
> Bid good day to the officer of the United States, and tell him that I appreciate the energy with which he has spoken of me and my companions in arms. Nothing can intimidate us; we run the same fortune, and our maxim is, that the goods of this world belong to the brave and valiant.
>
> The occupation of the Floridas[100] is a pledge that the course I follow, is conformable to the policy pursued by the United States.
>
> (Signed) RICHARD CŒUR DE LION."[101]

---

96 A 1,265 ton, 164-foot long, 38-gun frigate, USS *Constellation* was launched in 1797. In 1799, during the Quasi-War, it captured the French *L'Insurgente* and also took a pair of French privateers. A year later it fought a stalemate with the 52-gun *Vengeance*, and retook three captured American merchant craft. It served with distinction in the Barbary wars, during the campaigns against Caribbean piracy, and on many significant cruises afterwards. It was broken up in 1853 (Mooney, *Fighting Ships*, II:170–173).

97 Arauco is the name of a city, province, and adjacent bay on the Chilean coast; the island of Santa Maria (St. Mary's) is to the bay's west. One British account described the island thus: "Off Arauco Bay lies the low and dangerous island of Santa Maria" (Knight, *English Cyclopedia: Geography*, II:456). By 1820, St. Mary's was "a favorite watering-place of whalers . . . " (Heffernan, *Stove By a Whale*, 92).

98 Cabo de San Antonio, off the Peninsula de Guanahacabibes on Cuba's extreme western edge.

99 Corvettes are (Smyth, *Lexicon*, 215) "[f]lush-decked ships, equipped with one tier of guns: fine vessels for warm climates, from admitting a free circulation of air. The Bermuda-built corvettes were deemed superior vessels, swift, weatherly, 'lie to' well, and carry sail in a stiff breeze. The cedar of which they are chiefly built is very buoyant, but also brittle."

100 The United States had finalized an agreement with Spain earlier in the year over the annexation of Florida.

101 Opinions vary on the identity of this pirate, who took as a *nom de guerre* the nickname of Richard I (Richard the Lion Heart) of England (1157–1199). "He may have been one Dubois, who cruised in the Venezuelan-

But what is terrible; a letter received at Charleston, from a gentleman at Matanzas, Cuba, dated 27th Sept. says – "Three horrible events have just taken place. Three American vessels – two of them coming in, viz. the brig *John*, Smith, and the schooner *Milo*, of Bristol; the other the sloop *Collector*, of Rhode Island, bound out, HAVE BEEN CAPTURED at the entrance of this harbor by a launch fitted out here! and manned by nine villains, viz. one Portuguese, six Spaniards and two Englishmen. They killed the captain and two men of the sch[oone]r and then ordered her to the north-ward; they murdered all the crew of the brig, opened their entrails, hanged them by the ribs to the masts, and afterwards set fire to the vessel and all were consumed!! The sloop was more fortunate; the pirates contented themselves with severely beat-ing the crew and plundering her of the most valuable articles on board – they then collected the combustibles and set them on fire and left her, hoping, as in the case of the brig, to consume the vessel and crew together, but these last, fortunately, had strength sufficient to take to her long boat and have safely got back to Matanzas.[102]

On their arrival, they applied to the governor for protection, and after some delay, he allowed the Americans in the place to arm in pursuit of the pirates. Three boats' full set out in quest of them, and after a cruise of 36 hours, have just returned without success.

ooooo

[*Charleston City Gazette and Commercial Daily Advertiser*, 26 October 1821, 2]

From the *New-York Gazette*, October 20.

Capt. Davis arrived at Boston from Havanna, furnishes the following account of recent piracies in that neighbourhood: [. . .] "The schooner *Louisa*, Capt. Sherman, from Rhode Island, fell in with a boat and nine men, who boarded her with pistols and cut-lasses, struck the mate several times, drove them all below, threatened the captain's life if he did not say where the doubloons[103] were; – finding there were none, they took about 2000 pounds [of] cheese; the captain delivered his own money to them, about $150; they then robbed them of all their clothes, not even leaving the captain a shirt to put on; they hoisted out his long boat, filled her with the cargo, and what

---

101 commissioned brig *General Arisimendi*. After the 'Coeur de Lion' episode, Dubois and his crew reportedly stopped another American craft and 'told the story of the *Orleans*, but not that they themselves had written [the note]. They said that the humorous Richard Coeur de Lion had been none other than Jean Laffite.' Another candidate is Jose Gaspar, a mythical figure who reputedly operated from Florida's Charlotte Harbor between 1819 and 1822.He was said to have been a disgruntled Spanish naval officer who stole a warship and turned against his country, waging war on its shipping in the Americas. Legends said 'Gasparilla' killed most prisoners but kept the attractive females in a private harem. They also held that he met his end off Boca Grande Pass, at-tacked by an American warship disguised as an English merchantman. His vessel going down, Gaspar 'wrapped a piece of anchor chain about his waist and jumped into the sea.' Such an episode is not mentioned in contem-porary records" (Gibbs, *Dead Men*, 76–77).

102 Port (and bay – Bahia de Matanzas) on Cuba's north coast, east of Havana.

103 The Spanish gold doubloon was worth about £4 by late 1818 ("Monthly Commercial Report," *Monthly Maga-zine, or British Register* 322, Vol. 47(1), 1 February 1819, 74).

Pirates in an open boat attacking a ship in the West Indies (artist unknown).

they could not take in their own boat – the vessel then close[d] into the mouth of Matanzas. The commander of the boat dressed himself in the captain of the schooner's best clothes, hat and boots, and walking the quarter deck, looked at him-self with exultation.["]

"The brig *George*, of Boston, was robbed by an open boat of eight men only, armed with pistols and cutlasses. When they came on board they demanded 550 ounces[104] the captain had in his possession. It is presumed they must have intercepted some advice of the money being on board. After tearing the ceiling from the foot of the sternpost, then down the rudder case, they found the amount. They previously drove the people into the forecastle, where they secured them, and then threatened the captain's life if he did not disclose where the money was hid, which he refused, handing them at the same time a few doubloons of his own.["]

"The sloop *Collector*, French, of Bristol, Rhode-Island, was boarded by the same boat the day before, and after the pirates had abused and wounded most of the seamen of the sloop, and given the captain two saber cuts on the arm and a heavy stroke on the neck, they set fire to the cabin of the sloop, taking the long boat with them. Fortu-nately Captain French had not his stern boat lashed, and let it down directly on their leaving him, otherwise it would have been destroyed immediately, by the fire making from the cabin window. The *Collector* was bound from Matanzas to Rhode-Island,

---

104   For 1821, the average market price of gold per troy oz. was £3.894 (Jastram, *Golden Constant*, 324).

with a cargo of sugars, and Capt. French heard them say during the time he was in their power, [']Let us treat these damn'd rascals as we did the crew of the brig yester-day,['] from which he supposed they had murdered the crew of a vessel, or merely spoke thus to intimidate Capt. F[rench]. Some six or seven other vessels had been robbed by them and the people treated roughly – but not any robbed of large amounts. Several small vessels have been fitted out from Matanzas, and from Ha-vanna to put a stop to these depredations; and it is said the government mean[s] to fit out some small armed vessels.["]

ooooo

[*Charleston City Gazette and Commercial Daily Advertiser*, 14 November 1821, 2]

Captain French, of the sloop *Collector*, which was lately robbed by pirates on the coast of Cuba, has arrived at Bristol, and in a letter to the *Providence American*, states, that he saw two of the villains in custody before he left Matanzas. One of them was arrested in the country some miles from Matanzas, and was committed to prison; one other attempted to obtain the release of his comrade by the offer of a bribe of 100 doubloons to the principal Alcalde,[105] in consequence of which he was detected and secured by the vigilance of the Alcalde. Capt. F[rench] was called on to go into the prison, and see if he could select from a large number of culprits, the pi-rates who robbed his vessel. He identified them without hesitation, as did several of the crew who were admitted to the prison afterwards. Capt. F[rench] recognized one of his own shirts on the back of one of them, which on examination was found to have his name marked upon it, at full length. – Captain F[rench] remarks, "I have great confidence in the disposition of the Spanish officers at Matanzas to punish such atrocities as they deserve." *Boston Daily Advertiser,* Nov. 3.

---

105   The Spanish word *alcalde* "is usually rendered in English as 'mayor' but a Spanish-American alcalde is by no means identical in function, legal position, institutional descent, or psychology with a United States mayor. [. . .] The Spanish-American alcalde is the chief governmental official of a town or city and as such has princi-pally administrative functions, but combines with these judicial powers and duties to a greater extent than is customary for a mayor in the United States. The alcalde is usually an appointive official" (Fitzgibbon, "Glossary of Latin-American Constitutional Terms," 575, 576–577).

7

"They . . . took to their heels" – Kearny's *Enterprise* at Cape Antonio (1821–1822)

The Caribbean in the early 1820s had devolved into what one maritime historian has termed "a dangerous and semi-anarchic place, where a once powerful central authority had been replaced by a patchwork of warlords, revolutionary juntas and petty rulers."[1] Two factors brought the United States into closer engagement with the region's pirates. One was the American acquisition of Florida in early 1821, a development that gave Washington – hitherto deferential to Spain in the prosecution of Caribbean pirates – cause to be more assertive in the waters near its new territory. A second was a new spate of sea robberies later that year (see Chapter 6) that prompted a concerted naval response.[2] In September, a Baltimore newspaper reported that the brig *USS Enterprise* was, along with other navy craft, "about to sail in quest of these freebooters – the fag-end of what was recently called privateering."[3] The *Enterprise*, which earned fame in 1813 for defeating *HMS Boxer*, had been commanded since February 1815 by Lawrence Kearny, an American officer who would enjoy a long career as sailor, administrator, and diplomat.

Kearny's early role in the naval campaign peaked with the *Enterprise*'s raids on the Cabo de San Antonio, or Cape Antonio, on Cuba's extreme western edge, in October and December, 1821. In each case, as Patterson had done at Barataria in 1814, sailors went ashore in small boats to pursue fleeing pirates. The difference now was that Kearny took the chase onto Spanish territory. The international law concept of "hot pursuit" was far-off, so Kearny's action signaled a bolder, interventionist stance from Washington. A few months later, Secretary of the Navy Smith Thompson told Commodore James Biddle, head of the new West Indies Squadron, to ask Havana authorities for clearance to pursue pirates ashore. If permission was denied – as it would be – Biddle was still directed to take the chase onto Cuban soil, albeit in remote areas.[4]

A version of Kearny's October raid as seen from the pirate side may exist. In the set of confessions that James Jeffers, alias Charles Gibbs, gave out shortly before being hung in 1831, he claimed to have been present at Cape Antonio when the *Enterprise* attacked. His account is presented in chapter 9.

---

1 Konstam, *Piracy*, 273.
2 Allen, *Our Navy*, 20–23.
3 "Piracies," *Niles' Weekly Register*, 22 September 1821, 64.
4 Wheeler, *Pirate Waters*, 100.

Engagement between the Enterprise & Boxer, Off Monhegan, Sept. 4th 1813 (by Walter F. Lansil, courtesy of the Collection of William Vareika Fine Arts, Newport, Rhode Island).

ooooo

[*Charleston Courier*, 31 October 1821, 2]

Pleasing Intelligence.
CAPTURE OF THE PIRATES!
By the sch[oone]r *Mary-Ann*, Capt. Hillard, arrived yesterday, we received a Havana paper of the 24th inst. From which we have translated the following highly pleasing article:

"Havana, October 24, 1821.["]
   "Arrived from Liverpool, the American ship *Lucies*, Capt. [James] Missroon. On the 16th, this ship was taken possession of by the famous pirates who cruize off Cape St. Antonio, [and?] as these picaroons[5] were about plundering her, the U.S. brig *Enterprize*,[6] fortunately hove in sight, and succeeded in capturing the piratical fleet, consisting of four schooners and one sloop. The sea robbers had the audac-

---

5   From the Spanish word *picarón*, commonly translated as rogue.
6   USS *Enterprise* was launched in 1799 as an 84-foot long schooner carrying 12 6-pounder cannon. "During the Quasi-War it captured eight French ships and liberated 11 American vessels, and between 1801 and 1804 it distinguished itself in service against the Barbary pirates. During the War of 1812, the *Enterprise*, now rigged as a brig, fought and captured the brig HMS *Boxer* off Portland, Maine, both commanders losing their lives in the contest." In July 1823, "it grounded and broke up on Little Curaçao Island in the West Indies" (Morris and Kearns, *Historical Dictionary*, 89).

ity to hoist the red flag.[7] Besides the vessels captured, there was an open boat attached to the same gang, which effected her escape. – The prizes have been sent to Charleston, where the crews will be tried. The ship was brought in by a midshipman of said U.S. brig.["] [. . .]

Another Account.

We have been politely favored with the following extract from the Log-Book of the ship *Lucies*, Capt. Missroon, which was received yesterday in a letter from Capt. M[issroon] dated Havana, 24th Oct. 1821.

"Tuesday, Oct. 16 – At 5 a.m. when hauling[8] round Cape Antonio, saw a large brig ashore on the Cape; and when we came abreast of her, she hailed us, saying, ['T]his is the *Aristides*,[9] of Boston, from Liverpool, taken by the pirates two days since, and run ashore by them.['] At that instant, we were fired at by a pirate, and shortly after was boarded by her, three others in company, all under Spanish colors. As soon as they got on board, they drew their sabres, cocked their blunderbusses,[10] and drove us all below. After they had possessed themselves of our (officers and passengers) watches and other valuables, with blunderbusses at our breasts, threatening instant death in case of refusal, they then proceeded to break open the trunks of dry goods in the steerage; in the mean time [they] liberated some of our crew to bring the ship to anchor, which they did in three fathoms water. While we were confined in the cabin, we saw from the windows a large schooner and brig, standing close round the Cape, which appeared to be armed vessels; the brig at this time being near to the *Aristides*, taking off her crew, fired at one of the pirates that had run down from us in that direction. Our captors, on seeing this, precipitately left us, and began to tow and sweep their vessels in shore. At 8, the large schooner came up with and hailed us, under the Colombian

---

7   The red flag – a traditional signal that no quarter would be given in battle – was one of many designs pirates employed. The so-called "Jolly Roger," generally depicted as a black flag with white skull and crossbones, is well known, but in contemporary records "red or 'bloody' flags are mentioned as often as black flags until the middle of the eighteenth century" (Cordingly, *Under the Black Flag*, 116–117). The red flag was preeminent in the Caribbean in the early 1800s. "At Barataria, Jean Laffite was said to have sailed under a 'Red Flag of the River,' and many contemporaries preferred the same color scheme. In 1822 the USS *Shark* captured a pirate craft named *Bandera de Sangre* (Banner of Blood) and confronted another flying a red shirt for a flag. Some predators began pursuits flying American or English colors, replacing them with red ones if their prey failed to slow down" (Gibbs, *Dead Men*, 55).

8   To haul generally means to be sailing close to the wind, i.e., toward the direction from which the wind is blowing (Smyth, *Lexicon*, 371–372).

9   According to surviving registration data, *Aristides* was built in Quincy, Massachusetts, in 1820. It was listed at 291 12/95 tons, 97 feet 8 inches long, 25 feet 11 ½ inches broad. It had "Two decks, two masts, square stern, no galleries, a billethead" (WPA, *Ship Registers and Enrollments 1821–1830*, 37). The term billethead indicates *Aristides* had no figurehead, but rather had "a carved prow bending in and out" (Smyth, *Lexicon*, 101).

10 The blunderbuss, with its distinctive flaring barrel (which facilitated loading), originated in the seventeenth-century. It was a short-range weapon, firing buckshot, and easy to carry aboard a small boat conveying boarders (Frayler, "Arms Chest," 2).

flag; enquired if we had been taken by the pirates, and being answered in the affirmative, instantly opened a well directed fire upon them from a 24[-]pounder.
When the firing had ceased, she again hailed us to say if the brig astern did not
prove to be an American man-of-war, on our hoisting our signal, she would immediately come to our assistance – she then hauled off. This vessel proved to be the
Colombian armed sch[oone]r *La Cent[e]lla*,[11] commanded by Charles C. Hopner.
About 9, the brig, which proved to be the U.S. brig *Enterprize*, came up with us,
and inquired if we had got possession of our ship again? Being answered yes,
Capt. Kearn[e]y[12] demanded all the boats and men we could spare, to go in pursuit of the pirates; and in less than ten minutes, five armed boats left the *Enterprize*, pulling after them. – About 11, the boats being near to the sch[oone]rs, the
largest one being full of dry goods, was set fire to by themselves, and abandoned.
About half past 11, she was in a blaze to the mast-head, all sail being set. At
meridian she blew up. So ends this day.["]

"Wednesday, Oct. 17. – Begins with heavy squalls, thunder, lighting and rain. At 4
p.m. cleared up. Saw coming round the Point (Mangrove Point on the chart) the
other two schooners and a sloop, (no longer pirates) with American colors at their
mast-heads, prizes to the *Enterprize*. At 9, was boarded by Capt. Hopner, supplied
him with sundry articles of provisions, which he would not accept of on any other
terms, than paying even more than was demanded for them. At 10, Capt.
Kearn[e]y boarded us, from whom we learn that the *Aristides* will be totally lost;
her rudder and stern post is torn off, and four feet [of] water in the hold. The
British brig *Larch*, of St. Andrews [Canada] from Kingston for Havana, was taken at
the same time we were, and re-taken by the *Enterprize*. After Capt. Kearn[e]y had
dispatched the boats after the pirates yesterday, he stood[13] round the Cape with
the brig to the southward, and there captured another of the robbers, who had
taken a French brig the day before bound for Campeachy [Campeche]."

11 Spanish for thunderbolt. Hopner's command may have later turned pirate. On 15 January, 1825, the *New York Shipping and Commercial List* reported that the "Spanish brig '*Maceas*,' from Gibara, Cuba, for Cadiz, with a cargo of tobacco, was captured on the 3d ult. by the pirate schooner '*Centella*,' formerly a Colombian privateer" (quoted in Bradlee, *Piracy in the West Indies*, 158).
12 Lawrence Kearny (1789–1868) began his navy career in 1807 as a midshipman and by 1813 had made lieutenant. Following his successes in the early 1820s against Caribbean pirates he was given a similar task against Greek pirates operating in the Mediterranean. Promoted to captain in 1832, in 1840 he was put in charge of the East India Squadron. "Kearny made a positive impression on the Chinese leading to the first treaty signed between the United States and China in 1844." His later service included heading the Norfolk Navy Yard and the New York Navy Yard. He retired late in 1861 (Morris and Kearns, *Historical Dictionary*, 145–146). For a biography, see Carroll Storrs Alden, *Lawrence Kearny, Sailor Diplomat* (Princeton: Princeton University, 1936).
13 Synonymous with *sailed* – Smyth (*Lexicon*, 649) defines *stand* as "The movement by which a ship advances towards a certain object, or departs from it; as, 'The enemy stands in shore;' 'We saw three sail standing to the southward.'"

U.S. Brig Enterprise and Pirate Schooners, October 16, 1821 (watercolor by Irwin John Bevan, courtesy of the Mariners' Museum, Newport News, Virginia).

ooooo

[Kearny to Secretary of the Navy, 12 November 1821[14]]

U.S. Brig *Enterprise*
Charleston, S.C. Nov. 12th, 1821

Sir

I have the honor to report my arrival here from a cruise in the Bay of Mexico. Off Cape Antonio on the 10th ult. we had the fortune to capture four piratical Schooners and a Sloop. [T]hey were manned by Spaniards about 70 or 80 strong.

The pirates ran their vessels on shore when pursued by our boats and made their escape except one man now a prisoner on board this vessel.
One of the Schooners full of goods was burnt by the Pirates, another I ordered burnt for want of men to man her; she was in ballast.[15]

Two of the Schooners have arrived here with goods saved from the American Brig *Aristides,* a vessel they had run ashore and were plundering when we hove in sight.

---

14 National Archives Microfilm Publications, Microcopy No. 148, Letters Received by the Secretary of the Navy from Officers Below the Rank of Commander, 1802–1884, Roll 27, 1 August–31 December 1821 (Washington, DC: National Archives, 1959). In some transcription cases, the editor consulted an image of an undamaged version of the same document reproduced in Mooney, *Fighting Ships,* III:606–608.

15 A cargo vessel *in ballast* is one which "has discharged its cargo and has taken ballast on board" (Dear and Kemp, *Companion,* 29).

We also recaptured the American Ship *Lucies* from them with a full cargo from Liverpool.

The *Lucies* is now at the Havanna having been taken in by the Master in violation of my orders and against the direction of the prize masters. She was ordered for this port.

We also found an English Brig called the *Larch* in their possession. She being in ballast was given up to the Master and allowed to proceed on her voyage – We have come in to supply [ourselves?] with a cable and Anchor and a Launch[16] lost at Cape Antonio also to get some sails and rigging of which we are in great want.

My cruise from [here?] if with your approbation will be along the South side of Cuba where a number of Piracies are committed.

Your Instructions will find me at this place.

I have the honor to be
Your most obt. Servt.
Lawrence Kearny
Lt. U.S. Navy

The Hon. Mister Thompson, Sec[retar]y of the Navy[17]
P.S. The U.S. Schooner *Porpoise*[18] is off Cape Antonio.

ooooo

[*Charleston City Gazette and Commercial Daily Advertiser*, 12 November 1821, 2]

BALTIMORE, NOV. 5
The schooner *Sally & Polly*, [C]apt. Galloway, from Trinidad de Cuba,[19] is ashore on Thomas' Point.[20] Off Cape Antonio [it] was robbed by a pirate, of which [C]apt. Galloway makes the following report: –

["]At half past 6 p.m. in hauling round Cape Antonio, we discovered a small sail at anchor under the land. At 7 she got under way and stood towards us, firing muskets at us at intervals. At 8 p.m. they came alongside, hailed us, and ordered me

---

16   "The largest or long boat of a ship of war. . . . A launch being proportiona[l]ly longer, lower, and more flat-bottomed than the merchantman's long-boat, is in consequence less fit for sailing but better calculated for rowing and approaching a flat shore" (Smyth, *Lexicon*, 434.)

17   Smith Thompson (1768 to 1843) was a New York lawyer, legislator, and judge. After serving as Secretary of the Navy from 1819 to 1823, "he sat on the U.S. Supreme Court from 1824 to 1843" (Morris and Kearns, *Historical Dictionary*, 313).

18   Built in 1820, USS *Porpoise* was an 86-foot long topsail schooner carrying 12 6-pounder cannon. After initial West Indies service, it cruised against the African slave trade and in the Mediterranean (Mooney, *Fighting Ships*, V:353).

19   On Cuba's south coast.

20   On the Chesapeake Bay.

to come on board of them. – On answering that our boat would not float, they fired a volle[y] into us. Sent the mate and two men in the boat whom they detained aboard the pirate and returned the boat with ten armed men. They demanded where the money was – to which I answ[e]red, there was none on board. – They then dragged me forward, beating me with their swords, and hung me up on the starboard yard rope. After remaining a while they lowered me and dragged me towards the stern. They then commenced plundering and searching, taking every thing that suited them. Disappointed in finding no money, they ordered the vessel into the shore, threatening to throw over the cargo and burn the vessel if the money could not be found. In going in, the schooner grounded, when they commenced throwing the cargo overboard; finding that destruction to the vessel and cargo was inevitable I informed them there was money on board: and asked in case I gave it up whether they would assist me in getting the schooner off the shore. To this they answered in the affirmative, when by my order, the mate directed them to the money. They forced the schooner off by carrying an anchor ahead, when they departed with the money and plunder.["]

ooooo

[*Charleston Courier*, 13 November, 1821, 2]

We have been furnished by Captain [Joseph] Couthouy, late of the brig *Aristides*, of Boston, recently captured by the pirates off Cape Antonio, and run on shore, a particular account of the capture of his vessel, and the treatment he received from those ruffians, together with the subsequent capture of the piratical vessels. It does not differ from the accounts already published. He experienced the most inhuman treatment – was knocked down several times, and his life, that the lives of his crew were probably saved by the timely appearance of the *Enterprize*, which caused the pirates to abandon the brig with great precipitation. The *Aristides* had a very valuable cargo of dry goods, the whole of which, except what was stowed between decks, was destroyed by the vessel's being run on shore.

Capt. C[outhouy] also states that it was the intention of the pirates to have run the ship *Lucies* on shore, and murder all on board, which they no doubt would have effected, had not the *Enterprize* approached and fired a gun, on which they immediately abandoned her.

It was reported that the pirates had a short time before captured a French ship, and murdered all on board, including a lady passenger; and the fact of a lady's clothes being found on board of one of their vessels, stained with blood, is strong confirmation of the report.[. . .]

We are indebted to Lieut. Kearn[e]y for the following information:

The U.S. brig *Enterprize* on the 6th inst. boarded off the Double Headed Shot Keys,[21] the Colombian privateer *Congress*, Capt. Almeida, from a cruise off Cadiz, who reported that she had an engagement with a Spanish man of war brig, 2 schooners, and some gun-boats, off that place, which continued two hours.

The Colombian privateer *La Cent[e]lla*, was also boarded off Capt Antonio by the *Enterprize* on the 16th ult. and was on 6th inst. spoken by the *Congress* privateer off Matanzas, where she is now cruising. These vessels are regularly commissioned.

A CARD. – Merchant vessels passing Cape Antonio, should not approach the land nearer than to be seen from aloft, as the coast is infested with a number of piratical vessels and boats, who screen themselves from view under cover of the land, and wait the approach of vessels until they come within the usual distance, when passing the Cape.

The best course, on making the Cape, is N[orth] by W[est] until they get into lat[itude] 22, 30, N[orth] or about 30 miles north of the Cape.

ooooo

[*Charleston City Gazette and Commercial Daily Advertiser*, 17 November 1821, 2]

BOSTON, Nov. 5

Arrived, brig *Cobbossee Contee*,[22] Jackson, 28 days from Havanna. Sailed 8th ult. and same evening, about 4 miles from the Mor[r]o [Castle], was brought to[•] by a piratical sloop, with about 30 men; a boat with 10 men came on board and commenced plundering. They robbed the captain of his watch, 4 boxes segars, nearly all his clothing, as well as the mate's; and from the vessel all her spare rigging, cooking utensils, unrove part of the running rigging, cut the small cable, stove the compasses, cut up the masts' coats;[23] and from the cargo they took 9 bales cochineal [dye], and 6 boxes segars. The captain was beat most unmercifully, had a large broadsword broke across his back, (the piece he now has,) and a long knife run through the thick part of his thigh, by which he nearly bled to death; the mate was also beat severely, and was hung by the neck under the maintop. Capt. Jackson says he saw the same sloop laying at the Regla the day before. [. . .]

Captain Jackson, and many other ship masters, and other persons, have informed me, that this piratical system is openly countenanced by a considerable part of the inhabi-

---

21   A cay (or key) is a small island; the Double Headed Shot Cays, or keys, are part of a group of islands off Cuba's northern coast known collectively as Cay Sal (or Key Salt) Bank.

22   A lake in central Maine.

23   A coat was "A piece of tarred canvas nailed round above the partners, or that part where the mast or bowsprit enters the deck. Its use is to prevent the water from running down between decks" (Smyth, *Lexicon*, 197).

tants of Havanna many of whom have been heard to say in the most public places that it was a just retaliation on us for our interference in the suppression of the slave trade, and for allowing Patriot privateers to refit in our ports; and my informants have expressed their belief, that many persons of wealth and influence in Havanna were in the secret, and no doubt had knowledge of the departure of the pirates.[...]

ooooo

[*Charleston City Gazette and Commercial Daily Advertiser*, 8 December 1821, 2]

LETTER FROM CAPT. R. HENLEY TO SECRETARY OF THE NAVY.
U.S. ship *Hornet*, at sea, Oct. 30th, 1821.
Lat[itude] 19° 47', N[orth] Long[itude] 74° 05', W[est]

SIR – I have the honour to inform you, that, in pursuance of your orders, I remained at the appointed rendezvous, off the Capes of Virginia, until the evening of the 15th inst. when no vessels appearing to profit of the convoy offered them, I proceeded on my cruize. Having had bad weather and unfavourable winds, almost ever since, we did not get through Turks Island passage[24] until yesterday, when we fell in with and captured, off St. Domingo, the piratical armed schooner, called the *Moscow*, mounting one two[-]pounder. She has no commission, and a mixed crew of blacks and Spaniards – nineteen in number. I have put on board the necessary officers and men to navigate her, and have instructed Midshipman Kennon to proceed with her, and such part of her crew, as I have thought it safe to leave on board, to the first convenient port, agreeable to your general instructions, and deliver her over to the civil authority.[25]

We found on board a number of articles, evidently of her plunder, viz. such as watches, ladies' shawls, silk stockings, shirts, and other articles marked with initials. She has been out but a short time, as she had on board fresh fruit, &c. She was in pursuit of a merchant vessel the moment we came up with her.¶

I have the honour to be, Sir, with great respect, your obedient servant,

R. HENLEY[26]

The Hon. Smith Thompson, Sec. U.S. Navy.
(*National Intelligencer*, Nov. 30)

24 A channel between the West Indian islands of Caicos and Turks.
25 Efforts at prosecution appear to have been unsuccessful, to judge from the following item published several months later: "*Piracy*. Five men belonging to the crew of the *Mosca* [sic; *Moscow*], sent into Norfolk by the U.S. ship *Hornet* and charged with piracy, have been put upon their trial and promptly released – an act of piracy not being even attempted to be proved, though the character of the vessel was very suspicious" (*Niles' Weekly Register*, 8 June 1822, 239).
26 Robert Henley (1783–1828), a hero of the Battle of Lake Champlain in 1814; he would later command naval stations at Norfolk and Charleston (Mooney, *Fighting Ships*, III:298).

ooooo

[Charleston City Gazette and Commercial Daily Advertiser, 20 December 1821, 2]

PIRACY – Extract from the log-book of the sch[oone]r *Emily*, Capt. Robbins, arrived here yesterday from Matanzas: – "Dec. 12[th], (sea account) at 1 p.m. the sch[oone]r *Mary Rose* in company, half a mile astern, saw a small sch[oone]r 2 miles to leeward, supposed a drogher[27] from Havanna; at 2 p.m. distant 10 miles from Matanzas, standing N[orth] E[ast] by E[ast] close hauled,[28] the *Mary Rose* distant [3/4?] mile, observed the sch[oone]r which had then got in our wake, to tack,[29] which caused suspicion that she was a piratical cruizer. At half past 2 the *Mary Rose* hove to[e] – the sch[oone]r then came alongside and sent a boat with 10 men on board the *M[ary] R[ose,]* took possession of her, and stood in for the land. After the boat left her for the *Mary Rose*, she gave chase to us, and we observed her apparently full of men. At 3 p.m. they fired a musket at us – we hove to[e], when we were hailed and ordered to lower our foresail; we were then boarded by 9 men armed with muskets, cutlasses and knives, driven into the cabin, and confined. They then made sail on the sch[oone]r for the shore, the pirate in company. The crew appeared to be Spaniards. After being confined for a short time, one of the pirates, who spoke good English, came below and demanded of Captain Robbins the money on board. Capt. R[obbins] replied there was none; to which the pirate retorted, "[U]nless you deliver all the money you have, your coffee shall be taken and your vessel burnt," and then left us, in a state easier imagined than described, expecting nothing short of death. Shortly after he returned and ordered the captain and crew, six in number, and a French gentleman (passenger) on deck – immediately on reaching the deck we were driven forward and confined in the forecastle, after beating us with their muskets and pricking us with dirks – we found the forecastle pillaged of every thing, and the people's chests broken open. In the mean time they plundered the cabin of every article of value, breaking open every chest, trunk, &c and strewing the articles about in search of money. About 4 p.m. they opened the scuttle and ordered the captain and passengers on deck, as we supposed to be murdered, securing the scuttle afterwards so right as nearly to produce suffocation, and placing two centinels near it with drawn sabres, to prevent our rising. After keeping us confined in this manner until 8 p.m. we were ordered on deck to take in sail and let go the anchor, distant about ½ mile from land, which from appearance was the extreme east point of Matanzas harbor.

---

27 Variously spelled, a type of West Indian trading vessel.

28 The term *close hauled* refers to the "general arrangement or trim of a ship's sails when she endeavours to progress in the nearest direction possible contrary to the wind; in this manner of sailing the keel of square-rigged vessels commonly makes an angle of six points with the line of the wind, but cutters, luggers, and other fore-and-aft rigged vessels will sail even nearer" (Smyth, *Lexicon*, 192).

29 "*To tack.* To go about, to change the course from one board to another from the starboard to the port tack, or vice versâ. It is done by turning the ship's head suddenly to the wind, whereby her head-sails are thrown aback, and cause her to fall off from the wind to the other tack. The opposite to *wearing*" (Smyth, *Lexicon*, 672).

The pirates informed us they had let the *Mary Rose* go. Their schooner being near, the captain of this banditti ordered her along side of us, had her made fast, un-stowed our boat, broke open our hatches, and compelled our crew to pass the cof-fee from the hold to their vessel: – of 212 bags which we had on board, they robbed us of 210. During our confinement in the forecastle, they twice hung Capt. Robbins by the neck, in order to extort confession; and whilst we were passing out coffee the four commanders of this gang of robbers, which consisted of from 25 to 30 in number, were beating him most unmercifully with their swords. After the whole crew had satisfied themselves with beating Capt. R[obbins] and that there was no money except $344, which they had taken, having plundered the cabin of every thing, they sent for the cook (a black) to come into the cabin. – They, after demand-ing of him where the money was, beat him most cruelly with their swords, and let him go. The mate was then brought forth – six swords pointed at his breast, threat-ened with instant death – the same demands made, and after beating him so se-verely as scarcely to leave him able to stir, let go, and sent again to assist in getting out coffee. After plundering us of every thing they could find of any value, and rip-ping off the ceiling, in search of money, they cut our cable, then about 20 fathoms out, and ordered us to steer to the northward, for if we returned to Matanzas, and were again captured by them, death should be our portion: having plundered us of 210 bags of coffee, 150 lbs. new rigging, 2 pr. can-hooks,[30] 1 small bower anchor[31] and 20 fathoms cable, 1 kedge anchor,[32] half bbl. sugar, all our knives and forks, davit[33] tackle, blocks, falls,[34] charts, quadrants, boots, shoes, hats, all our stores, cooking utensils, &c &c.

ooooo

---

30   Can-hooks "are used to sling a cask by the chimes, or ends of its staves, and are formed by reeving the two ends of a piece of rope or chain through the eyes of two flat hooks, and there making them fast. The tackle is then hooked to the middle of the bight," the latter being "the loop of a rope when it is folded, in contradistinction to the end . . . " (Smyth, *Lexicon*, 99, 156).

31   Bower anchors, wrote Smyth (*Lexicon*, 124) are "[t]hose at the bows and in constant working use." Frayler ("Walk Away with the Cat," 1n.6) observed that the bowers "are the two primary anchors by which a ship rides at an-chor. They are stowed on either side of the bow for immediate deployment. A third and sometimes-larger anchor called the best (or spare) bower is also available. It is kept in reserve and firmly lashed in place."

32   "A small anchor used to keep a ship steady and clear from her bower-anchor while she rides in harbour, particu-larly at the turn of the tide" (Smyth, *Lexicon*, 417).

33   A davit is "[a] piece of timber or iron, with sheaves or blocks at its end, projecting over a vessel's quarter or stern, to hoist up and suspend one end of a boat" (Smyth, *Lexicon*, 234).

34   A fall referred to "the loose end of a tackle, or that part to which the power is applied in hoisting, and on which the people pull" (Smyth, *Lexicon*, 286).

[Kearny to Secretary Thompson, 18 December 1821[35]]

U[nited] States Brig *Enterprize*
Havana Dec. 18th 1821

Hon. Mister Thompson
Secretary of the Navy

Sir,
I have the honor to inform you that I have touched at this place (where we arrived on the 10th Inst.) for information in relation to piratical vessels [and] slave vessels &c.

It is reported to me that several small vessels sailed from this a few days since which are supposed to be of a piratical character. We sail this day in pursuit of them.

The ship *Lucies* recaptured by this vessel from the Pirates at Cape Antonio is yet here under trial for Salvage and as soon as the trial closes I will forward to the department the papers relating to the [the] case which at present it is necessary should be here.

I would respectfully suggest to you the propriety of a vessel of war of the United States of a more considerable force than the *Enterprize* occasionally touching at this Port. In my several visits here I have found that the commercial interest is much benefited by the presence of the Government vessels as they possess more weight with the government here than the commercial agents who are not acknowledged.

I have the honor to be
Your most ob^t Servt

Lawrence Kearny
Lt. U.S. Navy

ooooo

[Kearny to Commodore Patterson, 28 December 1821[36]]

Copy

U[nited] States Brig *Enterprize*
Off Cape Antonio,
December 28, 1821

Dear Sir:
I had the pleasure to write you a few days since from the Havana, at which place I

---

35 National Archives Microfilm Publications, Microcopy No. 124, Miscellaneous Letters Received by the Secretary of the Navy, 1801–84, Roll 91, 1821, Volumes 5–7, 23 August–31 December (Washington, DC: National Archives, 1960).

36 National Archives Microfilm Publications, Microcopy No. 124, Miscellaneous Letters Received by the Secretary of the Navy, 1801–84, Roll 91, 1821, Volumes 5–7, 23 August–31 December (Washington, DC: National Archives, 1960)

obtained information of a gang of Pirates sailing from thence on a Cruise, fitted out at the Regla Harbor, of Havana.

On the 21st inst. I fell in with them at this place, and Captured one of their Vessels, a Schooner of about 35 Tons, the Crew, about 25 in number escaped (unfortunately) by land having run their Vessel on Shore. They made a stand on shore protected by a Bank (a good natural breastwork) until our party got within musket shot when they deeming "prudence the better part of Valor" took to their heels thro' the well known intricate paths of the thick woods of the Cape and effected their escape.
We have mann'd the Vessel and p[ro]pose making an excursion up the coast within the Colorados reef[37] in pursuit of other piratical schooners which by reason of a fresh breeze [e]ffected their escape from the Boats of the Brig.

I succeeded in decoying them off from their rendezvous but not at a sufficient distance to make them prisoners.

We have made attempts to pursue them since, but owing to a severe north wind the surf has been so great we could not get the Tender (as I now call the prize) over the reef, behind which these Villa[i]ns make a harbour.

The Rendezvous is about four or five miles north of the Cape around a point easily discerned when passing that headland. The Tender with all on board had nearly been lost by the surf in an attempt to cross the reef a few days since – two Boats which I sent with her were capsized by a Breaker and by the greatest difficulty the lives were saved. One Boat however was lost. We have just rode out a heavy Norther which continued about 36 hours, it has now abated and the weather is such that when I again fall in with our Tender (prize) I hope to visit the Coast up as far as Cape Buenavista,[38] between which and the Cape these Villa[i]ns harbour – They are all Spaniards and are particularly inimical to Americans. My life and all my Officers' lives are openly threatened at Havana for having interfered with their speculations. I hope soon to bring some of them up with a "round turn".

We found the body of a murdered man at the Cape recently buried – he was an American or European, the fingers of one hand were cut off and his breast much lacerated. We found plundered goods (coffee & Segars) in the Huts built by the Pirates, also a number of papers, letters, American Seamen's protections,[39] &c. We burnt their

37 Located on the north coast of Pinar del Rio, Cuba, Los Colorados Reef is a large reef system. "The Colorados, so little known, and so much dreaded by mariners, is also erroneously laid down [e.g., located on nautical charts]; an error which frequently occasions a serious loss of lives & property" (Smith, *Atrocities of the Pirates*, 35).
38 Cape Buenavista, Cuba, on the island's western-most coast, located "on the northern point of the gulf of which Cape St. Antonio forms the southern horn" (Smedley et al., *Encyclopaedia Metropolitana*, XVII:423). An English navigator remarked that "Cape Buonavesta . . . is erroneously laid down as high and mountainous, whereas the land about it is not more than eighteen feet from the surface of the ocean; and that which is in general mistaken for it, lies a great way in the interior of the island, and six leagues to the eastward of the Cape" (Smith, *Atrocities of the Pirates*, 35).
39 A "seaman's protection" was a citizenship document issued to American sailors to prevent them from being impressed aboard British warships. See Dye, "Early American Merchant Seafarers," *passim*.

establishment and destroyed everything but their facility of fitting out piratical cruisers, which can never be done as long as the <u>Havana</u> & <u>Regla</u> exist.

With my best wishes for your good health and uninterrupted happiness of yourself and family, I remain, Dear Sir

           Your most Obt. Servt.

Signed   Lawrence Kearny

           U.S. Navy

Com. Patterson,
Comdg Naval Officer,
New Orleans Station.

[Postscript:] I have to add that several pieces of Wearing apparel were found in the Pirate huts so bloody as to leave but little doubt that Murder has been committed. Some shirts which were brought on board the *Enterprize* were covered with the stains of blood about the collar and breast.

It will also be recollected that on a former occasion a <u>female</u> dress was found in the same state among those infernal rascals.
(Signd) L.K.

ooooo

[*Niles' Weekly Register*, 5 January 1822, 304]

NAVAL. *Boston Dec. 26.* Arrived yesterday the Portuguese ship *Marianna Falora*, [C]apt. [V]entura Anacleto de Brito. She was from Bahia [Brazil] for Lisbon, and captured by the U.S. sch[oone]r *Alligator*,[40] [L]t. [Robert F.] Stockton, and ordered for this port, under the command of [L]t. Abbot. She came into port with the same pendant flying, and displayed in the same manner as when she attacked the *Alligator*.

Extract of a letter from [L]t. Abbot, of the navy, to [C]om. John Shaw, commanding naval officer in Boston, dated,

                            Boston harbor, Dec. 24, 1821.

"I have the honour to report to you my arrival at this place with the armed ship *Marianne Falora*, having on board all her crew as prisoners – 29 in number. "This vessel attacked the *Alligator* on the 5th Nov. (lat[itude] about 20 38, N[orth] lon[gitude] 30 W[est]) in a most outrageous and piratical manner; but was foiled in her attempt to capture her, and after an action of about an hour and a half, surrender[e]d to the *Alligator*.

---

40 Carrying twelve 6-pounder cannon, the 86-foot long, 198-ton schooner USS *Alligator* was launched in 1821. "It was lost when it ran aground on Craysfort Reef, Florida, on November 23, 1823" (Morris and Kearns, *Historical Dictionary*, 7).

"She is a ship of between 300 and 400 tons; mounting 4 long 12[-]pounders, 2 long 6[-]pounders, and 4 24[-]pound car[r]onades; 4 of which I was under the necessity of throwing overboard in a very heavy gale of wind in the Gul[f] Stream, on the 6th inst. in which gale we lost some of our spars and had our stern boat washed away.

"The prize crew consists of 16, including myself and two officers, midshipman George S. Blake, and Mr. J. Dixon master's mate; and it gives me pleasure to acknowledge their uniform, vigilant and correct conduct, and that they rendered me every possible aid.

"I will take the liberty to add, that the reason of the great length of the action, was in consequence of the long guns of the prize, and [C]apt. Stockton's desire to get along side before he commenced, (the wind being light) gave her the fight to herself for more than one hour."

It is most probable that this vessel will be given up. It does not appear that she was engaged in an illegal trade – she took the *Alligator* for a Buenos Ayrean privateer, an illegal pirate; but how the commander will reconcile himself in hoisting a signal of distress, as it seems he did do, to excite the attention of [C]apt. Stockton, who thereupon approached for the purpose of administering relief, and then to salute him with a broadside, we are at a loss to conjecture – and for which he has been rightly punished. The Portuguese ship is laden with sugar, cotton, &c and was on her voyage from Bahia to Lisbon. The officers and crew have been strictly examined at Boston, and promptly liberated, on the ground that there exited no proof of their having attacked the *Alligator* with a piratical intention, having acted under the impression that she was a privateer, &c.

The U.S. schooner *Tartar*,[41] [L]ieut. Crowley, arrived at Pensacola, affords the following particulars relative to the U.S. brig *Enterprize*, [C]aptain Kearn[e]y.

Captain Kearn[e]y having rescued the ship *Lucies* from the pirates, put a midshipman and some men on board, and ordered her to the Havana. On his arrival at Havana he found the *Lucies* in charge of a guard of Spanish soldiers under the orders of the captain-general, claiming her as under his jurisdiction. Capt. K[earny] repossessed himself of the ship, denying the right of the captain-general, and declaring that he would take her to the United States for adjudication. Whilst making his arrangements for this purpose, he was waited on by an officer of the government, and told that he would not be suffered to leave the port with the *Lucies*, and, if he persisted, his vessel would be sunk. This threat did not alter his determination, and shortly afterwards he made sail with his fleet, the *Enterprize*, *Lucies*

---

41 The *Tartar* had, in summer 1820, intercepted a group of about 20 sailors who had eluded "the vigilance of the officers at Charleston, and went to sea to join [Joseph] Almeida's privateer." They were "bought back, examined and committed to prison" ("Patriot recruits," *Niles' Weekly Register*, 5 August 1820, 416).

and piratical vessels,[42] resolved to carry his point at all hazards. He proceeded until he was nearly abreast of the Mo[r]ro [Castle],[43] when he was overtaken by another message from the captain-general, in which the captain-general offered to make himself personally responsible for the amount of salvage due the *Enterprize*, pledging himself to this effect. This was done with a view to conciliate, and [C]apt. K[earny] actuated by the same motives, yielded to the compromise, and gave up the *Lucies*.

---

42 Captured vessels, prizes to the *Enterprise*.
43 *El Morro*, or the Morro Castle, a fort guarding the harbor of Havana. According to an 1832 book, it "stands on a high rock, and is a triangular work, mounted with 40 pieces of heavy cannon, having a battery nearly level with the water at the foot of the rock . . . " (Bell, *System of Geography*, VI: 321).

8

"Her red flag [was] nailed to the mast" – The campaign against piracy in the Gulf and Caribbean (1822–1825)

The successful raids against the pirates of Cape Antonio opened what became a major anti-piracy effort by both the American and British navies. The Americans would in 1822 create a new force, the West India (or West Indies) Squadron under Captain James Biddle, specifically to attack Caribbean freebooters. To work in shallow coastal waterways where the pirates operated and hid, the American force employed smaller craft such as Lawrence Kearny's brig USS *Enterprise*, fresh from its successes in western Cuba, and the 12-gun schooners USS *Shark*, USS *Porpoise*, and USS *Alligator*. Captain David Porter assumed command of the squadron the following year, and added a "Mosquito Fleet" of smaller vessels to further aid in coastal operations. From the British side, the Caribbean pirates faced pressure from the Royal Navy's Jamaica Squadron, with warships such as HMS *Tyne*, HMS *Grecian* and HMS *Icarus*. American and British forces sometimes worked in unison, such as in a March 1825 episode which resulted in the capture of a pirate schooner, as detailed below.

The pirates often put up stiff resistance. The USS *Alligator*'s captain lost his life in a small boat assault near Cuba's Punta Hicacos in November 1822; a report included in this chapter notes how the pirates in that battle defiantly nailed their red flag to their mast. In the following September, pirates took the initiative against a craft being used as a tender to HMS *Tyne*, attacking it at night and being repulsed only after heavy fighting.

But in a sustained struggle the pirates could not compete with the professionals for discipline and resources. Inexorably the navies gained and held the upper hand. By the spring of 1825, when the entries in this chapter end, the age of large-scale piracy in the Gulf of Mexico and the Caribbean was coming to a close.

ooooo

[*Boston Columbian Centinel*, 19 January, 1822, 2]

MORE PIRACY.
NORFOLK, JAN. 10. – We are indebted to the polite attention of Capt. Saunders, of the sch[ooner] *James Monroe*, reported under our marine head, for the following account of piratical outrages recently committed on American commerce.

The sch[ooner] *Planet* (of Portland [Maine]), Capt. Dennison, arrived at the Balize 21st Dec. in 13 days from St. Thomas. On the 16th off Cape Antonio, was boarded by two piratical schooners of 15 or 20 men each, which robbed the captain of all the money he had on board, about $300, [38?] bags of coffee, 48 boxes of cider, took all the clothing and blankets belonging to the captain and mate, and flogged the captain severely, to extort from him where the balance of the money was concealed.

Capt. D[ennison] also informed Capt. S[aunders] that these pirates had previously captured the ship *Liverpool Packet* (of Portsmouth), Capt. Ricker, from Rio [de] Jan[ei]ro, bound to Havana, from which they robbed sixty thousand dollars, and took a boy from the ship to fill water casks for their use. This boy they afterwards put on board the *Planet*. When the *Planet* hove in sight, coming round the Cape, the pirates cut the cables of the ship and let her go, after putting on board the crew of the English brig *Alexander* (of Greenock) which they had captured and burnt some days previous, and the captain and steward of which, they had murdered.[1]

ooooo

[*Niles' Weekly Register*, 16 February 1822, 388–389]

"THE PIRATES ON THE COAST OF CUBA, &c."[. . .]
U.S. schooner *Porpoise*
Off the North Coast of Cuba, 20th January, 1822

SIR – Having completed the necessary equipments of this vessel, at New Orleans, on the 7th inst. and previously given public notice that I should sail from the Balize on the 10th, with convoy I have now the honor to inform you that I proceeded to sea on the day appointed with five sail under my protection. On the 15th, having seen the vessels bound to Havana and Matanzas safe to their destined ports, I made all sail to the westward, and on the following day boarded the brig *Bolina*, of Boston, Gorham master, from whom I received the following information: That on the day previous, his vessel was captured by pirates, and robbed of every material they could carry away with them, at the same time treating the crew and himself with inhuman cruelty. After supplying him from this vessel with what necessaries he required, I made sail for the land, and early the following morning, (Saddle Hill, on the north coast of Cuba, then bearing S[outh] by E[ast]) I dispatched our boats, with forty men, under command of [L]ieut. Curtis, in pursuit of these enemies of the human race.[2] The boats having crossed the reef, which here extends a considerable distance from the shore, very soon discovered, chased, and captured, a piratical schooner, the crew of which made their escape to the

---

1   Se the next entry, and that below from *Niles' Weekly Register*, 17 May 1823, for more on the *Alexander*.
2   See the discussion of *Hostis Humani Generis* in Chapter 10, note 20.

woods. [L]ieut. Curtis very judiciously manned the prize from our boats, and proceeded about ten miles to leeward, where it was understood, the principal depot
of these marauders was established. This he fortunately discovered and attacked.
A slight skirmish here took place, but, as our force advanced, the opposing party
precipitately retreated. We then took possession, and burnt and destroyed their
fleet, consisting of five vessels – one of them a beautiful new schooner, of about
sixty tons, ready for sea, with the exception of her sails. We also took three prisoners; the others fled to the woods.

In the affair just mentioned, the officers of the expedition state the enemy's loss
to be severe. Only one man was wounded in our boats – and it is worthy of remark, that this man was one of their own gang, then a prisoner in our possession,
and surrounded by our people.

The destruction of this place will, I trust, be of some service. From information by
me received, it was their principal depot, from whence they dispatched squadrons
to Cape Antonio. These returning, loaded with plunder, it was transshipped to Havana in vessels sent from there for that purpose. Stores and materials were collected on the spot, not only for repairing but building vessels.

The prisoners now on board are recognized by a seaman in my possession, who
was one of the crew of the English ship *Alexander*, of Greenock, lately burnt by
these pirates; and not content with destroying the vessel, they inhumanely
butchered her unfortunate commander. The seaman in question, I retain as an evidence in the case.[. . .]

JAMES RAMAGE.

Honorable Smith Thompson,
Secretary of the navy [. . .]

ooooo

[*Niles' Weekly Register*, 13 July 1822, 309–310]
A Tale of Terror.

New-Orleans, June 11.
Extract from the log-book of the brig Aurilla, *of N[ew] York, [C]aptain Wing Howland,
bound from Baltimore to New-Orleans.*

On the 15th May, finding the current in the Gulf too strong, it was thought best to
cross the Salt Key bank;[3] when about half over the bank, two schooners hove in sight,
which, at first view, were of a suspicious appearance. Immediately ordered all the negroes upon deck, thinking to frighten them off if they were pirates. They tacked and

---

3 See Chapter 7, note 21.

stood from us – the one astern hoisting a private signal, they soon after closed and bore down upon us – they brought us to with a shot, and fired into us after we had hove to; several grape shot passed over us, and others through our sails – we struck our colors, and all went below. They boarded us and filled[4] away for Salt Key, then in sight. At 12, brought us to anchor in 2½ fathoms water, under the island. On boarding us, they drove every person below except the captain, and put on the skylight and hatches.¶

[On the] 16th, the captain and his papers having been examined on deck, some of the pirates entered the cabin, where the mate and passengers were confined; they interrogated us as to the cargo and destination of the vessel, behaved politely, encouraged us not to feel alarmed, as they intended us no injury. The captain was then ordered into the cabin, after which the whole company were taken individually upon deck, and required to confess if there was money on board, and there being none, negative answers were of course given.¶

Having proceeded through the examination of the whole, threatening, at the same time, if they found any money, our lives should pay the forfeit, they again ordered us, with the crew, into the cabin, threw a blanket over the companion way, and placed a guard over us – the slaves were in the meanwhile kept in the hold, a guard posted over them. After the lapse of a quarter of an hour, during which the pirates were making preparations to torture us into a confession that we had money on board, we were again summoned upon deck, beginning with the sailors, then the captain, mate and passengers. (The passengers were called in the following order, viz. Stephen W. Wikoff, [C]aptain John Campbell,[5] Wm. Inskeep, Chas. A. Warfield, Wm. Campbell.) Those who remained behind in the cabin, from the sound of arms, the agonizing groans and the prayers of their fellow passengers who went before them, and from the termination of their wo[e]ful sufferings by the report of pistols, were convinced they were to suffer a cruel death. So regular and systematic were the arrangements, and so well calculated to inspire terror and to fill the breast of all with the most dreadful apprehensions, that every man marched upon the deck expecting to meet inevitable death.¶

We were all in succession ordered upon the deck and made to run the gauntlet through fifteen or twenty most ferocious and barbarous monsters disguised in the shape of human beings, from the cabin to the windlass, being beaten most cruelly and unmercifully with swords and pistols, until death would have been a welcome visitor. We were then ordered to sit upon the windlass, with our backs turned to them, there to be shot – they put the pistols to our heads and fired them – it is im-

---

4 To fill is to control the yards, using braces (ropes) "so that the wind strikes the after side of the sails, and advances the ship in her course, after the sails had been shivering [fluttering], or braced aback" (Smyth, *Lexicon*, 127, 295, 619).

5 Note that the vessel's captain is identified as Wing Howland in the introduction to this extract.

possible to describe our feelings, when, after the report of the pistols, we found ourselves still alive. This was the system of terror they adopted to compel us into a disclosure of our hidden riches, as they imagined. We were immediately, as we were
successively d[i]spatched, ordered into the forecastle, there to await their further
vengeance. Language fails to convey an adequate conception of our astonishment
and agreeable surprise when we beheld our fellow passengers, who we believed
were sacrificed to Spanish cupidity and sunk into their watery graves, still breathing
the breath of life, but whose countenances still communicated the cruel apprehension that harassed their minds.¶

In this place we remained ruminating upon our situations and anticipating the most
horrid consequences of Spanish barbarity. (It is worth while to mention, that, when
we were brought to the windlass, we found it bloody, those hellhounds of war having,
in order to convince us of the murder of our fellow passengers, killed a duck and
sprinkled its blood on and about the windlass.) A sailor, who had secreted himself,
being discovered, was barbarously beaten; the poor fellow believing that we were all
dead, in order to obtain some cessation of his tortures, told the pirates that he knew
Mr. Wikoff had a box of money in the hold; to get at this box they cut the cabin floor
away and broke a few of the lockers, but their search was in vain, for there was no
money; they then re-commenced to mal-treat the sailor, who persisted in declaring
that he knew there was a box of money on board; not being able to find it, they beat
the sailor most cruelly. Mr. Wikoff was then ordered on deck – as he was ascending a
ruffian stabbed him in the thigh with a stiletto – being on deck, he was again barbarously treated, being stabbed in several places and beaten with swords and pistols
– in vain he declared he had no more money – in vain he declared his ignorance of
there being any on board; to cap the climax of human suffering, they put a rope
around his neck and hoisted him up to the yard arm, then dropped him almost lifeless into the chains,[6] then struck him with swords, calling out for money; but he was
too far gone to answer – they again hauled him up to the yard arm, and when he
was apparently dead, they dropped him into the water, then drew him up and threw
him into the long boat, which was alongside the brig – when he was able to move,
they drew him on deck, and beat him back into the forecastle. At the sight of him,
bleeding profusely from several wounds, weakened from the loss of blood, and almost drowned, we all again were certain of undergoing the same cruel treatment. In
this horrid state of suspense we were suffered to remain for hours.¶

Being disappointed in the object of their pursuit, they commenced to plunder the brig
of every thing that was valuable – the captain of all the brig's papers, and his desk

---

6   Pronounced chain-wales or channels, *chains* refers to "a small platform on either side of a ship from which the
    leadsman took soundings to ascertain the depth of water." Also: the "wooden projections from the sides of square-
    rigged ships, abreast of each mast, which carry the chain-plates," these being metal strips bolted to the ship's side,
    which themselves "carry the deadeyes or rigging screws to which the standing rigging is secured" (Dear and
    Kemp, *Companion*, 96).

with all his private papers, and the passengers of all their valuable papers, and trunks, with all their contents; they robbed us all our clothing, watches, breast pins, and in fact of every thing except what we had on our backs. About the same time that they brought the *Aurilla* to anchor, they brought the brig *Hiram*, of Newport, [C]aptain Weeks, and, as near as we could ascertain, the captain and his crew suffered severely. About five hours after they had captured us, they saw three sail crossing the bank – they ordered the captain to remain until morning for further orders, and that if he attempted to violate his orders, all hands should be murdered and the brig set on fire; then made sail in chase of the three vessels, succeeded in capturing two of them, and then returned to the anchorage near us.¶

About 8 o'clock, p.m. they came on board of us again, ransacked the brig and took away every thing they could find, even of the most trifling consideration. At this time commenced scenes of brutal outrage and shocking immorality, which it is painful to record. With their stilettos in their hands they ravished the defen[s]eless negro women in the face of every person on board! Several of the woman who resisted the gratification of their beastly appetites, were forced by menaces to yield their bodies up to the most shocking indulgences. They returned to their vessels. During the night, different parties came on board and committed the same abominable excesses on the bodies of the women.

At day light, a large party came on board and made a thorough search through the brig – not the least thing or place was left unsearched. At this time they left us scarcely any thing on board – a short allowance of provisions and a few large boxes of furniture which they were unable to take away. They took also our colors, a new hawser[7] and the brig [was] robbed of every thing. It is impossible to conjecture what would have been our lot had they not have captured so many vessels about the same time. About 10 a.m. they ordered the captain to cut his cable, and be off immediately; the order was no sooner given than executed.¶

A short time after the cable was cut, and as we were making sail, we saw a boat, with a number of the pirates on board, approaching us – we experienced the most terrible apprehensions of a speedy death. For some minutes we remained in the agony of suspense, until they boarded us and demanded of the captain, in Spanish, his carpenter; but there being no carpenter on board, or attached to the vessel, the captain answered that there was no carpenter on board. However, they still persisted that there was one, and that if he was not delivered up immediately, they would murder all of us instantly. The ruffians fell to beating the captain, then the mate most unmercifully. In the mean time, some person said that an old negro man by the name of Simon, was the carpenter: they fell to beating him, drove him into the boat and took

---

7 "A large rope or cablet [a 120-fathom line], which holds the middle degree between the cable and towline, being a size smaller than the former, and as much larger than the latter" (Smyth, *Lexicon*, 151, 374).

him off. They left us about half after ten in the morning – all hands employed in repairing our rigging and stowing away what little cargo they could not take away; the
boxes, barrels and packages nearly all broken open, some of which were robbed of
part of their contents, and others torn to pieces. As to the quantity robbed we have
not been able to ascertain.

ooooo

[*Niles' Weekly Register*, 5 October 1822, 69]

West Indies. The Kingston, (Jam.) *Chronicle*, of Aug. 3, says – The following affidavit
details a most horrid and diabolical act of piracy and murder. – The circumstances
has been laid before the admiral, at which he expressed great abhorrence: he stated,
that the first brig of war he could get hold of would be stationed in the quarter where
the piracy was committed; and that he was in hopes that some of our cruisers would
capture one of those scoundrels, to enable him to make an example.

(COPY)

Jamaica, ss.
Personally appeared before me, one of his majesty's justices of the peace, Hugh
Hamilton, mariner, who, being duly sworn, maketh oath, and saith, he sailed as mate
on board the sloop *Blessing*, Wm. Smith, master, and had made three voyages from
Oracabessa, in this island, to St. Jago de Cuba; and that in the return of the fourth
voyage, about the beginning of the present month, (but cannot name the day), were
fallen in with by a long black sch[oone]r with black mouldings, (then), the name of
Emmanuel marked on her stern, and commanded by a white man, with a mixed crew
of color and countries, among whom were English and American; that after bringing
the sloop to, the privateer, or pirates' boat came along side, and took out the captain
and his son, with all the crew, and carried them on board of the schooner, leaving the
sloop in possession of his people; that he demanded of the captain his money or his
life. The captain persisted that he had none, but proffered him the cargo, which consisted of one hundred barrels of flour, and fifty tierces of corn meal; that, on the following day, not producing any money, a plank was run out in the starboard side of
the schooner, upon which he made [C]aptain Smith walk, and that, as he approached
to the end, they tilted the plank, when he dropped in to the sea, and there, when in
the effort of swimming, the captain called for his musket, and fired at him therewith,
when he sunk, and was seen no more![8] The rest of the crew were ironed below, with
the exception of his son, a boy about 14, who witnessed the fate of his father. In the
agony of tears and crying, the captain took the but[t] end of the musket and knocked
the boy on the head, thereafter took him by the foot and hove him overboard; that,

---

8 This is one of the few documented cases of pirates making a prisoner walk the plank.

on the day following this sad event, having previously taken out all the rigging, sails, &c &c of the sloop, he set her on fire and burnt her – and, on the same day, gave the crew, consisting of three others, and him, this deponent, (having stript us of every article but what we had on our backs), the jolly boat,[9] with a bucket of water, and one biscuit each person, without compass, which we asked for, but were refused by his saying, "he would sooner give *hell!* to be off, or he would sink them." Thus we parted, and in the afternoon of the same day was picked up by the schooner *Mary Ann*, belonging to Black River, and were landed at Port Morant on the 18th July.

(Signed) HUGH HAMILTON.

ooooo

[*Niles' Weekly Register*, 2 November 1822, 134]

A DESPERATE FIGHT. The brig *Patriot*, of New York, Horace T. Jacobs, master, on her voyage from Port au Prince to New Orleans, on the 7th of September, being off Cape Antonio, and in a dead calm, was attacked by a piratical schooner of about 60 tons, with a crew of from 45 to 50 men. After noticing the approach of the enemy, we find the following account of the engagement in a New Orleans paper: "Capt. Jacobs then tacked to the south and eastward and hauled up the courses,[10] and ordered preparations to be made for action, which was readily and unanimously obeyed; the universal good spirits which pervaded all hands, (consisting of ten men and a boy) were truly conspicuous. When the schooner was close under the stern [C]aptain Jacobs hailed her, upon which she fired a whole volley of musketry into the brig – and we in return commenced upon the schooner by firing the stern gun, which was under the direction of Mr. Johnson, the chief mate, which, with the musketry, did great execution amongst them. This gun was however dismounted the 3d round, and our colors were shot away at the same time, upon which the schooner set up a terrible shout to board from the bowsprit end; her boarders were covered by an abundance of musketry, but not withstanding their vast superiority they were very gallantly repulsed. She then set fire to the brig astern, by throwing fired wads[11] into the cabin windows and into the stern boat, which was happily extinguished without damage. She then made another attempt to board, but was equally unsuccessful. By this time her fire considerably abated, and we could perceive an almost clear deck on board of her, and that she manifested a willingness to get clear of us. She asked for quarters repeatedly, but it was suspected to be a trick, (and regarded as such), to get a sight of the people and knock them off. She had much difficulty in getting clear of the brig, as her jib-boom and some of her ropes forward had got foul of the brig's davi[t] and the stern

---

9   A compact boat "for small work, being about 4 feet beam [widest point] to 12 feet length, with a bluff bow and very wide transom [stern]" (Smyth, *Lexicon*, 413).

10   " . . . [S]ails hanging from the lower yards of the ship. . . . " (Smyth, *Lexicon*, 218).

11   Wads of paper or other combustible materials were normally tamped into cannon muzzles as part of the loading process to keep gunpowder and shot from spilling out.

boat's bow. Seven men could only be counted on her deck with the glass when she was a half mile off. The brig's rigging and sails are very much cut up: Captain Jacobs was wounded in the head by a musket ball and is supposed to have fractured his skull. He died of a lockjaw[12] and violent convulsive fits on the night of the 12th inst. He has left a wife who was on board in the action, to lament his loss; he had only been married a little more than three months. Mr. Johnson, chief mate, to whom reference has already been made, is the only surviving officer of the brig, and was wounded in the thigh by a musket ball. He is much to be praised for his good and persevering conduct. Mr. J.D. Walker, of New York, doing 2nd mate's duty, was killed in the action.["]

["]The following persons, comprising the crew of the said brig, to wit: Robert Greenoh, Thomas Stanley, Robert Mins, Henry Wilson, alias John Cotton, Henry Brown, Wm. Brown and Jerry Dedon, are deserving of every encouragement for their intrepid conduct against an unequal force, as well as their dutiful obedience throughout to Mr. Johnson, in bringing the brig hither.["]

ooooo

[*Niles' Weekly Register*, 7 December 1822, 211–212]

THE PIRATES OF CUBA. The following extract of a letter from an officer on board the United States schooner *Alligator*, to a friend in Washington City, may be regarded as a semi-official account of a melancholy event:

Extract. "I will now give you a brief account, in detail, of the pirate fight of the 9th inst. The *Alligator* was coming to anchor the morning previous in the port of Matanzas, when information was brought on board that an American brig and schooner had been captured some days before, and were then at anchor and in possession of a large gang of pirates in a bay on the east side of Point Hycacos,[13] about 15 leagues to the windward of Matanzas, and that the master of the brig and mate of the schooner had been sent in the preceding morning by the pirates to procure $7000 for the ransom of the two vessels, with which sum they were to return in three days on pain of their vessels being destroyed, and the officers and crew, remaining on board, treated with every severity their avaricious revenge could inflict.["]

---

12 Tetanus, or lockjaw, "results from infection of a wound by the bacterium *Clostridium tetani*, which produces a toxin (tetanus toxin). The toxin travels to the brain and spinal cord and causes the symptoms of the disease." These include "spasm of the jaw muscles, leading to difficulty in opening the mouth and swallowing ('lockjaw'); increasingly frequent, extremely painful muscle spasms, triggered by external stimuli such as touch, noise, or bright light, with the patient remaining fully conscious; spasms spreading to the chest, neck, and back; sweating; irritability; restlessness; [and] rapid pulse" (World Health Organization, *International Medical Guide for Ships*, 275).

13 Punta Hicacos, in Varadero, Cuba.

["]Having the master and mate on board, we immediately stood to sea, and proceeded to the release of their vessels. At day-light on the morning of the 9th inst. came to anchor off Point Hycacos and within one of the islands at the entrance of the bay, and about 10 or 12 miles distant from where the brig and schooner had been left at anchor, being hid from our view by intervening land. We then discovered, some little distance over small island, a ship, a brig, and schooner, lying at anchor, and, a little further to the leeward, a small schooner under sail, her deck apparently filled with men, and boats communicating between her and the vessels at anchor, the two last of which, at the same time, getting under way. With the boats of the *Alligator* chase was immediately made after the schooner, and she with her sweeps endeavoring to escape by doubling an island nearest Point Hycacos, and steering up the bay. The wind being light, after rowing three or four leagues, we had gained within reach, when the chase rounded, hoisted a *red flag*, and commenced a heavy fire of round and grape upon us. We soon regained her wake, and when within reach of our muskets commenced our fire, the men at the oars at the same time giving way to lay alongside and board on her quarter.¶

At this time, a second schooner, armed and filled with men, had commenced firing upon us, and passing some distance ahead, brailed up[14] her foresail on the starboard bow of the first, which we were now within pistol shot of, and had silenced her fire with our small arms, when her men took precipitately to their boats, four or five in number, towing on the larboard side, to get on board their consort, when our two boats (launch, [C]apt. [William Howard] Allen,[15] and cutter, [L]ieut. Dale) pulled away to cut them off. Seeing our object, they returned on board their vessel. We immediately regained our position astern to pull up and board on her quarters, returning their fire of small arms; and they again took to their oars, now on the starboard side, and escaped on board the other sch[oone]r Capt. Allen now directed a midshipman, with four men, in his gig, which was near us, to board and take possession of the first prize, and, with our two other large boats, towed immediately after the second, now reinforced with from 30 to 40 men in addition to her own, (which we have since understood to be from 60 to 80), all well furnished with small arms and boarding pikes, &c. and had gained within twice our boat's length of her stern and larboard quarter, sustaining and returning their fire, when the cutter began to veer off, and was falling round on her starboard bow, from the obstruction of killed and wounded at her oars, and the launch unable to keep way with the chase, from like causes, and [C]apt. A[llen] having previously been wounded by two musket balls, of one of which he died

---

14   Brailing is "to pull upon the brails," the latter being "ropes passing through leading blocks on the hoops of the miz[z]en-mast and gaff, and fastened to the outermost leech of the sail, in different places, to truss it close up as occasion requires" (Smyth, *Lexicon*, 128).

15   According to the monument erected in his memory in Hudson, New York (the place of his birth), Allen was born 8 July 1790, became a midshipman in 1804 and lieutenant in 1811. He served aboard USS *Argus* in its 1813 fight with HMS *Pelican* (in which it was captured). He was originally buried at Matanzas; his remains were moved to Hudson in 1833 ("Monument to Lieutenant Allen," *Niles' Weekly Register*, 14 September 1833, 40).

four hours after), both boats dropped along side the prize, and removed our killed (two) and wounded (five, two since dead) on board her. She was armed with one long 12 pounder, (on a pivot), two d[itt]o [i.e. long] 3-pounders, carriage guns, and two swivels – her *red flag nailed to the mast*. In the cabin and run were a number of bottles filled with powder, and slow matches through the corks, some of which having been lighted and extinguished, it appeared evident that the pirates had set fire to them on first leaving her, expecting she would blow up soon after our boarding, but, returning so instantly on board, they extinguished the matches, and the last time they were too closely driven in abandoning her, to take time to re-fire them.¶

The pirates now kept off, and in shore, where they were joined by another schooner, about three miles distance from us, of heavier armament than either of the others, and about thirty men on board, (according to our subsequent information), both, however, kept away under the land, and, with our prize, we stood out to the *Alligator*. Having buried our killed and taken the wounded on board, crews were sent to take possession of the brig and schooner in the bay, both of which had been cut adrift, and were found without any individual on board either. The next day, with those and the ship, brig and schooner we had first seen at anchor, all of which had been abandoned by the pirates on the *Alligator*'s coming in the morning previous, leaving orders for the two last to follow them into the bay on *pain of death*, we proceeded to Matanzas, where the remains of [C]aptain Allen were interred with military honors; an escort being furnished by the lieutenant-governor of the island and commander of Matanzas, who expressed much sympathy and regret for his death, and the deprecated, but increasing villainies that had caused it.["]

["]He had, the day previous to our first going in there, furnished arms, &c. to put on board a small American schooner, at the request of the Americans in that port, and gave her a commission to go out and re-capture the two merchant vessels. But I am digressing from my intended narrative, which, for the present, you must take as finished, only adding, that, while in Matanzas, we were informed that the pirates had lost in the action 14 killed, and that a great number were taken on shore the same afternoon wounded; among whom was the second in command, shot through the body, and since reported dead.["]

"I consider it the most hazardous and dangerous action in which I have been engaged. I cannot but deeply lament the fate of poor Allen, on whom a widowed mother and orphan sister [sic] were almost wholly dependent. Leaving them so, appeared to be his only regret in meeting his death; and his last wishes were, that the government, in whose service he had fallen, should, in requital, give due credit to his name, and extend its protecting aid to them."

The ship re-captured was the *William Henry*, of New-York, brigs *Sarah Morril*, and *Iris*, of Boston; one schooner belonged to Rochester and the other to Salem – these have since arrived in the United States, together with the pirate schooner captured. She is called the *Revenge*, and is a fine vessel. It is believed that 14 of the pirates were killed – one of their captains among them. Much respect has been paid to the memory of [L]ieut. [C]om. Allen at the various navy stations and ports of the United States. He was a very valuable officer.

There is a rumor that the British sloop of war *Tyne*[16] has had a severe fight with a large body of these villains, in which she lost 12 killed, besides wounded. But, it is said, that between 40 and 50 of the pirates were slain, and 29 of them taken prisoners.[17] [. . .]

ooooo

[*Niles' Weekly Register*, 12 April 1823, 82]

THE PIRATES. The brig *Alert*, from New Orleans, put into Havana, about 25 days since. On her arrival off the Mor[r]o [Castle] she was boarded by three piratical boats, and her captain and cook killed, and another man mortally wounded by the villains. No American vessel of war being in port, the wounded person was kindly attended by the surgeon of the British frigate *Hyperion*.[18] Every day seems to furnish new instances of the depredations of these men, and their spoils are openly disposed of at Matanzas &c. There is reason to believe that the crews of several vessels have been murdered by them. The details of their proceedings are shocking. The captain, mate and passengers of a French brig, were half-hanged, then half-drowned, and beaten and abused in the most shameful manner for hours, to make them discover if money was on board – and the vessel was visited by several small boats from the shore,

---

16 Launched in 1814, HMS *Tyne* was a 108-foot long ship, designated a 20-gun "sloop" (or sloop of war) as it was smaller than a frigate; this class of vessels was later re-rated to carry 28, then 26 guns. HMS *Tyne* began West Indies service in early 1821. It was sold in 1825 for £1,820 (Winfield, *British Warships*, 240).

17 Possibly a garbled reference to the 30 September 1822 pirate attack on the *Eliza*, a sloop hired to act as tender to HMS *Tyne*, while anchored at La Guajaba, which maritime historian Basil Lubbock placed "just west of Cayo Romana in the Old Bahama Passage." According to Lubbock's account: "The *Eliza* was manned by twenty six men headed by a master's mate, name[d] Hugh Nurse and a mid[shipman] named White; her only gun was a twelve-pounder carronade. She was attacked by the pirate schooner, *El Diableto*, mounting six broadside guns and with a complement of forty men, and the felucca *Firme Union*, of five guns and thirty five men. Here is a first-hand report of the fight:– 'At eight thirty p.m. the schooner brought up at a short distance, and without hailing, fired two shots at the *Eliza*. Mr. Nurse immediately opened a fire from his only gun, loaded with round and grape, supported by musketry; and after six rounds, the slaughter on the pirate's deck must have been great, as the cries of the wounded were hideous. The felucca now bore down between the schooner and the *Eliza*, with the evident intention of running alongside the latter, but which she frustrated by getting under her bow and instantly boarding. The defence of the freebooters was desperate: the captain and nine men were killed and the remaining part of the crew, with the exception of four men, two of whom were severely wounded, jumped overboard – She appeared to have been fully prepared for action. Shot were heating, and the men were armed with cutlasses, each having a long knife in his left hand. On our side two seamen were killed, and Mr. Nurse and six men sever[e]lly wounded. Perhaps in few actions of the kind has a greater degree of cool and determined gallantry been displayed.' The *Diableto* managed to escape, whilst the *Eliza* was desperately engaged in capturing the felucca" (Lubbock, *Cruisers, Corsairs and Slavers*, 75–76).

18 HMS *Hyperion* was a 143-foot long, 32-gun frigate launched in 1807; its service included capturing the American privateer *Rattlesnake* in 1814 (Winfield, *British Warships*, 174).

which were loaded with her cargo. In another instance, they used a lady in the same way. It is extremely dangerous now either to enter or leave the port of Havana. It is stated that to the eastward of Matanzas, the houses are filled with goods. In general, they ask only a doubloon for a horse load of merchandise. The following however, is the Matanzas *piratical price current*, carefully corrected, from actual sales, up to the last date. Russia sheeting, fair to good, 6 dollars; gin, per case one dollar and fifty cents; nails, per cask, four dollars; assorted invoices six hundred dollars, for eight thousand first cost.

The brig *Bellisarius*, of Kennebunk [Maine], has arrived at the Balize, for New-Orleans. When on her voyage from Port au Prince for Campeachy [Campeche], she was boarded off the harbor of the latter by a piratical schooner, of about 40 tons, and manned by 30 or 40 men, who asked for money, but the captain (Parkins) denied having any. They then stabbed him in several places and cut off one of his arms, when he told them w[h]ere the money was, (200 doubloons), which they took, and proceeded to murder him in the most inhuman manner. He was first deprived of the other arm and one of his legs. They then dipped oakum in oil, put some in his mouth and under him – set it on fire, and thus terminated his sufferings!!! The mate was stabbed with a saber in the thigh. They also robbed the brig of anchors and cables, sails, rigging, quadrants, charts, books, papers, and nearly all the provisions and water. On the passage from Campeachy to the Balize she was providentially supplied with provisions, &c. by several vessels which she fell in with, or her people must inevitably have perished.

The British cutter *Grecian*[19] has captured the famous pirate *La [G]ata*,[20] off the isle of Pines.[21] The cutter had 50 men, the pirate 100 men and 8 guns – it was believed that about 50 of the crew of the latter were killed, but only three prisoners were made, the rest made their escape on shore. Considerable quantities of goods were found on board the prize. The *Grecian* was conveying the prisoners to Jamaica, where, it seems, there is more law to reach cases of piracy than we have in the United States.

It would be sickening to relate all the cases of piracy and outrage that occur off the coasts of Cuba, and assassinations seem frequent even in Havana. A sailor belonging to the ship *Governor Tompkins* was lately found dead in the dock with a knife sticking in his neck, having been murdered by the Spaniards. A coroner's inquest was held over the body for which the captain of the ship had to pay the sum of $33.08.

---

19   The 10-gun HMS *Grecian* was a 69-foot long ex-revenue cutter, originally named *Dolphin* (Colledge, *Royal Navy*, 167).

20   *La Gata* (its name is Spanish for "cat" or "she-cat") was an 88-ton, 61-foot long schooner built at Baltimore in 1821 (Lubbock, *Cruisers, Corsairs & Slavers*, 80).

21   Isla de Pinos, or Isle of Pines, the former name of Isla de la Juventud (Isle of Youth), to the south of Cuba's western coast. Pinos, according to an 1832 book, "has several good and secure roads, but it is uninhabited, except by a few fishermen who occasionally dwell on its coasts. The only animals on it are goats, but it abounds in pastures and large trees. Pinos is about 42 miles long . . . " (Bell, *A System of Geography*, VI:322).

Captain David Porter, USN, possibly by John Trumbull (US Naval Historical Foundation, 80-G-K-17588).

ooooo

[Niles' Weekly Register, 19 April 1823, 98]

Com. Porter,[22] in the *Peacock*,[23] reached Matanzas about the 26th of March. He had divided his light squadron into four parts, to scour the coasts. The *Peacock* and two of the schooners had "left no hole or corner unsearched" for the distance of 300 miles – under severe duty, but without success. Several vessels of a suspicious character had been fallen in with, but nothing sufficient appeared to justify their detention. The pirates change their shapes daily. Their depredations are spoke[n] of as horrible –

---

22   David Porter (1780–1843) joined the U.S. navy in 1798; in February 1799 he saw action on *USS Constellation* in its Quasi-War battle with the French warship *L'Insurgente*. He was among those taken prisoner in Tripoli on the *Philadelphia*. He had a stellar War of 1812 record as captain of *USS Essex*, taking 400 prizes until defeated by British warships early in 1814. He was made commodore of the West Indies Squadron in 1823. In November, 1824, Porter invaded Fajardo, in eastern Puerto Rico, with 200 sailors and marines, "demanding an apology for the mistreatment of one of his officers . . . He threatened to shell 'Foxhardo' if his demands were not carried out. When Porter returned to the United States in early 1825 he was court-martialed for his actions and suspended from duty for six months." He subsequently resigned from American service and accepted the job of heading Mexico's navy, which he did from 1829–1829. Returning to the U.S, he became a diplomat and died in Turkey (Morris and Kearns, *Historical Dictionary*, 242, 244).

23   A 117-foot long, 509-ton, 22-gun "sloop of war," *USS Peacock* was launched in 1813. It defeated HMS *Epervier* in early 1814, and took 14 more prizes during a long cruise from June–October. It continued taking British craft as late as June 1815, its commander not knowing peace had been signed. It served as Porter's flagship in the West India Squadron. After many more cruises and operations, it was decommissioned in 1827 and broken up the following year (Mooney, *Fighting Ships*, V:240–241).

whole ships' crews are often murdered by them. A letter says – "We were surprised to hear, on our arrival, that the governor of the island (Cuba) had given orders to all the governors and commandants of districts, forbidding our entrance into any of the ports. It is to be hoped we may have no difficulty with them; but, if we do, the fault will not be on our side."

There was a fleet of American vessels at Matanzas, waiting for convoy; some had been ready for sea for twenty days – there was not a vessel on the coast to protect them. Com. Porter's presence secured it to them.

Some one in Philadelphia, who has kept a list of piratical acts since the cessation of hostilities in 1815, makes them amount to *three thousand and two*.[24] [. . .] It is also said that a battle took place [near Cape Antonio] between some British boats, from a sloop of war, and a schooner of six guns and sixty men, supposed to be the *Gata*. The pirate blew up – when the smoke dispersed, twenty five men were seen swimming in the water, to whom no quarter was given.[25]

ooooo

[*Niles' Weekly Register*, 26 April 1823, 114]

THE PIRATES. The account of the total destruction of the pirate *La [G]ata* by the British cutter *Grecian*, is fully confirmed – she was blown up; some of her crew, as they swam ashore, were assailed by the *Hyperion*, and nearly every one of them killed.

It is stated that a British sloop of war has captured a piratical vessel that had a crew of sixty men under command of the famous Laf[fit]e. He hoisted the bloody flag and refused quarter, and fought until nearly every man was killed or wounded – Laf[fit]e being among the former.[26]

The schooner *Pilot*, of Norfolk, was lately captured by the pirates off Matanzas – and her crew much abused; but they were put ashore, and the wretches went on a cruise in the prize, and captured and robbed two vessels within *two miles of the Mor[r]o*

---

24   This statement would be later disowned. See entry for 17 May.

25   According to Lubbock (*Cruisers, Corsairs & Slavers*, 76–77), the battle between the cutter HMS *Grecian*, under Lt. John Cawley, and the pirate vessel *La Gata* [commanded by one Josef Sabina] took place on 20 March 1823, among reefs to the east of the Isle of Pines. "The pirate schooner *La Gata*, it seems, was not entirely destroyed, as a quantity of prize goods were found in her hold. The [five] prisoners were taken back to Jamaica and hanged at Gallow's Point."

26   This is "clearly a garbled account," according to Davis (*Pirates Laffite*, 462–464, 642n67). Laffite was mortally wounded in a nighttime battle in the Gulf of Honduras in February, 1823, between his privateer *General Santander* and an unidentified schooner and brigantine. "Laffite had unwittingly taken on either Spanish privateers or warships, or perhaps elements of a British squadron patrolling for pirates. They might even have been pirates themselves, though, if so, they were unusually well armed."

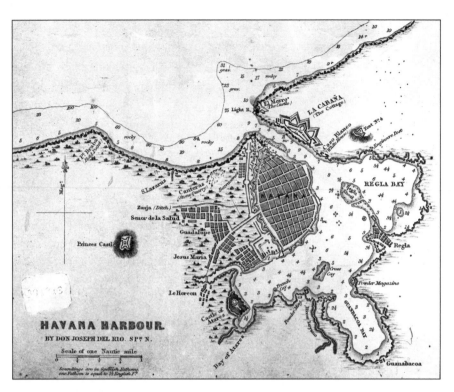

Map of Havana Harbor, Island of Cuba, the Morro Castle (El Morro) is visible at upper right center (courtesy of Mystic Seaport, G.W. Blunt Library Collection, #95-9-5).

castle, Havana – but, a few days after, the U.S. schooner *Jackall*[27] fell in with her and made a re-capture, securing, however, only one of the pirates, but several of them were killed in the action, fighting desperately. It is reported that five captures have been made by [C]om. Porter's squadron, which has been very actively employed. Some of the vessels had stopped at Port Allen, Thompson's Island, or Key West.[28] They had afforded convoy to many vessels, and the most of the pirates appeared to have retired for the present.

---

27 Porter in January 1823 bought the 47-ton, *Jackal* or *Jackall* in Baltimore for service with the "Mosquito Fleet." Commanded by Lt. T.H. Stevens, it mounted three guns, and was initially among several navy vessels "assigned to the northwestern coast of Cuba, where they searched each bay, inlet, and key and escorted merchantmen through the dangerous waters." After helping rescue the crew of the *USS Ferret* when it capsized in February, 1825, *Jackal* was found to be "seriously in need of repair, [and] was sold" (Mooney, *Fighting Ships*, III:482–483).

28 American navy officials attempted to re-name Key West both Allenton (for William Howard Allen, killed by pirates) and Thompson's Island (for the Secretary of the Navy). Allenton was also the name of a settlement on the island, evidently rendered here as "Port Allen" (Burke, *Streets of Key West*, 107–108; and Ticknor, "Yellow Fever," 214–215). From a contemporary description: "'Thompson's island' is about 7 miles long and 2 broad; it is located 75 miles N[orth] by W[est] from Havana, 85 from Matanzas, and about 30 from the main land of Florida. Its harbor, is a very fine one, and has long been the resort of vessels in rough weather, on which account it is considered as a very valuable acquisition to the United States. The east part lies open to the sea, the northern and western are surrounded by small sand keys. The port is said to be equal to any on the gulf of Mexico, for safety or depth of water, and may become the rendezvous of our navy employed in those seas" ("Valuable Acquisition," *Niles' Weekly Register*, 11 May, 1822, 176).

ooooo

[Niles' Weekly Register, 3 May 1823, 129]

HISTORY OF THE PIRATES. By way of Nassau, we learn that the boats of the British vessels of war *Tyne* and *Thracian*[29] had had a desperate fight with a pirate schooner called the *Zaragozana*,[30] having a crew of 70 or 80 desperadoes. After a sharp battle of 55 minutes, the British succeeded in boarding the pirate and securing 28 prisoners – 10 of her crew had been killed, and the rest escaped on shore. One seam[a]n was killed and five wounded on the other side. It was afterwards stated that sixteen of the fugitive wretches had been taken by a Spanish force from Barracoa.[31] The British have lately taken possession of certain persons detected in the act of purchasing goods of the pirates, and it was thought that they ought to be treated as principals.

Some particulars of the recapture of the *Pilot*, of Norfolk, have been received. The pirates had armed her with one gun, muskets, &c. for a cruiser. She was attacked by two of the cutters, under command of [L]ieut. [Cornelius] Stribling[32] – the fight lasted about 15 minutes, for she had 36 men on board. All these made their escape except two who were killed, and one taken prisoner, though hotly pursued by the marines. Not one man in the boats was injured.

Subsequent accounts say that twelve or fourteen bodies, of the crew of the piratical schooner *Pilot*, re-captured by the boats of the squadron, who were either killed or drowned at the time her re-captured, had drifted on shore near the spot, on the coast of Cuba, where she was taken.

At the latest date from this quarter, Com. Porter was at Matanzas, with the *Sea Gull*,[33] &c. and all the squadron was actually employed in pirate-hunting and convoying vessels.

ooooo

---

29 The 100-foot long HMS *Thracian* was launched in 1809 as an 18-gun "brig-sloop." It defeated French privateers in 1811 and 1814. Altered to a "ship-sloop" rigging design in 1822, it initially served in the West Indies under Commodore John W. Roberts, succeeded in mid-1823 by Commodore Andrew Forbes. (Winfield, *British Warships*, 300; Colledge and Warlow, *Royal Navy*, 404).

30 The fight, on 31 March 1823, took place outside the entrance to Puerta de Mata, which a modern authority places "on the eastern tip of Cuba"; the *Zaragozana* was a 115-ton, 76-foot long schooner built at Baltimore in 1820 (Wombwell, *Long War Against Piracy*, 48; Lubbock, *Cruisers, Corsairs & Slavers*, 79–80).

31 On the north coast of Cuba's eastern tip, off the Bahia de Miel.

32 Stribling (1796–1880) would later serve as superintendent of the U.S. Naval Academy and in various senior commands; during the Civil War he served the Union commanding the East Gulf Blockading Squadron. He held the rank of rear admiral at the time of his death (Mooney, *Fighting Ships*, VI:652–3).

33 Launched in 1818 as a civilian side-wheel steamer, the Navy purchased and renamed this 150-ton vessel in late 1822, fitting it with sails and five cannon. Its service with the West Indies Squadron ended in July 1825; it subsequently became a receiving ship for recruits in Philadelphia (Mooney, *Fighting Ships*, VI:402).

[*Niles' Weekly Register*, 17 May 1823, 163]

HISTORY OF THE PIRATES, &c. The depredations of the Cuba pirates have very nearly ceased, since the arrival of [C]ommodore Porter. The *Peacock* is laid up at Allentown [Key West], and her officers and crew dispersed among the small vessels, several of which have been added to the squadron, and all are actively employed. The commodore has made such arrangements, that he holds constant communication with all the vessels under his command, and an excellent system of operations appears to have been adopted. [. . .]

The Jamaica papers furnish us with the particulars of the capture of the piratical vessels *La Gata* and *Zaragozana*, by British cruisers. The former was blown up, and all or nearly all her crew perished – 80 or 90 in number. Of the crew of the latter 10 were killed, 15 wounded, 14 taken by the Spaniards on shore, and 28 brought to Jamaica for trial. There are between 40 and 50 prisoners now there, several other small vessels having been taken.

The noted pirate William Smith[34] has been recognized and arrested at Havana. It was supposed that he would be delivered up to the British.

The U.S. ship *Hornet*[35] and brig *Enterprize*, have sailed to join the squadron under [C]ommodore Porter. Our last accounts from the commodore say that he was at Havana in the steam galliot *Sea Gull*, keeping a sharp look-out for certain vessels supposed to be fitting at the Regla[5] for piratical expeditions, one of which, it is said, will have 150 men!

A letter from an officer of the U.S. schooner *Wild Cat*,[36] dated at sea, on the 27th ult. reprobates the conduct of those persons who publish, in the American papers, false and extravagant accounts of the capture and destruction of American vessels and murder of American citizens, even in sight of [C]ommodore Porter's squadron, &c. The outrages committed upon our commerce are quite sufficient, in themselves, without any undue attempts to swell the list, and exaggerate the enormities. Such misrepresentations are only calculated to cast a doubt over those barbarities which really

---

34   Smith allegedly in 1822 "plundered and burnt . . . the brig *Alexander*, of Glasgow, and murdered Captain Ferguson, her commander . . ." (*Independent Chronicle & Boston Patriot*, 14 May 1823, 2).

35   USS *Hornet* was launched in 1805 as a brig, but was "rebuilt and ship-rigged" in 1810–1811. It served in the War of 1812, slipping the British blockade of New London late in 1814. It "continued to attack British ships, unaware that the war was over. After a number of cruises in West Indian, European, and Caribbean waters, the *Hornet* left Pensacola on March 4, 1829, and was never seen again." It sank with no survivors off Tampico on a September storm (Morris and Kearns, *Historical Dictionary*, 127).

36   The U.S. Navy bought this shallow-draft, 48-ton schooner in 1822 for service in Porter's "Mosquito Fleet." Yellow fever outbreaks interrupted its routine of patrol and escort duty. It sank in an October, 1824 storm (Mooney, *Fighting Ships*, VIII:301).

exist.[37] The officers and crew of the *Wild Cat* were all in good health – she had under convoy 16 sail of vessels from Havana. [. . .]

ooooo

[*Niles' Weekly Register*, 14 June 1823, 240.]

"*Jamaica*. The captain [Cayatano Aragonez] of the pirate vessel *Zaragozana* ha[s] been found guilty of piracy. The crew were to be tried. It is probable that the whole of them will be executed."

ooooo

[*Niles' Weekly Register*, 21 June 1823, 245]

PIRATES. Two or three vessels are reported as having been lately captured by the pirates on the south side of Cuba – and it was feared that the crew of one of them had been murdered. The late master of one of the captured vessels had reached Havana. Several vessels of [C]om. Porter's squadron immediately sailed in quest of the offenders. It was rumored that a large piratical schooner was cruising off Campeachy, at the latter end of last month. [. . .]

The U.S. brig *Enterprize* has sailed from St. Thomas, in search of a piratical vessel said to be at the Five Islands.[38]

Twenty of the pirates lately sent to Jamaica, having been tried and found guilty, were executed on the 16th of May.[39]

ooooo

[*Niles' Weekly Register*, 12 July 1823, 304]

Pirates. The U.S. schooner *Ferret*,[40] [L]ieut. [C]om. T.M. Newell, has had an engagement with seven piratical boats, which he fell in with at Escondido about twelve miles west of Matanzas. The pirates being completely covered by a reef, hauled up their boats, and placed themselves behind the rocks – the *Ferret*, having but a small boat, could not send in more than six men. [L]ieut. Newell, finding it only a waste of am-

37 Footnote in original text: "It appears that the late presented enumeration of captures by the pirates, was the mere coinage of the brain of one of our editors – as he himself has confessed!"
38 A group of small islands in Trinidad's Gulf of Paria.
39 "The *Zaragozana* prisoners were all hanged on a gigantic gallows on the Palisadoes at Port Royal to the great satisfaction of [Jamaica Station commander] Sir Charles Rowley, who sailed for home very soon after, being succeeded by Vice-Admiral Sir Lawrence Halsted" (Lubbock, *Cruisers, Corsairs and Slavers*, 79).
40 A 51-ton schooner carrying three cannon, *USS Ferret* capsized in an 1825 gale, its survivors aided by USS *Jackal* (Mooney, *Fighting Ships*, II:402–403).

munition, left them and made sail for Matanzas in order to get a suitable boat and return back before they could make their escape – but, unfortunately, the contrary wind
and current frustrated him in his views. However, early the next morning, he fell in
with an English brig; the captain very readily furnished [L]ieut. N[ewell] with a boat
with which the *Ferret* immediately made for the same place but, on coming near, had
the mortification to find that the villains had decamped.

The British ship of war *Tamar*,[41] [C]apt. [Thomas] Herbert,[42] has captured a piratical
schooner, of two guns and fifteen men – and, also, re-captured the American brig
Tropic, which the pirate had taken.

ooooo

[*Niles' Weekly Register*, 2 August 1823, 340–341]

THE PIRATES OF CUBA. We have, almost every day, heard of something that evi-
denced that activity of [C]om. Porter and the officers and men under his command;
but, as yet, their industry and zeal was rather sh[o]wn in the *suppression* of piracy
than the *punishment* of it: at last, however, an opportunity has offered for inflicting
the latter, as detailed in the following letter, published in the *National Intelligencer*,
dated Matanzas, July 10 –

"I have the pleasure of informing you of a brilliant achievement obtained against the
pirates on the 5th inst. by two barges attached to [C]ommodore Porter's squadron, the
Gallinipper, [L]ieut. [W.H.] Watson, 13 men, and the *Musquito*, [L]ieut. [William]
Inman, 10 men.[43] The barges were returning from a cruise to windward; when they
were near Jugupa bay, 13 leagues to windward of this port, they entered it – it being
a rendezvous for pirates: they immediately discovered a large schooner under way,
which they supposed to be a patriot privateer; and as their stores were nearly exhausted, they hoped to obtain some supplies from her; they therefore made sail in
pursuit. When they were within cannon shot distance, she rounded to and fired her
long gun, at the same time r[a]n up the bloody flag, directing her course towards the
shore, continuing to fire without effect; when she had got within a short distance of
the shore she came to with springs on her cable,[44] continuing to fire; and when the

---

41 HMS *Tamar* was a 108-foot long, 26-gun 6th rate warship, launched in 1814. It was converted to a coal hulk in
1831 and sold six years later (Colledge and Warlow, *Royal Navy*, 396).

42 Sir Thomas Herbert (1793–1861), made a Knight of the Order of the Bath in 1841 for service in the First Opium
War. He was later vice-admiral and Member of Parliament ("Vice-Admiral Sir Thomas Herbert, KCB," *The Gentleman's Magazine and Historical Review*, October 1861, 445–446.

43 *Gallinipper* was a converted ship's boat, refitted with "sails and double-banked oars"; *Mosquito* was originally a
small cutter built for the frigate *Potomac*. Both saw extensive service with Porter's fleet (Mooney, *Fighting Ships*,
III:10–11 and IV:442).

44 Spring lines are used for adjusting a moored or docked vessel's angle relative to incoming waves. A spring line
may be attached to an anchor ("springing the rode") to turn the vessel into the waves of a surge to minimize the
rocking motion felt aboard (Pinney, "Springing the Rode," and correspondence with John Frayler, 6 March,
2011).

barges were within 30 yards, they fired their muskets without touching boat or man; our men gave three cheers, and prepared to board; the pirates, discovering their intention, jumped into the water, when the barge-men, calling on the name of 'Allen,' commenced a destructive slaughter, killing them in the water and as they landed; so exasperated were our men, that it was impossible for their officers to restrain them, and many were killed after orders were given to grant quarters: Twenty seven dead were counted, some sunk, five taken prisoners by the bargemen, and eight taken by a party of Spaniards on shore; the officers calculated that from 30 to 35 were killed. The schooner mounted a long nine[-]pounder on a pivot, and 4 fours,[45] with every other necessary armament, and a crew of from 50 to 60 men, and ought to have blown the barges to atoms, commanded by the notorious *Diableto* or Little Devil; this statement I have from [L]ieut. Watson himself, and it is certainly the most decisive operation that has been effected against those murderers, either by the English or American force.

This affair occurred on the same spot where the brave Allen fell about one year since."

Another account states that those who reached the shore, say they were not pirates but *fishermen* but the plea will hardly avail them. A third says that "Diableto" himself had escaped – that's a pity; but a fourth declares that he was killed – and that's well. The prize has been sent to Thompson's Island.

It is reported that [L]ieut. [F.H.] Gregory, of the *Grampus*,[46] has discovered a band of pirates, two or three hundred strong, and sent to [C]om. Porter for reinforcements, that he may attack them.

Twenty more pirates have been hung at Kingston, Jam[aica] and yet a large piratical brig is said to be cruising off the island! A British sloop of war has lately captured a pirate schooner off St. Domingo with a crew of 60 men, 200,000 dollars in specie, and other valuable articles on board; and the brig *Vestal*[47] has sent another pirate schooner to New Providence. "Old Tom," a famous pirate, has been hung at St. Bartholomew's. It is now regarded as certain that the brig *Mechanic*, of New York, was captured and burnt by the pirates, in the West Indies, and that her master and his crew, with several passengers, were murdered. The fact is stated to be confessed by some of the wretches now in prison in Cuba.

ooooo

---

45 I.e., four-pounder cannons.

46 Launched in August 1821, at 171 tons and 97-feet long USS *Grampus* was the largest of five schooners built especially for navy service in the West Indies. A year after its launch, *Grampus* captured a Puerto-Rico-based pirate brig, *Palmyra* (Mooney, *Fighting Ships*, III:130).

47 The only HMS *Vestal* listed as being in service at this time was a 10-gun brig, launched in Bombay in 1809 (Colledge and Warlow, *Royal Navy*, 429).

A felucca (artist unknown). See the note in Chapter 6 for more on this maritime design.

[*Niles' Weekly Register*, 26 June 1824, 270]

West Indies. The British ship *Hussar*[48] has arrived at Jamaica, from a cruise after the pirates off the isle of Pines. They had succeeded in destroying Pepe['s][49] felucca, a new vessel on her second cruise, with 3 guns; 2 schooners, a felucca-rigged boat, with a 3-pounder, a 36[-]feet row boat, and three large piratical canoes. They had killed several pirates and brought in five for trial – the remainder of the crews of the felucca were yet on the isle of Pines and could hardly escape, being hunted and watched under the orders of captain [John George] Graham,[50] of the *Icarus*.[51] The Cuba pirates seem especially hostile to English traders on the coast – and the most horrible murders are often added to robbery. Take the following account from the Montego (Jamaica) *Gazette*: –

> The sloop *Endeavor* sailed from hence some time since, to fish for turtle among the keys, and was fallen in with by a felucca[-]rigg[e]d vessel, who sent their boat on board. It appeared that a dog on board the *Endeavor* attempted to bite the first of the pirates who came on deck, and that the fellow immediately killed the

---

48 HMS *Hussar* was a 154-foot long 38-gun frigate launched in 1807; it served in both the East and West Indies at various times; it was sent to the Jamaica station in 1823 (Winfield, *British Warships*, 171).

49 Pepe, according to sources quoted in an 1829 article, "was, with other pirates, infesting the Isle of Pines when [Captain John George Graham] was endeavouring, by order of the government, to extirpate them. A boat's crew of Captain Graham's fell into their hands, and, under the direction of Pepe, every person on board was murdered." Pepe met his end by accident, "amusing himself firing in the woods, when his gun burst and shattered his arm. Subsequently a British marine came upon him, and pursued him with his arm in a sling. Pepe swam a river, the marine did the same, but Pepe escaped. Next day Pepe was found dead not far from the river, with maggots in his arm, mortification having caused his death" ("Pepe the Pirate," *Phrenological Journal and Miscellany*, 6(21) Aug. 1829, 98, 100–101).

50 Graham's commission as captain dated from 3 October 1825 (*A List of the Flag Officers*, 33). He was on the retired list by January 1854, at which time he was "promoted to be Retired Rear-Admiral" (Behan, *Bulletins*, 136).

51 The 10-gun brig-sloop HMS *Icarus* had been launched at Portsmouth in 1814 (Colledge and Warlow, *Royal Navy*, 192).

dog. James Whittaker, the captain of the *Endeavor*, remonstrated with him for having killed the dog. The other said, ["]I will serve you the same,["] and instantly stabbed him three times in the breast, and threw him overboard. Whittaker beginning to swim, he leveled his musket and shot him in the shoulder: finding he still continued to swim, he got in the boat and pulled after him, hauled his head up on the gunnel [gunwale] of the boat, and cut his throat, when he immediately sunk. He then returned on board the *Endeavor*, and, with the other pirates, killed all the crew (3 other persons) except David Smith, who jumped overboard and succeed in getting on shore.

ooooo

[*Niles' Weekly Register*, 20 November 1824, 189–190]

THE PIRATES. The brig *Laura Ann*, of New York, has been captured off the coast of Cuba by the pirates, who murdered all the crew except one, who concealed himself below. After they had plundered the brig, they set fire to her and abandoned her – and the man who had secreted himself, then made his escape through the flames and swam to the shore. Several other vessels are mentioned as missing, the crews of which are supposed to have been all murdered.

Norfolk, November 12. Captain Banks, of the schooner *Princess Ann*, arrived at this port on Wednesday from Havana, whence she sailed on the 1st inst. was informed, just before his departu[r]e, that the Colombian private armed schooner *La Zulma*, had had an engagement off Point Yeacos [Punta Hicacos] with two piratical schooners, and after a severe conflict, succeeded in capturing one of them, and sinking the other. – Fifteen of the crew of the captured schooner were found dead on the decks after the action; and all on board the one sunk, went down with her – not one was saved, The Colombians had ten men killed. There were two other schooners in company with them when first discovered by the *La Zulma*, but they made off, and stood in towards the land.

(The commander of the *La Zulma* has been very polite and kind in giving protection and convoy to many American vessels, and exceedingly active in harassing the Spaniards. He had made several prizes.)

OFFICIAL CORRESPONDENCE
U.S. Sch[oone]r *Porpoise*, Matanzas, 24th Oct. 1824.

SIR: I have the honor to inform you, that, after leaving the convoy from Havana, I stretched in for this port, where I anchored on the evening of the 18th. On inquiry, I was informed, no piracies had been recently committed in this vicinity. I, however, determined to dispatch the boats secretly from the harbor, and examine the adjacent bays and inlets. On the night of the 19th, I placed them under command of [L]ieut. Hunter, and acting [L]ieut. Johnson, with orders to examine about Point Yeacos [Punta Hicacos], Sewappa [Siguapa] bay, and Cam[a]rioca, places long notorious as a retreat for pirates. On the evening of the 22d, [L]ieutenant Hunter returned with a piratical schooner of one carriage gun one new American cutter, and two other boats; one, having three men on board, he captured in Sewappa bay; every appearance justified the suspicion of piracy. The persons informed [L]ieut. Hunter their vessel had been taken by armed men, the boat they were in given in exchange, with a promise of returning in a few days, and restoring their vessel. The next day, off Cam[a]rioca, [L]ieut. Hunter discovered a suspicious schooner standing to sea, in chase of a vessel in sight – on his approach the sch[oone]r tacked and made for the shore, closely pursued by the boats. The crew abandoned the vessel, and fled to the wood, where they were sought for in vain. She proved to be a pirate mounting one gun and small arms. From the number of nautical instruments, trunks of clothing, rigging and sails, with three sets of American colors, found on board, she must have robbed several vessels; from stains of blood on the cloth[e]s and other articles on board, I fear the unfortunate persons to whom they belonged must have been murdered – no papers were discovered which could lead to the name of the vessel or vessels captured; several articles of clothing were marked "[C]aptain Shaw" – a number with the initials "A.S."; A bag on board was lettered "brig Morning Star's letter bag;" one waistcoat contained in the pocket a printed card, "Mrs. Loris' boarding-house, Charleston, S.C." and appeared to have been newly printed. A medicine chest on board was put up in New York. I have delivered the prisoners to the governor of Matanzas, and shall furnish him all the testimony in my power which can throw any light on their character. The schooner I sent out last night under command under command of acting [L]ieut. Brown in hopes of decoying some of her former comrades. I sail with convoy to-morrow, and after joining the prize at sea, shall proceed to Thompson's Island for supplies, and return to the protection of commerce on this coast. I trust, sir, should the prize be sufficiently fortunate to meet with pirates, I shall have the pleasure to give a satisfactory account of them.

I do myself the honor to enclose the correspondence relative to the capture of the vessels and prisoners.

I have the honour to be, respectfully, sir, your ob't servant,

[Lt.] CH. W. SKINNER[52]

To the hon. Samuel L. Southard, secretary of the navy.

---

52 Commander of the *Porpoise*.

(COPY)

To his excellency Don Cecelio Ayillor, governor of Matanzas:

U.S. sch[oone]r Porpoise, Matanzas, 23d Oct. 1824

I deliver to your excellency three men, captured by a detachment of my boats, a few days since, under circumstances justifying a belief of their having committed piracy. An armed schooner was also captured, which the prisoners claim as their property, alleging, in explanation, that their vessel had been forcibly seized by armed men, and, in exchange, they had received from the pirate his vessel, with a promise to return in a few days and restore their original property. Under this expectation they were anxiously awaiting her arrival. Fortunately for humanity, my boats encountered her. From the quantity of clothing, goods, and nautical instruments, found on board, she must have robbed several vessels, and from stains of blood on cloth[e]s, &c. most probably murdered the unfortunate people who fell into their hands. We found on board also, three sets of American colors. These enormities call loudly for punishment. It affords me pleasure to deliver these people to your excellency, as I am well persuaded, from your well known regard to justice, they will meet the punishment due their crimes.
If your excellency will inform me when you will receive them, they shall be landed under an escort.

I enclosed to your excellency the papers found on board; and have the honor to be, respectfully your excellency's obedient servant,

C.W. SKINNER.

(COPY)

The governor of Matanzas' Answer.

I have just received your statement of this day, relative to the capture of a small vessel, whose crew ran to the sea shore, suspected, with much reason, to be pirates, not only on account of their flight and equipment, but of some crimes committed by them. In consequence thereof, I will give my orders to receive, on the wharf, at 4 o'clock in the afternoon, the three men which you captured, and that you promised to remit me. I hope that, to-morrow, between ten and eleven, you will have the kindness to send to this government the officer and marine guards that joined in the capture of the vessel, to hear their respective information[6], as the beginning of the summary. I hope, also, that for their examination you will please send the clothes stained with blood, and other articles and arms, all of which will serve for the inquiry or search, and which will be returned whenever you require it, after the matter is finished.

I now put you in mind that the papers that you mentioned in your statement have not come to hand.

I declare to you that your recommendable services to the cause of humanity, and in favor of our commercial relations, will be worthy of praise to the superior government. And for my part, I promise you, with all the justice of the laws, and my firmness to observe them, that I will contribute to the most to the extermination of those wicked men.

With the greatest regard, I am, dear sir, yours, &c.

CECELIO AYILLOR.

To the com[mander] of the American sch[oone]r of war Porpoise.

(COPY)

U.S. schr. Porpoise, *Matanzas, 24th Oct. 1824.*
To his excellency Don Cecelio Ayillor, governor of Matanzas:

I had the honor to receive your excellency's reply to my communication, in relation to the prisoners made by this vessel, and have delivered them agreeably to your wishes. The papers which I neglected to send, I have forwarded immediately, on discovering the omission. The clothes stained with blood, and many other articles, were in a condition so filthy, I caused them to be thrown into the sea. For a corroboration of the testimony which you will receive this day, I beg leave to refer your excellency to the Spanish officer, and his interpreter, who came on board the moment of arrival, and to whom the articles alluded to were exhibited.

I have the honor to be, your excellency's obedient servant,

C.V. SKINNER.

ooooo

[U.S. Senate, 18th Congress, 2nd session, *In Senate of the United States, December 30 1824*, 1–2[53]]

UNITED STATES' COMMERCIAL AGENCY.
Be it known, that, on the day of the date hereof,[54] before me, John Mountain, Vice Commercial Agent of the United States of America, at the city of Havana, personally came and appeared George Brown, of New York, seaman, aged twenty-one years and upwards, who, being duly sworn by me, according to law, upon his solemn oath, did depose, declare, and say, that he was acting and employed in the capacity of seaman, on board of the brig *Laura Ann*, of New York, ––––––– Shaw, master, last from Buenos Ayres, with a cargo of jerked beef, bound to the port of Havana; that, on the night of the 20th day of October last past, they made the island of Cuba, and on the

---

53 Senate Document 6. Serial Vol. 108 (Washington, D.C.: Gales & Seaton, 1825).
54 16 November 1824.

next morning, being the 21st day of October, when about twelve miles to leeward of Matanzas, they were boarded by an open boat, with twelve men, armed with muskets, cutlasses, pistols, and knives, who ordered the captain into the cabin, fired two pistols, and drove the mate and seamen into the forecastle, and, in a few minutes, ordered three of the men out of the forecastle, and compelled them to take in the studding sails, and brace up the yards, and running the vessel close in shore, near to Port de Canase, came to anchor, and, for an hour, the vessel beat heavy on the rocks; at this time, a schooner boat, armed with one gun and 28 to 30 men, also armed, came along side, appearing to be a party with the boat's crew, came on board and joined them, immediately ordered the second mate on board the schooner, and to make two masts for the boat; he, accordingly, obeyed their orders, and went on board.¶

The pirates now numbered about 40 men; they called the captain upon deck, and asked him where his money was; the captain replied that he was a poor man, and had not any money; they tied him (the captain) to the windlass, and beat him very severely, then untied him, and driving him into the forecastle, called the mate upon the deck, tied him to the windlass, and beat him in a like manner; then driving him below, ordered all the sailors to come upon deck: after the sailors came up, they were ordered aloft to furl the sails, which being done, they were again ordered into the forecastle; after all hands being below about an hour, three seamen were ordered upon deck; this deponent being one of the three, he went up into the foretop to un-reef[55] the maintopsail braces;[56] it being in the dusk of the evening; as this deponent came down, he saw that the pirates were running the captain up to the larboard fore yard arm, being hung by the neck; as soon after as possible, this deponent r[a]n into the forecastle, and immediately the mate was called upon deck, and this deponent heard him only say, "Oh God!" They then called the cook upon deck, afterwards the sailors, one at a time; this deponent stowing himself away in the coal hole, where he remained hid, notwithstanding they searched for him with lanterns, without finding him, until he was compelled to leave his hiding place by the fire; when, on his going upon deck, and finding the vessel on fire, and burning as far forward as the fore-hatch, he dropped himself overboard, under the vessel's bows, and swam ashore, distant about sixty yards, accompanied by two sharks, one swimming on each side of him.¶

After reaching the shore, and walking about three miles, he being much fatigued, lay in the wood for the night, and, on the following morning, saw the same piratical boat board and take possession of a brig under American colors, this deponent remaining

---

55 *Reef* in this case refers to "The means of shortening a sail to the amount appropriate to the strength of the wind, and the same word is also used as a verb to describe this action" (Dear and Kemp, *Companion*, 460).

56 *Braces* are "ropes or wire ropes rove to the ends of all yards in a square-rigged ship by which the yards are braced, or swung, at different angles to the fore-and-aft line of the ship to make the most of the wind" (Dear and Kemp, *Companion*, 64).

in the wood until the next morning, when he commenced his walk, making for Matanzas, keeping near the sea shore; coming to a small river, where there were many stores and small schooners, he swam across the river, and in the continuation of his walk, fell in with a small town, or place, and twenty persons, who, after questioning this deponent, who he was, and where he was going, some of them threatening to take his life, suffered him to proceed, and, on Saturday night, the 24th, reached a farm house, where he remained until Monday morning, when the farmer, having to send produce of his farm to Matanzas, on horses, and this deponent's feet being much cut, allowed him to ride on one of the horses, and at about 10 o'clock of the same day, he reached Matanzas.

GEORGE BROWN
X
his mark.

[...]

JOHN MOUNTAIN.

ooooo

[*Niles' Weekly Register*, 30 April 1825, 139–140]

Lieut. [C]om. Sloat to the secretary of the navy.[57]
U.S. Schooner Grampus
St. Thomas, 12th March, 1825

Sir: I have the honor to report [...] that having learned that several vessels had been robbed by pirates near Foxardo, and that two sloops of this place, and one of Santa Cruz, had been taken by them, and two of them were equipped and cruising as pirates, I obtained two small sloops at this place, free of expense, by the very cordial co-operation of his excellency, governor [P.] Von Scholten, of St. Thomas, who promptly ordered the necessary documents to be issued, and imposed a temporary embargo, to prevent the transmission of intelligence to the pirates, which sloops I manned and armed, under the command of lieutenants Pendergrast and Wilson, for the purpose of examining all the small harbors of Crab Island, and the south coast of Porto Rico.¶

We sailed on the 1st of March, and examined every place as far to the westward as Ponce, without success, although we got frequent information of them. We anchored at Ponce on the evening of the 3d, and took our men and officers on board; the next morning, at 10 o'clock, a sloop was seen off the harbor, beating to the eastward,

---

57   Samuel L. Southard, secretary of the navy from 1823–1829.

which was very confidently supposed to be one of those fitted out by the pirates. I again got one of the sloops and manned her, under the command of [L]ieut. Pendergrast, accompanied by acting [L]ieutenant Magruder, Dr. Biddle and midshipman Stone, with twenty-three men, who sailed in pursuit the next day, at 3 o'clock.¶

They had the good fortune to fall in with her in the harbor of "Boca de Inferno," which is very large and has many hiding places, where an action commenced, which lasted forty-five minutes, when the pirates ran their sloop on shore, and jumped overboard: two of them were found killed, and ten of those which escaped to the shore were taken by the Spanish soldiers, five or six of whom were wounded, and amongst them the famous piratical chief Cofrecinas [Roberto Cofresi], [58] who has long been the terror of the coast, and the rallying point of the pirates in this vicinity. As near as we can ascertain, he had fifteen or sixteen men on board, and was armed with one four[-]pounder, and muskets, pistols, cutlasses and knives, for his men.¶

The sloop was got off, and arrived safe, with our tender, at this place, last evening; and I am happy to add, that none of our people received any injury, and all have returned in good health, notwithstanding their exposure to the sun and rain, for eleven days, without the possibility of getting below. I have much pleasure in stating to you, that I received every assistance from the authorities of Ponce, whilst there, and that they showed every desire to promote the success of the expedition. [59] [. . .]

JOHN D. SLOAT. [60]

ooooo

---

58 Born in 1791 in Cabo Rojo, Puerto Rico, Cofresí (1791–1825) reputedly shared some of his piracy proceeds with the poor. "Many Puerto Ricans still consider Cofresí a hero" (Banting, *Puerto Rico*, 8). Sloat reported to Southard on 5 April 1825 that Cofresi and ten others were convicted and executed by firing squad on 30 March: "They all, except one, met their fate in the most hardened manner. The celebrated Cofrecinas reused to be blindfolded, saying, that he himself had murdered at least three[-] or four[-]hundred persons, and it would be strange if, by this time, he should not know how to die. From his and other confessions, twenty-eight others have been taken, and seventeen are to be executed in a few days, and the remainder in a short time after. Those already executed have been beheaded and quartered, and their parts sent to all the small ports round the island to be exhibited" (*Niles' Weekly Register*, 30 April, 1825, 142).

59 The governor of Puerto Rico, Miguel De La Torres, authored a letter for Sloat directing Spanish officials to give the American officer "all the necessary aid" on his mission (translated and reprinted in *Niles' Weekly Register*, 30 April 1825, 141).

60 John Drake Sloat (1781–1867) "was appointed Midshipman in the United States Navy on 12 February 1800. He was sailing master of *United States* under Commodore Decatur and was promoted to Lieutenant for conspicuous gallantry in the capture of HMS *Macedonian* on 25 October 1812. He cruised in *Grampus, Franklin, Washington,* and *St. Louis,* between 1815 and 1831 and commanded the Pacific Squadron between 1844 and 1846, rendering efficient service on the coast of California in the early part of the Mexican War. Under his direction, the American flag was hoisted on 7 July 1846 above Monterey, symbolizing the conquest of that part of California by the United States" (Mooney, *Fighting Ships*, VI: 531.

[*Niles' Weekly Register*, 30 April 1825, 138–139]

Capture of Pirates, &c.
[L]ieut. [C]om. M'Keever to [C]om. [Lewis] Warrington

U.S. STEAM GALLIOT SEA GULL,
Thompson's Island, April 1, 1825.

SIR: I have the honor to give you a detailed report of the late cruise on which I sailed from Matanzas, immediately after the reception of your orders of the 19th ultimo, taking with me the barge *Gallinipper*.

At Stone Key,[61] I met his B[rittanic] M[ajesty's] ship *Dartmouth*,[62] under the command of the [H]on. [C]apt. [James A.] Ma[u]de, and was informed by him that some of his boats were then cruising to windward in company with H.B.M. schooners *Union* and *Lion*.[63] Continued our course, and fell in with them the next evening at Cadiz bay.[64] As they were also in search of pirates, but without any particular or certain information of their haunts, of which I was possessed, I deemed it proper to propose a co-operation, it being perfectly understood that I was to have the conducting of the enterprise. This proposition was cheerfully acceded to: and, requesting that the schooners should not leave Cadiz bay, to go to windward, within three days, I left the *Sea Gull* under charge of [L]ieut. Rudd, and took with me, independent of the barge, which was well[-]manned, two small cutters, with five men in each; and, in company with a British barge and two cutters, under charge of [L]ieut. Ward, of the *Dartmouth*, we made the westernmost point of the entrance of Sagua La Grande,[65] where we were detained 48 hours, in consequence of strong head winds. The day after we arrived there, our water being nearly expended, the British barge and *Gallinipper*, [L]ieut. Cunningham, sailed in quest of some, although it was blowing a heavy gale from the eastward; and on the evening of the same day, the *Gallinipper* was capsized in a squall; but, with the assistance of [L]ieut. Ward and his crew, our officers and men were saved, and the vessel righted; she rejoined me, with the intelligence of the accident, a few hours after it happened, having lost part of her arms, ammunition and provisions.¶

---

61 Probably Cayo Piedras off the Hicacos Peninsula.
62 HMS *Dartmouth* was a 145-foot long, 36-gun frigate launched in 1813; it was sent to Jamaica in 1824. Three years later, in Mediterranean service, it lost six killed and eight wounded at the Battle of Navarino (Winfield, *British Warships*, 167).
63 Both HMS *Lion* and HMS *Union* appear to have gone into Royal Navy service in 1823; the former was sold in 1826; the latter was wrecked in the West Indies two years later (Colledge and Warlow, *Royal Navy*, 230, 422).
64 "Cadiz is situated in Cadiz bay, on the N[orth] coast of Cuba, 164 miles E[ast] of Havannah, and about 10 miles E[ast] of Cadiz river" (Bell, *A System of Geography*, VI:322).
65 A bay, a river, and a city on Cuba's north coast all bear this name; the mouth of the river was the scene of a fight, in June 1822, between boats of the 12-gun USS *Shark* and a pirate schooner.

Notwithstanding this very serious misfortune, after pledging myself to procure provisions, we determined not to abandon the pursuit of our object but upon the very last extremity. Accordingly, the next morning, the 25th ult., the wind abating, we made another effort, and gained the mouth of the river Sagua La Grande about noon. At this place I found a fisherman, and compelled him, much against his inclination, to pilot us to the Key of Jutia Gorda, one of the places of our destination, and at about 4 p.m. descried the masts of a vessel lying nearly concealed by the bushes, under said Key.¶

We immediately pushed for her, and when we approached within hail, she hoisted Spanish colors, and ordered us to keep off, or she would fire into us, having her guns trained, and matches lighted, with which they made several ineffectual attempts to fire the gun pointed upon the advancing boat. The channel being very crooked and narrow, the boats grounded several times. At length, one of the British cutters succeeded in passing the bar, and as two boats abreast could not approach, the officers and crews of the others were ordered to jump overboard and wade to the shore, where, taking a commanding position on the bank of the inlet in which she was anchored, and within twenty yards of her, I ordered her commander instantly to come on shore, and not fire at his peril.¶

After much hesitation, and reiterated threats to fire upon us, he obeyed. By this time every one on board was in great confusion. Instead of coming to me, he and a man who had accompanied him, attempted to make their escape. The commander, however, was seized, but his companion fled to the mangrove bushes. I now directed him to order his colors to be hauled down, and to surrender his vessel and crew. He did order his colors to be struck; but at the same moment, a musket or pistol was fired at the cutter, then close alongside, which was immediately returned, and a general fire ensued. The leader of the band, availing himself of the confusion, attempted flight. I fired at him, and wounded him; he fell – but rising very soon, and attempting to fight his way through our men with a long knife, he received several other wounds, and was retaken. Many of the pirates, in endeavoring to make their escape by jumping overboard to gain the mangrove bushes, were shot; whilst others, seeing no chance of escape, were driven below by the boarders and musketry from shore.¶

On taking possession of her, she proved to be a schooner, mounting two six-pounders, on pivots, four large swivels, and several blunderbusses, and completely equipped for a complement of 35 men, which was the least number she could have had on board, as we took 19 prisoners and can account for 8 killed. Several effected their escape into the mangrove bushes; and we are induced to believe that others were killed, whose bodies are supposed to have floated out to sea, unobserved, as there was a strong ebb tide. Among the prisoners are six wounded, one of whom is their chief, and calls himself Antonio Ripol. We were fortunate in having but one man wounded, a British marine, who received a slight cut in the arm.

After securing the prisoners, we searched the schooner, and discovered that, with the evident intention of blowing us up, they had placed lighted cigars in and near the magazine, which were soon carefully removed. We also found many articles on board, of American produce, (and to all appearance but recently taken, as the cases were quite new and clean:) New York hats, shoes, flour, rice, cheese, butter, lard, &c, &c, and to confirm their character, if there had been the least shadow of doubt remaining, we found the counterpart of these articles concealed in a thicket about twenty yards from the vessel, which was approached by a meandering path, and could only be discovered by careful search, so cautious were they in their operations. The following morning at daylight, [L]ieutenant Ward and myself took with us three boats and proceeded to windward, leaving [L]ieutenant Cunningham in charge of the prize, prisoners, &c. We soon after discovered a large schooner-rigged "Regla boat," gave chase, and at 11 a.m. the crew finding we were gaining fast upon them, made for the nearest mangrove island, jumped overboard, and effected a precipitate retreat to the bushes, leaving everything standing, with a keg of gunpowder, open, near the galley-fire, and quantities of it strewed over the vessel. The powder was instantly thrown overboard, and the fire extinguished. She proved to be the boat whose crew had murdered the five men belonging to the American brig *Betsey*, that was wrecked on the Double Headed Shot Key, in December last.[66] After a long and ineffectual search among the mangrove bushes, for the fugitives, we took the boat in charge, and pushed on to the Key la Cosimera, whence they sailed from in the morning, being their place of resort and establishment. This we burnt, and returned to Jutia Gorda, at midnight, the officers and men being nearly exhausted; the latter having been at their oars from daybreak.

The schooner and boats being laden with the property found secreted in the woods and elsewhere, we set fire to the buildings on the Key, consisting of two very large huts, and some out-houses. At this place was an old man, of more genteel appearance than the rest, whose situation was so suspicious, that I thought proper to bring him with me. I have since discovered that he is the commandant of Sagua la Grande, and in some way intimately connected with these pirates: his papers I transmit to you, separate from those found on board the vessel. [. . .]

[ISAAC] McKEEVER [. . .][67]

---

66   For a contemporary account of this event, see *Narrative of the Shipwreck of the Brig Betsey, of Wiscasset, Maine, and Murder of Five of her Crew by Pirates, on the Coast of Cuba, Dec. 1824, By Daniel Collins, one of the only two Survivors* (Wiscasset: J. Dorr, 1825).

67   Isaac McKeever figured in the 1814 assault on Barataria documented in Chapter 6; by 1852 he had the rank of Commodore ("Naval," *United Service Journal* 5(8), 7 August 1852, 62); by 1856 he was commandant of the Norfolk Navy Yard (*Register of the Commissioned and Warrant officers of the United States Navy*, 112).

9

"No evidence of a 'contrite heart'" – The *Vineyard* mutiny and the piracy confessions of "Charles Gibbs" (1830–1831)

The pirate "Charles Gibbs" – the alias for Newport, Rhode Island-born James Jeffers – is an enigmatic figure in American piracy lore. Tales of his privateering and piratical careers – he claimed to have been one of the Cape Antonio raiders Lawrence Kearny's *Enterprise* attacked in late 1821 – stem largely from his own "confessions" to a New York magistrate a few weeks before his execution; they were being liberally augmented well into the late 20th century.

Jeffers, who kept up the Gibbs alias until shortly before he and Thomas Wansley were hanged for mutiny and murder aboard the brig *Vineyard*, claimed to have taken about 40 ships over his earlier career. The scale of such alleged activities later elevated him to an upper tier in some American piracy histories. But while his story is plausible, his claims are hard to verify, and even before his hanging he was caught in lies about his alleged War of 1812 service – something subsequent chroniclers often overlooked. His response was that he had falsified certain details solely to shield his identity, for the sake of a family that had thought him long dead. He went to the gallows retracting none of his piratical confessions, yet still denying having committed the murder aboard the *Vineyard* for which he was convicted.

This chapter provides four texts that help provide some balance to later exaggerated histories of Charles Gibbs. All appeared originally in the *New York Journal of Commerce*. They include two accounts from Jeffers' and Wansley's trial for the *Vineyard* mutiny and the murder of the vessel's master and mate; the controversial and influential "confessions" document in full; and an article about the pair's execution on Ellis Island, in which the writer notes Jeffers' final confrontation with Kearny, who reportedly pronounced him genuine.

ooooo

[*New York Journal of Commerce*, 10 March 1831, 2]

TRIAL FOR MURDER AND PIRACY. – Thomas J. Wansley,[1] colored man, 23, a native of Delaware, steward[2] of the brig *Vineyard*,[3] and Charles Gibbs,[4] 32, a native of Rhode

Island, were tried and found guilty of murder in the U.S. Circuit Court, – the former on Monday for the murder of William Thornb[er], captain of brig – and the latter on Tuesday, for the murder of William Roberts, the mate, on the high seas, on the night of 23d November last.[5] The testimony given upon the trial was so nearly the same with that published by us at the time of the arrest of the prisoners, that it is unnecessary to repeat it except in a summary form.

It appeared in evidence that the brig *Vineyard*, William Thornb[er], master, sailed from New Orleans for Philadelphia with a crew of eight persons, viz. William Roberts, mate, Charles Gibbs, John Brownrigg,[6] Robert Dawes,[7] Henry Atwell, A. Church, Thomas J. Wansley, and Jas. Talbot, most of whom were shipped at that port. During the passage, on the 5th day out, Wansley, the steward, informed the crew that there was

---

1   "Born on December 8, 1807, as the eldest offspring of his mother's second marriage, Thomas Wansley went to work at a young age. He grew to be an admitted 'seducer . . . gambler, and Sabbath-day breaker,' and was also 'undutiful to his mother,' who was still alive at the time of the subsequent *Vineyard* trial. An observer deemed Wansley handsome, 'a light mullatto'[sic] whose features 'approach but little towards those which distinguish the African race.' The description continued, 'He is about five feet ten inches in height—his well knit limbs convey the idea of great personal strength, and I have no hesitation in saying that I have seen but few persons of any colour who to my mind bear a more striking resemblance to the statue of the Apollo Belvidere, which . . . has been considered as the most perfect model of manly beauty.' His various jobs included work as a servant for a chaplain named McGlaughlin, who provided him with religious instruction, and about a year spent aboard the 74-gun USS *Delaware*. Wansley joined it in early 1828 in Norfolk, Virginia, and was paid off and discharged on February 6, 1830, in the same port. The *Delaware*'s muster rolls and payrolls list Wansley as ordinary seaman, but he later said he had served as steward or servant to the *Delaware*'s purser, Silas Butler. . . . Wansley would double as steward and deckhand while serving aboard the *Vineyard*" (Gibbs, *Dead Men*, 99–100).

2   "The steward is the captain's servant, and has charge of the pantry, from which everyone, even the mate himself, is excluded. These distinctions usually find him an enemy to the mate, who does not like to have anyone on board who is not entirely under his control. The crew do not consider him as one of their number, so he is left to the mercy of the captain" (Dana, *Two Years Before the Mast*, 12).

3   According to surviving registration data, the *Vineyard* was built at Kennebunk, Maine, in 1822. It was listed at 159 48/95 tons, 85 feet 4 inches long, with a breadth of 23 feet, 5 inches. It had "One deck, two masts, square stern, no galleries, a billet head" (Works Progress/Work Projects Administration, *Ship Registrations and Enrollments, Boston and Charlestown 1821–1830*, 553–54).

4   James Jeffers, alias Charles Gibbs, was probably the same James Jeffers born in Newport on 5 Nov., 1798 to ship captain and former Revolutionary War privateer Samuel Jeffers and his wife Elizabeth Drew. James was the fifth of their eight children and their third son (Gibbs, *Dead Men*, 17).

5   Few details emerged about Thornber (whose name was routinely given as "Thornby") or Roberts in press accounts of the *Vineyard* case), other than that both were freemasons, and that Thornber was engaged to a woman who lived on John Street in New York City ("Mutiny and Murder," *Baltimore Patriot*, 4 December 1830, 2; and "Postscript," *Baltimore Patriot*, 6 December 1830, 2).

6   Born about 1789 in Cumberland, England, Brownrigg's "career included stints forced aboard three British warships (HMS *Gloucester*, HMS *Dreadnought*, and HMS *Thames*), each of which he deserted. . . . An observer described him as having 'a rather heavy and lugubrious countenance, though expressive of a degree of honesty. . . . He is rather under the middle size, and muscular, has light hair and bushy whiskers, yet, in his general appearance, there is nothing to distinguish him from the usual ordinary seamen. His *Vineyard* shipmates called him 'Jack' or 'the old man,' and he sometimes acted in capacity of second mate" (Gibbs, *Dead Men*, 102).

7   "Born in December 1812, Dawes was the son of a Lancaster, England, shoemaker. He was sandy haired and of below-average height; one observer described him as 'a good looking young man.' In 1826, aged thirteen and with his father's permission, he went to sea. Dawes first set foot in the United States in 1829 . . . " In mid-1830 he signed on, at $8 per month, the *Lexington*, which worked the Boston-New Orleans-Liverpool route; Jeffers joined it, probably in either Boston or Liverpool, and he and Dawes both left the *Lexington* in New Orleans and signed on to the *Vineyard* (Gibbs, *Dead Men*, 98).

The mutiny aboard the Vineyard (19th century illustration, artist unknown).

money on board, which led to a combination to murder the captain and mate, take possession of the vessel, and divide the money. The night of the 23d November was fixed on for the perpetration of the deed. That night, while Dawes was at the helm and Brownrigg aloft, Wansley, who was called by Dawes to trim the lamp, struck the Captain with a pump-brake on the back of the head, which leveled him, and followed up the blow with others until he was dead. Gibbs and Wansley then took him by the head and feet and threw him overboard. The murder of the mate was assigned to Atwell and Church. They stood by the companion-way, waiting for him to come out of the cabin, and as he, hearing the noise, was hastening up to ascertain the cause, they struck him over the head with a club. He turned and ran below, followed by Gibbs, who being unable to find him in the dark, returned, took out the binnacle light, and proceeded again in search of him. He found him bleeding below, dragged him on deck, and held him firmly, while Atwell and Church beat him over the head. Before he was dead, the three seized and hove him overboard. He did not sink immediately, but swam after the vessel, crying for help for three or four minutes. They then took possession of the vessel, and promising not to injure Talbot, Brownrigg and Dawes, if they proved true to them, proceeded to open the kegs and divide the money. They found about $50,000 on board, which was distributed equally among all. They then steered a north-easterly course towards Long Island, and when they had arrived within 15 miles South of Southampton Light,[8] they scuttled the brig, set fire to her, and took to the boats. Gibbs, Wansley, Dawes and Brownrigg, were in the long boat,

---

8   On east Long Island.

The Vineyard mutineers burying the money on Great Barn Island (19th century illustration, artist unknown).

and Talbot, Church and Atwell, in the jolly boat. It blowed very hard, and the jolly-boat was upset, and her crew drowned. Those in the long boat, in order to save themselves, found it necessary to throw over more than half of the money they had, and finally succeeded in reaching Pelican Island,[9] whence they crossed to Great Barn Island,[10] buried the money, and went to the house of Mr. Samuel Leonard. Soon after they reached Mr. Leonard's house, Brownrigg gave information respecting the murder and robbery, and the next day, when they left the island, they were arrested at the house of Mr. Johnson, and committed to Flatbush jail.

The evidence of the guilt of the prisoners was full and conclu[s]ive. Their own confession of the crime, gratuitously made to Messrs. [Henry W.] Merritt and [William F.] Ste[ph]enson,[11] who had the custody of them from Flatbush to this city, could have left not the semblance of a doubt on the mind of any person who heard the testimony of those officers. And we learn from a person[s] who re[-]conveyed them to the Penitentiary on the night of the conviction of Gibbs, that both freely admitted that Brownrigg and Dawes had given a faithful relation of the circumstances, except in some trifling particulars.

---

9   Pelican Beach on Barren Island.
10 Wards Island.
11 Police officers; Merritt was also the deputy keeper of Bridewell prison in New York City (Gibbs, *Dead Men*, 112–113).

There was nothing peculiar in their deportment during the trial. The iron visage of Gibbs was occasionally darkened with a transient emotion, but he had evidently abandoned all hope of escape, and sat the greater part of the time with his hands between his knees, calmly surveying the scene before him. Wansley was more agitated, and trembled visibly when he rose to hear he verdict of the Jury. We are informed that Gibbs has declared his intention of avoiding the ignominy of the gallows, if possible, and it will therefore be well for those who are entrusted with his custody, to take such precautions that he cannot add the crime of suicide to the already black catalogue of his offences.

A motion in arrest of judgment was made to the Court yesterday morning, but it was overruled, and notice given that sentence would be pronounced on Friday.

ooooo

[New York Journal of Commerce, 12 March 1831, 2]

SENTENCE OF THE PIRATES. – The prisoners, Thomas J. Wansley and Charles Gibbs, were conducted into the Court room yesterday morning, to receive the sentence of the law for the murder of William Thornb[er], captain, and William Roberts, mate, of the brig *Vineyard*, on the high seas, on the night of the 23d of November. The avenues leading to the room were filled with a dense crowd, who seemed to have an irresistible curiosity to witness the last appearance of the unhappy convicts before an earthly tribunal. Their demeanor was more composed than was expected, and there was no indication of remorse or anguish in their features at the prospect of their inevitable doom.

The U.S. District Attorney[12] moved for judgment upon Thomas J. Wansley, and he was accordingly put to the bar. Judge [Samuel R.] Betts[13] addressed him as follows: – "You were indicted by the Grand Jury in behalf of the U.S. for the wil[l]ful murder of Captain William Thornb[er], on board of the brig *Vineyard*, on the high seas. You were tried and found guilty of the murder. Have you any thing to say why judgment should not be pronounced upon you according to law?" The prisoner replied in a firm tone of voice, that he had a few words to say. He had often understood that great prejudices existed in respect of color, and he had seen it to his sorrow. Antipathies against blacks existed in the breasts of white men, who thought them worthy of less justice. The same influence extended to Jurors, and was seen in the District Attorney, by the preference he had shown in taking the two white men as witnesses against him. The greatest part of the testimony against him, he said, was false; but he would not say

12 The prosecutor was James A. Hamilton, third son of Alexander Hamilton; he later (1829) served briefly as acting secretary of state. (Malone, *Dictionary of American Biography*, VIII:188–89).
13 Betts was about 44 at the time; a former Congressman, he had been admitted to the New York bar in 1809, became a judge in 1823, and a federal judge in 1826. For a biography, see Georgina Betts Wells, *Life and Career of Samuel Rossiter Betts* (New York: Sloog, 1934).

there would be any injustice in taking his life. His agitation here so overpowered him that he declined saying any thing more; but the Judge encouraged him and he proceeded. He said he was not acquainted with any one of the crew when he shipped, and that he saw the money put on board the brig. He mentioned it, and when it reached the ears of Atwell, he said, "[L]et's have it." A few days afterwards, Atwell told him that they were determined to take the brig and have the money; and when he found that the whole crew had joined in the conspiracy, he was induced to take a part in it, from a belief that his own life would otherwise be in danger.

Charles Gibbs was then asked what he had to say, and replied in a firm, unembarrassed manner, that he wished to explain how far he had participated in the transaction. "I was a stranger to all the crew when I went on board the brig, but Dawes and Church. Atwell first mentioned about the money, and wished me to aid in getting it, but I refused. Some days afterwards, when it was again proposed, I agreed. Brownrigg and Dawes also agreed to take the brig, and the lives of the mate and captain. A few days afterwards, I tried to abolish their determination, and all consented but Dawes and Atwell. I told them I would break the nose of the first man that insisted on taking life, and it would have been well for me, if I had stood to my resolution; for then I should not have been here. This man (alluding to Wansley) agreed to strike the captain, and I helped to throw him overboard; but of the murder of the mate I am innocent. I now commit myself to the care of that God who knows all hearts, and the hearts of false swearers."

His Honor Judge Betts then proceeded to address the prisoners. The Court, he said, had listened to their appeal, and although there might be something in their story, it admitted enough to confirm the justice of their sentence. Wansley had conceived that his color had exerted a baneful effect upon his cause; but if he would look back and review the proceedings he could find the charge on which he had been convicted, supported by the most ample proof; and even admitting that both Dawes and Brownrigg had sworn falsely, did not the conspiracy prove beyond a doubt, that he was a free, voluntary, and active agent in depriving two fellow beings of their lives, who had given him no cause of offence, nor provocation? If there were the shadow of a belief that the proceedings were perverted to produce his conviction, the Court would allow another opportunity to him to be heard. But there was no uncertainty in the case and his very address to the Court showed the judgment to be true. There was generally, in such cases, something palliative, and something to call forth human sympathy: – some heat of passion, and long smothered resentment. Was it so in this case? Had Capt. Thornb[er] offered any provocation, or what offence had the mate given? None. They confided in the fidelity of the crew, and had done no act, wounding or offensive to the feelings of either.

Gibbs had declared that he did not throw the mate overboard, but was he not there aiding by his presence and assisting? The very reaching of his hand would have saved him. It was murder in law, and murder in his heart. The testimony proved that both had been guilty, not only of murder, but of robbery, revolt, and the piratical destruction of the vessel; and had they been tried on any of those charges, they must have been convicted, and the judgment of the law would have been death.

["]It now only remains,["] said the Judge, ["]to pronounce that judgment which the law exacts at the hands of the Court. The judgment is, that you, Thomas J. Wansley, and you, Charles Gibbs, be taken hence to the place of your confinement, and thence to the place of execution, and that you be hanged by the neck until you are dead, and that the Marshal cause this sentence to be executed on the 22d day of April next, between the hours of 10 in the morning and 3 in the afternoon.["]

The Judge proceeded to remark that it was in the power of the Court to have ordered an immediate execution, but that it had been deemed advisable to defer it for a period of 6 weeks. That brief interval was not allowed for the purpose of giving them any hope of pardon. The justice and humanity of the law exacted punishment, and it would be in vain for them to suffer their minds to be deluded by any such expectation. There were many affecting and distressing considerations, arising from the relation in which they now stood to the world. Did they realize it, and could they understand that they were in a condition desperately hopeless? In his closing remarks he should address them; he hardly knew how to do it, in the manner which he considered best calculated to penetrate their hearts. It had no doubt occurred to their minds that it was a dreadful thing to die – it was dreadful in old age, when the faculties and feelings were worn out: the individual still clung to life. It was doubly so in youth and manhood: the soul shrunk from its earthly termination, and could hardly submit to the stern decree. If they had gone through all the scenes and perils of their vocation and escaped those feelings, they could do so no longer. And it would be well for them to ask themselves, what would be their condition after death? The period allowed them would afford them time to consult their own reflections, and the humanity of the Marshal would allow them to communicate with such pious men as might be disposed to administer to them the consolation of religion, preparatory to their final departure.

The prisoners were then delivered into the custody of the Marshal, and reconveyed to prison.

We are credibly informed that Gibbs is not the real name of the prisoner who passes by that name. He admits this, and further states, that he formerly commanded a Buenos Ayrean privateer, in which he made several cruises. During the last Spring he took passage for Gibraltar, and thence for Algiers, in the hope of procuring a situation on board some of their corsairs; but he found it impossible to elude the vigilance of the French blockading squadron, and proceeded to Tunis. His attempt was unsuccessful there, and he was compelled to return to Gibraltar. He sailed thence for Boston, and afterwards to New-Orleans, where he shipped as one of the crew of the *Vineyard*.

ooooo

[*New York Journal of Commerce*, 7 April 1831, 2]

Confessions of Gibbs the Pirate

The criminal who stands convicted of the murder of William Roberts, mate to the brig *Vineyard*, on the high seas, on the 23d of November last, and who is to be executed on the 22d inst. is a native of the State of Rhode Island. As the name by which he is known the community is Charles Gibbs, we shall accordingly designate him by that name, in the history of his bloody atrocities which is here subjoined.

Soon after his arrest, and before his trial, he expressed a desire to Henry W. Merritt, one of the Police marshals, to make some communications to a magistrate respecting his career and crimes. The officer made known his wish to James Hopson,[14] Esq., one of the Police Magistrates of his city, and that gentleman, presuming that a develop[e]ment of the circumstances attending his piracies would be highly important and valuable to the mercantile community, proceeded to the prison at Bellevue,[15] to receive his confession. The disclosures made to that gentleman will be found in the sequel. The other details presented in the following narrative, were communicated to Mr. Merritt, Police Officer, the deputy keeper of Bridewell,[16] and another person, at different times, and were committed to paper by them on the spot, very nearly in the his own language. That they are all true we do not undertake to affirm; but that they are in the main, founded in truth, we do most sincerely believe. Some of them are so strongly corroborated by circumstances, as to leave hardly a doubt on the minds of the most sceptical.

The first account which he gives of himself is, that his father obtained a situation for him in the United States sloop-of-war *Hornet*, Capt. [James] Lawrence, during the last war with England, in which vessel he made two cruises; in the last of which she captured and sunk the enemy's sloop of war *Peacock* off the coast of Pernambuco, after an engagement of 20 min. –– On the arrival of the *Hornet* in the U.S., Capt. Lawrence was assigned by the government to the command of the frigate *Chesapeake*, then lying in Boston harbor, and Gibbs accompanied him to that ill-fated

---

14 Hopson (1773?–1854) was a local police magistrate who had no connection with Jeffers's case. His obituary ran in the *New York Times*, 11 April 1854, 8.

15 On the East River at 26th Street and First Avenue, Bellevue prison "was a 50-by-150 feet rectangular stone building dating to 1816. It shared the 20-acre, stonewall-enclosed plot with an almshouse and hospital – which would take over the entire site in 1848. Its correctional innovations included a grain-processing treadmill known as a 'stepping wheel,' on which both male and female inmates toiled. The entire complex was known for disease and overcrowding" (Gibbs, *Dead Men*, 135).

16 The Bridewell prison was "a cheerless graystone edifice, two stories high, with basement, a front and rear pediment, which stood a little west of the present [1872] City Hall. It was erected for the confinement of vagrants, minor offenders, and criminals awaiting trial, in 1775, just in time to serve as a dungeon for the struggling patriots of the Revolution. . . . The Bridewell was finally demolished, and much of the material used in the erection of the Tombs [prison] in 1836" (Richmond, *New York and its Institutions*, 512, 515).

vessel in the month of April, 1813. "Early in the month of May," says he, "we received a challenge from Capt. [Philip] Broke, of the frigate *Shannon*, and we instantly made preparation to go to sea, and risk a battle. We stood down the harbor about 11 o'-clock, and commenced the action about 3, p.m. off Cape Ann. It lasted about 30 minutes, with great slaughter, especially on board the *Chesapeake*. I escaped miraculously, with only a sabre wound upon my nose, the only wound I ever received in my life. The loss of the *Chesapeake* was 65 killed dead, and 100 wounded – one half mortally. We were taken into Halifax, where I remained about four months."[17]

After his exchange, he abandoned all idea of following the sea for a subsistence, went home to Rhode Island, and remained there a few months, but being unable to conquer his propensity to lead a roving life, he entered on board a ship bound to New Orleans and thence to Stockholm. On the homeward passage they were compelled to put into Bristol, England, in distress, where the ship was condemned and he proceeded to Liverpool, and returned to the United States in the ship *Amity*, Capt. Maxwell. Shortly after his return home, the death of an uncle put him in possession of about two thousand dollars, with which he established himself in the grocery business in Boston. This undertaking was far from being profitable, and he was often under the necessity of applying to his father for assistance, which was always afforded, accompanied with good advice and his blessing. The stock was finally sold at auction, for about 900 dollars, which he soon squandered in ale-houses and among profligates.[18] His father hearing of his dissipation, wrote affectionately and earnestly to him to come home, but he stubbornly refused, and went to sea again, in the ship *John*, Capt. Brown, bound for the Island of Margarita.

After their arrival, he left the ship, and entered on board the Colombian privateer *Maria*, Capt. Bell. They cruised for about two months to the Bay of Mexico, around Cuba, but the crew becoming dissatisfied in consequence of the non-payment of their prize-money, a mutiny arose, the crew took possession of the schooner, and landed the officers near Pensacola. A number of days elapsed before it was finally decided by them what course to pursue. Some advised that they should cruise as before, under the Colombian commission; others proposed to hoist the Black Flag. The cruised for a short time without any success, and it was then unanimously determined to hoist the black flag, and declare war against all nations. Their bloody purpose was not carried however, into immediate execution. They boarded a number of vessels, and allowed them to pass unmolested, there being no specie on board, and their cargoes not being convertible into any thing valuable to themselves. At last one

---

17   "Even allowing for exaggeration of losses, particularly the number of mortally wounded, [James Jeffers'] pretended first-person account is reasonably close to the accepted historical one" (Gibbs, *Dead Men*, 31). For a modern account of the battle, see Guttridge and Smith, *The Commodores*, 211–215.

18   Interestingly, a provision store co-owned by a Charles Gibbs and one Abel Barnes existed circa 1816–19, on India Wharf in Boston. It was "either a remarkable coincidence or more likely proof that Jeffers, like many liars, drew on real things when inventing stories" (Gibbs, *Dead Men*, 9, 33).

of the crew named Antonio, suggested that an arrangement could be made with a man in Havana, that would be mutually beneficial; – that he would receive all their goods, sell them, and divide the proceeds. This suggestion being favorably received, they ran up within two miles of the Mor[r]o Castle, and sent Antonio on shore to see the merchant and make a contract with him. – Previous to this, Gibbs was chosen to navigate the vessel. – Antonio succeeded in arranging every thing according to their wishes, and Cape Antonio was appointed as the place of rendezvous. The merchant was to furnish drogers to transport the goods to Havana, which was done by him for more than three years.

The *Maria* now put to sea, with a crew of about 50 men, principally Spaniards and Americans, with every hope of infamous success. The first vessel she fell in with was the *Indispensable*, an English ship, bound to Havana, which was taken and carried to Cape Antonio. The crew were immediately destroyed: those who resisted were hewn to pieces; those who offered no resistance, were reserved to be shot and thrown overboard. Such was the manner in which they proceeded in all their subsequent captures. The unhappy being that cried for mercy in the hope that something like humanity was to be found in the breasts even of the worst of men, shared the same fare with him who resolved to sell his life at the highest price. A French brig, with a valuable cargo of wine and silk, was taken shortly after: the vessel was burnt and the crew murdered.

The sanguinary scenes through which Gibbs had passed now effectually wrought up his desperation to the highest pitch, and being as remarkable for his coolness and intrepidity as he was for his skill in navigation, he was unanimously chosen to be their leader in all their future enterprizes. To reap a golden harvest without the hazard of encountering living witnesses of their crimes, it was unanimously resolved to spare no lives and to burn and plunder without mercy. They knew that the principle inculcated by the old maxim that "dead men tell no tales," was the only safe one for them, and they scrupulously followed it. Gibbs states that he never had occasion to give orders to begin the work of death. The Spaniards were eager to accomplish that object without delay, and generally every unhappy victim disappeared in a very few minutes after they gained the deck of a vessel.

He now directed his course towards the Bahama Banks, where they captured a brig, believed to be the *William* from New York [bound] for some port in Mexico, with a cargo of furniture; destroyed the crew, took her to Cape Antonio, and sent the furniture and other articles to their friend at Havana. Sometime during this cruise, the pirate was chased for nearly a whole day by a[n] U.S. ship, supposed be the *John Adams*; they hoisted Patriot colors,[19] and finally escaped. In the early part of the summer of 1817, they took the *Earl of Morla*, an English ship from London, with a cargo

---

19   I.e., one of the flags used by the insurgent Latin American republics.

of dry goods. The crew were destroyed, the vessel burnt, and the goods carried to the Cape. There they had a settlement with their Havana friend, and the proceeds were divided according to agreement.

Gibbs then repaired to Havana, introduced himself to the merchant, and made further arrangements for the successful prosecution of his piracies. While there, he became acquainted with many of the English and American naval officers, enquired respecting the success of their various expeditions for the suppression of piracy, and made himself acquainted with the speed of their vessels, and all their intended movements.

On his arrival at Cape Antonio, he found that his comrades were in a state of complete muti[n]y and rebellion, and that several of them had been killed. His energy checked the disturbance, and all agreed to submit to his orders, and put any one to death who should dare to disobey them.

During the cruise which was made in the latter part of 1817 and the beginning of 1818, a Dutch ship from Cura[ç]oa[20] was captured, with a cargo of West India goods, and a quantity of silver plate. The passengers and crew, to the number of 30, were all destroyed, with the exception of a young female about 17, who fell upon her knees and implored Gibbs to save her life. The appeal was successful, and he promised to save her, though he knew it would lead to dangerous consequences among his crew. She was carried to Cape Antonio, and kept there about two months; but the dissatisfaction increased until it broke out at last into open mutiny, and one of the pirates was shot by Gibbs for daring to lay hold of her with a view of beating out her brains. Gibbs was compelled in the end to submit her fate to a council of war, at which it was decided that the preservation of their own lives made her sacrifice indispensable. He therefore acquiesced in the decision and gave orders to have her destroyed by poison, which was immediately done.

The piratical schooner was shortly afterwards driven ashore near the Cape, and so much damaged that it was found necessary to destroy her. A new sharp built schooner was in consequence provided by their faithful friend in Havana, called the *Picciana*, and d[i]spatched to their rendezvous. In this vessel they cruised successfully for more than four years. Among the vessels taken and destroyed, with their crews, were the *Belvidere, Dido*, a Dutch brig, the British barque[21] *Larch*, the other vessels

---

20 "Curacco or Curassou, as it is generally called, is about thirty miles long, and ten in breadth. Though it is naturally barren it produces a considerable quantity both of sugar and tobacco, and here are besides very great salt works, which furnish a good deal to the English islands, and for which there is a considerable demand from our colonies on the continent; but the trade for which this island is chiefly valuable, is that which in time of war is carried on between them, the English, and the French; and the counterband [contraband] which is carried on between them and the Spaniards at all times" (Burke, *European Settlements*, II:51).

21 Accounts from 1821 describe the *Larch* as a brig, as is later noted in this paragraph. Smyth (*Lexicon*, 79) held that the term barque or bark was "a general name given to small ships, square-sterned, without head-rails." However, it also referred to a three-masted vessel with schooner-rigging (i.e., fore-and-aft sails) on its mizzen mast.

American 19th century barque Mendota (artist unknown).

enumerated in the list furnished to Justice Hopson, and many others whose names are not recollected. They had a very narrow escape at one time, from the English man-of-war brig *Coronation*.[22] In the early part of October, 1821, they captured the ship *Lucius* [*Lucies*] of Charleston, took her to Cape Antonio, and were busily engaged in landing her cargo, when the U.S. brig *Enterprise*, Capt. Kearn[e]y, hove in sight, an discovering their vessels at anchor, sent in her barges to attack them. A serious engagement followed; they defended themselves for some time behind a 4[-]gun battery, but in the end, were defeated with considerable loss, and compelled to abandon their vessels and booty, and fly to the mountains for safety. In the list of vessels destroyed, as stated in the confession to Justice Hopson, Gibbs speaks of this ship as the *Caroline* of Charleston. But he afterwards recollected that it was the *Lucius*, and proceeded to state a variety of circumstances, which prove beyond a question the correctness of his recollections. By a recurrence to newspaper files, we find that such a ship was captured by the pirates of Cape Antonio in Oct. 1821, and was shortly after retaken by the U.S. brig *Enterprise*, Capt. Kearn[e]y, while the pirates were landing her cargo. Gibbs states that according to the best of his belief only one of the crew had been killed at the time they were forced to abandon the ship. The

---

22 The Royal Navy had no vessel named *Coronation* at this time; however, the 100-foot long "brig-sloop" HMS *Carnation* was in service from 1813–1836; it spent 1822–1825 at Jamaica (Winfield, *British Warships*, 305). Captained by Edward Walcot, it was near Cape Antonio in August, 1822, when it encountered the English brig *Industry* after it had been ransacked and released by a pirate schooner (Smith, *Atrocities of the Pirates*, 135–37).

same account says that the British brig *Larch* of St. Andrews, from Kingston for Havana, was taken by the pirates, and recaptured at the same time by the *Enterprise*. This is doubtless the *Larkin* spoken of by Gibbs in the confession made to Justice Hopson, which we here subjoin:

ooooo

City Prison and Bridewell, March 6, 1831

Question. Charles Gibbs, – my name is Mr. Hopson. I understand from Mr. Merritt you wished to see me. He told me so some ten or twelve days since, and the weather being so cold, I have put off coming until now. He informed me you wished to make some communications which you would not make to any other person.

Ans. – I have.

Ques. – Gibbs, are you going to tell me the truth, or is it to amuse me, and make me write a long story that will not amount to any thing.

Ans. – I shall tell nothing but the truth; and it is only on condition that you will swear not to divulge any thing I may say, when I am on my trial, and at no time after, if I should get clear.

My reply was (says Mr. Hopson), that I should not take my oath, but I would give him my word that it should be kept a secret according to his request.

Under this promise he stated as follows: – that he commenced piracy in the year 1816, in the schooner *Sans Sou[cis]*,[23] belonging to the Island of Margarita, and that since that time, has been in several other vessels engaged in the same business. That many of his comrades are now living in the United States, but whose names he never would mention: That they had taken from many vessels large sums of money, and various articles of merchandise. He had no doubt he had been concerned in robbing forty different vessels; and on reflection, could mention many of the names. He then gave me the names of the following vessels:

Brig *Jane*, of Liverpool; cargo dry goods. – Crew destroyed, vessel burnt.[24]

Brig (name forgotten), of New York, from the Spanish Main[e]; took money from her. Crew destroyed, vessel burnt.

23 French for "without worries." But elsewhere Jeffers tells Hopson that he began his criminal career in 1816 on a privateer called *Maria* – and the newspaper narrative mentions only the latter vessel. "Was Jeffers 'remembering better' as execution approached? The slip might signal that he could not keep his story straight, a fact a critical reader must keep in mind. But as a distinction was made between the privateer (the *Maria*) and the pirate (the *Sans Soucis*) it is conceivable that only one vessel was involved, its name changing as it shifted careers" (Gibbs, *Dead Men*, 54).

24 See the entry from *Lloyd's List*, 16 May 1817, in Chapter 6, for a candidate for the *Jane*, which on that occasion (at least) survived its encounter with pirates.

Brig *Belvidere*, of Boston, taken in the Gulf; crew and vessel destroyed. [25]

Two French Brigs, in the Gulf of Mexico; money taken – crews and vessels destroyed.

Ship *Providence*, of Providence; took from her $10,000. She was suffered to pass, as Examinant could not consent to destroy his own townsmen.

Ship *William*, of Salem; took from her dry goods and money. Crew and vessel destroyed.

Bark *Dido*, of Bremen; took from her dry goods. Vessel and crew destroyed.

Bark *Larkin*, of London; took from her a large quantity of dry goods. Vessel and crew destroyed.

Genoese brig, name unknown; took from her a large quantity of plate, some gilt[-]edge paper, and from twenty to thirty piano fortes.

A French ship, cargo wine; vessel and crew destroyed.

The *William Dawson*, of New York; boarded her and let her pass.

Ship *Earl of Morla*, of London; took from her dry goods and money. Vessel and crew destroyed.

Ship *Indispensable*, of London; took from her dry goods and money. Vessel and crew destroyed.

A Dutch Ship from Cura[ç]oa, bound to Holland. There were thirty passengers in her; some of them were females. Took a large quantity of plate, destroyed the vessel, and all on board except a young girl, the daughter of one of the families. (Afterwards told me that she was poisoned.) Took her to the West end of Cuba, Cape Antonio, where we had a rendezvous, and where we had a small fort that mounted four guns. We kept her about two months, and she was then killed; and this circumstance hurt his feelings more than any act of his life; and which is the only act he can say he was sorry for. The girl was about 17 or 18 years of age; her father, mother, and all her relations were on board the vessel.

There were many other vessels taken and destroyed, and among them, Americans. Every thing valuable was taken from them, and vessels and crews destroyed. The goods were sent to a Spanish House in the Havana, who sold them. We had a contract with the House, and received half the proceeds.

While I was in the schooner *Margarita*, we took the American ship *Caroline* [i.e., the *Lucies*], and run her on shore at Cape Antonio, (Cuba.) The United States

---

25 A Beverly, Mass.-registered *Belvidere* existed; it was stopped once in 1821 and robbed; it successfully fought off pirates who attacked it in 1822 (Lamson, *Autobiography*, 254–55, 260). Other vessels that appear on Jeffers' lists of admitted captures are assessed in Gibbs, *Dead Men*, 126–131.

armed vessel, the *Enterprize* came along shortly after, and before we had a chance of taking any thing out of her, the crew or some of the crew of the *Enterprize* landed; we had a fight with them, some of our men were killed, and I believe some of theirs. We were beaten and driven to the mountains, where we remained some days. We then separated; some got to Trinidada, south side Cuba; others got to the Havana. The crew of the *Enterprize* destroyed our fort, took the goods from the *Caroline* and our two vessels, the *Margaretta* and *Picciana*, which were principally dry goods. The cargo of the *Caroline* was dry goods principally, as appeared from the bills of lading.

(Here is a long statement given of the monies taken, and where secreted.)

Ques. – Gibbs, why were you so cruel as to kill so many persons, when you had got all their money, which was all you wanted?

Ans. – The laws are the cause of so many murders.

Ques. – How can that be? [W]hat do you mean?

Ans. – Because a man has to suffer death for piracy; and the punishment for murder is no more. Then you know, all witnesses are out of the way, and I am sure if the punishment was different, there would not be so many murders.[26]

Ques. – Have you any objections to tell[ing] me the names of any persons who have been concerned in piracy, or who received the gains of pirates?

Ans. [–] There are many now in the U[nited] States, but I will not mention their names. I know that when I was cruising, the Governor of the Isle of Pinos was concerned with pirates, and I won't mention any others.

Here we separated (says Justice Hopson) and he wished me to call and see him again, which I promised.

I visited him again on the 19th March. At that visit, nothing but conversation took place. I asked him many questions; he conversed with great freedom; repeated to me the vessels he first informed me had been robbed and destroyed. At this visit I questioned him about the following vessels, at the request of Mr. Amos Butler,[27] who handed me a list of them, viz: – *Mary Augusta* from Antwerp to Mobile? [Gibbs] said he had no recollection of her.

---

26 Thomas More's *Utopia* (33) includes criticism of societies assigning identical punishments for robbery and murder. This provoked a robber "to kill him whom else he would have but robbed. For the murder being once done, he is in less fear and in more hope that the deed shall not be betrayed or known, seeing the party is now dead and rid out of the way, which only might have uttered and disclosed it. But if he chance to be taken and descried, yet he is in no more danger and jeopardy than if he had committed but single felony. Therefore while we go about with such cruelty to make thieves afraid, we provoke them to kill good men."

27 Then about 52, Butler, who lived on Murray Street, owned the *Mercantile Advertiser* newspaper, based on Wall Street (Gibbs, *Dead Men*, 126).

Dutch vessels from Europe for Cura[ç]oa? To this question he said that in the year 1822, a Dutch ship and a bark were taken off the Bahama Bank, and two days after they (the pirates) run in under the Mo[r]ro Castle. Their vessel was a privateer schooner, with a Big Gun amidships, which they had under cover. After they had been in port two days, two boats' crews came in and said their vessels had been taken, off the Bahama Bank.

Providence of Providence? Two times, once from Liverpool to N[ew] York, and once from Mobile to N[ew] York, stopped her once, as well be seen by his first account. Br. Brig *Discover*, two years ago from Jamaica to St. Johns[?] Knew nothing of her. Brig *Transit*, Ellet, from Trinidad to N[ew] York, two years ago? Knows nothing of her. *Candace* from Boston to Sumatra, in 1824, robbed of $19,000? Knows nothing of her.

Topaz in 1828 from Calcutta, crew murdered? Knows nothing of her.

I then left him, under the promise that I would come and see him again. He set the following Wednesday week.

I again visited him on Wednesday morning, 23d March, and then told him I expected all he had told me could not be true; and as I had a list of the various vessels he said had been plundered, and the crews murdered, I wished him to go on and repeat them again, and such others as he could recollect. Here follows the account, as given this day:

Brig *William*, of N[ew] York,	vessel and crew destroyed.
Bark *Larkin*, of London	[ditto]
Brig *Belv[i]dere*, of Boston	[ditto]
Ship *Indispensable* of London	[ditto]
Ship *Earl of Morla*, of London	[ditto]
Two French brigs, on Bahama Banks	[ditto]
A Genoese brig, from Straits	[ditto]
A N[ew]York brig name forgotten	[ditto]
A French ship from Europe	[ditto]
Dutch Ship, on South Cuba, cargo dry goods	[ditto]
Dutch ship *Dido*	[ditto]
D[itt]o brig from Europe	[ditto]

Providence of Providence, took out $10,000, and let her pass because the crew were his townsmen.

Bark *Transit*, in year 1824 or 25, cargo molasses, vessel and cargo[28] destroyed. Commenced in the year 1816, in the privateer *Maria*, Capt. Bell, of the Port of Margarita, in the Island of Santa Martha.[29] Capt. Bell was from somewhere up North River, at or near Hudson. Took the vessel from the officers, and set them on shore at Pensacola.

The *Picciana* was sent to Cape Antonio for them, from the Havana; won['t] tell by whom.

The ship that he mentioned as having been run on shore at Cape Antonio, was the *Caroline* of Charleston, from Liverpool – (Gibbs afterwards recollected that this ship was the *Luciur* [*Lucies*].)

I then withdrew from the prison, and left Merritt with him

When I saw Merritt afterwards, he informed me that Gibbs had given him an account of himself up to the time he commenced piracy.

Delivered to Mr. Merritt, March 31st, 1831, at the request of Gibbs.

ooooo

On one occasion Gibbs states that he cruised for more than three weeks off the Capes of the Delaware, in the hope of falling in with the *Rebecca Sims*, a Philadelphia ship, bound for Canton. They knew that she would have a large quantity of specie on board, but they were disappointed in their booty. The ship passed them in the night.

Sometime in the course of the year 1819, he states that he left Havana and came to the United States, bringing with him about $30,000. He passed several weeks in this city, and then went to Boston, whence he took passage for Liverpool in the ship *Emerald*. Before he sailed, however, he had squandered a large part of his money by dissipation and gambling. – He remained in Liverpool a few months, and then returned to Boston in the ship *Topaz*, Capt. Lewis. His residence in Liverpool at that time is satisfactorily ascertained from another source besides his own confession. A female now in this city was well acquainted with him there, where, she says, he lived like a gentleman, with apparently abundant means of support. In speaking of his acquaintance with this female, he says "I fell in with a woman, who I thought was all virtue, but she deceived me, and I am sorry to say that a heart that never felt

28 Possibly the writer intended "crew" instead of cargo.
29 Something may be garbled here: Santa Marta is a Colombian port; Margarita is an island off the Venezuelan coast.

abashed at scenes of carnage and blood, was made a child of for a time by her, and I gave way to dissipation to drown the torment. How often when the fumes of liquor have subsided, have I thought of my good and affectionate parents, and of their God-like advice! But when the little monitor began to move within me, I immediately seized the cup to hide myself from myself, and drank until the sense of intoxication was renewed. My friends advised me to behave myself like a man, and promised me their assistance, but the demon still haunted me, and I spurned their advice."

He subsequently returned to Boston, sailed for Havana, and again commenced his piratical career. In 1826, he revisited the United States, and hearing of the war between Brazil and the Republic of Buenos Ayres,[30] sailed from Boston in the brig *Hitty* of Portsmouth, with a determination, as he states, of trying his fortune in defence of a republican government. Upon his arrival, he made himself known to Admiral Brown, and communicated his desire to join their navy. The admiral accompanied him to the Governor, and a Lieutenant's commission being given him, he joined a ship of 34 guns, called the *Twenty Fifth of May*.[31] "Here," says Gibbs, "I found Lieutenant Dodge, an old acquaintance, and a number of other persons with whom I had sailed. When the Governor gave me the commission, he told me they wanted no cowards in their Navy, to which I replied that I thought he would have no apprehension of my cowardice or skill when he became acquainted with me. He thanked me, and said he hoped he should not be deceived; upon which we drank to his health and to the success of the Republic. He then presented me with a sword, and told me to wear that as my companion through the doubtful struggle in which the Republic was engaged. I told him I never would disgrace it, so long as I had a nerve in my arm. I remain[d]ed on board the ship in the capacity of 5th Lieutenant for about four months, during which time we had a number of skirmishes with the enemy. Having succeeded in gaining the confidence of Admiral [William] Brown,[32] he put me in command of a privateer schooner, mounting 2 long 24[-]pounders and 46 men. I sailed from Buenos Ayres, made two good cruises, and returned safely to port. I then bought one half of a new Baltimore schooner, and sailed again, but was captured seven days out, and carried into Rio Janeiro, where the Brazilians paid me my change. I remained there until peace took place, then returned to Buenos Ayres, and thence to New York.

After the lapse of about a year, which he passed in traveling from place to place, Gibbs states that the war between France and Algiers attracted his attention. Knowing

---

30 The "Cisplatine War" between Brazil and Buenos Aires, capital of the United Provinces of the River Plate, was over possession of what became modern Uruguay. For a modern study, see Vale, *War Betwixt Englishmen*.

31 Admiral William Brown (see below) purchased the aging merchantman *Comercio de Lima* at the start of the war and renamed it *Veinticinco de Mayo* (25th of May) for the 1810 date from which Argentina marked independence. As Brown's flagship, Argentine sources describe it as a *fragata* (frigate) or *corbeta* (corvette) carrying 28–36 guns (Carranza, *Campañas navales*, II:263, 266, 277, and IV:178. 185, 186, 189).

32 Irish-born Brown was head of the navy of the United Provinces of the River Plate. For a biography, see John De-Courcy Ireland, *Admiral from Mayo: A Life of Almirante William Brown of Foxford, Father of the Argentine Navy* (Dublin: Burke, 1995).

that the French commerce presented a fine opportunity for plunder, he determined to embark for Algiers and offer his service to the Dey. He accordingly took passage from this port in the *Sally Ann*, belonging to Bath, [Maine][33] landed at Barcelona, crossed to Port Mahon,[34] and endeavored to make his way to Algiers. The vigilance of the French fleet prevented the accomplishment of his purpose, and he proceeded to Tunis. There finding it unsafe to attempt a journey to Algiers across the desert, he amused himself with contemplating the ruins of Carthage,[35] and reviving his recollections of her war with the Romans. He afterwards took passage to Marseilles, and then to Boston. From Boston he sailed to New Orleans, and there entered as one of the crew of the brig *Vineyard*. To a question why he who had been accustomed to command, should enter as a common sailor on board the *Vineyard* he answered that he sought employment to assuage the horrors of reflection.

He solemnly declares that he had no agency in the murder of the mate, for which he was tried and convicted, and is unable to understand how he could be found guilty, when he stood by and looked passively on the scene of destruction. He readily admits, however, his participation in the mutiny, revolt and robbery, and in the murder of Capt. Thornb[er]. He often asks if he should not be murdered in the streets, if he had his liberty, and was recognized, and frequently exclaims, "Oh, if I had got into Algiers, I never should been in this prison to be hung for murder."

Though he gives no evidence of a "contrite heart" for the horrible crimes of which he confesses himself guilty, yet he evidently dwells upon their recollection with great unwillingness. If a question is asked him, "[H]ow were the crews generally destroyed"? he answers quickly and briefly, and instantly changes the topic either to the circumstances that attended his trial, or to his exploits in Buenos Ayres. Since his trial, his frame is somewhat enfeebled, his face paler, and his eyes more sunken; but the air of his bold, enterprising and desperate mind still remains. In his narrow cell, he seems more like an object of pity than vengeance; if affable and communicative, and when he smiles, exhibits so mild and gentle a countenance, that no one would take him to be a villain. His conversation is concise and pertinent, and his style of illustration quite original.

To correct the impression which some of our public prints have thrown out that Gibbs, like other criminals, is disposed to magnify and exaggerate his crimes, it may be well to state that a few days since a chart of the West Indies (Jocelyn's) was handed him, containing the names of about 90 vessels which were boarded and

---

33 A candidate for this *Sally Ann* was a 175-ton brig "built at Topsham in 1824." It sank in a gale in late 1839 while sailing from Matanzas to Wilmington, North Carolina (Baker, *Maritime History of Bath, Maine*, I:250–251).

34 The Spanish port of Mahón on the island of Minorca.

35 A literary device of the era apparently used to refer to the North African/Iberian/Mediterranean region. Consider the editor's note inserted into the following passage: "The following are extracts from three letters from the present squadron in the Mediterranean – 'The mind in ruminating over the remains of antiquity, (the writer is immediately alluding to the ruins of Carthage) which abound every where in this part of the globe, is naturally led to consider the frailty and vanity of man'" ("Our Naval officers," *Niles' Weekly Register*, 24 May 1817, 200).

plundered by pirates from 1817 to 1825, with a request that he would mark those of whose robbery he had any recollection. The chart was returned with but one mark, and that upon the ship *Lucius* of Charleston. – When questioned afterwards in regard to that vessel, he gave such an account of her, and of her subsequent re-capture by the *Enterprize*, as left no doubt respecting the truth of his statement. Had he been desirous of increasing the black catalogue, here was so fine an opportunity, that he would undoubtedly have availed himself of it. He has repeatedly stated that he was concerned in the robbery of more than forty vessels, and in the destruction of more than twenty, with their entire crews. Many of those destroyed had passengers on board, which makes it probable that he has been an agent in the murder of nearly FOUR HUNDRED HUMAN BEINGS!!

Gibbs was married in Buenos Ayres, where he now has a child living. His wife is dead. By a singular concurrence of circumstances, the woman with whom he became ac-quainted in Liverpool, and who is said at that time to have borne a decent character, is now lodged in the same prison with himself. He has written her two letters since his confinement, both of which are before us. They indicate a good deal of native tal-ent, but very little education. The spelling is bad, and no regard is paid to punctuation, capitals, &c. One of these letters we subjoin to gratify the perhaps innocent curiosity which naturally is felt to know the peculiarities of a man's mind and feelings under such circumstances, and *not* for the purpose of intimating a belief that he is truly penitent. The reader will be surprised with the apparent readiness with which he makes quotations from Scripture.

Bellevue Prison,[36] March 20, 1831

It is with regret that I take my pen in hand to address you with these few lines, under the great embarrassment of my feelings, placed within these gloomy walls, my body bound with chains, and under the awful sentence of death. It is enough to throw the strongest mind into gloomy prospects, but I find that Jesus Christ is sufficient to give consolation to the most despairing soul. For he saith that he that cometh to me I will in no wise cast out.[37]¶

But it is impossible to describe unto you the emotions of my feelings. My breast is like the tempestuous ocean, raging in its own shame, harrowing up the bottom of my own soul. But I look forward to that serene calm when I shall sleep with kings and counsel[l]ors of the earth.[38] There the wicked cease from troubling, and there the weary be at rest. There the prisoners rest together; they hear not the voice of the oppressor.¶[39]

---

36 [Footnote in original text:] We have thought best to correct the spelling and punctuation. In other respects the letter stands as it was written. – *Edits. J.C.*
37 John 6:37.
38 Job 3:13–14.
39 Job 3:17–18.

And I trust that there my breast will not be ruff[l]ed by the storm of sin, – for the thing which I greatly feared has come upon me.[40] I was not in safety, neither had I rest; yet trouble came.[41] It is the Lord, let him do what seemeth to him good.[42] ¶

When I saw you in Liverpool, and a peaceful calm wafted across both our breasts, and justice no claim upon us, little did I think to meet you in the gloomy walls of a strong Prison, and the arm of justice stretched out with the sword of the law, awaiting the appointed period to execute the dreadful sentence. I have had a fair prospect in the world, at last it budded and brought forth the gallows. I am shortly to mount that scaffold, and to bid adieu to this world, and all that was ever dear to my breast. ¶

But I trust when my body is mounted on the gallows high, the heavens above will smile and pity me. I hope that you will reflect on your past, and to fly to that Jesus who stands with open arms to receive you. Your character is lost it is true. [But w]hen the wicked turneth from the wickedness that they have committed, they shall save their soul alive.[43] ¶

Let us imagine for a moment that we see the souls standing before the awful tribunal, and we hear its dreadful sentence, ["D]epart ye cursed into everlasting fire.["][44] Imagine you hear the awful lamentations of a soul in hell. It would be enough to melt your heart, if it was as hard as adamant. You would fall upon your knees and plead for God's mercy, as a famished person would for food, or as a dying criminal would for a pardon. ¶

We soon, very soon, must go the way whence we shall ne'er return.[45] Our names will be struck off the records of the living, and enrolled in the vast catalogues of the dead. But may it [sic] ne'er be numbered with the damned. I hope it will please God to set you a[t] your liberty, and that you may see the sins and follies of your life past. ¶

I shall now close my letter with a few words which I hope you will receive as from a dying man: and I hope that every important truth of this letter may sink deep in your heart and be a lesson to you through life.

> Rising griefs, distress my soul,
> And tears on tears successive roll. –
> For many an evil voice is near,
> To chide my woes and mock my fear;

---

40 Job 3:25
41 Job 3:26.
42 A phrase employed several times in the Books (1 and 2) of Samuel.
43 Ezekiel 18:27.
44 Matthew 25:41.
45 Job 16:22

And silent memory weeps alone,
O'er hours of peace and gladness flown,[46]

> I shall remain your sincere friend.
> CHARLES GIBBS

ooooo

[New York Journal of Commerce, 23 April 1831, 2]

EXECUTION OF THE PIRATES. – James D. Jeffers, alias Charles Gibbs, and Thomas J. Wansley, convicted of the murder of the captain and mate of the brig *Vineyard*, underwent the last penalties of the law, on Ellis' Island yesterday at 12 o'clock. They were brought out from the prison at Bellevue, at 8 in the morning, under the direction of Thomas Morris, Esq., U.S. Marshal, and conveyed to the place of execution, in the steam boat *Bellona*, attended by a detachment of marines from the Navy Yard. They arrived at the island about 10, but the execution was delayed until 12 o'clock, at their special request. The interval was wholly devoted to religious services in which both the wretched criminals participated, with great apparent earnestness. They *seemed* penitent,[47] particularly Wansley; and in their supplications to the throne of mercy, acknowledged that the punishment which awaited them, was justly due to the horrid crimes they had committed. After they had taken their stand under the gallows, and the ropes had been adjusted around the necks, they shook hands with the clergymen and officers in attendance, and took leave of the spectators in the most affecting manner, praying fervently that others would take warning by their fate. The Rev. Messrs Kent and Carter offered up prayers in their behalf, and a hymn was given out, which they commenced singing, but before it was finished, the signal was given, the cord cut, and they were launched into eternity. Wansley appeared to die instantly; but Gibbs struggled very much, for three or four minutes, and expired in great agony. Their bodies remained hanging on the gallows, for the space of about 40 minutes, when they were cut down, and delivered to the surgeons for dissection.

The whole scene was in the highest degree solemn and affecting. It was difficult to estimate the number of spectators, who amounted to many thousands, and covered the whole island. There was very little disorder; no more than would necessarily arise from the presence of a large multitude, collected into one dense mass, and all eager to witness the doom of the criminals.

---

46 Part of an Episcopal Hymn, based on the 42nd Psalm as paraphrased by John Bowdler, *Select Pieces in Verse and Prose* (London: G. Davidson, 1816), I:60.

47 [Footnote in original text:] Such appearances, in circumstances like the present, we always regard with suspicion. We know it is perfectly easy for Omnipotence to change the heart of the vilest sinner, and at the twelfth hour if He please; but we are equally well satisfied that this is not his usual mode of dealing with his creatures, and that as men *live*, so they may expect to die.–*Eds J.C.*

To the last, Gibbs confirmed the statement published by us respecting his horrid atrocities, in nearly every particular. He admitted that what he had communicated in regard to his being on board the *Hornet* and *Chesapeake* was unfounded, and declared that his sole object in making such representations was to conceal his true name, and prevent his friends from being visited with the stigma that his crimes would cast upon them. He said if he had confessed that he first went to sea in the brig *Brutus* from Newport in 1816, that then he might easily have been traced and identified as James D. Jeffers.[48]

We are informed from the most respectable authority that he has made a full disclosure of all the accomplices, aiders and abettors in his piracies, and that it is the intention of the person who has the information in his possession, to proceed to Washington and communicate it without delay to the President. When published, says our informant, *"it will astound the people of this nation."*[49]

There are various circumstances which have come to our knowledge since the confession was published, which tend strongly to corroborate the statement which Gibbs has given of his piratical career. He was visited in prison by Capt. Kearn[e]y , who commanded the U.S. brig *Enterprise* when she recaptured the ship *Lucius* and another [ship, and?] in the course of their conversation referred to numerous incidents that occurred there, which none but a person present could have known. He enquired of Captain K[earny] if he found some warm coffee on board of the ship when he took possession of her? [W]hich being answered in the affirmative, he added, with a half smile "[Y]ou didn't drink any of it!" intending to convey the idea that it was prepared and poisoned for their destruction. We learn from a gentleman who was present at the interview, that Capt. Kearn[e]y was fully satisfied that he had been a pirate, and a participator with the Cape Antonio free booters in the commission of many of their horrible outrages upon the lives of their fellow beings.

The appearance of a suspicious vessel off the Capes of the Delaware several years ago, about the time that the *Rebecca Sims* sailed on one of her voyages to the East

---

48 A Newport-based *Brutus*, a 197-ton brig, existed. "Built at Freetown, Massachusetts, in 1815, the *Brutus* was 77 feet long and 24 feet across at its widest point. . . . Registration documents noted that it had 'two decks, two masts, no figurehead.' Many co-owners are listed between its first registration in March 1816 and its 1825 loss on a Florida reef. Its first master was Charles Gorton of Newport, born circa 1778 and described on surviving crew lists of the era as almost six feet tall, with a dark complexion and brown hair. He had captained merchant ships since at least 1812, when he took the Newport brig *German Peggy* to Havana. He returned there during 1815 in three different craft, bringing back a cargo of molasses to Newport in January 1816 while captaining the schooner *Eliza*. Two months later Gorton, then thirty-eight, took the recently launched *Brutus* to Charleston, taking ten days to get there. If James Jeffers accompanied him on this trip, he likely got off in Charleston. His name does not appear on the crew list Gorton filed with Charleston's customs collector on April 26, when the *Brutus* sailed for Copenhagen to pick up hemp and iron to transport back to Newport. Nor does Jeffers appear on documents Gorton filed for the *Brutus*'s November 23 trip to Bonavista. Could Jeffers have taken the *Brutus* to Charleston early in 1816 and never looked back?" Gibbs, *Dead Men*, 34–35.
49 The individual was probably politician James Coggeshall, a Newport native who indeed delivered a report to President Andrew Jackson (Gibbs, *Dead Men*, 137–138).

Indies, and the robbery of the ship *Providence*, as spoken of by Gibbs, have been fully confirmed to us.

The demeanor of the two criminals while standing under the gallows, was in general accordance with their different temperaments. Wansley's frame was visibly agitated, though his voice was firm and his countenance composed. He clearly felt, as he was forewarned by Judge Betts in his impressive sentence, that it was a dreadful thing to die. Gibbs stood erect and firm, and looked around two or three times to observe the manner in which it was designed to effect his death. He evinced not the slightest tremor, and met his fate with a very different feeling from what was generally antici-pated.

10

"Demons in the Shape of Men" – The taking of the *Mexican* and its aftermath (1832–1835)

Although Captain Pedro Gibert claimed the Spanish nobility title of *Don*, it was self-given. An ex-Colombian privateer, he went into smuggling and slave-trading using what historian Angus Konstam called "the perfect vessel for the job – a fast 150-ton Baltimore clipper (schooner) called the *Panda*, crewed by a dozen men who didn't have too many scruples."[1] Like Gibert, they also found it easy to slip into piracy when the opportunity presented itself.

Many Caribbean pirates, in fact, started their careers on slavers; some returned to the trade in response to naval pressure in the early- and mid-1820s. An 1829 editorial noted: "Slavers are generally fast sailing craft, manned with a motley mixture of all nations, of unprincipled characters and piratical dispositions; and already exiled from the society of honest men, and desperadoes by profession, they are reckless of consequence. If they chance to meet any unarmed vessel, with specie, they have no objection to making her a prize. They are well armed and full of men, so that resistance in case of such an attempt would be useless. The crime once committed, they are off in a moment— they paint their sides of a different stripe, and if the same ship should meet again it would be impossible for her to identify them."[2]

The *Panda*'s robbery of the Salem-based *Mexican*, during one such voyage of ill-repute in 1832, is one of the era's last recorded episodes of Caribbean piracy, an echo of crimes that had reached their peak a decade earlier. However, that no lives were lost aboard the *Mexican* was unintended. The pirates torched the brig with its crew barricaded belowdecks – they were able to escape and douse the fire before it became unmanageable. Later, a British warship captured some of the *Panda*'s crew off the African coast and brought them to Salem.

The 14-day trial that ended in several hangings revolved around the testimony of Joseph Perez, Gibert's steward, who became a witness for the prosecution: one alleged pirate killed himself before the trial began. Several published versions of the *Panda* trial

---

1 Konstam, *Piracy*, 282.
2 *Salem Gazette*, 18 December 1829, quoted in Bradlee, *Piracy in the West Indies*, 138–39, see also 147; and Lubbock, *Cruisers, Corsairs and Slavers*, 86.

transcript exist, offering varying levels of sometimes contradictory detail. One is reproduced herein largely intact; extracts from another appear in several places.

ooooo

[*Salem (Mass.) Gazette*, 16 October 1832, 3]

The brig *Mexican*, Capt. Butman, which sailed from this port about six weeks since for South America, returned on Friday, having been fallen in with by a pirate, and robbed of TWENTY THOUSAND DOLLARS in specie, besides the property of the officers and crew – the sails and rigging of the vessel injured – the officers and crew of the Mexican were also shamefully maltreated, and had a very narrow escape from a HORRIBLE DEATH! – This daring and high handed outrage upon the high seas is calculated to excite fears for the safety of other vessels bound on the same track, and particularly our outward bound Indiamen.

It is hoped this outrage will stimulate our Government to greater vigilance in looking after these demons in the shape of men – our public ships and light vessels of war should be constantly on the watch for them – and a compact should be entered into with other Governments for the adoption of measures to ferret them out and bring them to punishment.

The *Mexican* is owned by Joseph Peabody, Esq. The property, we learn, was insured. The following is Capt. Butman's statement, which we copy from the *Advertiser* of Saturday.

PIRACY AND ROBBERY

On the 20th September, in lat[itude] 33.00 N[orth] lon[gitude] 34 30 W[est] at 2 ½ a.m. saw a vessel which passed across our stern about half a mile from us. At 4 a.m. saw her again passing across our bow, so near that we could perceive that it was a schooner with a fore top sail and top gallant sail. As it was somewhat dark she was soon out of sight. At daylight saw her about five miles off the weather[3] quarter, standing on the wind on the same tack we were on – the wind was light at S[outh-]S[outh-]W[est], and we were standing about S[outh-]E[ast]. At 8 a.m. she was about two miles right to windward of us; could perceive a large number of men on her deck, and one man on the fore top gallant yard looking out; was very suspicious of her, but knew not how to avoid her. Soon after saw a brig on our weather bow steering to the N[orth-]E[ast]. By this time the schooner was about three miles from us and four points forward of the beam. Expecting that she would keep on for the brig ahead of us we tacked to the westward, keeping a little off from the wind to make good way through the water, to get clear of her if possible. She kept on to the East-

---

3   The weather side of a vessel is that facing the wind. The opposite is leeward (Smyth, *Lexicon*, 723–4).

ward about ten or fifteen minutes after we had tacked, then wore round,[4] set square
sail, steering directly for us, came down upon us very fast, and was soon within gun
shot of us – fired a gun and hoisted Patriot colours[5] and backed[6] main topsail. He ran
along to windward of us, hailed us to know where we were from, where bound, &c.
then ordered me to come on board in my boat. Seeing that he was too powerful for
us to resist, I accordingly went and soon as I got along side of the schooner, five ruffians instantly jumped into my boat, each of them being armed with a large knife and
told me to go on board the brig [i.e., the *Mexican*] again; then they got on board they
insisted that we had got money and drew their knives, threatening us with instant
death and demanding to know where it was. As soon as they found out where it was
they obliged my crew to get it up out of the run upon deck, beating and threatening
them at the same time because they did not do it quicker. – When they had got it all
upon deck, hailed the schooner, and they got out their launch and came and took it
on board the schooner, viz: – ten boxes containing twenty thousand dollars; then returned to the brig again, drove all the crew into the forecastle, ransacked the cabin,
overhauling all the chests, trunks, &c. and rifled my pockets taking my watch, and
three doubloons which I had previously put there for safety; robbed the mate of his
watch and two hundred dollars specie – still insisting that there was more money in
the hold. Being answered in the negative, they beat me severely over the back, said
they knew that there was more, that they should search for it, and if they found any
they would cut all our throats. They continued searching about in every part of the
vessel for some time longer, but not finding any more specie, they took two coils of
riggings, a side of leather, and some other articles, and went on board the schooner,
probably to consult what to do with us – for, in eight or ten minutes they came back,
apparently in great haste, shut us all below, fastened up the companion-way, fore-
scuttle and afterhatch-way, stove our compasses to pieces in the binnacles, cut away
tiller-ropes,[7] halliards,[8] braces,[9] and most of our running rigging,[10] cut our sails to
pieces badly; took a tub of tarred rope yarn and what combustibles they could find
about deck, put them in the camboose house and set them on fire; then left us tak-

---

4   Tacking and wearing (or veering) are two different forms of changing a ship's direction. "In tacking it is a neces-
    sary condition that the ship be brought up to the wind as close-hauled, and put round against the wind on the
    opposite tack. But in veering or wearing, especially when strong gales render it dangerous . . . the head of the
    vessel is put away from the wind, and, turned round 20 points of the compass instead of 12, and, without strain
    or danger, is brought to the wind on the opposite tack" (Smyth, *Lexicon*, 710–711).
5   In his testimony, presented below, witness Joseph Perez identified this as a Colombian flag.
6   "*To back a sail*. To brace its yard so that the wind may blow directly on the front of the sail, and thus retard the
    ship's course" (Smyth, *Lexicon*, 66).
7   The ropes that link the vessel's wheel or helm to the tiller, the large wooden bar used to turn the rudder (Smyth,
    Lexicon, 683).
8   Halliards, also Halyards or Haulyards, are "The ropes or tackles usually employed to hoist or lower any sail upon
    its respective yards, gaffs, or stay . . . " (Smyth, *Lexicon*, 363).
9   "The braces are ropes belonging to all the yards of a ship; two to each yard, rove through blocks that are stropped
    to the yards, or fastened to pendants, seized to the yard-arms. Their use is either to square or traverse the yards
    horizontally; hence, *to brace the yard*, is to bring it to either side by means of the braces" (Smyth, *Lexicon*, 127).
10   Rigging elements are "termed 'standing' which are comparative fixtures, and support the masts, &c; and those
    'running,' which are in constant use, to trim the yards, and make or shorten sail, &c" (Smyth, *Lexicon*, 573).

ing with them our boat and colours. When they got along side of the schooner they scuttled our boat, took in their own, and made sail, steering to the Eastward.

As soon as they left us, we got up out of the cabin scuttle, which they had neglected to secure, and extinguished the fire, which if it had been left a few minutes, would have caught the mainsail and set our masts on fire. Soon after we saw a ship to leeward of us steering to the S[outh]E[ast], the schooner being in pursuit of her did not over take her whilst she was in sight of us.

It was doubtless their intention to burn us up altogether, but seeing the ship, and being eager for more plunder they did not stop fully to accomplish their design. She was a low strai[gh]t schooner of about one hundred and fifty tons, painted black with a narrow white streak, a large head with the horn of plenty painted white, large main-topmast but no yards or sail on it. Mast[s] raked[11] very much, mainsail very square at the head, sails made with split cloth and all new; had two long brass twelve[-] pounders and a large gun on a pivot amidships, and about seventy men who appeared to be chiefly Spaniards and mulattoes.

JOHN G. BUTMAN

ooooo

[From *A Report of the Trial of the Spanish Pirates Before the United States Circuit Court . . .* , 3–4]

EARLY in the month of June last [1834], intelligence reached this country, that [H]is Britannic Majesty's brig of war *Curlew*,[12] Capt. [Henry Dundas] Trotter,[13] while cruising off the coast of Africa for slavers, had fallen in with, and captured, the Spanish schooner *Panda*, and that several of the crew of that vessel had been identified as the individuals who robbed the brig *Mexican*, of Salem, on the 2[0th] of September [1832], while on her voyage from that port to Rio Janeiro. A part only of the crew, it was stated, had been secured and taken to England; the remainder having escaped to the shore, where they were protected by the natives.

On the 26th of August [1834], the British gun-brig *Savage*[14] arrived in the harbor of Salem, having on board the prisoners named in the title page of this report.[15] Her

---

11 Slanted.
12 HMS *Curlew* was the last in a series of "brig-sloop" type vessels of that name in the Royal Navy. It was built at Woolwich in 1830 and carried 10 guns (Colledge and Warlow, *Royal Navy*, 98).
13 Trotter (1802–59) "entered the navy in 1815; was made a lieutenant on the 9th Jan. 1823; promoted to the command of the *Britomart* sloop, Feb. 20th, 1826; and appointed to the *Curlew*, fitting out for the African station, July 22d, 1830" (Marshall, *Royal Navy Biography*, IV/II:180). Trotter "survived the disastrous Niger expedition of 1841 and reached admiral's rank (retired)" (Blake, *Evangelicals in the Royal Navy*, 290n38).
14 HMS *Savage* was a sister vessel to *Curlew*, sharing the same "brig-sloop" design. Like *Curlew*, it was launched in 1830 and carried 10 guns (Colledge and Warlow, *Royal Navy*, 360).
15 e.g., Pedro Gibert, Bernardo De Soto, Francisco Ruiz, Nicola Costa, Antonio Ferrer, Manuel Boyga, Domingo De Guzman, Juan Antonio Portana, Manuel Castillo, Angel Garcia, Jose Velazquez, and Juan Montenegro alias Jose Basilio De Castro. Another prisoner, Manuel Delgardo, committed suicide before the trial.

commander, Lieutenant Loney, waited upon the authorities of Salem, and after the usual formalities, surrendered his charge into their hands; stating that the English government waived their right to try and punish the prisoners, in favor of the United States, against whom the principal offence had been committed.

A primary examination was held in the Town Hall at Salem, his Honor Judge Davis, presiding; and the prisoners were directed to be transferred to the jail at Boston, there to await their trial at the October term of the United States Circuit Court. This was done, and on the 23d of October they were brought up at Boston, arraigned, furnished with copies, in Spanish and English, of the indictment found against them, and allowed three days to consider and determine upon their pleas. At the expiration of that time, they again appeared before the court, and severally pleaded "Not Guilty." Their pleas were then recorded, and the 11th of November appointed as the day of trial.

ooooo

Trial of the Twelve Spanish Pirates of the Schooner Panda, *a Guinea Slaver, Consisting of Don Pedro Gibert, Captain; Bernardo de Soto, Mate; Francisco Ruiz, Carpenter; Antonio Ferrer, the tattooed Cook; Nicola Costa, Manuel Boyga, Domingo de Guzman, Juan Antonio Portana, Manuel Castillo, Angel Garcia, Jose Velazquez, and Juan Montenegro, Seamen, for Robbery and Piracy, committed on board the Brig* Mexican, *20th Sept. 1832* (Boston: Lemuel Gulliver, 1834).

United States Circuit Court

His Honor Joseph Story, LL.D. }
[His Honor] John Davis, LL.D. } Presiding.

Counsel for the Government,
   Andrew Dunlap,[16] Esq., *District Attorney.*

Counsel for the Prisoners,
   David Lee Child,[17] Esq.
   George S. Hillard,[18] Esq.

16 "Andrew Dunlap was born in Salem in 1794; graduated from Harvard College in 1813. He was for several years United States attorney for the district of Massachusetts. He was the author of Dunlap's *Admiralty Practice*. He died in 1835" (Northend and George, *Memorials*, 252).
17 Journalist and attorney Child (1794–1874) "had fought in Spain against the Bourbon monarch and endured two libel prosecutions for his newspaper attacks upon Jacksonian poiticians." Irrespective of his defense of the slaver's crew, he (with his wife, author Lydia Maria Child) became a prominent anti-slavery writer and editor (Mayer, *All on Fire*, 107, 128, 131, 188, 221, 255, 620).
18 George Stillman Hillard (1808–1879) graduated from Harvard College in 1828, and was later "admitted to the bar and acquired an extensive practice." He was a Massachusetts legislator, a delegate to the state's 1853 constitutional convention, and U.S. district attorney in Massachusetts from 1866–1870. The author of several published works, he also served as associate editor of the *Boston Courier* (Wilson and Fiske, *Appleton's Cyclopedia*, III:207–208).

His Excellency Don Antonio G. Vega, *Spanish Consul*.

Stephen Badlam, Esq., *Sworn Interpreter*.

William H. P[e]yton, Esq., Joseph Tavers, Esq., *Interpreters of the Spanish and Portuguese Languages*.

Jonas L. Sibley Esq., *Marshal*.

Horatio Bass, Esq., *Deputy Marshal*.

Boston, Tuesday, Nov. 11, 1834, at 9 o'clock a.m., the prisoners, consisting of Don Pedro Gibert, and his mate Bernardo De Soto, with ten of his crew chained together in pairs, were placed at the bar.

The Clerk then read the indictment in English, and Mr. Badlam read it to the prisoners in Spanish.

[**Editor's note:** The indictment charged that Pedro Gibert, Bernardo de Soto, Francisco Ruiz, Nicola Costa, Antonio Ferrer, Manuel Boyga, Domingo de Guzman, Juan Antonio Portana, Manuel Castillo, Angel Garcia, Jose Velazquez, and Juan Montenegro (alias Jose Basilia de Castro), on 20 September, 1832, "with force and arms did feloniously and piratically" board the *Mexican*; place its captain John Groves Butman "in great bodily fear and danger of his life"; and steal ten boxes containing $2,000 each belonging to Joseph Peabody.]

To this indictment the prisoners one and all plead Not Guilty.

The Clerk then proceeded to empan[^]el the Jury for the trial; and [twelve] Jurors, after eighteen were peremptorily challenged by Don Pedro Gibert, and twenty by Bernardo De Soto, were sworn. [. . .]

[Part I: Initial Testimony for the Prosecution]

The District Attorney now opened the cause on the part of the government in substance as follows:[19]

May it please your Honors and Gentlemen of the Jury,

On this solemn occasion twelve men of a foreign nation, unacquainted with our language, are placed at the bar of this tribunal to answer for the crime of piracy, or robbery, and depredation on the high seas. This is an offence against the universal law of

---

19 This trial transcript consists of an at-times confusing mix of direct quote, summarization, and paraphrase, with reporter's remarks interspersed throughout, sometimes italicized, sometimes set apart in brackets (replaced here by parentheses). When the reporter's input was discernible within testimony, it was italicized in an effort to lend clarity and consistency. In some cases, quotation marks have been silently eliminated when deemed unnecessary and/or misleading (such as when placed around evident paraphrasing).

William Kidd (as depicted by illustrator
Howard Pyle).

society; – a pirate being, according to Sir Edward Coke, *hostis humani generis*.[20] As
therefore he has renounced all the benefits of society and government, and has re-
duced himself afresh to the savage state of nature, by declaring war against all
mankind, all mankind must declare war against him; so that every community hath a
right, by the rule of self defence, to inflict that punishment upon him which every individual would in a state of nature have been otherwise entitled to do, for any invasion of his person or personal property. Piracy is every where pursued and punished
with death. It is of no importance, for the purpose of giving jurisdiction in cases of
piracy, on whom or where a piratical offence is committed. A pirate who is one by the
law of nations may be tried and punished in any country where he may be found, for
he is reputed to be out of the protection of all laws. Thus if the prisoners were con-

---

20 Often translated as "enemy of mankind," *Hostis Humani Generis* has long been cited as an international legal condemnation of pirates. The term is sometimes attributed to Cicero (*On Duties*, 385) who actually used the phrase
communis hostis omnium – "common foe of all the world." As suggested here, it may have originated with English
jurist Coke (1552–1634) who in his *Third Part of the Institutes of the Laws of England* (113) used the phrase "*Pirata
est hostis humani generis*." Examples of American understandings of *Hostis Humani Generis* as an international
principle can be traced into the colonial era. In 1717, Boston cleric Cotton Mather (*Instructions to the Living*, 17)
admonished one of Samuel Bellamy's pirate crew: "All Nations agree, to treat your Tribe, as the Common Enemies of Mankind, and Extirpate them out of the World." At the 1723 Newport, Rhode Island trial of Charles
Harris and his crew, the prosecutor remarked that: "This sort of Criminals are engag'd in a perpetual War with
every Individual, with every State, Christian or Infidel; they have no Country, but by the nature of their Guilt,
separate themselves, renouncing the benefit of all lawful Society, to commit these heinous Offences: The Romans
therefore justly held 'em, *Hostis [H]umani Generis*, Enemies of Mankind . . . " (*Tryals of Thirty-Six Persons for
Piracy*, 3). See also Goodwin, "Universal Jurisdiction and the Pirate," 989–990.

victed of the crime for which they are now indicted in their own country, the punishment would be the same as in this, and all civilized nations, which is death.

By the Act of Congress, April 30, 1790, if any person, upon the high seas, or in any river, haven, or bay, out of the jurisdiction of any particular state, commit[s] murder or robbery, on board a vessel, he shall be deemed a pirate and a felon, and shall suffer death. Since then two additional acts have been passed, both of which make the punishment of this offence capital.

A piratical vessel may sail under pretence of being engaged in commerce having lawful papers; or with a commission from some nation for a specific purpose; and when so engaged commit the crime of Piracy. The celebrated Capt. Kidd sailed under a commission to take Pirates in the Indian Seas, and when so engaged he captured and robbed a Mahometan ship, for which offence he was taken and sent to England, tried and hung in chains at Execution Dock.[21]

After defining the statutes and quoting the precedents applicable to the present case to be found in the books, he gave a brief and pertinent detail of the robbery and piracy on board the Mexican: *which he expected to prove in the case. Also the capture of the prisoners by an English Brig of War: and their subsequent conveyance to this country. He concluded, by extol[l]ing in high terms, the nice sense of justice entertained by the British Government, and its scrupulous regard for the rights of nations.*

Joseph Peabody, Esq., sworn: Is owner of the Brig *Mexican*. Shipped ten boxes of specie, containing two thousand dollars each. The boxes were marked P. – The brig sailed the 28th August, 1832. She arrived back in 42 days, being robbed of the specie. I have been engaged in the West India trade for forty years. I formerly sailed myself to and from the Havana. Passages vary from ten to thirty days. Vessels bound from Cuba to Africa do not steer a strai[gh]t course across the Atlantic, but follow the Gulf Stream until they get as far north as Lat[itude] 30 or 34. A fast sailing vessel leaving the Havanna on the 20th, and a dull sailing vessel leaving Salem on the 29th of the month would be likely to meet in the spot where the *Mexican* was robbed. The Bill of Lading, and Register produced in Court are the genuine ones.

Capt. John Groves Butman, sworn: I commanded the Brig *Mexican*. I sailed on the 29th Aug. 1832, and had twenty thousand dollars in specie[22] on board, stowed down in the run. On the 20th Sept. lat[itude] 33 lon[gitude] 34. 30 fell in with a schooner,

---

21 Engaged as a pirate-hunter, Kidd in 1698 seized the Armenian-hired, Indian-owned *Quedagh Merchant*, captained by an Englishman. Its traveling under French documents technically made it a lawful prize, as Britain was then at war with France. The capture became central at Kidd's politically influenced trial for piracy; he was hanged in chains in 1701.

22 Hard currency, generally in the form of gold or silver coins.

Baltimore clipper, 1820
(artist unknown).

she passed across our bow at 4 a.m.; she was a Baltimore clipper, low, straight and long; at day-break she was on our weather quarter standing from us, after daylight she tacked and stood towards us, between 9 and 10 she was on our weather bow. The wind then shifted a little, we tacked ship because we did not like the appearance of the strange sail. We now perceived a man stationed in her foretop on the look-out; shortly after the schooner squared her sails and stood directly down upon us. When within gunshot she fired a gun to leeward, I now hove to; when a little to windward of us she hailed me. Her distance from us was 30 or 40 yards. I now saw two guns on deck and a large number of men; he asked where we were from, where bound, and what our cargo was on board, I answered our cargo was saltpetre and tea. I was now ordered on board, I took four of my men and went in the boat to her; when we got to her gangway they ordered me to come on board at the fore chains, when we got to the chains five of the schooner's crew jumped into our boat and ordered us back to the brig; none of my crew went on board the schooner. When we got back to the brig they all rushed on deck and ordered me down into the cabin, I went down and they followed me. As soon as I turned round two of them drew their knives on me and stabbed them at my throat, exclaiming, ["]Money, Money,["] in broken English. I was now very much alarmed, and called the mate and crew to come down and get the money out from the run under the cabin floor.

They beat my crew with their knives to make them work quick. After the money was got up they insisted I had more, and pulled over all the chests, boxes, and berths, and told me if they found any they would cut my throat, I was now left alone in the cabin. Soon after as I attempted to go on deck, one of them drove me back and struck me with the speaking trumpet. Saw the boat going to the *Panda*, and return with 12 or 15 men. Heard them jump on board and close up the hatchways, soon after this heard a great noise as if the mainsail had fallen, soon after a spar was thrown on deck. We were now all fastened below, and half suffocated with smoke coming down from the camboose. From the cabin window we saw them return to the *Panda*. They carried one of our spars on board and sunk my boat, they now made sail. We now got on deck through the cabin sky-light, and found every thing in confusion. All the standing and running rigging was cut away, the mainsail cut into ribbons and hanging over the camboose, the camboose burnt half up, in it was a tub of rope yarns, on fire, and other combustibles. In a few moments the fire would have reached the mainsail and set the masts on fire, all the sails were cut up badly. I cannot swear to the identity of any of the prisoners at the bar, I can swear that there was a man[23] chained to one of the prisoners in Salem who drew his knife on me.

Cross Ex[amination]: I should say the schooner was 150 tons burden, the guns appeared to be 12 pounders. There was 50 or 60 men on board, could not swear there was a gun amidships.

Stephen Badlam: I saw Manuel Delgardo, the man identified by Capt. Butman. He cut his throat in the jail, with a bit of glass, I saw him after death.

Benjamin Brown Reed: I was first mate of the *Mexican*. In the morning when I came on deck to stand watch, about 4 o'clock, the second mate told me a vessel had passed astern of us about an hour before. Asked him to pass up the glass, took it and went on the forecastle. Saw her standing for us, went down and told the captain, I thought the vessel wanted to hail us. They were on the starboard tack, she appeared full of men, and manoeuvered in a suspicious manner. The captain now called me, and we consulted where the money should be put. I told him it was no use to do any thing with it as every one on board knew where it was, as they saw it taken on board in Salem harbour, and if we denied having it, and they should find it, we would only fare harder. While we were talking, the 2d mate came down and said they were chasing us, and had fired a gun. Ran on deck and saw the smoke of her gun. The captain ordered our brig to be hove to, and we hoisted American colors. The schooner now hailed us, there was a man on the foretop gallant yard, he was there from our first seeing the pirate in the morning, till we lost sight of her in the afternoon. I reached the manropes to them and saw the knives in their sleeves. We were now all called into the cabin. The Spaniards came up and threatened to cut our throats with their knives, they made us go down one at a time, and beat us to make us get the money out quick, they made such a flustration that it was some[ ]time before we could do any thing. Two men got into the run to get the money out, but could not work for

---

23 Manuel Delgardo, who later committed suicide (*A Report of the Trial of the Spanish Pirates Before the United States Circuit Court* . . . , 10).

want of room; at last after great confusion the steward lifted up the boxes and we passed them on deck. They hailed the *Panda* and said there was plenty of money on board. The boatswain kicked me forward, and then kicked me down the forecastle, called me up, sent me down again, and placed a man over me as guard. I begged hard for my life, he asked me what o'clock it was, and before I could get it [a watch] out, he snatched it from me, he demanded my money, sent a man to get it from the wood pile on deck where it had been hid before they boarded us. They asked for our chronometer,[24] and struck the captain so hard with the speaking trumpet as to bend it all up, they drove us all down the hatchway and made all the hatches fast; we kept quiet till the pirate got to a great distance; when we got up through the cabin skylight, the camboose was all on fire. The mainsail soon would have caught, and the masts would soon have gone by the board, and we should have all been burnt up. Two of the men are now present who boarded the *Mexican*. *The witness now went and put his hand on Francisco Ruiz, and said,* "[T]his is the man that was stationed at the forecastle to keep me down." *Manuel Boyga was the other. These two men now rose and with the fiercest gesticulations denied what the witness had asserted.* I saw another person at Salem who boarded us, he cut his throat in jail.

Cross Ex[amination]: The Capt. at first thought the men on board the *Panda* were the dead eyes[25] of the lower rigging. We thought she was a pirate and tried to avoid her. The boatswain had a bunch [swelling] on his nose,[26] some of the Pirates shifted their clothes on board, putting on ours and leaving theirs. One of the Pirates had on cowhide shoes. The long knives were about a foot in length.

Benjamin Larkum: I shipped as boy on board the *Mexican*, I can recognize two of the prisoners at the bar. *The witness went and put his hand on Ruiz the piratical carpenter.* I saw that man with the first boat['s] crew that came on board. I went in the boat with Capt. Butman on board the pirate. When we got back I stayed in the boat and bailed her out. I heard a great noise on board, was frightened and crept into the head. I thought they were murdering our crew. I was not frightened when the schooner first hailed us, but when I saw their knives in their sleeves when they boarded us, I was scared.

Cross Ex[amination]: I should think the pirate about 150 tons, I could see the figure head from the place where I concealed myself.

24 "A valuable time-piece fitted with a compensation-balance, adjusted for the accurate measurement of time in all climates, and used by navigators for the determination of the longitude" (Smyth, *Lexicon*, 186).

25 A dead-eye was a round, flat, circular wood block "fixed to the channels by the chain-plate: it is pierced with three holes through the flat part, in order to receive a rope called the lan[y]ard, which, corresponding with three holes in another dead-eye on the shroud end, creates a purchase to set up and extend the shrouds and stays, backstays, &c., of the standing and top-mast rigging" (Smyth, *Lexicon*, 235).

26 According to another source of trial testimony, this witness said: "Among the men who came on board from the schooner was the boatswain; was about five feet in height, stout, and wore large whiskers; had a bunch on his nose" (*A Report of the Trial of the Spanish Pirates Before the United States Circuit Court* . . . , 12).

John Battis: I am 18 years old, I was with the *Mexican*. I can swear to the identity of two of the prisoners. *He went up and put his hand on Ruiz and Boyga. They rose with great indignation and exclaimed in the most savage manner,* "[Y]ou lie, you say you saw us." [Battis:] I first recognized these men on board the *Savage* in Salem harbour.

Thomas Fuller: Was a seaman on board the *Mexican*. I think there is one person here whom I recognize to be one of the pirates that robbed us. *Fuller went up to identify Ruiz, and struck him a terrible blow, and then retreated back very suddenly.*[27] *The prisoners all resented this with great indignation.*

The court reprimanded the witness for his uncourteous recognition. [Fuller:] "I am not certain he [Ruiz] is one,[28] I think he is, I saw him beat the steward with an oak baton in the forecastle."

Cross Ex[amination]: Had no more enmity for him than the rest. *Mr. Dunlap now said to Fuller,* [I]f you had struck lighter your evidence would have been harder.

Benjamin Daniells: I can identify one person who boarded us, it is Ruiz the carpenter. *He put his hand on him in a gentle manner.* I am positive he was one who boarded us, he drove us around the vessel. I was much alarmed when they drew their knives on us.

Thomas C. H. Ridgely – Black Cook: When the pirates came on board the *Mexican*, I had a good chance to see them come in the gang way. I was lying my body over the camboose, had my feet on some spars. I saw Antonio Ferrer, the black man, on the fore top sail yard of the *Panda*, saw the scars[29] on his face. The vessel sometimes came within a few feet of us, and then yawed off.[30] *Antonio [Ferrer] now rose and said,* "[Y]ou must have fine eyes to see that distance."

John Lewis – Black Steward: This is the man that beat me down in the half deck with an oak baton, *putting his hand on Ruiz.* He beat me because I would not tell him where the money was.

Cross Ex[amination]: He broke the baton into three pieces in striking me. I lifted the money out of the run. *Mr. Child to Lewis.* What have you and the cook been talking

---

27 According to *A Report of the Trial of the Spanish Pirates Before the United States Circuit Court . . .* (13), Fuller "went up to him [Ruiz] and struck him rather rudely upon the shoulder."

28 In *A Report of the Trial of the Spanish Pirates Before the United States Circuit Court . . .* (14), Fuller said "Recollect Ruiz perfectly well."

29 A defense counsel would later describe these as tattoos.

30 A yaw is a "quick movement by which a ship deviates from the direct line of her course towards the right or left, from unsteady steering" (Smyth, *Lexicon*, 741).

about since you have been confined in the same room? [*Lewis:*] We have been talking about nothing. *(A Laugh.)*

[Part II: Perez's testimony]

Joseph Perez, one of the Panda's crew taken for a United States' Evidence.

Mr. Dunlap requested Mr. Badlam, the interpreter, to say to Perez – "You are now put to the bar as a witness; and if you tell the truth, the whole truth, and nothing but the truth, you will not be prosecuted."

Judge Story instructed Mr. Badlam to repeat Mr. Dunlap's proposition to Perez, by one sentence at a time, and to add: "If you do not tell the truth, the whole truth, and nothing but the truth, you will be liable to be prosecuted as much as any other of the Pirates" – *and to add the distinct question to him* – "Are you willing to testify upon these conditions?"

This question being answered in the affirmative, a Bible, certified by the Bishop to be such, was produced, and with his left hand on the New Testament portion of the Scriptures, and the right one raised, he was sworn according to the most solemn form known.

Judge Story then asked, through the interpreter: "Do you believe God will punish you, if you testify falsely?"

Perez answered affirmatively, and the examination proceeded; he testified as follows, with the exception of such omissions, as are not deemed essential:–

Joseph Perez: I was born in the island of Margueritta, in Colombia;[31] am about 22 years old. I was taken to Havana in a vessel, a prisoner, and stayed there four months. Afterwards, about two years and four months ago, I joined the *Panda* at Havana; Pedro Gibert, now present, was her commander; Bernardo de Soto, present, was her mate; Francisco Ruiz, present, was her carpenter; *all* of the prisoners were of the crew, but all the crew are not here. When we sailed from Havana, there were 30 in all, including the officers. When we sailed from the mouth of the harbor, in passing Mor[r]o Castle we were hailed– "[W]here bound?" We answered, to St. Thomas and Principi,[32] on the coast of Africa, and our Captain's name given "Pedro Gibert." We

---

31 Margarita, off the coast of modern Venezuela, which from 1819–1831 was part of Bolivar's *Gran Colombia.*
32 São Tomé and Príncipe, the latter also referred to herein as Prince's Island or variants of that name. Both housed what one British official termed "Slave Factories" (Commodore Sir G.R Collier to the Lords of the Admiralty, 27 Dec. 1821, in *British and Foreign State Papers*, 215). An 1834 book observed that Prince's Island, "twenty-eight leagues distant to the S[outh] S[outh] W[est] of Fernando Po, is nearly eight leagues long, and six broad. It is the ordinary rendezvous of the Guineamen, the harbour being considered the best in this group of islands. The air is

sailed at 8 in the morning, somewhere about the 20th or 26th of August. We first spoke a corvette on the 20th of September, at 4 in the morning. I first saw the American brig, heading south; the Captain was asleep; it was the 2d mate's watch; the captain got up and ordered the schooner to be put about; we tacked ship and stood for the brig. When it began to be more light, the brig altered her course to west, with all sails set; our schooner then set all her sails. I was stationed in the foretop; at half past 6 I sung out, "A sail;" it was to windward of the American brig; I should call it a schooner[-]brig. About 8, the *Mexican* altered her course and sailed south; the *Panda* loosened her sails and stood for the brig; a sailor on board went forward to the bows and fired a musket: the *Mexican* hove to, and hoisted an American flag: the *Panda* hoisted a Colombian flag. A sailor, who spoke English, hailed the brig, "Where do you come from?" "From Boston," was the answer.

A boat from the brig, with four men and an officer, rowed to our schooner—came on the larboard side.[33]

The 3d mate, boatswain, carpenter and one sailor got into the brig's boat, and went to the brig – that is, four men of the Spanish schooner embarked in the boat for the American brig. There the carpenter sits (*here arose a brief, but most ferocious gabbling between the witness and Ruiz, who appeared ready to fly at each other's throats*) – the 3d mate ran away at Nazareth[34] – the boatswain died at Fernando Po,[35] a prisoner – Delgardo was the name of the sailor, and he died in Boston Jail. The people of the brig went below in the forecastle – the 3d mate took the speaking trumpet and sung out to the captain of our schooner: "There is on board what you wish; what you are looking for; she carries $20,000, as put down in the papers of the vessel; the money is in 10 boxes, containing $2000 each." The boatswain held up a handful of dollars and showed them to the captain, and afterwards threw them into

---

healthy and agreeable; the water excellent. Many fresh and clear streams descend to the coast; a small lake occupies the summit of a high mountain in the middle of the island. . . . The city, built near the north-east point, contains two hundred houses of one story, two churches, and a convent; there are about fifty whites, the remaining population consists of mulattoes and free negroes, who maintain a great many slaves. A small fort, guarded by Portuguese exiles, defends the entrance of the harbour. At twenty leagues distance south-west of Prince's Island, under the equator, is the Island of Saint Thomas: it is twelve leagues in length, and seven in its greatest breadth, with fifteen thousand inhabitants, the greater part negroes or mulattoes. The northern part is composed of high mountains, terminating in peaks, always enveloped in clouds, which, at a distance, look like smoke, and have been taken by voyagers for perpetual snow. . . . " (Malte-Brun, *System of Universal Geography*, II:150).

33 The left, or port, side of the vessel.
34 River on the west coast of Africa; a contemporary source placed its mouth 13 leagues north-east of Gabon's Cape Lopez (Purdy, *Memoir*, 100).
35 Now called Bioko; a volcanic island in the Gulf of Guinea. At this time the British had established bases on the island. From an 1834 book's description: Fernando Po "is eight leagues long, from north-east to south-west, and about three wide. It is represented as very high, woody, frequently covered with clouds, very fertile in sugar-canes, cotton, tobacco, manioc, sweet potatoes, fruits and other commodities bartered here for iron bars and wine. . . . The ordinary anchorage, where ships take in wood and water, is only an open road on the northern side" (Malte-Brun, *System of Universal Geography*, II:150). For a modern history, see I. K. Sundiata, *From Slaving to Neoslavery: The Bight of Biafra and Fernando Po in the Era of Abolition, 1827–1930* (Madison: University of Wisconsin, 1996).

the sea. The captain sung out, "Very well, very well; let her be well searched, and let it all come on board."

The $20,000 were brought on board; it was money; I saw it with my own eyes from the top; the schooner's launch towed the American boat to the schooner ¼ I looked so intently at what was going on in the brig, that the captain scolded me, and sent another man up to look out; four men then went on board the brig; they were Garcia, Montenegro, Castillo, and Ruiz, (*all in court*). I was in the tops; told the captain there was a sail in sight; "Where away?" said he.¶

"Astern of the American brig."¶

"How close?"¶

"So nigh, I can see her 3 masts."

At this time, one of my comrades in the American brig was standing guard over the forecastle, with a handspike; the captain sang out to take them (*brig's crew*) out of the forecastle, and shut them up in the cabin; the 3d mate, with a sword, and a sailor, with a knife, then chased them after from the forecastle to the cabin; the people were shut below with a padlock. After they were all shut up below, saw smoke; they all then started for the schooner, bringing a keg of butter and one of lard; when about half way to the schooner, 3d mate and boatswain got out of the American boat and knocked her bottom out with something heavy; when our launch was hoisted, we turned a gun towards the brig, and made a round turn across her bows. . . .

The *Panda* first made Cape Monte,[36] on the coast of Africa, then Port Bazaar,[37] sta[ye]d there some days, took in water, &c. one morning saw a frigate running down with all sails set – our captain then ordered all the knives to be taken away from the crew – the frigate saw us, and sailed on the other tack – our captain ordered us to weigh anchor, and with a light wind and oars we got out from Grand Bazaar – went to Cape Lopez[38] – thence to the river Nazareth, in November, and left me ashore there to look after the slaves, the schooner sailed to the Isle of Principi, in January. When they came back from Principi, they came running away, and they ran the schooner

---

36 A 19th century account places Cape Monte (Cape Mount) sixteen leagues from Cape Mesurado, near Monrovia, Liberia: "Cape Monte (Mount) is represented as the paradise of Guinea, watered with rivulets and springs, spreading into vast meadows and plains, interrupted by groves perpetually green; the leaves of which resemble laurel. Rice, millet, and maize, are produced in greater abundance than in any other part of Guinea; and orange, lemon, almond, and palm trees, are the spontaneous productions of the soil" (Hugh Murray, *Western Africa*, II:283–286, cited in "Swedish Project of a Colony on the Western Coast of Africa," *The African Repository* 27(8), August 1851, 246).

37 This location, which the witness later calls Grand Bazaar, may be Buchanan in modern Liberia, once known as Grand Bassa (Room, *Alternate Names*, 36).

38 Peninsula on Gabon's coast.

ashore, on the beach of Cape Lopez – the captain came ashore at Nazareth – I was his servant, and while setting the table I heard him tell the boatswain that he had to fly from Principi because the news of the American brig robbery had reached there – he had bought $250 dollars' worth of provision, which he was obliged to leave, the schooner remained at Nazareth about 4 months, – when the English hove in sight with their boats, the carpenter went into the cabin, took up the after scuttle, and put a brimstone match to a bag or keg of powder – the rest of the crew had all gone ashore – the carpenter then left in a canoe. Before he left he took the papers of the schooner, and brought them with him. The captain and men all went to the negro barracks, and remained there till the English vessel went to sea.

The British brig took the schooner off to sea, but both came back again, and came to an anchor; the English commander came on shore, and demanded the captain, mate, and carpenter; captain hid himself in a negro hut; the commander demanded them of the black king; he refused to deliver them up; the captain of the brig began to fire on the town from the pivot gun of the schooner *Panda*, a 12[-] or 16[-] pounder, till she caught fire during the bombardment. After the English went away, the money was hid in a barrel, on the beach, on the right side of the river; the captain that day gave orders to move back into the woods as the English boats were coming down upon us; we took the money to Cape Lopez, and buried it there; I went after it there again by the captain's orders, with Boyga, Castillo, Ruiz, and Velasquez; while Castillo and I were digging up the money, the others began to count it; I said there were too many musquitoes here to throw away time in counting the money; one of them replied, that it was the captain's orders to count it, and leave five thousand dollars there for him. After his $5,000 were left, there were about $6,000 which we took to the negro barracks. We divided this money between us. . . . We were sitting in a dark room; the carpenter and captain up stairs talking; the carpenter came down, and said, "The captain is going to divide the money, and if *all* did not go and get their share, there would be the devil to pay." They all then went and got their share. . . .

I delivered myself up at Fernando Po – myself, Castillo, Montenegro and Garcia, and Delgardo, went there together in a boat – was taken in an English transport to Ascension,[39] Sierra Leon[e], back again to Fernando Po, then to Principi, back to Ascension, where I found the rest of the prisoners in custody. We five were taken to Plymouth, in England, in the merchant schooner *Hope*, and then put on board a 74[-gun warship] – while on board of the 74, the other prisoners were also brought in by the British man-of-war brig *Curlew*, and put on board of the 74 with us, and we were all brought to this country in the 10[-]gun brig *Savage*.

---

39   A volcanic island in the South Atlantic, midway between Brazil and central Africa. A British possession, it housed a Royal Navy base.

"The Pirates carrying Rum on Shore to purchase Slaves" (19th century illustration, artist unknown).

Joseph Perez – (*cros[s]-ex[amination]*): The cargo of our schooner consisted of 60 pipes new rum[40] – bales of clothing, 30 bundles, all sizes – some dry goods – pieces of cloth – 250 muskets – powder – flints – boxes of swords and cutlasses – 1 barrel knives – 2 boxes axes – beads, necklaces – I shipped for $20 per month – able seamen had $25. . . . It is customary in all vessels going and returning from the coast of Africa to have a man in the tops – the *Panda* was painted black with a white streak – billet head – before she left Nazareth, the billet head was taken off, and an awkward piece of wood put on – we made her a two topsail schooner – she left Havana a foretopsail schooner – 3 or 4 days after the robbery she put up her maintopsail – we saw an hermaphrodite brig while we were robbing the *Mexican* – then a ship, which we ran away from – some of the sailors said she was a man-of-war – don't know whether she chased us or not, but she came nearer – saw the captain take a pistol, which came from the American brig, out of the third mate's hand, and throw it overboard – Captain Gibert said he did not want any such thing on board – wanted nothing but money. . . . The third mate had a sword – the sailors had knives ground sharp at the point, like daggers – it is customary to give the men jackknives, but the men themselves bring long knives in their bags.

That day the captain said to the men – "Boys, take off your hats and put on your caps, and change about." Those that were obedient took their hats off, and those that were not kept theirs on. . . . I cannot read Spanish, much less English – all the letters of the alphabet which I know is, P, D, O and U, (*witness then explained that he*

---

40 A pipe consisted of two hogsheads, for a total of about 126 gallons (Flett, "Arithmetic Exercise Book," 5).

meant written or Italian characters – he succeeded in making out nearly all the let-ters in print, and read a number of words correctly in the Spanish translation of the indictment.) I want to tell how I got $250 – the boatswain [$]500 – Delgardo [$]300 – Montenegro [$]250, and the mate $2,400 – he confessed his guilt in Sierra Leon[e.] *([A]t this point the witness spoke so fast that it was impossible to interpret, or take down his testimony – he was therefore repeatedly interrupted, till losing all patience, he exclaimed in English – "I will say, and by G-d I will" – and when checked again, misunderstood a remark, and drew the inference that he was ren-dering himself liable to the same punishment as the other prisoners, by what he was testifying. He in consequence became excited, and was made quite frantic by Capt. Gibert's remarking to him, that he took him on board of his schooner out of charity. The interpreters were requested to take him out and tranquilize him, by an explana-tion. When they returned, Judge Story requested the interpreters to assure him, if la-boring under any delusion of danger, of his perfect safety. Mr. Child objected to any such intimation being given, but Mr. Dunlap moved that he be assured that the faith and honor of the government pledged to him by its legal officers, should be faithfully kept. Mr. Child replied, with great vehemence, to this motion, and concluded by say-ing –* "I believe the unhappy men at this bar are totally innocent of the crime they are charged with – I believe them to be the victims of one of the foulest plots that was ever contrived." *The assurance, however, was given, and the confidence of the wit-ness being restored he proceeded.)*

... There was nothing said about dividing the money till the English had taken the schooner. The captain had $4000 of the money in his trunk when he ran her ashore. The captain bought a watch, valued at $400, and a shaving machine, worth $400, from Prince['s] Isle – knew they were bought with the stolen money, because the vessel had not a quarter of a cent, when she left Havana – [I] was [the] captain's steward. .... The negro interpreter took the money the captain had, at the time the English came to Nazareth, and hid it in his own yard – we buried $11,000 at Cape Lopez – don't recollect the day we dug it up again – left $5000 for the captain – does[n']t recollect the day, because he was so afraid of being made a prisoner – had never been in such a dirty scrape before – we five that went to Fernando Po threw our money overboard, because the boatswain said it would be our own condemna-tion – when the captain called me to receive my share of the money, it was laying by his side on the floor – $250 – he said, "You may want a little money to buy clothes, and you may go, as you have been wanting to go this long time." The captain had a knife in his bosom – I believe his intention was to kill any one who refused to take his share of the money – the boatswain had $500 – Garcia $400 – Castillo $250 – Montenegro $250 – Delgardo $300 – the mate, De Soto, $2,400 – the 3d mate ran away at Lopez, and the captain sent him $1000, by the carpenter – there was no rule agreed upon for dividing the money – the captain was the sole owner, and did as he had a mind to with it – he had one lot of $4000, and another of $5000 – don't know what become of the rest.

. . . When [the] carpenter failed to blow up the schooner on the beach, [the] captain asked why he did not spread powder on the deck, tie a string to the lock of the gun, and as he rowed ashore give it a slant, and thus fire it off among the powder on the deck, and so set fire to her – had purchased 60 slaves – the schooner was to carry 450 slaves. . . .

At Fernando Po, I denied that I belonged to the *Panda* at first, but when put under oath I confessed that I did belong to her – by advice of [the] boatswain, we agreed to say we belonged to the Spanish brig *Little Negro*, which was cast away – the boatswain continued to say so, till confronted by a Portuguese, who had seen him on board of the *Panda*, when he owned it; when examined there I was put into a room by myself – Delgardo also confessed – the Governor made him sign a paper – they never offered me anything – it was my own fear that made me declare – they said if I lied, and it turned out that I belonged to the *Panda*, I should be hung – my heart failed me, and I told the whole story. They had a newspaper there containing an account of the robbery of the *Mexican*. When I spoke of the $20,000, one of the clerks took up the paper, and said "True," and threw it down on the table.

I did not come here bribed. – I did not say, when I saw the boatswain dead at Fernando Po, "God forgive me for bearing false witness against him." … On board the *Victoria*, 74,[41] at Plymouth, the captain [Gibert] and mate [de Soto] told me to say I knew no English, and to deny every thing. Captain conversed with all the prisoners. I told the Cook, Ferrer, that the Captain wanted all of them to deny everything, so that he himself might turn king's evidence, and that the captain had offered to, – the captain and mate have tried several times to get me to deny every thing. … Perico was the name of the sailor who hailed the *Mexican* in English – they say he died when the schooner went to Principi. … I was on board of a Spanish schooner when Morillo[42] commanded the Spanish forces, but I don't know how old I was. (*This answer was given to a question that was propounded to him, in a variety of forms, and he broke out – "I don't want to be bothered with these questions in this way – I know they come from the prisoners.*") I was taken into Havana in the brig *Eagle* a prisoner, – I was cabin boy of her, – we were taken because we had slaves on board. Costa was on board the *Eagle*. – Costa was cabin boy on board the *Panda*, – heard Costa say that Ferrer was a slave. I did not know when I shipped that there was any intention of robbery – all vessels bound to the coast of Africa have to report their crew to the general of marine, but our crew was not inspected by him – I don't know the reason why our crew did not go to his office – I did not know the captain then; if I had, I should sooner have stopped ashore, and ate dirt, than have gone with him – saw the

---

41 Though Victoria became Queen of Great Britain in 1819, no warship would be named for her until 1839. What may have been intended was a reference to the 74-gun HMS *Victorious*, on receiving ship duties after 1826, broken up at Portsmouth in 1862 (Colledge and Warlow, *Royal Navy*, 430–431).

42 Spanish General Pablo Morillo was the principal commander against Bolivar's forces until a truce was negotiated in 1820 (Harvey, *Liberators*, 134, 186–187).

carpenter give the captain the schooner's papers, in the barracoon (*negro barracks*), but don't know what became of them after – the schooner sailed from Havana under a Spanish flag. Before we robbed the *Mexican* we robbed an English vessel; hailed the English corvette, and asked if they could sell us a topmast, as our main topmast was not up; then asked the captain to come on board, but the English answered that his boat leaked. The third mate, boatswain, &c. went on board of the English vessel; the third mate hailed the schooner, and said that there was *not* on board *what* he wanted; they took some leather, lemons, cordials, rigging, a spyglass, cabin curtains, and monkey jackets.[43]

The crew obeyed every command of the captain, and after the robbery of the *Mexican*, the captain was still *greater* and *greater*. We had been out about 8 days.

We did not commit any other robbery after robbing the *Mexican*; but at Sesto[44] the captain wanted to sink a Spanish schooner laying there – he got the gun all ready, and fixed the tackle to the anchor to weigh it, but the sea was too heavy and he gave it up.

In answer to the question – "Have you ever received any money since you were taken?" *Perez replied*; [Y]ou are trying to do with me what the Spanish consul tried to do in England; trying to make me confess that I was bribed.

Mr. Child: Have you ever confessed that you were drunk when you gave your declaration at Fernando Po?

Perez: The scoundrel that says so is a liar.

In answer to Mr. Dunlap: [T]he papers brought ashore from the schooner by the carpenter and given to the captain, were put in a tin box, all wet. In the negro barracks, when the English brig was in sight, I heard De Soto say to the third mate, that he had been up all night making up a false log book, so as to make it appear, that the schooner came a different way than she did come. I went to school eight months; they tried to make me read printed letters; I can read print a little, but can neither write nor read writing. The 3d mate, who I saw at the negro hut after he left, gave as a reason for running away that news of the robbery of the *Mexican* had reached Principi.

[Part III: Silvera's Testimony]

Anastasio Silvera: I was born at St. Catherine,[45] in the Brazils; am 23 years old; I belonged to the *Panda*; I joined her at Princes Island on the 9th of February, 1833; Don

---

43 "A warm jacket for night-watches, etc" (Smyth, *Lexicon*, 482).
44 Possibly Sasstown (or Sosstown), a port in modern Liberia (Cohen, *Columbia Gazeteer*, III:3462).
45 The state of Santa Catarina.

Pedro Gibert was captain, and De Soto was mate (*witness identifies all the prisoners as belonging to the crew of the* Panda*)*; I went on board at nine in the morning, and the schooner sailed in half an hour after; went to Cape Lopez, and thence to the river Nazareth; the river is 4 or 6 leagues from Lopez; she ran ashore at Lopez, and the carpenter said he was going to set her on fire; the captain sent me and the other Portuguese taken on board at Princes Island ashore; they got her off again; I did not go up the river with her; the captain sent me on board after she got up the river; at Nazareth the captain and mate lived ashore in a barracoon – 8 or 9 of the crew lived on board; the rest lived on shore; the cargo we were going to take were slaves; when the English boats came into the river on the 4th of June, the carpenter told us to jump into the boat and go ashore, as he was going to set fire to the schooner; but the carpenter came on shore without setting her on fire, whether through fear because the English boats were so near, or not, I do not know; the carpenter was the last man on board, he came on shore in a canoe after the crew left in the boat; I went to the barracoon where the captain was, at Nazareth town; I sta[ye]d there one day, when the captain turned me and the rest of the Portuguese away, and said it was because he had nothing to support us with; I went to a negro house and sta[ye]d 9 or 10 days; the *Panda* went out of the river, but came back in 10 or 15 days; there was a Portuguese schooner laying there; I asked the captain of her if he would give me a passage to Princes Island, and he said he would. The English captain was on board of the Portuguese schooner, at this time, and pressed me, and I was taken on board of the *Panda*, a prisoner; the next day the English commenced firing on the town from the *Panda*, and upon firing the second gun she blew up; they put me and the rest of the Portuguese on board of a little Portuguese sloop that lay there, from which I was taken on board the *Curlew*; Domingo and I, when we first left the *Panda*, went back in the country together, but on the same day he left me and said he was going back to the *Panda*, but I don't know whether he did go on board of her or not, as I did not see him after.

Cross-examined: Before I joined the *Panda*, I had been at Princes Island a month and a half, on board of a Brazilian brig – the brig had been there, I think, over fifteen days – I did not see her till two or three days after she had been there – it was in the month of January, but what day I don't know – the captain of the *Panda* was to give me $120 for the voyage round to Nazareth and back to Havana – one of the others shipped for the same wages – she was a two-topsail schooner, had a [B]ray pivot-gun,[46] and two carronades – the head was neither a fiddle-head[47] nor a billet-head – it was long and slim, and turned up at the end – the main topsail yards were smaller than the fore yards – had twelve men on board when I first went on board – after-

---

46 "Some carronades were fitted on the 'non-recoil' principle. This was invented by Bentham, the Inspector General of Naval Works, though a slightly different version, devised by a ship's carpenter named Bray, was used aboard improvised gunboats at the siege of Acre in 1799" (Lavery, *English Ships of War*, 132).

47 "When there is no figure; this means that the termination of the head is formed by a scroll turning aft or inward like a violin. . . . " (Smyth, *Lexicon*, 293).

wards I saw seven more at the barracoon (*see testimony of Perez*) – the custom-house boat was along side, when I went on board, but I do not know that the custom-house officers overhauled her – I think Ferrara,[48] the Governor of the Island, was the consignee of the *Panda*'s cargo – I heard that the mate was sick at the Governor's house – I heard no report of the piracy of the *Mexican* at Princes[s] Island – I never saw any money on board – we were not chased while going to Lopez – saw no vessel while going from Princes Island to Lopez.

When we were going to leeward of the Cape Lopez, the schooner touched, or dragged on the bottom; we passed one gun forward,[49] and got her off into deep water and anchored – remained two days; the captain then said she was unseaworthy, and not fit to make the voyage to Havana, and must be ran ashore, and set fire to – and he gave that as a reason for weighing anchor, and going up the river so quick; when she got to Nazareth the mate said there was 4 feet of water in her; saw no money taken out of her at the time she was anchored of Cape Lopez – muskets, pistols, swords, beef, bottles of gin, &c. were taken out. She lay about a gun shot to the leeward of Cape Lopez – I am certain that she ran ashore; I was on board and ran a line ashore; at Nazareth I was kept ashore to take care of the slaves; lead them to bathe, and give them water and victuals; the 3d mate went away in an English hermaphrodite brig, in February or March – the day the third mate went ashore, he and the boatswain had a quarrel, in which the boatswain received a small wound – I don't know where – I do not know that the 3d mate went away because he had wounded the boatswain; I don't know what trade the English brig was engaged in – nor where she went.

The prisoners all told me that they abandoned their cargo to trade in slaves – *(the witness describes the attack on the Panda, and escape of her crew, precisely as [the] other witnesses)* – one or two muskets were fired from the English boats, *(Mr. Child here contradicts Mr. Peyton's interpretation, but Mr. Tavers, the native Portuguese, confirms Mr. Peyton)* –I can only swear that they fired one, two, or three – they were very near when we first saw them – the schooner lay at anchor in a bite [bight] or cove – the English did not open a fire as soon as they got round the point, but pulled directly for the schooner, with an English flag – as soon as they got on board of the schooner they fired a gun, and another in the evening, but I don't know what for – I don't know of any money having been buried by any of the crew of the *Panda* – *(interpretation challenged by Mr. Child, and Mr. Peyton was sustained by Mr. Tavers, in*

48 One Ferrara Gomez, reputedly heavily involved in slave-trading, had been governor of Prince's Island circa 1819 and retained influence even after "the Portuguese were shamed into a pretense of removing this man . . . " ("Art. III" ["Fernando Po – State of the Slave Trade"], *Quarterly Review*, Vol. XXVI, No. LI [October 1821], 68). In the early 1830s, a British naval officer wrote of a "Señor Ferrara, a Portuguese, possessing the largest property and greatest influence in the island" and who was "officiating in [the] absence" of the governor; Ferrara's wife was the "queen" of Prince's Island (Leonard, *Records of a Voyage*, 119–120, 125).

49 To shift the weight within the vessel and thereby free it from the shallows.

his interpretation) – I don't know whether the English searched for money or not – I don't know where the captain of the *Panda* was taken prisoner – sailed from the river Bonney[50] to Fernando Po, where the Captain of the *Curlew* heard that there were five of the *Panda*'s crew there – I went ashore there – remained 34 or 35 days; I never went on board of the *Curlew* again – I went, with Montenegro, Garcia, and Castillo, now here, and Perez and Delgardo not here, to Ascension, in an English transport.

It was in August I left Fernando Po in the transport – arrived there about 30 days before the *Curlew* – at Ascension I was put on board of an English man-of-war *Flora*,[51] and went to Sierra Leon[e] with the other five – went from there to Fernando Po – thence to the river Camarone [Camaroon]; thence to Princes Island; then transferred to another English brig *Trinado*, and went back to Ascension, and found the *Curlew* there; then put on board of the *Esperanza*, and went to England; don't recollect the length of the voyage; touched at St. Michael's; stopped two days; *thinks the voyage lasted 60 days*; I did not see the other prisoners at Ascension; only the five; I was always a prisoner; I was always the first that they put in irons, when we were ironed; we were all called up and put to work in the day time; to wash deck, sheet home,[52] or set the sails,[53] or clew them up;[54] on board of the *Curlew*, we were two or three days in irons; when first taken into the other vessel, slept the first night in irons; when we got to sea the irons were taken off; at Ascension we were kept four days in jail ashore, in irons; at Sierra Leon[e], we were kept ashore two days, taking declarations, (*i.e. depositions;*) at St. Michael's we slept in the forecastle with a sentry over us; when we arrived in England, we were not put in chains.

I never heard Perez (*United States' evidence, already examined*) say any thing about the testimony he had given or was to give in this case – never heard any one talk to Perez about it – whenever I saw Perez talking, I always cleared out – I did not like his conversation – he always spoke blackguard about my father and mother – *mocha palav[e]ra*[55] – the whole of them would blackguard one another about each other's fathers and mothers. (*Mr. Peyton here explains that among Spaniards, when they get angry with each other, they always abuse each other's parents.*) I heard Perez say, in the presence of some of these prisoners, that they had robbed the American brig –

50 The Bonny River had become one of "the great Marts" for slave-trading by the early 1820s. It was navigable by larger vessels: "Bonny, though it may be considered a bar River, is nevertheless accessible to Ships of 400 or 500 tons" (Commodore Sir G.R Collier to the Lords of the Admiralty, 27 December 1821, in *British and Foreign State Papers*, 202).

51 No HMS *Flora* appears to have been in service between 1809 and 1844 (Colledge and Warlow, *Royal Navy*, 146).

52 "The order, after the sails are loosed, to extend the sheets to the outer extremities of the yards, till the clue [or clew] is close to the sheet-block" (Smyth, *Lexicon*, 614). The clew is, "in a fore-and-aft rig, the lower after-most corner of the sail; in a square-rigged ship, the two lower corners of the square sail" (Dear and Kemp, *Companion*, 113).

53 "A sail is set when it is hoisted and sheeted home to the wind" (Dear and Kemp, *Companion*, 510).

54 The process of employing the "clew lines," which are the "lines or tackles used in square-rigged ships to haul the clews of the square sails up to their yards" (Dear and Kemp, *Companion*, 113).

55 "Ugly talk" in Portuguese.

and they at that time owned it; Perez also said that the declarations he had made at Fernando Po he would always stick to.

Perez said he confessed because it was the truth, and the other prisoners said it was true; they said so more than twenty times on board of the *Esperanza* on her way to England; the first time I heard of the robbery of the *Mexican* was on board of the *Panda*, after she was captured; I learnt it from one of the Portuguese who shipped with me; he said the carpenter told him; at Fernando Po, they all five wanted to confess, but made such a noise that they would not let them; a great many things that Perez would say, they would say was true, and at other things he would say, they would cry out it was a lie; they would get mad with each other during the examination, and call each other rascals; no promises made to them to induce them to confess; would not even give me a shirt; if it had not been for the goodness of the English sailors, I should not have had any thing to cover my flesh; no threats were made; no musket ever pointed at the black man, to my knowledge; at Fernando Po, in the Governor's house, he asked the whole of the five if they had robbed the *Mexican*; they said they had; the English captain was present; the first day they denied it.

When the English captain came on shore at the river Nazareth, I saw the Captain and crew of the *Panda* go back into the forest which borders on the town – the captain went one way and the crew another; I never knew Captain Trotter to give wine or rum to Perez; I never heard Perez say that what he had confessed (*told*) about the piracy was all a lie; I never heard Perez say to the prisoners: "I would rather take your lot than mine." We Portuguese all told Captain Trotter that we shipped in Princes Island, in reply to him, when he asked us if we came from Havana in the *Panda*. I don't know why the *Esperanza* was captured; her boatswain, cook, and a negro were taken to England. The English talked about sending them to this country, but the Portuguese consul interfered and prevented it; I don't know what became of them; I was present when the boatswain of the *Panda* died at Fernando Po; I never heard Perez say any thing about him after his death; I have not conversed with any one about this matter since I came to America; I do not know that several of the prisoners have had offers of liberty if they would testify against the rest of the crew; I don't know that any of them have had offers of clothing and a conveyance to their own country if they would testify; I feel quite certain that I have had no conversation about these matters with other persons than the prisoners, either here or in England, except with the Spanish Consul in this city; he asked me something about the death of the boatswain.

[Part IV: Quentin's Testimony]

George H. Quentin: I am an officer in the British navy, I am a master's assistant (*i.e. midshipman*) – came to Salem in the 10[-]gun brig *Savage*, on the 27th of August, direct from Portsmouth, England[56] – the prisoners were received on board at Spit-head.[57] I was attached to the brig *Curlew*, commanded by Henry Dundas Trotter; I be-longed to her about 3 years and a half; had been at Cape of Good Hope; arrived on the coast of Africa in January, 1833; touched at Princes Isle in March; in May, at Princes Isle, we received information that a piracy had been commit[t]ed on the *Mexi-can*, and that a vessel, answering the description, contained in the *Salem Gazette*,[58] of the pirate schooner, was laying in the river Nazareth.

We then sailed for the river Nazareth, and arrived there on the 4th of June; three of our boats, armed, went up the river with about forty men; Capt. Trotter himself com-manded the boats; I was in one of them: just after daylight, we observed the schooner laying at anchor; we pulled up, but kept out of sight as much as possible: when we got within a mile of her, we hoisted a "union jack;" we were at that moment behind a point of land. A[s] soon as we hove in sight of the schooner, her whole crew left her, except one man, and we soon saw him go off in a canoe. Capt. Trotter then chased the canoe, but could not come up with her, and returned to the schooner. I was the first who boarded the schooner; there was not a soul on board; saw nothing but smoke issuing from the cabin; one man went down, and found a slow match, made of brimstone and cotton, burning in the magazine, where there were fourteen or sixteen quarter casks of powder; it was hauled from the cabin burning; the fire was immediately put out with water; the hatch was off the magazine. The captain gave or-ders to look for the schooner's papers and log-book and all other papers: one of the men found a few notes in the cabin; I searched, but found no papers; none were found: the notes were taken possession of by Capt. Trotter. We bent the sails[59] of the schooner, and went down the river with her; had her in our possession ten or eleven days. She was a long, two-topsail schooner, figure-head cut off; raking masts, sharp like a Baltimore clipper, no name on her stern, had a slave deck, grated hatchway.

On the 6th day we went to [Cape] Lopez; three days after the schooner blew up, killing 2 officers and 2 men; we supposed a spark from the gun fell into the maga-zine; we went to Lopez in search of the pirate-crew; we obtained Simon Domingo, a Portuguese, before we came down the river; the natives brought him off in a canoe, the same day; four other Portuguese were taken from the schooner *Esperanza*, but I

---

56   A port city some 60 miles south of London, Portsmouth hosted (and continues to host) a major Royal Navy dockyard and base. For a contemporary history and description, see Slight and Slight, *Chronicles of Portsmouth*.

57   "Before the mouth of Portsmouth Harbour, runs out (like a vast court before the front gate of a castle) the noble roadstead of Spithead. It takes its name from a sand-bank, which extends from the right side of the Harbour, run-ning towards Southsea Castle, and ending in a point which is called the Head of the Spit, or Spithead. Round the point under the batteries of the Castle passes the Channel, through which all ships which go from Portsmouth Harbour into Spithead Road must sail. Spithead stretches five or six leagues, a[n]d is well secured from every wind by the folding of the Isle of Wight over to the Hampshire coast." *Gilpin's Tour Through Hamp-shire*, quoted in Slight and Slight, *Chronicles of Portsmouth*, 103.

58   See the first entry in this chapter.

59   Bending a sail "is to extend or make it fast to its proper yard or stay" (Smyth, *Lexicon*, 95).

don't know at what time; Silvera, the Portuguese, was picked up at Lopez. Captain Trotter sent a boat to demand the pirate captain and crew, and the king promised to give them up. The next morning I was sent ashore for them, and the king's son came down and said [that t]he men would be brought down as soon as the son had gone to dinner, meaning at 12 o'clock; they were not brought down.

In August we went to Fernando Po, and found five of the pirate's crew there; saw Perez there; – again to [Cape] Lopez; I went in the *Esperanza*, a schooner we had taken; we obtained there Don Pedro, the captain, Ferrer, the black cook, Costa, the boy, and Joseph Velasquez; an English bark, trading there, who had some of our men on board, captured them. At St. Thomas's Island, we took De Soto, the mate, Ruiz, the carpenter, Boyga, and another; all were first put on board of the *Curlew*, but five went to England in the *Esperanza*, and the rest in the *Curlew*; all taken to Plymouth first, thence to Portsmouth, and thence to America.

Cross-ex[amination]: The *Esperanza* [was] taken because she was suspected of aiding and abetting the *Panda*, by giving a passage to her crew and their money. I found on board of the *Panda* a United States ensign and pennant – 2 Spanish ensigns, 1 French ensign, and a Danish or Portuguese – she had a great quantity of round shot on board, besides canister[60] and chain shot – there were also double-headed shot,[61] and grape[.][62] I never saw chain shot or grape shot on board of a trader on the coast of Africa before. There was a musket or two fired at the canoe with the carpenter in it, when leaving the schooner – the fire was not returned – I do not know that the crew of the *Panda* ever carried on hostilities against the English–there was some firing on shore among the black fellows, but I do not know that any of our men were there, we never fired among the negro canoes – I am sure the pivot gun was not fired among them – none of our men were ever flogged for firing at the canoes; three or four days after the capture some of them were flogged for drunkenness and insolence to the commander – there were nine casks of rum in the hold of the *Panda*, and they broached one and got drunk – when the *Panda* blew up I was a mile and a half from her, going to the brig; a small trading Portuguese schooner rendered assistance; I do not know that any of the *Panda*'s crew assisted in saving the lives of any of our people that were blown into the river. I am sure, certain, that the *Panda*'s figure-head was cut off; I went to the bows to see; it was cut off smooth like the stern of a boat. I think there was a Spanish consul at Plymouth; a gentleman came on board there, who was said to be the consul; only saw him about five minutes; captain Trotter was

---

60 "Canister was scrap metal (langrage) and/or musket balls packed in tin canisters with sawdust. It was intended for use at the closest ranges against personnel" (Tucker, *Handbook*, 11).

61 Tucker (*Handbook*, 11) classified chain shot (two cannonballs linked by a chain) and double-headed shot (two halves of a cannonball linked by an iron bar) as types of "disabling shot, which was fired high to damage the sails and rigging of an opponent. . . . "

62 "Grape consisted of smaller balls positioned around a stand and enclosed in canvas, wound with rope so that it rather resembled a cluster of grapes; the balls separated when fired. Grape was used at short range against personnel and small craft" (Tucker, *Handbook* 11).

sick with a fever several times on the homeward voyage; I have no knowledge that Capt. Gibert ever gave Capt. Trotter a Protest; the letters B.S. and some other initials were on the diamond ring taken from the mate; I do not know that the other letters stood for his wife's name; there was hair in it; I was not present when Capt. Trotter took the mate's watch from him: our orders were to cruize on the coast of Africa till further orders; we were retarded in waiting for orders; as soon as they were received, I did not perceive but what Capt. Trotter availed himself of every wind and circumstance to reach England.

[Part V: Domingo's Testimony]

Simon Domingo, one of the Panda's crew, who joined her on the coast of Africa: I was on the coast of Africa between two and three years ago – went from Brazil to Princes Island in the Portuguese schooner *Harriet* – while at Princes Island, I shipped in a Portuguese brig, and went to Bahia – I returned to Princes Island in another brig – I left her in Princes Island, and Capt. Pedro Gibert asked me if I would ship on board of his schooner *Panda* – Don Pedro Gibert was her commander – Bernardo de Soto was mate, Ruiz was carpenter – Antonio Ferrer was cook, all the rest of the prisoners here belonged to her crew then – it was on the 9th of February, 1833 – we went to the river Nazareth, there dropped two anchors and moored her – bent the sails and sent down the maintopsail yard, she lay there four months – the Captain and officers went ashore, were engaged in buying slaves – I was taken prisoner, because I had said the *Panda* had robbed an American brig; four English boats came on board of the *Panda*; the carpenter set her on fire, and all the crew jumped into a boat and went ashore; I don't know how he set her on fire; I saw him run to the galley with a bag of powder, and I was scared, and got into the boat; the same day I went on board the *Panda* again; the English had possession of her, I heard from all the prisoners here that the *Panda* came from Havana.

Cross-ex[amination]: I was born on the Cape de Verds [i.e., the Cape de Verde islands]; I heard some of the crew confess to the captain of the English brig that they had robbed the *Mexican*; they had a Portuguese for an interpreter; they were the first five that were captured; Domingo Guzman confessed; he is a South American Indian, and as I knew some Indian I interpreted for him; at Fernando Po, before a Justice, Montenegro, Garcia, Castillo, Perez, Delgardo, and the boatswain confessed; they did not have the same names then that they have now; they were all sworn.

Mr. Child[s]: During the four months you were laying in the river Nazareth before the capture of the *Panda*, did you ever hear the crew of the *Panda* say any thing about the robbery of the *Mexican*[?]

Mr. Dunlap: I object to that question; it is an improper one; it is dangerous to the prisoners; for if answered in the negative it amounts to nothing, but if answered in the affirmative, it must be fatal to them.

Mr. Child[s]: I am not afraid of the answer.

Mr. Dunlap then withdrew his objection, and the witness proceeded.

[Domingo]: I never heard them say any thing about it then; the English captain sent me with an officer and Velasquez and the cook to look for the money, they took us to the place where the money had been buried, but it was gone; we then went into the forest to look for it; we did not look in the town for it. When the Spanish captain was taken at Cape Lopez, the English captain obtained some of the money, but I don't know how much it was; it was in a small bag. I never received any of that money from the English captain; I never received any money from him but one dollar for bread money, as I had been on short allowance.

Mr. Child: Did not the English captain call all the crew up on deck, one by one, and give them some of the money taken from the captain of the *Panda*; and did you get some then?

Domingo: No, he did not. Before Gibert's money came on board, the captain said that to those who did not take any bread, he would at the end of the month, give the value of the bread in money. . . . When Captain Trotter went to demand the pirate crew, they went back into the woods, and the negroes formed on the beach armed; the negroes were not excited against the English, but only informed them that the pirates had gone back into the country. They did not keep the captain in irons, but when they came to a port to take in provisions, they put him in irons. After the first day I was taken out of irons to wait on the others who were in irons. . . . There were no presents offered to the five who confessed, nor were there any threats used to make them confess. . . . Bernardo de Soto went from the river Na[a]zareth to St. Thomas, in the *Esperanza*, to purchase another vessel; and that was the reason she was captured.

[Part VI: Testimony of Budd, Bacon, Jellison and Peyton]

George Budd, Esq., A Captain in the U.S. Navy: I have been in the navy 29 years. Have commanded vessels in the West India station – have been to the Havana – vessels bound from Havana to Africa come as far north [as] 31 or 35 deg[rees] Lat[itude]. A Baltimore clipper leaving Havana on the 20th and a merchant vessel leaving Salem on the 29th would be likely to meet about the time and spot on which the *Mexican* was robbed. The route is the common thoroughfare to Africa. I have crossed the Atlantic in a clipper in 12 days. These kind of vessels are not so common as they were 18 years ago. They are used chiefly for illicit purposes. They carry very little cargo, and sail at a great expense, so they are unprofitable to owners unless engaged in a contraband trade. Our ships of war generally sail ten knots at most an hour.

Captain Joseph V. Bacon: I have been acquainted with nautical affairs 30 years, I have generally been engaged in the trade between Boston and Havana, Matanzas, &c.

The winds that prevail in the Atlantic Ocean in the months of August and September, are generally from the west and south-west. A vessel from the Havana usually gets through the Bahama channel in four or five days.

Zacharia Jellison: I have made ten passages to the West Indies. I went as passenger – am acquainted with the navigation of those seas – I have made the passage from Salem to the Havana. There is a great probability, of two vessels of the description of the *Mexican* and *Panda*, meeting in the latitude and longitude marked out.

William H. Peyton (interpreter sworn as a witness): I was once mate of a Spanish brig 4 years; her tonnage in Spanish measure was ninety-five tons; but when she was measured in Charleston, she was declared to be one hundred and twenty tons; I have been three voyages to Africa from Havana; on the first voyage I was quarter-master, on the second, 2d mate, and on the 3d, I was mate; have been in service since 1819 – I think it is likely that vessels sailing in the latter part of August from Salem and Havana would fall in with each other in latitude 32 N[orth] and longitude 37 W[est] if they fell in at all – I mean about that latitude and longitude; that is, they would be in the same region of the ocean. (*Mr. Child, after this answer was given, objected to the question which drew it out, and said he did "not want Mr. Dunlap to play the part of cloud-compelling Jupiter, but wished to have the clouds of testimony gather naturally."*) [*Peyton*] The farthest North we were went was latitude 32 – the ordinary passage is eight days, to get out from the Bahamas – I should shape my course to the eastward, to keep clear of the trade winds, and get into the variable winds, to bring up my *northing*.

(*Mr. Peyton was subjected to a long cross-examination respecting the length of various voyages, and parts of voyages, to different ports in Africa; but as it related almost entirely to a portion of the ocean which the* Panda *could only have traversed in her last voyage, subsequent to the robbery of the* Mexican, *we cannot perceive that it can have much, if any, bearing on the case, at bar. Mr. Peyton stated that the natives of several ports in Africa will take dollars in payment of articles, but they are not current among themselves and they only use them in making purchases of traders to their ports.*)

[*Peyton*:] I was five months a prisoner on the Island of Ascension. I was in Havana from June last till December – I saw the *Panda* there, anchored in the man-of-war grounds – she laid a mile from the town from which I saw her – she was rigged as a two top-sail schooner then, Baltimore clipper built, masts raked off about fifteen or twenty degrees, very low, appeared to be very deeply laden – it was in August that I saw her – the cargo of an African trader from Havana, so far as I know, is rum, tobacco, dry goods, muskets, pistols, powder, flints, cutlasses, Spanish dollars, &c.

When a captain of a merchantman is fitting out a vessel in the Havana, he obtains a number of sailors to work on board of her for a dollar a day and found;[63] the day before she clears, the boatswain generally picks out the smartest for the crew; the next day they sign the papers; they then go to the office of the general of Marine, and are reviewed, and their licenses are examined; Spanish sailors are obliged to serve three years on board of a man of war, and when that term is out they receive a license to go where they please for the following three years. Their licenses are always examined before they can clear, to see if their term of liberty has expired; if it has expired, or is about expiring, they are sent on board of a man-of-war; if it has not expired, they are permitted to sail in the merchantmen. The first voyage I went, the sailor's wages were from 30 to 35 dollars per month; on my second voyage, from 40 to 45 dollars, but on my last only 20 to 25 dollars. It is usual for all African traders to take out money. I never knew but one vessel to go out without money, but she was overhauled and brought back, and the boxes marked money were found to contain nothing but brickbats. . . . I never heard Perez threaten the prisoners when he came into court. When he was raving, the prisoners jumped up, and said to him – "You'll be fixed yet," and shaking their finger at him; he replied, "[Y]ou'll be fixed." That is the only time he said any thing like a threat.

[Part VII: Ship's papers]

Mr. Badlam then commenced reading the ship's papers; the first was a "royal passport," dated 29th of April 1831, permitting Captain Pedro Gibert to take a cargo of lawful merchandise direct to St. Thomas and Princes Island, the owners of the ship "to be made manifest to Capt. Gibert, and all other vassals of mine", signed "I, the King." The captain is expressly notified, in a note attached to this passport, that the vessel must not be employed to trade in new negroes, otherwise called raw negroes, – that is negroes not taught.

Paper 2: Mo[r]ro Passport, dated Havana, August 18, granting a passport to make this particular voyage, in which the captain is called a Catalonian, and the mate a Cor[s]ican, and the whole crew, to the number of 30 enumerated. The pass winds up with a long chapter of wholesome marine morality. On the back of it is written, of the *Panda*, "she carries, solely for the defence of the vessel, one brass pivot gun, of 16 [i.e., a 16-pounder]; 2 gunnades of 12,[64] in her battery, 24 muskets, 32 swords, 4 pairs of pistols, and corresponding munitions."

Paper 3: Bill of sale of the *Panda*, of 98 Spanish tons, dated August 7, 1832, to Bernardo de Soto, for $54,000, signed by Joseph Benedict Pardo, the former owner.

---

63 I.e., food and provisions provided over and above the salary.
64 According to Smyth (*Lexicon*, 357), a gunnade was "a short 32-pounder gun of 6 feet, introduced in 1814; afterwards termed the shell-gun." As this text refers to a 12-pounder, *gunnade* here may be used as a synonym for carronade.

Paper 4: Invoice of cargo, a very full and choice one, precisely suited for the African trade.

Paper 6:[65] Contract between the captain and owners; the captain's wage to be $100 per month, and 10 per cent on the Cargo, and $3 a head for every slave he brings.

Paper 7: Instructions to Capt. Gibert, to act according to his discretion, after consulting with his mate Bernardo de Soto, and to use due diligence, upon reaching his port of destination, to procure a return cargo: and to see that "meekness and tenderness be observed on board," and to "avoid all suspicious looking vessels." On his return, he is instructed "to enter Matanzas at night in silence, and, if hailed, say that you are from St. Thomas, in ballast" and that there are certain officers there, who are advised of their wishes, and will instruct him what is proper for him to do.

When the reading of these papers was concluded, Mr. Dunlap announced to the court, that the testimony in behalf of the Government had all been introduced.¶

[Part VIII: Defense witnesses]

The examination of witnesses for the offence [sic] was then commenced, by calling to the stand Juan B. Aranzai, captain of the Spanish merchantman Conde de Villanueva, laying in this port; he was examined at great length, by Mr. Child, upon routes, of voyages, rates of sailing, and distances of ports, and the general usages of the African trade. He confirmed, in the main, the government witnesses respecting the route from Havana to the coast of Africa, making no other variance than what might be naturally occasioned by the prevalence of different winds.

The witness [Aranzai] testified that Captain Gibert bore a high character in Havana. Mr. Dunlap then asked the witness what he himself traded in, when on the African coast, and he replied "sometimes in black ivory;" but, being more closely pressed to explain what he meant by "black ivory," he admitted, that when he could not get a cargo of real ivory, he took one of slaves.

Santiago Elonzo: I have been an officer 3 years; have made voyages to Africa from Cadiz and Havana, have sailed in a clipper; clippers sail faster than other vessels, for they are built for nothing else but sailing, and not to carry cargoes – I can get eleven and a half knots out of a clipper with the same wind that I can only get six with, in my present brig.

Judge Story: Suppose a vessel sailed from Salem for Rio Janeiro on the 29th of August, and the schooner *Panda* sailed from Havana for Africa on the 20th[. W]ould they be likely to meet, or not?

---

65   Paper 5 is not mentioned in the transcript.

Witness: I think it hardly possible for them to meet, as the schooner must get ahead of the brig; for I once knew a clipper to reach the Cape de Verd[e] in 30 days. A brig from Salem, for Rio Janei[r]o, would cross the Equator from 21 to 28 West, and the schooner would be in 12, at the same time. (*The witness has been in the slave trade; and was a custom house officer in Havana four years.*) I was acquainted with Captain Gibert, and he bears a very good character in the best mercantile houses in Havana. – When I was clerk in the custom house, in Havana, in 1827, I know that Capt. Gibert was a member of a mercantile house – he used to enter goods consigned to the house – the merchandise in their store was worth $10,000 – I am not much acquainted with Bernardo de Soto, but have always heard merchants, concerned in the African trade, speak highly of him; he owned a schooner – afterwards purchased the *Panda*, and went out in her – the *Panda* once arrived at Havana with 420 slaves. *In reply to a question, by Mr. Dunlap, the witness says it was in the slave trade in which Bernardo de Soto gave satisfaction to the merchants.*

Joseph Smith: I have been 25 years in the United States Navy, besides being in the merchant service before.– [I] was 5 years a midshipman – 14 years a lieutenant, and a master commandant ever since. (*Having ascertained the rate of sailing of the* Mexican, *Captain Smith is of opinion, that the* Panda *would beat her 25 per cent.*) It is not at all impossible, but only improbable, that the *Mexican*, sailing from Salem on the 29th, and the *Panda* from Havana on the 20th, would meet, provided that both vessels improved their time to the best advantage. (*Mr. Peyton was here called by Mr. Child, to say whether a vessel could go to Cape Mount, in Africa, in 14 days, from lat[itude] 33, long[itude] 34.30, where the* Mexican *was robbed; – Mr. Peyton was of opinion that she could not go in less than 28 or 30 days. Perez testified that the* Panda *made Cape Mount in 14 days after the robbery.*) *In reply to Mr. Dunlap –* If the brig and schooner would meet at all, it would be where the brig was robbed.

Capt. Beethold: A vessel bound to Rio from Salem, and one from Havana to Cape Mount, would probably meet where the brig and schooner met – the distance from Havana being enough greater to make up for the greater speed of the schooner.

In reply to Mr. Dunlap – If the schooner made all possible speed, she might get a little further to the eastward (than lon[gitude] 34) – but if she did not take every advantage in her power, she might not get quite so far east; but my general opinion is, that they would meet about there, as that is the general thoroughfare.

Capt. Faucon: Been to sea 12 years – *is master of a vessel, never sailed in a sharp vessel* – have understood that the speed of such vessels is about 30 percent faster than other vessels. Supposing that the brig and schooner, sailing according to date stated, took advantage of every thing, it would be improbable, but not impossible for them to meet.

Samuel Austin Turner: Have been six years in the U.S. Navy – is acquainted with the brig *Mexican*; the schooner would sail 9 knots, with the same winds that would carry the *Mexican* only 6, but in a fresh breeze, in which the *Mexican* would go eight knots, the schooner would exceed her only about one knot. From some calculations which I have made, the *Mexican* and *Panda*, under given data, would not approach each other nearer than one hundred miles – that is, taking it for granted, that they both avail themselves of every advantage.

W.S. Bruce is somewhat acquainted with Bernardo de Soto. Has resided several years in the Havana, and his knowledge of the prisoner commenced in the fall of '31. De Soto was then the captain of the Spanish brig *Leon*, from Philadelphia to Havana. During one of his voyages from Philadelphia to the latter place, he saved and brought in the crew and passengers of the American ship, *Minerva*, which had taken fire.[66] The passengers were thirty or forty in number (chiefly Irish) going to New Orleans or Mobile. De Soto's conduct was very highly spoken of at the time in Havana, and he was presented with a piece of plate by the merchants of New Orleans. Don't know that any one has asked him (De Soto) to become a witness against the rest of the prisoners. District Attorney did not request me to go to him. Did not intimate to me his wish or willingness that de Soto should be a witness. Should not have conjectured any thing of the kind from the District Attorney's conversation. Formed my opinion of the District Attorney's wishes from what was told me by a third person. That person was Charles W. Story.[67] I told de Soto that he had better become a witness.

Mr. Dunlap: Had you ever conversed with me before you saw de Soto?

Witness: Yes, both before and afterwards.

Mr. D[unlap]: Recollect yourself.

Witness: You did not say any thing particular the first time.

Mr. D[unlap]: Did you ever converse with me more than once?

Witness: No.

---

66 "HAVANA, Oct. 25. – Loss of Ship *Minerva*. – Arrived Spanish brig *Leon*, from Philadelphia, bringing in the crew and passengers (18 of former and 49 of latter) of ship *Minerva*, Putnam, of Salem. This vessel sailed from New York 12th inst. for New Orleans, with a cargo of stone, lime, naval stores, brandy, wine, oil and dry goods, and on the morning of 21st struck on the shoals about 2 miles E[ast] b[y] S[outh] from the Western Little Isaac. The crew immediately commenced getting out the cargo. At 4 p.m. the *Leon*, (which had been in sight since 11) anchored about 2 miles off, and sent her boat, with offers of assistance. Next morning some of the passengers went on board the brig. At 5:30 p.m. the wind having increased, and the ship surging and striking very heavy, the leak gained fast, and the masts were cut away. At 6:15, fire broke out in the hold, fore and aft, the water coming in contact with the lime, which immediately communicated with the oil and liquors, and in two minutes she was in flames, when those on board had barely time to escape into the *Leon*'s boat and to a raft which had been constructed, with the loss of almost their entire baggage" (*Salem Gazette*, 18 November 1831, 3).

67 A local attorney of that name appears in Massachusetts records; see for example, Nahum Capen, ed., *The Massachusetts State Record and Year Book of General Information* (Boston: James French, 1849), III:99.

Mr. D[unlap]: Did you not upon that occasion state to me what had passed between yourself and de Soto?

Witness: Yes.

Mr. D[unlap]: Then, of course, sir, you never conversed with me before you saw de Soto.

In reply to a question from Mr. Hillard as to the state of public opinion in Havana in relation to persons engaged in the slave trade, the witness said that the being so engaged was not considered to disparage any man's character.

Stephen Badlam. Has had a conversation with Joseph Perez, the government witness. About the 1st of October last was requested by the District Attorney to accompany him to the gaol for the purpose of interpreting between him and the prisoners. Witness and the District Attorney went into a room under the court, and directed the turnkey to bring in Perez. This was done, and witness then stated to the prisoner that the gentleman present, Mr. Dunlap, was the Attorney for the District, and had called, as the time of trial was approaching, to have some conversation with him. When I told Perez this, continued Mr. Badlam, he declared that all he had previously said was false; that he had had a good deal of wine given to him, and had been told that if he became a witness he would not be considered in the light of the other prisoners, but be kept as a witness. He by this time appeared much out of humor, and said rapidly, as if in a passion, "I will not be a witness any longer, but will take my chance with the others." I think he also said, that the English had deceived him, by telling him that he would not be kept a prisoner, while in reality he was now as much a prisoner as the others. I think when he said this he did not refer to any individuals in this country, but to the English. I cannot swear that he mentioned the English, but it is my impression that he did so. I have no doubt myself upon this point. I told Mr. Dunlap what the prisoner had said, and Mr. D[unlap] replied, "Very well, he may do as he pleases; if he does not like to be a witness we can do without him." Perez then cooled down, did not appear in such a passion as previously, and said that when he went before the judge he would tell the whole truth.

Mr. Dunlap said he should be happy to state any thing within his knowledge in relation to this matter; indeed he considered such a course to be his duty. After having had with Perez the conversation just alluded to by Mr. Badlam, and having noticed the state of his (Perez's) mind, he did not think it safe to leave the case for the government in its then state. He had therefore caused Nicola Costa to be brought in, and after telling him that he was under no obligation to state any thing, and that all he (the District Attorney) could promise him was that nothing he might say should be used against him, asked if he was willing to become a witness for the United States. The prisoner's reply was, "that they were all innocent, and that no robbery had ever been committed by them upon the *Mexican.*" I then, *said Mr. Dunlap*, called in Domingo Guzman, and afterwards Antonio Ferrer, (*the black cook*) but found them both in the same story as Costa. As a last resort, I then sent for Bernardo de Soto, the mate, but succeeded as ill with him as with the others. I was influenced in sending for Costa and Guzman by considerations as to their youth; as regarded the black, by compassion for his ignorance and degraded condition; and I selected de Soto in consequence of his having performed the act of humanity which has been alluded to (*saving the persons on board the* Minerva.)

Mr. Child said the District Attorney had been influenced in this affair by the honorable feelings he supposed him to possess, and begged him to accept his (Mr. C[hild]'s) sincere thanks for the course pursued.

Mr. Dunlap in reply to Mr. Child, said that when the offer of becoming a witness was made to de Soto, the latter returned for answer that he was willing to testify, but could only do so to his own innocence. He (Mr. D[unlap]) thought de Soto answered evasively, and therefore immediately ceased conversing with him.

[Part IX: Closing arguments]

Mr. Hillard arose and addressed the Jury for two hours in the most eloquent manner.

You are called upon to exercise your vocation in a case, a parallel to which we should seek in vain, in the criminal annals of this, and I had almost said in those of any other state or country. It is a serious thing gentlemen, to sit in judgment, for life or death upon a single person. Such a duty requires the most clear state of the understanding, the most careful attention to facts, lest through rashness or prejudice we pass sentence on the innocent, and commit judicial murder. Instead of one, you are now called upon to decide the fate of twelve persons. By your verdict, will it be determined whether the individuals who now sit before you in the fullness of life shall continue to exist or taste the bitterness of Death. The extraordinary spectacle is now presented of a number of prisoners tallying exactly with the jury.

Mr. Hillard after arguing upon the improbability of the prisoners being the crew that robbed the Mexican, *and giving an interesting account of Bernardo de Soto's act of humanity in relieving the American ship on fire, concluded with an eloquent appeal in behalf of Antonio Ferrer, the black, and the boy Costa.*

If, gentlemen, *said he*, you deem with me that the crew of the *Panda* (supposing her to have robbed the *Mexican*) were merely servants of the captain, you cannot convict them. But if you do not agree with me, then all that remains for me to do is to address a few words to you in the way of mercy. – It does not seem to me that the good of society requires the death of all these men, the sacrifice of such a hecatomb[68] of human victims, or that the sword of the law should fall till it is clogged with massacre. Antonio Ferrer is plainly but a servant. He is set down as a free black in the ship's papers, but that is no proof that he is free. Were he a slave he would in all probability be represented as free, and this for obvious reasons. He is in all probability a slave, and a native African, as the tattooing on his face proves beyond a doubt. At any rate he is but a servant. Now will you make misfortune pay the penalty of guilt? Do not, I entreat you, lightly condemn this man to death. Do not throw him in to make up the dozen. The regard for human life is one of the most prominent proofs of a civilized state of society. The Sultan of Turkey may place women in sacks and throw them into the Bosphorus without exciting more than an hour's additional conversation at Constantinople.[69] But in our country it is different. You well remember the excitement produced by the abduction and death of a single individual; the convulsion which ensued, the effect of which will long be felt in our political institutions. You will ever find that the more a nation becomes civilized, the greater becomes the regard for human life. There is in the eye, the form, and heaven[-]directed countenance of man something holy that forbids he should be rudely touched.

The instinct of life is great. The light of the sun even in chains, is pleasant; and life, though supported but by the damp exhalations of a dungeon, is desirable. Often too we cling with added tenacity to life in proportion as we are deprived of all that makes existence to be coveted.

> The weariest and most loathed worldly life
> That age, ache, penury and imprisonment
> Can lay on Nature, is a Paradise
> To that we fear of *Death*.[70]

Death is a fearful thing. The mere mention of it sometimes blanches the cheek and sends the fearful blood to the heart. It is a solemn thing to break into the "bloody house of life." Do not, because this man is but an African, imagine that his existence is valueless. He is no drift wood on the ocean of life. There are in his bosom the same social sympathies that animate our own. He has nerves to feel pain, and a heart to throb with human affections, even as you have. His life, to establish the law or to further the ends of justice, is not required. Taken, it is to us of no value; given to him it is above the price of rubies.

---

68 Hecatomb is derived from a Greek word meaning one hundred. It originally meant the "sacrifice of a hundred oxen; afterwards, of a hundred beasts of any sort. ... Some explain the word as a poetical figure, denoting, in general, a sacrifice of many victims" (Lieber, *Encyclopedia Americana*, VI:215).
69 A reputed Ottoman practice discussed and often romanticized in the period's English literature (DelPlato, *Multiple Wives, Multiple Pleasures*, 169–171).
70 Spoken by Claudio in William Shakespeare's *Measure for Measure*, Act III, Scene 1.

And Costa, the cabin boy, only 15 years of age when this crime was committed. Shall he die? Shall the sword fall upon his neck? Some of you are advanced in years. You may have children. Suppose the news had reached you that your son was under trial for his life in a foreign country – and every cabin boy who leaves this port may be placed in the situation of this prisoner – suppose you were told that he had been executed because his captain and officers had violated the laws of a distant land; – what would be your feelings I cannot tell, but I believe the feelings of all of you would be the same, and that you would exclaim with the Hebrew, "My son! my son! would to God that I had died for thee."[71] This boy has a father; let the form of that father rise up before you and plead in your hearts for his offspring. Perhaps he has a mother, and a home. Think of the lengthened shadow that must have been cast over that home by his absence. Think of his mother, during those hours of wretchedness when she has felt hope darkening into disappointment, next into anxiety, and from anxiety to despair. How often may she have stretched forth her hands in supplication, and asked, even the winds of heaven, to bring her tidings of him who was away! Let the supplications of that mother touch your hearts and shield their object from the law.

Mr. Child closed the Defence on the part of the Prisoners in an ingenious and elaborate argument of twelve hours.

He commenced by reading numerous statements showing how extremely difficult it was to identify persons, and what little dependence could be placed on evidence of this sort. He cited many authorities for the defence. He argued at great length upon the statements of the government witness Perez, and animadverted strongly against the manner in which he had given his testimony, and the great degree of hatred and revenge he exhibited on the stand; his utter want of veracity in saying he could not read his alphabet, but, after being pressed on that point, read whole sentences fluently; his saying rum had been given him at Fernando Po, and telling since "what he had said was all a lie." He spoke strongly in favor of the crew because there was no rule of division; the Captain and Mate keeping as much of the plunder as they chose. And Captain Trotter had not treated the crew of the *Panda* as Pirates, having kept them in irons but a short time. The statement of Bernardo De Soto's sitting up all night to make a false log-book should have no weight; if he had, it would be produced here. In the printed statement of Captain Butman, the *Panda*'s figure head is said to be very large, with a horn of plenty on it;[72] the witness Silvera, who saw it in the river Nazareth, says there was nothing carved on it. Mr. Quentin says it was off smooth like the stern of a boat. With respect to the capture of the Schooner, something explanatory of the conduct of her company may be said. Being unexpectedly and suddenly surrounded with a squadron of hostile boats, they fled for safety; – and, if they did attempt to blow her up, there is nothing very blam[e]able. Many a brave spirit, incapable of yielding to defeat, has ascended from the ruins of his gallant vessel.

---

71   2 Samuel 18:33.

72   See the first entry (from the *Salem Gazette*) in this chapter.

After arguing and endeavouring to refute and lessen the weight of the government testimony, he concluded by making a powerful appeal in favor of Antonio Ferrer and the boy Costa.

Mr. Dunlap, District Attorney, closed the cause on the part of the government in a most eloquent argument of six hours.

He began by saying that there was no doubt the Mexican *was robbed by pirates. The great question was whether the captain and crew of the* Panda *were the individuals who committed the robbery.* She sailed from Havana about the 20th. The witnesses prove that captain Gibert and Bernardo de Soto were her chief officers, and the prisoners at the bar were all of her crew. The crew of the *Mexican* make this probability certain by identifying some of the prisoners who were proved to be of the *Panda*'s crew. This is not circumstantial evidence, it is proof positive. *Mr. D[unlap] argued that the* Panda *sailed with the intention of committing piracies*; Bernardo De Soto was not the real owner; he stands in their shoes; the real owners are veiled. The instructions are not signed; there is piracy in every line of them. The contract with the Captain is in the same hand writing as the unsigned instructions. The cargo of the vessel is worth only $10,000, and going to Africa to buy 450 slaves. The cargo would not pay the wages of the crew for 10 months. She was to get the $30,000 to buy the slaves by robbing vessels, without doubt. With these instructions Captain Gibert is told to sail from St. Thomas in ballast, to enter with great secre[c]y into the harbor of Matanzas by night, and hold intercourse with certain persons indicated in his instructions. He was allowed to cruise where he pleased. He was left without any control but his own will. The slave trade is the twin-brother of piracy, for all the piracies of our day are committed by slave dealers. By the large share of the money kept by the Captain it proves that it was reserved for the owners. At the time the figure head was altered, no news had reached Africa of the piracy. He had it altered to elude pursuit when the news did come. It shows the prisoners were conscious of guilt by throwing the money overboard.

After drawing the attention of the jury to the boy Costa and Antonio Ferrer, he concluded by passing an eloquent eulogium on the conduct of Captain Trotter and the British navy generally.

Judge Story, in a luminous Charge of six hours summed up the evidence on both sides of the cause. The papers, charts and documents were given to the jury and they retired to agree upon a verdict.

Editor's Note: After 20 hours of deliberation, the jury convicted Pedro Gibert, Don Bernardo de Soto, Francisco Ruiz, Manuel Boyga, Manuel Castillo, Angel Garcia, and Juan Montenegro. The jury acquitted Nicolo Costa, Antonio Ferrer, Domingo de Guzman, José Velasquez, and Juan Antonio Portana. The jury also recommended "the Merciful consideration of the government" on behalf of de Soto in consideration of his efforts to save those aboard the *Minerva*.[73]

["Domestic. From the *Boston Post of Friday*." Pittsfield Sun, 18 June 1835, 2].

EXECUTION OF THE PIRATES.

Pursuant to previous arrangement, Captain Don Pedro Gibert, and Juan Montenegro, Manuel Castillo, Angel Garcia, and Manuel Boyga, were yesterday morning summoned to prepare for their immediate execution, agreeably to their sentence, for having, while belonging to the schooner *Panda*, committed piracy, by robbing the brig *Mexican*, of Salem, of $20,000, and afterwards attempting to destroy the crew and all evidence of their crime, by setting fire to the vessel.¶

It is understood, that, when the prisoners became thoroughly convinced that there was no longer any grounds to hope for a further respite, they entered into a mutual agreement to commit suicide on Wednesday night. Angel Garcia made the first attempt, in the evening, by trying to open the veins in each arm, with a fragment of a bottle, but was discovered before he could effect his purpose, and a stricter guard was afterwards maintained upon all of them during the remainder of the night, and every thing removed with which they might be supposed to renew any attempt upon their own lives. Yesterday morning, however, about 9 o'clock, while the avenues of the jail responded with the heavy steps of a host of acting marshals, and the "busy note of preparation" struck solemnly upon the ears of the spectators within reach of its echo, Boyga succeeded in inflicting a deep gash on the left side of his neck with a piece of tin. The officer's eye had been withdrawn from him scarcely a minute, before he was discovered lying on his pallet, with a peculiar trembling of his knees, which induced the officers to examine if any thing had suddenly happened to him. They found him covered with blood, and nearly insensible; medical aid was at hand, and the wound was immediately sewed up, but Boyga, who had fainted from loss of blood, never revived again.¶

Two Catholic clergymen, the Rev. Mr. Varella, a Spanish gentleman, & pastor of the Spanish congregation, at New-York, and the Rev. Mr. Curtin, of this city, were in close attendance upon the prisoners during the whole morning; and at ¼ past 10, under the escort of the Marshal and his deputies, accompanied them to the gallows, erected on an insulated angle of land in the rear of the jail.

When the procession arrived at the foot of the ladder, leading up to the platform of the gallows, the Rev. Mr. Varella looking directly at Capt. Gi[l]bert, said – "Spaniards, ascend to Heaven." Gi[l]bert mounted with a quick step, and was followed by his comrades at a more moderate pace, but without the least perceptible indication of

---

73   A Report of the Trial of the Spanish Pirates Before the United States Circuit Court . . . , 75.

hesitancy. Boyga, unconscious of his situation and destiny was carried up in a chair, and seated beneath the rope prepared for him. Gibert, Montenegro, Garcia and Castillo all smiled subduedly as they took their appointed stations on the platform. Judging only from Gibert's air, carriage and unembarrassed eye, as he glanced at the surrounding multiage, & surveyed the mechanism of his shameful death, he might have well been mistaken for an officer in attendance, instead of one of the doomed. – With the exception of repeating his prayers after the clergyman, he spoke but little. Soon after he ascertained his position on the stage, he left it, and, passing over to the spot where the apparently lifeless Boyga was seated on the chair, he bent over his shoulder and kissed him very affectionately. He then resumed his station, but occasionally turned round to Mr. Peyton the interpreter, and the clergyman. Addressing his followers, he said – "Boys, we are going to die; but let us be firm, for we are innocent." To Mr. Peyton, removing his linen collar, and handing it to him, he said – "This is all I have to part with – take it as a keepsake. I die innocent, but I'll die like a noble Spaniard. Good bye, brother, we die in the hope of meeting you in Heaven." Montenegro and Garcia, tho' exhibiting no terror, vociferated their innocence, explaining – "Americans we are not *culpable* – we are innocent; but we forgive all who have injured us." Castillo addressed himself to an individual, whom he recognized in the front rank of the officers below the stage, and said – "Adieu my friend – I shall see you in Heaven – I do not care so much about dying, as to have the Americans think I am guilty," (culpable). All of them expressed great satisfaction at the intelligence of De Soto's reprieve.

The Marshal [Jonas L. Sibley] having read the warrant for their execution, and stated that De Soto was respited for 60 days, and Ruiz for 30,[74] the ropes were adjusted round the necks of the prisoners and a slight hectic flush spread over the countenance of each; but not an eye quailed, nor a limb trembled, nor a muscle quivered. As the cap was about to be drawn over Gibert's face, the Spanish priest fervently embraced him, and during the operation of covering the faces of the others, the Rev. Mr. Curtin advanced to the railing of the stage, and read a brief declaration on behalf of the prisoners, addressed to the citizens of America assembled, setting forth, that as at the trial they had declared their innocence, so did they now continue to do so. – Boyga's cap and rope were adjusted, as he sat, supported by an officer, in the chair, which was so placed as to fall with the drop. At a quarter before 11, after every preparation was completed, and while they were repeating to themselves, in scarcely audible tones, their prayers, Dep. Marshal [Horatio] Bass suddenly cut the small cord, which restrained the spring, and the platform fell without even the creaking of a hinge. In falling, Boyga's chair struck against the bodies of the Captain and Garcia. Boyga struggled slightly once after his descent, and Montenegro and Castillo but little; Captain G[ibert] did not die quite so easily, the rope [sic – knot] being placed behind

---

74 DeSoto received a presidential pardon on 6 July 1835; Ruiz was hung 11 September 1835 (Ellms, *Pirates Own Book*, 144, 145).

A pirate hanging after execution
(George Albert Williams, 19th
century).

his neck.[75] Garcia struggled most and longest –
about 3 minutes. After being suspended 30 minutes, the physicians in attendance pronounced
them dead, and they were cut down, and placed
in black coffins, in readiness in the yard.

After the execution was over, Ruiz, confined in his
cell, attracted considerable attention, by his ma-
niac shouts and singing. At one time, holding up a
piece of blanket, stained with Boyga's blood, he
gave utterance to his ravings in a sort of recitative,
the burden of which was, *"This is the red flag my
companions died under."*

The crowd assembled on this occasion is estimated at from 20[,000] to 30,000, and occupied
every point that afforded the least opportunity for
witnessing the execution. The roofs of a couple of
sheds, contiguous to the jail yard, gave way beneath the pressure of the numbers who had
seated themselves on them, and there were 2 or
3 avalanches of men and boys, some of whom
were considerably injured. The sensation created
by their fall was the only appearance of disorder
manifested by the multitude during the whole
scene. One of the proprietors has preferred a verbal claim against the U.S. Marshal,
for damages done by the crowd to his shant[y]!!!

Some hundred or two, forgetful of the approach of the rising tide, posted themselves,
quite early, on the foundation of a branch of the [Boston and] Lowell Rail Road,[76]
and, unable to retreat, as the crowd on shore increased in density, they were compelled to retain their position, till the flowing tide came up even above their knees. –

75 In a judicial hanging the large knot on the noose is intended to be placed so as to "strike behind the left ear, instantly knocking the doomed unconscious. If things work to perfection, just the right number of small bones of
the cervical vertebrae in the neck are broken so that the head is not ripped off. The bones should then collapse
on the spinal cord, cutting off oxygen to the brain and paralyzing the rest of the body. Rapid brain death follows.
That makes for the ideal clean hanging, but it doesn't happen all that often" ("Execution methods," Sifakis, *Encyclopedia of American Prisons*, 80).
76 From an 1833 travel guide: "The Boston and Lowell Rail Road . . . commences at the basin of the canal in
Lowell, and crosses the Charles river at Boston over a wooden viaduct, on the west side of Warren bridge. The
length of the road is 25 miles, and the inclination on no part of the route exceeds 10 feet in a mile. For the present, there will be but a single track, with the necessary number of turn-outs; but provision is made for another
track, if required. . . . Medford, 4 miles from Boston, is on the Mystic river; 3 miles from which is the handsome
village of Charlestown. . . . One mile farther, the Charlestown bridge intervening, is the City of Boston . . . "
(*Traveller's Guide*, 366).

About a dozen were hemmed into a corner up to their middle in mud and water, but no worse accident happened to them.

Nothing could exceed the regularity of the proceedings within the area, on which the execution took place, under the direction of Marshal Sibley. The calm and unassuming deportment of the Catholic clergymen was very generally acknowledged by all present, & met the entire approbation of the Marshal and his deputies, with whom they necessarily had much intercourse.

The Spanish Consul having requested that the bodies might not be given to the Faculty, they were interred last night, under the personal direction of Marshal Sibley, in the Catholic burial-ground at Charlestown.[77]

There being no murder committed with the piracy, the laws of the United States do not authorize the Court to order the bodies to be given to the surgeons for dissection.

---

77   According to the Charlestown (Mass.) Historical Society, the Catholic Cemetery was established in 1833. It is now known locally as the Bunker Hill Catholic Cemetery, and is situated behind St. Francis de Sales Church (dedicated in 1862) on Bunker Hill Street. The pirates' graves are unmarked.

Bibliography

A List of the Flag Officers & Other Commissioned Officers of His Majesty's Fleet with the Dates of Their Respective Commissions (London: Hartnell, 1831).

Allison, Robert J., *The Crescent Obscured: The United States and the Muslim World, 1776–1815* (Chicago: University of Chicago, 1995).

Allston, Frank J., *Ready for Sea: The Bicentennial History of the U.S. Navy Supply Corps* (Annapolis, Md.: Naval Institute, 1995).

Andress, David, *The Terror: Civil War in the French Revolution* (London: Little Brown, 2005).

An Interesting Trial of Edward Jordan, and Margaret his Wife, who were Tried at Halifax, N.S. Nov. 15th, 1809, for the Horrid Crime of Piracy and Murder . . . (Boston: 75 State Street and 52 Orange Street, 1809).

A Report of the Trial of the Spanish Pirates Before the United States Circuit Court, With an Appendix containing several Documents never before published, and a correct likeness of each (3rd edition) . . . (Boston: Russell, Odiorne and Metcalf, 1834).

Augur, Helen, *The Secret War of Independence* (New York: Duell, Sloan and Pearce, 1955).

Baker, William Avery, *A Maritime History of Bath, Maine and the Kennebec River Region*. 2 vols. (Portland: Marine Research Society, 1973).

Baer, Joel H., *British Piracy in the Golden Age*, 4 vols. (London: Pickering and Chatto, 2007).

Banner, Stuart, *The Death Penalty: An American History* (Cambridge: Harvard University, 2003).

Banting, Erinn, *Puerto Rico: The People and Culture* (New York: Crabtree, 2003).

Bauer, Elizabeth Kelley, *Commentaries on the Constitution, 1790–1860* (New York: Columbia University, 1952).

Behan, T.L., compiler, *Bulletins and Other State Intelligence for the Year 1854*, Part 1 (London: Harrison, 1855).

Bell, James, *A System of Geography, Popular and Scientific*, Vol. VI (Glasgow: Fullarton and Co., 1832).

Beveridge, Albert J., *Life of John Marshall*, 4 vols. (Boston: Houghton-Mifflin, 1916–1919).

Blake, Richard, *Evangelicals in the Royal Navy, 1775–1815* (Woodbridge: Boydell, 2008).

Boswell, James, *Life of Samuel Johnson, LLD*, 8th edition, Vol. III (London: Cadell and Davies, 1816).

Boyd, Julian P., ed., *Papers of Thomas Jefferson*, Vol. I, 1760–1776 (Princeton, NJ: Princeton University, 1950).

Bradford, Gershom, *The Mariner's Dictionary* (New York: Weathervane Books, NY, 1952).

British and Foreign State Papers, 1821–1822 (London: Harrison, 1829).

Brooks, Francis, *Barbarian Cruelty, Being a true history of the distressed condition of the Christian captives under the tyranny of Mully Ishmael emperor of Morocco* . . . (Boston: Phillips, 1700).

Buman, Nathan A., *To Kill Whites: The 1811 Louisiana Slave Insurrection* (M.A. thesis, Louisiana State University, 2008).

Burdick, William, *Massachusetts Manual, or, Political and Historical Register for the Political Year June 1814 to June 1815*, Vol. I (Boston: Callender, 1814).

Burke, Edmund, *An Account of the European Settlements in America*, Vol. II, 3rd edition (London: Dodsley, 1760).

Burke, J. Wills, *Streets of Key West* (Sarasota, FL: Pineapple Press, 2004).

Carr, E.H., *What Is History?* (New York: Vintage, 1961).

Carranza, Angel Justiniano, *Campañas navales de la República Argentina.* 2nd ed., 4 vols. (Buenos Aires: Secretaría de Estado de Marina, 1962).

Carylye, Thomas, *Life of Friedrich Schiller* (London: Chapman and Hall, 1845).

Carey, Mathew, *A Short Account of Algiers and of its Several Wars Against Spain, France, England, Holland, Venice, and Other Powers of Europe . . .* 2nd ed. (Philadelphia: For Mathew Carey, 1794).

Chipman, Donald, and Harriet Joseph, *Spanish Texas, 1519–1821* (Austin: University of Texas, 2010).

Christensen, Lawrence, *Dictionary of Missouri Biography* (Columbia: Univ. of Missouri, 1999).

Cicero (M. Tulli Ciceronis, *On Duties*, Walter Miller translator (London: Harvard University, 1997).

—————, *Orationes Selectae*, J. A. Ernesti and C. Anthon, eds. (London: Priestley, 1837).

Cohen, Saul, ed., *Columbia Gazetteer of the World*, 3 vols. (New York: Columbia University, 2008).

Coke, Sir Edward, *Third Part of the Institutes of the Laws of England . . .* (4th ed., London: Crooke et al, 1669).

Colledge, J.J., and Ben Warlow, *Ships of the Royal Navy* (Newbury, UK: Casemate, 2010).

Cordingly, David, *Under the Black Flag: The Romance and the Reality of Life among the Pirates* (New York: Harcourt Brace, 1995).

Cousins, James, "Weights and Measures in England versus the Decimal and Metric Systems," *Science*, 20:512 (25 November, 1892), 298.

Dana, Richard Henry, *Two Years before the Mast* (New York: Buccaneer, 1984).

Davis, William C., *The Pirates Laffite: The Treacherous World of the Corsairs of the Gulf* (Orlando: Harcourt, 2006).

de La Rochefoucauld, François, *Réflexions ou Sentences et Maximes Morales* (Paris: Barbain, 1675).

DelPlato, Joan, *Multiple Wives, Multiple Pleasures: Representing the Harem, 1800–1875* (London: Associated University Presses, 2002).

Deutsch, Eberhard, "The United States vs. Major General Andrew Jackson," *American Bar Association Journal*, Sept. 1960, 966–972.

Dye, Ira, "Early American Merchant Seafarers," *American Philosophical Society Proceedings*, 120 (1976) 331–360.

Duyckinck, Evert Augustus, and George Long Duyckinck, *Cyclopaedia of American Literature*, 2 vols (New York: Scribner, 1856).

Ellms, Charles, *The Pirates Own Book* (New York: Dover, 1993).

Esposito, John, ed., *The Oxford Encyclopedia of the Modern Islamic World*, 4 vols. (Oxford: Oxford University, 1995).

Exquemelin, Alexandre O., *The Buccaneers of America*, translated by Alexis Brown. (Mineola, NY: Dover, 2000).

Foss, John, *A Journal, of the Captivity and Sufferings of John Foss . . .* (Newburyport: Angier, 1798).

Fitzgibbon, Russell H., "Glossary of Latin-American Constitutional Terms," *The Hispanic American Historical Review*, 27:3 (August 1947), 574–590.

Frayler, John, "Armed to the Teeth" [informational staff memo] (Salem, Mass.: Salem National Maritime Historic Site, March 16, 2001.

—————, *The Arms Chest.* Pickled Fish and Salted Provisions, 7:1 (Salem,Mass.: Salem Maritime National Historic Site, March 2005.

—————, *The Medicine Chest.* Pickled Fish and Salted Provisions, 6:3 (Salem, Mass.: Salem Maritime National Historic Site, April 2004.

—————, *Walk Away with the Cat, Walk Away with the Fish.* Pickled Fish and Salted Provisions 4:4 (Salem, Mass.: Salem Maritime National Historic Site, July 2003.

Flett, T. M., "An Early Nineteenth Century Arithmetic Exercise Book," *Mathematical Gazette*, 45:351 (Feb., 1961), 1–8.

French, Christopher J., "Productivity in the Atlantic Shipping Industry: A Quantitative Study," *Journal of Interdisciplinary History*, 17:3 (Winter, 1987), 613–638.

Frohock, Richard, "Exquemelin's Buccaneers: Violence, Authority, and the Word in Early Caribbean History," *Eighteenth-Century Life*, 34:1 (Winter 2010), 56–72.

Gannett, Ezra Stiles, *A Good Old Age: A Sermon Occasioned by the death of Hon. John Davis, LL.D* . . . (Boston: Crosby & Nichols, 1847).

Gibbs, Joseph, *Dead Men Tell No Tales: The lives and legends of the pirate Charles Gibbs* (Columbia, S.C.: University of South Carolina Press, 2007).

Gill, John, *A Collection of Sermons and Tracts*, Vol. III (London: George Keith, 1778).

Goodwin, Albert, *The New Cambridge Modern History: 1763–93* (Cambridge: Cambridge University, 1976).

Goodwin, Joshua Michael, "Universal Jurisdiction and the Pirate: Time for an Old Couple to Part," *Vanderbilt Journal of Transnational Law*, 39 (2006), 973–1011.

Gulliver, Lemuel, *Supplement to the Report of the Trial of the Spanish Pirates, with the Confessions or Protests Written By them in Prison* . . . (Boston: Dickinson, 1835).

Guttridge, Leonard F., and Jay D. Smith, *The Commodores* (Annapolis, Md.: Naval Institute Press, 1986).

Grahame, Arthur, "The Evolution of Naval Guns and Armor," *Popular Science*, December 1943, 51–57.

Gray, Lewis C., *History of Agriculture in the Southern United States to 1860*, Vol. I (Washington: Carnegie Institution, 1933).

Grose, Francis, *Classical Dictionary of the Vulgar Tongue*, 2nd edition (London: Hooper, 1788).

Hague, William, *William Wilberforce: The Life of the Great Anti-Slave Trade Campaigner* (London: Harper, 2007).

Hainsworth, Roger, and Christine Churches, *The Anglo Dutch Naval Wars 1652–1674* (Phoenix Mill, Gloucestershire: Sutton, 1998).

Hall, Luella J., *The United States and Morocco, 1776–1956* (Metuchen, NJ: Scarecrow Press, 1971).

Harvey, Robert, *Liberators: Latin America's Struggle for Independence, 1810–1830* (New York: Overlook, 2000).

Heffernan, Thomas Farel, *Stove by a Whale: Owen Chase and the Essex* (Middletown, CT: Wesleyan University, 1990).

Hervey, James, *Meditations and Contemplations* (London: Tegg, 1856).

Hess, Earl J., *The Rifle Musket in Civil War Combat: Reality and Myth* (Lawrence: University Press of Kansas, 2008).

Hirsch, Adam Jay, *Rise of the Penitentiary: Prisons and Punishment in Early America* (New Haven: Yale University, 1992).

The Holy Bible, Conteyning the Old Testament, and the New (King James Version) (London: Robert Barker, 1611).

Hopkins, James F., *The Papers of Henry Clay: Volume III – Presidential Candidate, 1821–1824* (Lexington: University of Kentucky, 1963).

Horgan, Lucille E., *Forged in War: The Continental Congress and the Origin of Military Supply and Acquisition Policy* (London: Greenwood, 2002).

Jastram, R.W., *The Golden Constant: The English and American Experience 1560–2007* (Cheltenham: Edward Elgar Publishing/World Gold Council 2009).

Kauffman, C. H., *The Dictionary of Merchandise, and Nomenclature in all Languages* (Philadelphia: Humphreys, 1805).

Kelbaugh, Paul R., "The Tobacco Trade in Maryland, 1700–25," *Maryland Historical Magazine*, 26 (1931), 16–17.

Kerber, Linda K., *Toward an Intellectual History of Women* (Chapel Hill, NC: University of North Carolina, 1997).

King, Edward, *The Great South* (Hartford, Conn.: American, 1875; reprint, New York: Arno, 1969).

King, Irving, *Coast Guard Under Sail: The U.S. Revenue Cutter Service,1789–1865* (Annapolis: Naval Institute, 1989).

Konstam, Angus, *Piracy: The Complete History* (London: Osprey, 2008).

Knudson, Jerry W., "The Jeffersonian Assault on the Federalist Judiciary, 1802–1805; Political Forces and Press Reaction," *American Journal of Legal History*, 14(1) January, 1970, 55–75.

Knight, Charles, *English Cyclopedia: Geography*, Vol. II (London: Bradbury, Evans & Co., 1866).

Lambert, Frank, *The Barbary Wars* (New York: Hill and Wang, 2005).

Lamson, Zachary G., *Autobiography of Capt. Zachary G. Lamson, 1797 to 1814* (Boston: Clarke, 1908).

Lavery, Brian, *The Arming and Fitting of English Ships of War, 1600–1815* (London: Conway Maritime, 1987).

Leeman, William P., *The Long Road to Annapolis: The Founding of the Naval Academy and the Emerging American Republic* (Chapel Hill: University of North Carolina, 2010).

Leiner, Frederick C., *The End of Barbary Terror* (Oxford: Oxford University, 2006).

Leonard, Peter, *Records of a Voyage to the Western Coast of Africa in His Majesty's Ship Dryad* (Edinburgh: Andrew Shortrede, 1833).

Lenfesty, Thompson, and Tom Lenfesty Jr., *Dictionary of Nautical Terms* (New York: Facts on File, 1994).

Lever, Darcy, *The Young Sea Officer's Sheet Anchor* (Mineola, NY: Dover, 1998).

Lieber, Francis, ed. *Encyclopedia Americana*, Vol. VI (Philadelphia: Carey and Lee, 1831).

London, Joshua E., *Victory in Tripoli* (Hoboken, NJ: Wiley, 2005).

Mair, John, "Description of Virginia Commerce," (Excerpt from *Book-keeping Modernized*, 3rd Edition, 1784) *William and Mary Quarterly*, 14(2) (Oct., 1905), 87–93.

Madison, James, *Calendar of the Correspondence of James Madison* (New York: Franklin, 1970 [reprint]).

Malone, Dumas, ed. *Dictionary of American Biography*, Vol. 8 (New York: Scribners, 1932).

Malte-Brun, M., *A System of Universal Geography, or a Description of All the Parts of the World on a New Plan*, Vol. 2 (Boston: Samuel Walker, 1834).

Marcus, Maeva, and James R. Perry, *Documentary History of the Supreme Court of the United States, 1789–1800*, Vol. 1, part 1 (New York: Columbia University, 1985).

Marshall, John (I) et al, *Papers of John Marshall*, Vol. 9 (Chapel Hill: Univ. of North Carolina, 1974).

Marshall , John (II), *Royal Navy Biography*, Vol. IV, part II (London: Longman, Rees, Orme, Brown, Green, and Longman, 1835).

Martin, Tyrone G., *A Most Fortunate Ship: A Narrative History of Old Ironsides* (Annapolis: Naval Institute, 1997).

Mather, Cotton, *Pastoral Letter to the English Captives in Africa from New-England* (Boston: Green and Allen, 1698).

—————————, *Instructions to the Living, from the Condition of the Dead* (Boston: Allen, 1717).

Maxwell, Kenneth, *Naked Tropics: Essays on Empire and Other Rogues* (London: Routledge, 2003).

Mayer, Henry, *All on Fire: William Lloyd Garrison and the Abolition of Slavery* (New York: St Martin's, 1998).

McCusker, John J., *Money and Exchange in Europe and America, 1600–1775* (Chapel Hill: University of North Carolina, 1992).

McKee, Christopher, *A Gentlemanly and Honorable Profession: The Creation of the U.S. Naval Officer Corps, 1794–1815* (Annapolis: Naval Institute Press, 1991).

Merriam-Webster's Biographical Dictionary, rev. ed. (Springfield: Merriam-Webster, 1995).

Merriam-Webster's Collegiate Dictionary, 10th ed. (Springfield: Merriam-Webster, 1999).

Merriam-Webster's Geographical Dictionary, 3rd ed. (Springfield: Merriam-Webster, 2001).

Miller, Nathan, *Broadsides: The Age of Fighting Sail, 1775–1815* (New York: Wiley, 2000).

Mooney, James L., ed., *Dictionary of American Naval Fighting Ships*. 9 vols. Washington, D.C.: U.S. Navy, 1959–1991).

More, Thomas, *Utopia*. Translated by Ralph Robinson (New York: Knopf, 1992).

Morris, Allen, *Florida Place Names: Alachua to Zolfo Springs* (Sarasota, FL: Pineapple Press, 1995).

Morris, James, and Patricia Kearns, *Historical Dictionary of the United States Navy* (London: Scarecrow, 1998).

Muscat, Joseph, and Andrew Cuschieri, *Naval Activities of the Knights of St. John, 1530–1798* (Malta: Midsea, 2002).

Mushabac, Jane, and Angela Wigan, *Short and Remarkable History of New York City* (New York: Fordham University, 1999).

Nicholson, Edward, *Men and Measures: A History of Measures, Ancient and Modern* (London: Smith, Elder & Co., 1912).

Nolfi, Edward A., *Legal Terminology Explained* (London McGraw-Hill, 2009).

Northend, William, and Edward George, *Memorials of the Essex Bar Association* (Salem, MA: Newcomb and Gauss, 1900).

Owsley, Frank, and Gene Smith, *Filibusters and expansionists: Jeffersonian Manifest Destiny, 1800–1821* (Tuscaloosa: University of Alabama, 1997).

Parker, Richard B., *Uncle Sam in Barbary: A Diplomatic History* (Gainesville: University Press of Florida, 2004).

Paullin, Charles, *Commodore John Rodgers* (New York: Arno, 1980).

Partridge, Eric, *Dictionary of American Slang & Unconventional English*, 8th ed. (New York: MacMillan, 1984).

Pinney, Tor, "Springing the Rode," http://www.tor.cc/articles/rode.htm.

Preyer, Kathryn, "Jurisdiction to Punish: Federal Authority, Federalism and the Common Law of Crimes in the Early Republic," *Law and History Review*, 4(2) (Autumn, 1986), 223–265.

Purdy, John, *Memoir, Descriptive and Explanatory, to Accompany the New Chart of the Ethiopic or Southern Atlantic Ocean . . .* (London: Laurie, 1822).

Sappol, Michael, *A Traffic of Dead Bodies: Anatomy and Embedded Social Identity in Nineteenth Century America* (Princeton: Princeton University, 2002).

Rainsford, Marcus, *An Historical Account of the Black Empire of Hayti* (London: Cundee, 1805).

Register of the Commissioned and Warrant Officers of the United States Navy (Washington: Nicholson, 1856).

Reese, George, "The Court of Vice-Admiralty in Virginia and Some Cases of 1770–1775," *Virginia Magazine of History and Biography*, 88:3 July, 1980, 301–337.

Rodriguez, Antonio Gómez "Louis Aury: Héroe Naval de la Gran Colombia. O la diferencia entre corsarios y piratas," http://www.encolombia.com/medicina/enfermeria/enfermeria7104-louis.htm.

Room, Adrian, *Alternate Names of Places* (Jefferson, N.C.: McFarland, 2009).

Rubin, Alfred P., *Ethics and Authority in International Law* (Cambridge: Cambridge University, 1997).

Rutherford, Samuel, *A Free Disputation against Pretended Liberty of Conscience . . .* (London: Crook, 1649).

Schonhorn, Manuel, ed., *A General History of the Pyrates* (New York: Dover, 1999).

Sifakis, Carl, *The Encyclopedia of American Prisons* (New York: Facts on File, 2003).

Simpson, A., and E.S.C. Weiner, eds., *Oxford English Dictionary*, 2nd ed., 20 vols. (Oxford: Clarendon, 1989).

Slight, Henry, and Julian Slight, *Chronicles of Portsmouth* (London: Lupton Relfe, 1828).

Smedley, Edward, Hugh James Rose, Henry John Rose, eds., *Encyclopaedia Metropolitana; or, universal dictionary of knowledge*, Vol. XVII. (London: Fellowes et al, 1845).

Smith. Aaron, *Atrocities of the Pirates* (New York: Lyons, 1999).

Smith, Whitney, *Flag Lore of all Nations* (Brookfield, CT: Millbrook, 2003).

Smyth, W. H., *The Sailor's Lexicon* (New York: Hearst, 2005).

Spain, Charles A., Jr., "Flags of the Texas Revolution," *Handbook of Texas Online* (http://www.tshaonline.org/handbook/online/articles/msf02).

Stevens, Michael E., and Steven B. Burg, *Editing Historical Documents: A Handbook of Practice* (London: Sage, 1997).

Stinson, Joseph W., "Opinions of Richard Peters (1781–1817)," *University of Pennsylvania Law Review and American Law Register*, 70:3, March, 1922, 185–197.

Story, William W., *Life and Letters of Joseph Story*, Vol. I (Boston: Little, Brown, 1851).

Sugden, John, "Jean Lafitte and the British Offer of 1814," *Louisiana History*, 22 (1979): 159–67.

Teeters, Negley, *Cradle of the Penitentiary: The Walnut Street Jail at Philadelphia, 1773–1835* (Philadelphia: Pennsylvania Prison Society, 1955).

Ticknor, Benjamin, "An Account of the Yellow Fever which Prevailed at Thompson's Island, in the Year 1824," *North American Medical and Surgical Journal*, 3(6) April 1827, 213–233.

Traveller's Guide through the Middle and Northern States and the Provinces of Canada, 5th ed. (Carvill, NY: Davison, 1833).

Tryals of Thirty-Six Persons for Piracy, . . . (Boston: Samuel Kneeland, 1723).

Tucker, Spencer, *Handbook of 19th Century Naval Warfare* (Stroud, U.K.: Sutton, 2000).

Turley, Hans, *Rum, Sodomy and the Lash: Piracy, Sexuality, and Masculine Identity* (New York: New York University, 1999).

Vale, Brian, *War betwixt Englishmen: Brazil against Argentina on the River Plate, 1825–1830* (London: Tauris, 2000).

Viel, John, *The Florida Keys* (Sarasota, Florida: Pineapple Press, 1999).

Vogel, Robert C., "Jean Laffite, the Baratarians, and the Battle of New Orleans: A Reappraisal," *Louisiana History*, 41:3 (Summer, 2000), 261–276.

——————, "The Patterson and Ross Raid on Barataria, September 1814," *Louisiana History*, 33:2 (Spring, 1992), 157–170.

Votaw, Homer C., "The Sloop-of-War *Ganges*" *United States Naval Institute Proceedings*, 98:7 (July 1972), 82–84.

Wheeler, Jacob, *Reports of Criminal Law Cases with Notes and References* . . . , 3 vols. (New York: Banks, Gould & Co., 1851).

Wheeler, Richard, *In Pirate Waters* (New York: Crowell, 1969).

Williams, Neville, *Captains Outrageous* (London: Barrie and Rockliff, 1961).

Wilson, James Grant and John Fiske, eds., 6 vols., *Appleton's Cyclopedia of American Biography* (New York: Appleton, 1892).

Winfield, Rif, *British Warships in the Age of Sail, 1793–1817* (Barnsley, Yorkshire: Seaforth, 2010).

Wombwell, James A., *The Long War Against Piracy* (Fort Leavenworth, Kansas : Combat Studies Institute Press, 2010).

Works Progress/Work Projects Administration. *Ship Registers and Enrollments of Boston and Charlestown*, Vol. 2: 1821–30 (unpublished material compiled in 1939 by the Survey of Federal Archives Division of Women's and Professional Projects (WPA) and the National Archives; held at the Phillips Library of the Peabody Essex Museum in Salem, Mass.

World Health Organization, *International Medical Guide for Ships*, 3rd edition (Geneva: World Health Organization, 2007).

Zacks, Richard, *Pirate Coast: Thomas Jefferson, the First Marines, and the Secret Mission of 1805* (New York: Hyperion, 2005).

Index

AN
INDEX MAP
to the following
SIXTEEN SHEETS,
being
A COMPLEAT CHART
of the
WEST INDIES,
WITH
Letters in the Margin, to direct the placing the different Sheets
in their proper Places.

London Printed for Robt. Sayer, Map & Printseller.

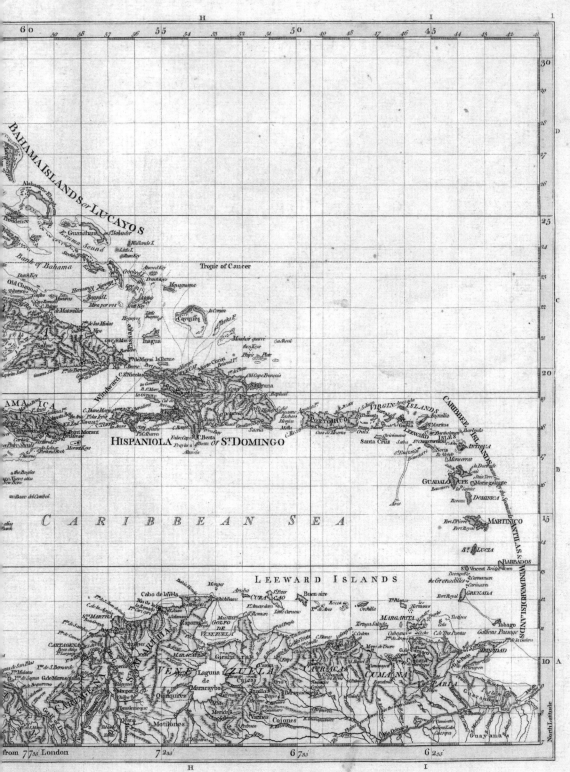